COLOSSIANS
A Commentary

COLOSSIANS

A Commentary

Petr Pokorný

Translated by
Siegfried S. Schatzmann

HENDRICKSON
PUBLISHERS
PEABODY, MASSACHUSETTS 01961-3473

Original German edition *Der Brief des Paulus an die Kolosser*. Theo-
logischer Handkommentar zum Neuen Testament 10/I, © 1987 Evangelische Verlagsanstalt GmbH Berlin. English translation copyright
© 1991 by Hendrickson Publishers, Inc.
P.O. Box 3473
Peabody, Massachusetts 01961–3473
Printed in the United States of America

ISBN 0-943575-38-9

Library of Congress Cataloging-in-Publication Data

Pokorný, Petr.
    [Brief des Paulus an die Kolosser.   English]
    Colossians: a commentary / Petr Pokorný.
       p.   cm.
    Translation of: Der Brief des Paulus an die Kolosser.
    Includes bibliographical references and indexes.
    ISBN 0-943575-38-9
    1. Bible. N.T. Colossians—Commentaries.   I. Bible. N.T.
Colossians. English. Revised Standard. 1991. II. Title.
BS2715.3.P6513   1991
227'.7077—dc20   91-2971
                                             CIP

Table of Contents

In Place of a Foreword

I wish to express my gratitude to my wife, Dr. phil. Věra Pokorná, for her many suggestions, her concrete assistance in preparing the manuscript, and especially for the inner support which I have received from her and from my children.

I also thank the editors of this commentary series, Dr. theol. habil. Joachim Rohde and Dr. sc. Christian Wolff, for their advice which I always welcomed.

My gratitude also belongs to the editor of this volume, Mr. Peter Sänger, together with his wife Ilsemarie, both of whom I came to treasure during our joint venture as experts, theologians, and people.

Prague, September 18, 1985
Petr Pokorný

Abbreviations

1. Old and New Testament

Gen.	Genesis
Exod.	Exodus
Lev.	Leviticus
Num.	Numbers
Deut.	Deuteronomy
Josh.	Joshua
Judg.	Judges
Ruth	Ruth
1 Sam.	1 Samuel
1 Kings	1 Kings
1 Chron.	1 Chronicles
Ezra	Ezra
Neh.	Nehemiah
Esther	Esther
Job	Job
Ps(s).	Psalms
Prov.	Proverbs
Eccles.	Ecclesiastes
Song of Sol.	Song of Solomon
Is.	Isaiah
Jer.	Jeremiah
Lam.	Lamentations
Ezek.	Ezekiel
Dan.	Daniel
Hos.	Hosea
Joel	Joel
Amos	Amos

Obad.	Obadiah
Jon.	Jonah
Mic.	Micah
Nah.	Nahum
Hab.	Habakkuk
Zeph.	Zephaniah
Hag.	Haggai
Zech.	Zechariah
Mal.	Malachi
Matt.	Matthew
Mark	Mark
Luke	Luke
John	John
Acts	Acts
Rom.	Romans
1 Cor.	1 Corinthians
Gal.	Galatians
Eph.	Ephesians
Phil.	Philippians
Col.	Colossians
1 Thess.	1 Thessalonians
1 Tim.	1 Timothy
Titus	Titus
Philem.	Philemon
Heb.	Hebrews
James	James
1 Pet.	1 Peter
1 John	1 John
Jude	Jude
Rev.	Revelation

The manuscripts of the NT are abbreviated according to Nestle-Aland (see bibliography: Primary Sources).

2. Non-Canonical Writings

with the Apocrypha (i.e., deuterocanonical books) of the OT

Acts Andr.	Acts of Andrew
Acts John	Acts of John
Acts Thom.	Acts of Thomas
Bar.	Baruch

Barn.	*Barnabas*
1 Clem.	1 Clement
Did.	*Didache*
Ep. Apost.	Epistula Apostolorum
1 Enoch	*Ethiopian Enoch*
Ign.	Ignatius
Eph.	*Letter to the Ephesians*
Phld.	*Letter to the Philadelphians*
Pol.	*Letter to Polycarp*
Rom.	*Letter to the Romans*
Trall.	*Letter to the Trallians*
Jos. Asen.	*Joseph and Aseneth*
Jub.	*Jubilees*
Macc.	Maccabees
Odes Sol.	Odes of Solomon
Herm.	Hermas the Shepherd
Man.	*Mandate*
Sim.	*Similitudes*
Vis.	*Vision*
Pol. *Phil.*	*Polycarp to the Philippians*
Pss. Sol.	Psalms of Solomon
Pss. Thom.	Psalms of Thomas
Sib. Or.	Sibylline Oracles
Sir.	Sirach
T. 12 Patr.	Testament of the Twelve Patriarchs
TBenj.	*Testament of Benjamin*
TJud.	*Testament of Judah*
TLevi	*Testament of Levi*
Tob.	Tobit
Wis.	Wisdom of Solomon

3. Judaic Writings

The *Tractates of the Mishnah and Talmud* are abbreviated as in Biller-beck (see bibliography: Commentaries).

Philo	Philo of Alexandria
Conf. Ling.	*On the Confusion of Tongues*
Decal.	*On the Decalog*
Ebr.	*On Drunkenness*
Fug.	*On Flight and Finding*

Leg. All.	Allegorical Interpretation
Migr. Abrah.	On the Migration of Abraham
Mut.	On the Change of Names
Opif.	On the Creation
Somn.	On Dreams
Spec. Leg.	On the Special Laws
Quis Her.	Who is the Heir
PsPhocyl.	Pseudo-Phocylides

Dead Sea Scrolls

CD	Damascus Document
1QH	Hodayot (Thanksgiving Hymns)
1QM	War Scroll
1QpHab	Pesher on Habakkuk
1QS	Manual of Discipline
1QSa	Appendix A to Manual of Discipline

4. Nag Hammadi Texts

NHC II/2	Nag Hammadi Codex II, Second Tractate; after the semicolon follows the number of the column and of the line. The count of the codices and of the tractates follows that of J. M. Robinson (see bibliography: Primary Sources)
1 Apoc. Jas.	(First) Apocalypse of James
Apoc. Adam	Apocalypse of Adam
Ap. John	Apocryphon of John
Asclepius	Asclepius 21–29
Auth. Teach.	Authoritative Teaching
Ep. Jac.	Epistula Iacobi apocrypha
Treat. Res.	Treatise on the Resurrection
Gos. Eg.	Gospel of the Egyptians (NHC III/2 = IV/2)
Gos. Phil.	Gospel of Philip
Gos. Thom.	Gospel of Thomas (cited by logia)
Gos. Truth	Gospel of Truth
Exeg. Soul	Exegesis of the Soul
Ogd. Enn.	De Ogdoade et Enneade
Orig. World	On the Origin of the World
Trim. Prot.	Trimorphic Protennoia
Steles Seth	Three Steles of Seth
Trac. Trip.	Tripartite Tractate
Treat. Seth	Second Treatise of the Great Seth

5. Classical Writers and Church Fathers

Apul.	Apuleius
Aristoph.	Aristophanes
Aristot.	Aristotle
Arnob.	Arnobius
Artemid.	Artemidor
Athan.	Athanasius
Aug.	Augustine
Chrys.	Chrysostom
Clem. Al.	Clement, of Alexandria
Corp. Herm.	*Corpus Hermeticum*
Exc. Stob.	Excerpts Stobaei Hermetica
Diod. Sic.	Diodorus Siculus
Diog. Laert.	Diogenes Laertius
Diogn.	Diognetus
Epict.	Epictetus
Epiph.	Epiphanius
Euseb.	Eusebius
Hippol.	Hippolytus
Hom.	Homer
Iren.	Irenaeus
Jos.	Josephus
Just.	Justin Martyr
Apol.	*Apology*
Liv.	Livy
Luc.	Lucian
Marc. Aurel.	Marcus Aurelius
Orig.	Origen
Oros.	Orosius
Orph. Hymn.	Orphic Hymns
Plato	Plato
Phaedr.	*Phaedrus*
Resp.	*Republic*
Sympos.	*Symposium*
Plin.	Pliny the Elder
Plut.	Plutarch
PsArist.	Pseudo-Aristotle
PsDion.	Pseudo-Dionysius
PsPhocyl.	Pseudo-Phocylides
Sen.	Seneca
Soph.	Sophocles
Exc. Stob.	Excerpta ex Stobaeo
Suet.	Suetonius

Tat.   Tatian
Virg.   Virgil
Xenoph.   Xenophon

The common abbreviations are used for the writings of these authors
(see *TDNT*: Index). On the papyri and other texts, consult the bibliography: Primary Sources.

6. Collections, Journals, and Bible Translations

AHAW	Abhandlungen der Heidelberger Akademie der Wissenschaften
AnBib	Analecta Biblica
ANRW	Aufstieg und Niedergang der römischen Welt
ASNU	Acta Seminarii Neotestamentici Upsaliensis
AThANT	Abhandlungen zur Theologie des Alten und Neuen Testaments
ATR	*Anglican Theological Review*
BBB	*Bonner biblische Beiträge*
BerlÄgUrk	Berliner ägyptische Urkunden (see bib.: Primary Sources: Helbling)
BevTh	Beiträge zur evangelischen Theologie
BhTh	Beiträge zur historischen Theologie
BLNT	Begriffslexikon zum Neuen Testament
BSt	Biblische Studien
BWANT	Beiträge zur Wissenschaft vom Alten und Neuen Testament
BZ	*Biblische Zeitschrift*
BZNW	Beihefte zur Zeitschrift für die neutestamentliche Wissenschaft und die Kunde der älteren Kirche
ConNT	Coniectanea neotestamentica
CBQ	*Catholic Biblical Quarterly*
CEP	Tschechische ökumenische Übersetzung der Bibel
CNT	Commentaire du Nouveau Testament
CV	Communio viatorum
EKK	Evangelisch-katholischer Kommentar zum Neuen Testament
ExpT	*Expository Times*
EÜ	Einheitsübersetzung der Heiligen Schrift

EvQ	*Evangelical Quarterly*
EvTh	Evangelische Theologie
EWNT	Exegetisches Wörterbuch zum Neuen Testament
FrankfThSt	Frankfurter theologische Studien
FRLANT	Forschungen zur Religion und Literatur des Alten und Neuen Testaments
HNT	Handbuch zum Neuen Testament
HThK	Herders Theologischer Kommentar zum Neuen Testament
HTR	*Harvard Theological Review*
ICC	International Critical Commentary
IDB	*Interpreter's Dictionary of the Bible*
IDBSup	Supplemental volume to *IDB*
JBL	*Journal of Biblical Literature*
JB	Jerusalem Bible
JR	*Journal of Religion*
JThSt	Jüdische Schriften aus hellenistisch-römischer Zeit (see bibliography: Primary Sources)
JTS	*Journal of Theological Studies*
KEK	Kritisch-exegetischer Kommentar über das Neue Testament
KNT	Kommentar zum Neuen Testament
LB	Linguistica Biblica
Luth.	Luther translation (1975)
MPG	Migne — Patrologia Graeca
MPL	Migne — Patrologia Latina
NCBC	New Century Bible Commentary
NEB	New English Bible
NHS	Nag Hammadi Studies
NovT	*Novum Testamentum*
NTA	Neutestamentliche Abhandlungen
NTD	Das Neue Testament Deutsch (Neues Göttinger Bibelwerk)
NTDErg	Das Neue Testament Deutsch — Ergänzungsreihe
NTS	*New Testament Studies*
NTSMS	New Testament Studies Monograph Series
NTTS	New Testament Tools and Studies
QD	Quaestiones disputatae
RAC	Reallexikon für Antike und Christentum
RevExp	*Review and Expositor*
RGG	Religion in Geschichte und Gegenwart

RGVV	Religionsgeschichtliche Versuche und Vorarbeiten
RHPR	*Revue d'Histoire et de Philosophie Religieuses*
RNT	Regensburger Neues Testament
RSV	Revised Standard Version
RTP	*Revue de Théologie et de Philosophie*
SBLDS	Society of Biblical Literature Dissertation Series
SBM	Stuttgarter biblische Monographien
SBS	Stuttgarter Bibelstudien
SHAW	Sitzungsberichte der Heidelberger Akademie der Wissenschaften
SJT	*Scottish Journal of Theology*
StANT	Studien zum Alten und Neuen Testament
StNT	Studien zum Neuen Testament
SUNT	Studien zur Umwelt des Neuen Testaments
StVTPsepigr	Studia in Veteris Testamenti Pseudepigrapha
SuppluralNovTest	Supplements to Novum Testamentum
SuppluralNumen	Studies in the History of Religions. Supplements to Numen
Supp.RivBibl	Supplementi alla Rivista Biblica
TEV	Today's English Version
ThB	Theologische Bücherei
TheolViat	Theologia Viatorum
ThF	Theologische Forschung
ThHK	Theologischer Handkommentar zum Neuen Testament
ThLZ	*Theologische Literaturzeitung*
ThSt	Theologische Studien
TDNT	*Theological Dictionary of the New Testament*
TDOT	*Theological Dictionary of the Old Testament*
TZ	*Theologische Zeitschrift*
TOB	Traduction oecuménique de la Bible
TrThSt	Trierer theologische Studien
TT-Ps	Texts and Translations. Pseudepigrapha Series
TU	Texte und Untersuchungen
UTB	Uni-Taschenbücher
VC	*Vigiliae Christianae*
WF	Wege der Forschung
WMANT	Wissenschaftliche Monographien zum Alten und Neuen Testament
ZdZ	Die Zeichen der Zeit
ZKTh	*Zeitschrift für katholische Theologie*

| ZNW | *Zeitschrift für die neutestamentliche Wissenschaft und die Kunde der älteren Kirche* |
| ZThK | *Zeitschrift für Theologie und Kirche* |

7. Other Abbreviations

adj.	adjective
adv.	adverb
acc.	accusative
act.	active
aor.	aorist
art.	article
BCE	before Common Era
cath.	catholic
CE	Common Era
cent.	century
cf.	compare
ch(s).	chapter(s)
cod.	codex
col.	column
copt.	coptic
Corp.Paul.	Corpus Paulinum
diss.	dissertation
ed.	edition, editor
e.g.	for example
esp.	especially
etc.	et cetera, and so forth
f(f).	following page(s)
fig.	figure
fragm.	fragment
FS	Festschrift
gen.	genitive
Gk.	Greek
Heb.	Hebrew
ibid.	ibidem, in the same place
id.	idem, the same
i.e.	that is
impf.	imperfect
impv.	imperative
ind.	indicative
inf.	infinitive

Lat.	Latin
loc. cit.	loco citato, in the place cited
LXX	Septuagint
masc.	masculine
MS(S)	manuscript(s)
n.s.	new series
NT	New Testament
OT	Old Testament
p(p).	page(s)
p	papyrus
pass.	passive
perf.	perfect
pres.	present
probl.	problem
ptc.	participle
R.	Rabbi
transl.	translated, translator
v(v).	verse(s)
vol.	volume
→	see interpretation of the reference indicated by arrow

Bibliography

§*Primary Sources*

In the references to the primary sources the common, most widely used text division is generally used. When there are no significant text variations in the respective pericope, the primary sources used are not cited. In the following, only the more recent and less common editions of primary sources, or their translations, are referenced, namely, those which I have cited or used together with the more frequently noted texts. On the details of the editions with single citations, consult the notes. In the citations of the Syrian and Egyptian texts, I follow W. G. Kümmel, et al., eds., *Jüdische Schriften aus hellenistisch-römischer Zeit I-V*, Gütersloh, 1973ff.

(Analecta) E. Preuschen, ed.: *Analecta II. Zur Kanonsgeschichte* (Samml. ausgew. kirchen- und dogmengesch. Quellenschriften I, 8, 2), Tübingen, 1910.

(Esseni) E. Lohse, ed. and transl.: *Die Texte aus Qumran*, Darmstadt, 1971.

(Hermetica) A. J. Festugière and A. D. Nock, eds. and transl.: *Corpus Hermeticum I-IV*, Paris, 1960², 1954.

(Jos. Asen.) M. Philonenko, ed. and transl.: *Joseph et Aséneth* (Studia Post-Biblica 13), Leiden, 1968.

(Textus judeochristiani) A. F. J. Klijn and G. J. Reinink, eds.: *Patristic Evidence for Jewish-Christian Sects*, NovTSup 36, Leiden, 1973.

(Scripturae judaeorum aevi hellenistici) W. G. Kümmel, ed.: *Jüdische Schriften aus hellenistisch-römischer Zeit I-V*, Gütersloh, 1973ff.

(Nag Hammadi) *The Facsimile Edition of the Nag Hammadi Codices I-XII*, Leiden, 1972.

Ménard, J. E., transl.: *L'Evangile de Vérité* (NagHamSt 2), Leiden, 1972.

Nagel, P., ed. and transl.: *Das Wesen der Archonten aus Codex II der gnostischen Bibliothek von Nag Hammadi* (Wiss. Beitr. der M. Luther Univ. 1970/6), Halle, 1970.

Böhlig A. and F. Wisse, ed. and transl.: *Nag Hammadi Codices III,2 and IV,2—The Gospel of the Egyptians* (NagHamSt 4), Leiden, 1975.

Parrot, D. M., ed. and transl.: *Nag Hammadi Codices V,2-5 and VI with Papyrus Berolinensis 8502,1 and 4* (NagHamSt 11), Leiden 1979.

(Novum Testamentum) post Eb. Nestle and Erwin Nestle, ed. K. Aland, M. Black, C. M. Martini, B. M. Metzger, A. Wikgren: *Novum Testamentum Graece*, Stuttgart, 1979²⁶.

Aland K., M. Black, C. M. Martini, B. M. Metzger, A. Wikgren, eds.: *The Greek New Testament*, New York, 1975[3] (abbrev. UBS[3]).
H. J. Frede, ed.: *Vetus Latina, Epistula ad Collosenses* (Vet. lat. 24/3), Freiburg, 1966–71.
(Odae Salomonis) J. H. Charlesworth, ed. and transl.: *The Odes of Solomon* (TT 13 Ps 7), Missoula, 1977[2].
(Orphici) O. Kern, ed.: *Orphicorum Fragmenta*, Berlin, 1922.
(Papyri) R. Helbing, ed.: *Auswahl aus griechischen Papyri* (Samml. Göschen 625), Berlin/Leipzig, 1924[2].
(Pseudo-Aristotle) W. L. Lorimer, ed.: *Aristotelis libellumde mundo* (Collection Budé), Paris, 1933.
(Pseudo-Phocylides) P. W. van der Horst, ed. and transl.: *The Sentences of PseudoPhocylides* (SVTP 4), Leiden, 1978.
(Tatianus) E. Schwartz, ed.: *Tatiani oratio ad Graecos* TU 4, Leipzig, 1888.
(Psalmi Thomae) P. Nagel, ed. and transl.: *Die Thomaspsalmen des koptisch-manichäischen Psalmbuches* (Quellen NF 1), Berlin, 1980.

§*Commentaries*

Some less significant commentaries which I do not cite because they were not available to me or because I did not use them throughout, are cited in the bibliographies of E. Lohse (see below) and E. Schweizer (see below). The most exhaustive listing of the older commentaries is found in H. Oltramare.

The commentaries are cited by author's name only. If no page reference is given, consult the respective text reference.

Abbott, T. K. *Epistle to the Ephesians and to the Colossians*. ICC. Edinburgh (1897), 1977, reprint.
Alford, H. *The Greek New Testament III*. Cambridge, 1871[5] (with several later reprints).
Beare, F. W. "The Epistle to the Colossians," in *The Interpreter's Bible* XI. New York/Nashville, 1955, pp. 131–241.
Beet, J. A. *A Commentary to St. Paul's Epistles to the Ephesians, Philippians and to Philemon*. London, 1890.
Bengel, J. A. *Gnomon Novi Testamenti*. Berlin, 1860, new third ed.
(Bible) *Traduction oecuménique de la Bible. Edition intégrale: Nouveau Testament*. Paris, 1977.
Bieder, W. *Der Kolosserbrief (Prophezei)*. Zürich, 1943.
(H. L. Strack—)Billerbeck, P. *Kommentar zum Neuen Testament aus Talmud und Midrasch I–V*. Munich, I:1969[5]; II–IV:1965[4]; V:1969[3].
Bratcher, R. G. and E. A. Nida. *A Translator's Handbook on Paul's Letters to the Colossians and to Philemon*. Helps for Translators XX. Stuttgart, 1977.
Braun, H. *Qumran und das Neue Testament I. Die Katene von Matthäus bis Apokalypse*. Tübingen, 1966.
Bunkhardus, J. P. *Dissertatio in ep. S. Pauli ad Colossenses I*. Zürich, 1697.
Caird, G. B. *Paul's Letters from Prison*. New Clarendon Bible. Oxford, 1981[2].
J. Calvini in omnes Novi Testamenti epistulas commentarii II. Halle, 1834, editio altera.
J. Chrysostomi in Epistulam ad Colossenses commentarius. MPG 62. Paris, 1862, pp. 207–392.
Conzelmann, H. *Der Brief an die Kolosser*. NTD III, vol. 8, pp. 130–154. Göttingen, 1962.

Dibelius, M., rev. by H. Greeven. *An die Kolosser, Epheser, an Philemon.* HNT 12. Tübingen, 1953.

Ernst, J. *Die Briefe an die Philipper, an Philemon, an die Kolosser, an die Epheser.* RNT. Regensburg, 1974.

Ewald, P. *Die Briefe des Paulus an die Epheser, Kolosser und Philemon.* KNT X. Leipzig, 1910².

Gnilka, J. *Der Kolosserbrief.* HTKNT X/1. Freiburg, 1980.

(Griechische Kirche) K. Staab, ed. *Pauluskommentare aus der Griechischen Kirche.* NTA—15. Münster, 1933.

Haupt, E. *Die Gefangenschaftsbriefe.* KEK VIII⁸–IX⁷. Göttingen, 1902.

Houlden, J. L. *Paul's Letters from Prison.* The Pelican NT Commentary. Harmondsworth, 1970.

Hugédé, N. *Commentaire de l'Epître aux Colossiens.* Geneva, 1968.

(Kralická bible—Kralice Bible) *Nový zákon s veškerými výklady Bratříceských z roku 1601.* Prague, 1875.

Lightfoot, J. B. *Saint Paul's Epistles to the Colossians and to Philemon.* London (1868) 1900 reprint.

Lindemann, A. *Der Kolosserbrief.* Zürcher Bibelkommentare 10. Zürich, 1983.

Lohmeyer, E. *Die Briefe an die Philipper, an die Kolosser und an Philemon.* KEK IX¹³. Göttingen, 1964. Supplement by W. Schmauch.

Lohse, E. *Colossians and Philemon.* ET by W. R. Poehlmann and R. J. Karris. Hermeneia. Philadelphia, 1971.

P. Lombardi Collectanea in epistulam ad Colossenses. MPL 192. Paris, 1880, pp. 257–288.

Martin, R. P. *Colossians. The Church's Lord and the Christian Liberty.* Exeter, 1972.

Martin, R. P. *Colossians and Philemon.* NCBC. Grand Rapids/London, 1981².

Masson, Ch. *L'épître de Saint Paul aux Colossiens.* CNT 10/2. Neuchâtel/Paris 1950.

Metzger, B. M. *A Textual Commentary on the Greek New Testament.* London/New York, 1971.

Meyer, H. A. W. *Critical and Exegetical Handbook to the Epistles to the Philippians and Colossians and to Philemon.* ET by J. C. Moore and rev. W. P. Dickson. 1884⁶. Reprint, Peabody, 1983.

Moule, C. D. F. *Epistles of Paul the Apostle to the Colossians and to Philemon.* Cambridge Greek NT Commentary. Cambridge, 1962³.

Oecumenii (Oikumenios) Pauli Apostoli ad Colossenses epistula. MPG 119. Paris, 1881, pp. 1–56.

Oltramare, H. *Commentaire sur les épîtres de S. Paul aux Colossiens, aux Ephésiens et à Philémon I.* Paris, 1891–92.

Peake, A. S. "The Epistle to the Colossians," in *The Expositor's Greek Testament.* London, 1910, pp. 475–547 (with subsequent new editions).

Schiwy, G. "An die Kolosser," in *Weg ins Neue Testament III,* ed. G. Schiwy. Würzburg, 1968, pp. 373–391.

Schlatter, E. *Die Briefe an die Galater, Epheser, Kolosser und Philemon.* Erläuterungen zum NT 7. Stuttgart, 1963 (reprint).

Schmidt, P. W. and F. v. Holzendorff. *Protestanten-Bibel Neuen Testaments.* Leipzig, 1879³.

Schweizer, E. *The Letter to the Colossians, to Philemon and to the Ephesians.* ET by A. Chester. Minneapolis, 1982.

Scott, E. F. *The Epistles of Paul to the Colossians, to Philemon and to the Ephesians* Moffat Commentary. London, 1930.

Soden, H. v. *Die Briefe an die Kolosser, Epheser, Philemon. Die Pastoralbriefe.* Hand-Kommentar zum NT III/1. Freiburg/Leipzig, 1893[2].

Souček, J. B. *Epištola Pavlova Kolossenským.* Prague, 1947.

Staab, Z. *Die Thessalonicherbriefe. Die Gefangenschaftsbriefe.* RNT 7, 1. Regensburg, 1969[5].

Thompson, G. H. P. *The Letters of Paul to the Ephesians, to the Colossians and to Philemon.* The Cambridge Bible Commentary. Cambridge, 1967.

Westcott, B. F. *A Letter to Asia.* London, 1914.

Wilckens, U., *Das Neue Testament übersetzt und kommentiert.* Edited by W. Jetter, E. Lange, and R. Pesch. Hamburg/Köln/Zürich, 1970.

Wohlenberg, G. "Die Briefe Pauli aus seiner römischen Gefangenschaft," in *Kurzgefasster Kommentar zu den Heiligen Schriften Alten und Neuen Testaments* B/IV. Munich, 1895[2], pp. 1–121.

§*Other Sources*

See also the bibliographies on Col. 1:15–20, on the excurses § 13 and 18, as well as the works cited in full in the notes. The works listed in this section are cited in abbreviated form in the notes.

Ahrens, Th. *Die ökumenische Diskussion kosmischer Christologie seit 1961.* Dissertation Lübeck, 1969.

Aletti, J. N. *Colossiens 1:15–20.* AnBib 91. Rome, 1981.

Bandstra, A. J. *The Law and the Elements of the World. An Exegetical Study in Aspects of Paul's Teaching.* Kampen, 1964.

Bauer W., W. F. Arndt, F. W. Gingrich, and F. W. Danker. *Greek-English Lexicon of the New Testament and other Early Christian Literature.* Chicago, 1979[2].

Baur, F. C. *Paul, the Apostle of Jesus Christ: His Life and Work, His Epistles and Teachings,* 2 vols. ET by A. Menzies. Ed. by E. Zeller. London/ Edinburgh, 1875–76.

Bénoit, P. "Rapports littéraires entre les épîtres aux Colossiens et aux Ephésiens," in *Neutestamentliche Aufsätze.* FS J. Schmid. Regensburg, 1963, pp. 11–22.

Berger, K. "Apostelbrief und apostolische Rede," ZNW 65 (1974), pp. 190–231.

Berger, K. *Exegese des Neuen Testaments.* UTB 658. Heidelberg, 1977.

Best, E. *One Body. A Study in the Relationship of the Church to Christ in the Epistles of the Apostle Paul.* London, 1955.

Binder, H. *Der Glaube bei Paulus.* Berlin, 1968.

Blass, F., A. Debrunner, and R. W. Funk. *A Greek Grammar of the New Testament and Other Early Christian Literature.* Chicago, 1961.

Bornkamm, G. "Baptism and New Life in Paul (Romans 6)," in *Early Christian Experience.* ET by Paul L. Hammer. London, 1969.

Bornkamm, G. "The Heresy of Colossians," in F. O. Francis and W. A. Meeks, *Conflict at Colossae,* Missoula, 1975, pp. 123–145. ET of Bornkamm, G. "Die Häresie des Kolosserbriefs," *TLZ* 73 (1948), pp. 11–20.

Bornkamm, G. "Die Hoffnung im Kolosserbrief. Zugleich ein Beitrag zur Frage der Echtheit des Briefes," in *Studien zum Neuen Testament und zur Patristik. Erich Klostermann zum 90. Geburstag dargebracht.* TU 77. Berlin: Akademie, 1961, pages 56–64. Reprinted in *Geschichte und Glaube 2. Gesammelte Aufsätze.* Vol. 4. BEvT 53. Munich: Kaiser, 1971, pages 206–231.

Bousset, W. and H. Gressmann. *Die Religion des Judentums im späthellenistischen Zeitalter.* HNT 21. Tübingen, 1966[4].

Bouttier, M. "Remarque sur la conscience apostolique de St. Paul," in *OIKONOMIA.* FS O. Cullmann. Ed. by F. Christ. Hamburg/Bergstedt, 1967, pp. 100–108.

Brox, N. *Falsche Verfasserangaben. Zur Erklärung der frühchristlichen Pseudepigraphie.* SBS 79. Stuttgart, 1975.

Brox, N., ed. *Pseudepigraphie in der heidnischen und jüdischen Antike.* WF 484. Darmstadt, 1977.

Bruce, F. F. "St. Paul in Rome; 3. The Epistle to the Colossians," *Bulletin of the John Rylands Library* 48 (1966), pp. 268–285.

Bujard, W. *Stilanalytische Untersuchungen zum Kolosserbrief.* StUNT 11. Göttingen, 1973.

Burger, Ch. *Schöpfung und Versöhnung. Studien zum liturgischen Gut im Kolosser- und Epheserbrief.* WMANT 46. Neukirchen/Vluyn, 1975.

Caragounis, Ch. F. *The Ephesian Mysterion.* CB—NT 8. Lund, 1977.

Christ, F. *Jesus Sophia. Die Sophia-Christologie bei den Synoptikern.* AThANT 57. Zürich, 1970.

Colpe, C. "Zur Leib-Christi-Vorstellung im Epheserbrief," in *Judentum—Urchristentum—Kirche.* BZNW 26. Berlin, 1960, pp. 172–187.

Colpe, C. *Die religionsgeschichtliche Schule. Darstellung und Kritik ihres Bildes vom gnostischen Erlösermythus.* FRLANT 78. Göttingen, 1961.

Conzelmann, H. *Der Brief an die Epheser.* NTD III/8. Göttingen, 1962, pp. 56–91.

Conzelmann, H. *An Outline of the Theology of the New Testament.* ET by J. Bowden. New York, 1969.

Conzelmann, H. and A. Lindemann. *Interpretation of the New Testament. An Introduction to the Principles and Methods of NT Exegesis.* ET by S. Schatzmann. Peabody, 1988.

Coutts, J. "The Relationship of Ephesians and Colossians," *NTS* 4 (1957–58), pp. 201–207.

Daecke, S. M. *Teilhard de Chardin und die evangelische Theologie.* Göttingen, 1967.

Dahl, N. A. "Formgeschichtliche Beobachtunen zur Christusverkündigung in der Gemeindepredigt," in *Neutestamentliche Studien für R. Bultmann.* BZNW 21. Berlin, 1957[2], pp. 3–9.

Deichgräber, R. *Gotteshymnus und Christushymnus in der frühen Christenheit.* StUNT 5. Göttingen, 1967.

Deissmann, A. *Light from the Ancient East.* ET by R. Strachan. Grand Rapids, 1927.

De Wette, W. M. L. *Lehrbuch der historisch-kritischen Einleitung in die kanonischen Bücher des Neuen Testaments.* Berlin, 1860[6].

Dilschneider, O. A. *Christus Pantokrator. Vom Kolosserbrief zur Ökumene.* Berlin, 1962.

Duncan, G. S. *St. Paul's Ephesian Ministry.* London, 1929.

Dupont, J. *La connaissance religieuse dans les épîtres de Saint Paul.* Univ. cath. lov. diss. II–40. Louvain/Paris, 1949.

Eckart, K. G. "Exegetische Beobachtungen zu Kol. 1:9–20," *TheolViat* 7 (1050–60). Berlin/Stuttgart, 1960, pp. 87–106.

Ellis, E. E. "Paul and his Co-Workers," *NTS* 17 (1970–71), pp. 437–452.

Ernst, J. *Pleroma und Pleroma Christi. Geschichte und Deutung eines Begriffs der paulinischen Antilegomena.* BU 5. Regensburg, 1970.

Fischer, K. M. *Tendenz und Absicht des Epheserbriefes.* Berlin, 1973.
Francis, F. O. "The Christological Argument of Colossians," in *God's Christ* (see below), pp. 192–207.
Frankemölle, H. *Das Taufverständnis des Paulus.* SBS 47. Stuttgart, 1970.
Gaugler, E. *Der Epheserbrief.* Ausl. ntl. Schriften 6. Zürich, 1966.
Gnilka, J. *Der Epheserbrief.* HTKNT 10/2. Freiburg, 1971.
Gnilka, J. "Das Paulusbild im Kolosser- und Epheserbrief," in *Kontinuität und Einheit.* FS F. Mussner. Ed. by P. G. Müller and W. Stenger. Freiburg, 1981, pp. 179–193.
Gnilka, J. *Der Philemonbrief.* HTKNT 10/4. Freiburg, 1982.
Grässer, E. "Kolosser 3:1–4 als Beispiel einer Interpretation secundum homines recipientes (1967)," most recently in *Text und Situation.* Ed. by E. Grässer. Gütersloh, 1973, pp. 123–151.
Hahn, F. *Christologische Hoheitstitel.* FRLANT 83. Göttingen, 1963.
Harder, G. *Paulus und das Gebet.* Neutest. Forschungen I/10. Gütersloh, 1936.
Harrison, P. N. *Paulines and Pastorals.* London, 1964.
Hegermann, H. *Die Vorstellung vom Schöpfungsmittler im hellenistischen Judentum und Urchristentum.* TU 82. Berlin, 1961.
Hennecke, E. and W. Schneemelcher, eds. *New Testament Apocrypha,* 2 vols. ET and ed. by R. McL. Wilson. London, 1963–65.
Holtzmann, H. J. *Einleitung in das Neue Testament.* Freiburg, 1886[2].
Holtzmann, H. J. *Kritik der Epheser- und Kolosserbriefe.* Leipzig, 1872.
Hooker, M. D. and S. G. Wilson, eds. *Paul and Paulinism.* FS C. K. Barrett. London, 1982.
Hooker, M. D. "Were there false teachers in Colossae?" in *Christ and Spirit in the New Testament.* FS C. D. F. Moule. Ed. by B. Lindars and S. S. Smalley. Cambridge, 1973, pp. 315–331.
Jenni, E. and C. Westermann. *Theologisches Handwörterbuch zum Alten Testament* I–II. Munich/Zürich, 1971 and 1976.
Jervell, J. *Imago Dei. Gen. 1:26 im Spätjudentum, in der Gnosis und in den paulinischen Briefen.* FRLANT 76. Göttingen, 1960.
Jervell, J. and W. A. Meeks, eds. *God's Christ and his People.* FS N. A. Dahl. Oslo/Bergen/Tromsö, 1977.
Jülicher, A. and E. Fascher. *Einleitung in das Neue Testament.* Tübingen, 1933.
Käsemann, E. *Leib und Leib Christi.* BhTh 9. Tübingen, 1933.
Käsemann, E. "A Primitive Christian Baptismal Liturgy," in *Essays on New Testament Themes.* ET by W. J. Montague. Ed. by E. Käsemann. Philadelphia, 1964.
Käsemann, E. "Kolosserbrief," in *RGG*[3] III, pp. 1727–1728.
Käsemann, E. "Erwägungen zum Stichwort "Versönungslehre im Neuen Testament," in *Zeit und Geschichte.* FS R. Bultmann. Ed. by E. Dinkler. Tübingen, 1964, pp. 47–59.
Kertelge, K., ed. *Paulus in den neutestamentlichen Spätschriften.* QD 89. Freiburg, 1981.
Kippenberg, H. G. "Ein Vergleich jüdischer, christlicher und gnostischer Apokalyptik," in *Apocalypticism in the Mediterranean World and the Near East.* Ed. by D. Hellholm. Tübingen, 1983, pp. 751–768.
Kramer, W. *Christos – Kyrios – Gottessohn.* AThANT 44. Zürich, 1963.
Kremer, J. *Was an den Leiden Christi noch mangelt. Eine interpretationsgeschichtliche und exegetische Untersuchung zu Kol. 1:24b.* BBB 12. Bonn, 1956.

Kümmel, W. G. *Introduction to the New Testament.* ET by H. C. Kee. Nashville, 1975.

Kuhn H. W. *Enderwartung und gegenwärtiges Heil.* StUNT 4. Göttingen, 1966.

Lähnemann, J. *Der ◂Kolosserbrief. Komposition, Situationen und Argumentation.* StNT 3. Gütersloh, 1971.

Lamarche, P. "Structure de l'épître aux Colossiens," *Biblica* 56 (1975), pp. 453–463.

Lindemann, A. *Die Aufhebung der Zeit. Geschichtsverständnis und Eschatologie im Epheserbrief.* StNT 12. Gütersloh, 1975.

Lindemann, A. "Bemerkungen zu den Adressaten und zum Anlass des Epheserbriefes," *ZNW* 67 (1976), pp. 235–251.

Lindemann, A. *Paulus im ältesten Christentum.* BhTh 58. Tübingen, 1979.

Lindemann, A. "Die Gemeinde von "Kolossä,'" in *Wort und Dienst* N. F. 16 (1981), pp. 11–134.

Lohse, E. "Christologie und Ethik im Kolosserbrief," in *Apophoreta.* FS E. Haenchen. BZNW 30. Berlin, 1964, pp. 157–168.

Lohse, E. "Christusherrschaft und Kirche im Kolosserbrief," *NTS* 11 (1964–65), pp. 203–216.

Lohse, E. "Pauline Theology in the Letter to the Colossians," *NTS* 15 (1968–69), pp. 211–220.

Löwe, H. "Bekenntnis, Apostelamt und Kirche im Kolosserbrief," in *Kirche.* FS G. Bornkamm. Tübingen, 1980, pp. 299–314.

Lüdemann, G. "Zum Antipaulinismus im frühen Christentum," *EvTh* 40 (1980), pp. 437–455.

Lüdemann, G. *Paulus, der Heidenapostel I. Studien zur Chronologie.* FRLANT 123. Göttingen, 1980.

Lüdemann, G. *Paul, Apostle to the Gentiles.* ET by F. Stanley Jones. Philadelphia, 1984.

Lührmann, D. *Das Offenbarungsverständnis bei Paulus und in den paulinischen Gemeinden.* WMANT 16. Neukirchen, 1965.

Mack, B. L. *Logos und Sophia. Untersuchungen zur Weisheitstheologie im hellenistischen Judentum.* StUNT 10. Göttingen, 1973.

di Marco, A. "Der Chiasmus in der Bibel," *LB* 44 (1979), pp. 3–76.

Martin, R. P. *Reconciliation. A Study of Paul's Theology.* New Foundations Theological Library. Atlanta, 1980.

Marxsen, W. *Introduction to the New Testament.* ET by G. Buswell. Philadelphia, 1970.

Maurer, Ch. "Die Begründung der Herrschaft Christi über die Mächte nach Col. 1:15–20," in *Wort und Dienst* N. F. 4 (1955), pp. 72–93.

Mayerhoff, E. Th. *Der Brief an die Kolosser, mit vornehmlicher Berücksichtigung der drei Pastoralbriefe kritisch geprüft.* Edited by J. L. Mayerhoff. Berlin, 1838.

Meeks, W. A. "In One Body: The Unity of Humankind in Colossians and Ephesians," in *God's Christ and his People.* Edited by J. Jervell and W. A. Meeks, pp. 209–221.

Meeks, W. A., ed. *Zur Soziologie des Urchristentums.* Munich, 1979.

Merklein, H. *Das kirchliche Amt nach dem Epheserbrief.* StANT 33. Munich, 1973.

Merklein, H. "Paulinische Theologie in der Rezeption des Kolosser- und Epheserbriefes," in *Paulus in den neutestamentlichen Spätschriften.* Edited by K. Kertelge. QD 89, pp. 25–69.

Müller, U. B. *Zur frühchristlichen Theologiegeschichte. Judentum und Paulinismus in Kleinasien an der Wende vom ersten zum zweiten Jh. n. Chr.* Gütersloh, 1976.

Munro, W. "Col. 3:18–4:1 and Eph. 5:21–6:9: Evidence of a Late Literary Stratum?" *NTS* 18 (1971–72), pp. 434–447.

Mussner, F. *Christus, das All und die Kirche.* TrThSt 5. Trier, 1955.

Neugebauer, F. *In Christus ἐν Χριστῷ: Eine Untersuchung zum paulinischen Glaubensverständnis.* Berlin, 1961.

Nilsson, M. P. *Geschichte der griechischen Religion I–II.* Handbuch der Altertumswissenschaft V/1–2. Munich, 1955² and 1961².

Norden, E. *Agnostos theos. Untersuchungen zur Formengeschichte religiöser Rede.* Leipzig/Berlin, 1923².

O'Brien, P. T. *Introductory Thanksgiving in the Letters of Paul.* NovTSup 49. Leiden, 1977.

Ochel, W. *Die Annahme einer Bearbeitung des Kolosserbriefes im Epheserbrief.* Würzburg, 1934.

Ollrog, W. H. *Paulus und seine Mitarbeiter.* WMANT 50. Neukirchen/Vluyn, 1979.

O'Neill, J. C. "The Source of Christology in Colossians," *NTS* 26 (1979/80), pp. 87–100.

(Pauly) K. Ziegler and W. Southeimer, eds. *Der kleine Pauly. Lexikon der Antike I–V.* Munich, 1979².

Penna, R. *Il "Mysterion" Paolino.* Supplural RivBibl 10. Brescia, 1978.

Percy, E. *Die Probleme der Kolosser- und Epheserbriefe.* Lund, 1946.

Pfitzner, V. C. *Paul and the Agon Motif.* NovTSup 16. Leiden, 1967.

Pokorný, P. *Der Epheserbrief und die Gnosis.* Berlin, 1965.

Pokorný, P. *The Genesis of Christology.* ET by M. Lefébure. Edinburgh, 1987.

Reicke, Bo. "The Historical Setting of Colossians," *RevExp* 70 (1973), pp. 429–438.

Reitzenstein, R. *Hellenistic Mystery–Religions: Their Basic Ideas and Significance.* ET by J. E. Steely. Pittsburgh, 1978.

Reitzenstein, R. and H. H. Schaeder. *Studien zum antiken Synkretismus aus Iran und Griechenland.* Studien der Bibliothek Warburg 7. Leipzig/Berlin, 1926.

Robinson, J. A. T. *The Body. A Study in Pauline Theology.* London, 1952.

Roller, O. *Das Formular der paulinischen Briefe.* BWANT 58. Stuttgart, 1933.

van Roon, A. *The Authenticity of Ephesians.* NovTSup 39. Leiden, 1974.

Sand, A. "Überlieferung und Sammlung der Paulusbriefe," in *Paulus in den neutestamentlichen Spätschriften,* ed. K. Kertelge. QD 89, pp. 11–24.

Sanders, E. P. "Literary Dependence in Colossians," *JBL* 85 (1986), pp. 28–45.

Schenk, W. "Christus, das Geheimnis der Welt als dogmatisches und ethisches Grundprinzip des Kolosserbriefes," *EvTh* 43 (1983), pp. 138–155.

Schenke, H. M. "Die neutestamentliche Christologie und der gnostische Erlöser," in *Gnosis und Neues Testament.* Edited by K. W. Tröger, pp. 205–229, Berlin, 1973.

Schenke, H. M. and K. M. Fischer. *Einleitung in die Schriften des Neuen Testaments I.* Berlin, 1978.

Schille, G. *Frühchristliche Hymnen.* Berlin, 1962.

Schille, G. *Das älteste Paulusbild. Beobachtungen zur lukanischen und zur deuteropaulinischen Paulus-Darstellung.* Berlin, 1979.

Schillebeeckx, E. *Christus und die Christen.* Translated. Freiburg, 1977.

Schlier, H. *Der Brief an die Epheser.* Düsseldorf, 1962³.

Schlier, H. *Principalities and Powers in the New Testament.* New York, 1961.

Schmid, J. *Zeit und Ort der paulinischen Gefangenschaftsbriefe.* Freiburg, 1931.

Schmidt, K. L. "Die Natur- und Geistkräfte im Paulinischen Erkennen und Glauben," in *Eranos-Jahrbuch* 14 (1946), pp. 87–143, Zürich, 1947.

Schmidt, T. *Der Leib Christi* (Σῶμα Χριστοῦ). *Eine Untersuchung zum urchristlichen Gemeindegedanken.* Leipzig, 1919.

Schmithals, W. *Gnosticism in Corinth.* ET by J. E. Steely. Nashville, 1971.

Schmithals, W. "On the Composition and Earliest Collection of the Major Epistles of Paul," in *Paul and the Gnostics.* ET by John Steely. Nashville, 1972.

Schnackenburg, R. "Die Aufnahme des Christushymnus durch den Verfasser des Kolosserbriefes," in *EKK Vorarbeiten* 1, pp. 33–50. Zürich/Neukirchen, 1969.

Schnackenburg, R. *Epheserbrief.* EKK 10. Zürich/Neukirchen, 1982.

Schrage, W. *Die konkreten Einzelgebote in der paulinischen Paränese.* Gütersloh, 1961.

Schrage, W. *The Ethics of the New Testament.* ET by David E. Green. Philadelphia, 1988. ET of *Ethik des Neuen Testaments.* NTDSup 4. Göttingen, 1982.

Schubert, P. *Form and Function of Pauline Thanksgiving.* BZNW 20. Berlin, 1939.

Schwanz, P. *Imago Dei als christologisch-anthropologisches Problem in der Geschichte der alten Kirche.* Arbeiten zu Kirchengeschichte und Religionswissenschaft 2. Halle, 1970.

Schweitzer, A. *The Mysticism of Paul the Apostle.* ET by W. Montgomery. New York, 1953.

Schweizer, E. "Die Kirche als Leib Christi in den paulinischen Antilegomena (1961)," in *NeoT,* pp. 293–316. Edited by E. Schweizer. Zürich/Stuttgart, 1963.

Schweizer, E. "Die "Mystik" des Sterbens und Auferstehens mit Christus bei Paulus (1966)," in *Beiträge zur Theologie des Neuen Testaments,* pp. 183–203. Zürich, 1970.

Schweizer, E. "Christus und Geist im Kolosserbrief," in *Christ and Spirit in the New Testament.* FS C. D. F. Moule. Edited by B. Lindars and S. S. Smalley, pp. 297–313. Cambridge, 1973.

Schweizer, E. *TDNT* VII:1024–1044; 1045–1094.

Schweizer, E. "Zur neueren Forschung am Kolosserbrief (seit 1970)," *Theol. Berichte* 5 (1976), pp. 163–191.

Schweizer, E. "Gottesgerechtigkeit und Lasterkataloge bei Paulus inkl. Kol und Eph," in *Rechtfertigung.* FS E. Käsemann. Edited by J. Friedrich et al., pp. 461–477. Tübingen, 1976.

Seeberg, A. *Der Katechismus der Urchristenheit.* Introduction by F. Hahn. Munich, 1966.

Sellin, G. " 'Die Auferstehung ist schon geschehen.' Zur Spiritualisierung apokalyptischer Terminologie im Neuen Testament," *NovT* 25 (1983), pp. 220–237.

Siber, P. *Mit Christus leben.* AThANT 61. Zürich, 1961.

Speyer, W. "Religiöse Pseudepigraphie und literarische Fälschung im Altertum," in *Pseudepigraphie in der heidnischen und jüdischen Antike.* Edited by N. Brox. WF 484, pp. 195–263.

Stegemann, E. "Alt und Neu bei Paulus und in den Deuteropaulinen Kol-Eph," *EvTh* 37 (1977), pp. 508–536.

Steinmetz, F. J. Protologische Heils-Zuversicht. Die Strukturen des soteriologischen und christologischen Denkens im Kolosser- und Epheserbrief. FrankfThSt 2. Frankfurt, 1969.

Suhl, A. Paulus und seine Briefe. StNT 11. Gütersloh, 1975.

Tannehill, R. C. Dying and Rising with Christ. A Study in Pauline Theology. BZNW 32. Berlin, 1966.

Usami, K. Somatic Comprehension of Unity: The Church in Ephesians. AnBib 101. Rome, 1983.

Vielhauer, Ph. Geschichte der urchristlichen Literatur. Berlin/New York, 1975.

Vögtle, A. Die Tugend- und Lasterkataloge im Neuen Testament. NTA 16/4–5. Münster, 1936.

Wagner, G. Das religionsgeschichtliche Problem von Röm. 6:1–11. AThANT 39. Zürich, 1962.

Wegenast, K. Das Verständnis der Tradition bei Paulus und in den Deuteropaulinen. WMANT 8. Neukirchen, 1962.

Weiss, H. "The Law in the Epistle to the Colossians," CBQ 34 (1972), pp. 294–314.

Weiss, H. F. "Paulus und die Häretiker. Zum Paulusverständnis in der Gnosis," in Christentum und Gnosis. Edited by W. Eltester. BZNW 37, pp. 116–128. Berlin, 1969.

Weiss, H. F. "Gnostische Motive und antignostische Polemik im Kolosser- und Epheserbrief," in Gnosis und Neues Testament. Edited by K. W. Tröger, pp. 311–324. Berlin, 1973.

Weiss, H. F. "Taufe und neues Leben im deuteropaulinischen Schrifttum," in Taufe und neue Existenz. Edited by E. Schott, pp. 53–70. Berlin, 1973.

Wengst, K. Christologische Formeln und Lieder des Urchristentums. StNT 7. Gütersloh, 1972.

Wengst, K. "Versöhnung und Befreiung. Ein Aspekt des Themas 'Schuld und Vergebung' im Lichte des Kolosserbriefes," EvTh 36 (1976), pp. 14–26.

Wibbing, S. Die Tugend- und Lasterkataloge im Neuen Testament. BZNW 25. Berlin, 1959.

Wikenhauser, W. J. and J. Schmid. Einleitung in das Neue Testament.

Wiles, A. P. Paul's Intercessory Prayers. NTSMS 24. Cambridge, 1974.

Windisch, H. Paulus und Christus. Untersuchungen zum NT 24. Leipzig, 1934.

Wolff, Ch. Der erste Brief des Paulus an die Korinther II. ThHK 7/2. Berlin, 1982.

Zeilinger, F. Der Erstgeborene der Schöpfung. Untersuchungen zur Formalstruktur und Theologie des Kolosserbriefes. Vienna, 1974.

Zeilinger, F. "Die Träger der apostolischen Tradition im Kolosserbrief," in Jesus in der Verkündigung der Kirche. Edited by A. Fuchs. Studien zum NT und seiner Umwelt A/1, pp. 175–190. Linz, 1976.

§Supplemental Bibliography

Aland, Kurt. "The Problem of Anonymity and Pseudonymity in Christian Literature of the First Two Centuries," JTS 12 (1961), pp. 39–49.

Bandstra, A. J. "Did the Colossian Errorists Need a Mediator?" in New Dimensions in New Testament Study, ed. Longenecker, R. N. and Tenney, M. C. Grand Rapids: Zondervan, 1974, pp. 329–343.

Bartchy, S. Scott. MAΛΛON XPHΣAI: *First Century Slavery and the Interpretation of 1 Corinthians 7.21*. SBLDS 11. Missoula: Scholars Press, 1973.

Bauckham, R. J. "Colossians 1:24 Again: The Apocalyptic Motif," *EvQ* 47 (1975), pp. 168–170.

Bénoit, P. *Epîtres de Saint Paul aux Philippiens, aux Colossiens, à Philémon, aux Ephésiens*. La Sainte Bible. Paris: Editions du Cerf, 1949.

Best, E. *A Historical Study of Exegesis of Col 2, 14*. Rome: unpublished thesis, 1956.

Bowen, C. R. "Are Paul's prison letters from Ephesus?" *AJT* 24 (1920), pp. 112–135, 277–287.

Bowen, C. R. "The Original Form of Paul's Letter to the Colossians," *JBL* 43 (1924), pp. 177–206.

Bradley, J. "The Religious Life-Setting of the Epistle to the Colossians," *StBibT* 2 (1972), pp. 17–36.

Brown, R. E. *The Semitic Background of the Term "Mystery" in the New Testament*. FBBS 21. Philadelphia: Fortress, 1968.

Bruce, F. F. in Simpson, E. K., and Bruce, F. F. *Commentary on the Epistles to the Ephesians and the Colossians*. NICNT. Grand Rapids: Eerdmans, 1957.

Burney, C. F. "Christ as the 'APXH of Creation," *JTS* 27 (1926), pp. 160–177.

Candlish, J. "On the Moral Character of Pseudonymous Books," *The Expositor* Ser. 4, Vol. 4 (1891), pp. 91–107, 262–279. In Brox, *Pseudepigraphie*, 7–42.

Cannon, G. E. *The Use of Traditional Materials in Colossians*. Macon, Georgia: Mercer, 1983.

Carson, H. M. *Colossians and Philemon*. TNTC. London: Tyndale, 1960.

Craddock, Fred B. "All Things in Him: A Critical Note on Col. 1:15–20," *NTS* 12 (1966), pp. 78–80.

Crouch, J. *The Origin and Intention of the Colossian Haustafel*. FRLANT 109. Göttingen: Vandenhoeck & Ruprecht, 1972.

Davies, W. D. "Paul and the Dead Sea Scrolls: Flesh and Spirit," in *The Scrolls and the New Testament*, ed. K. Stendahl. New York: Harper, 1957, pp. 157–182.

Deissmann, A. *Paul: A Study in Social and Religious History*. Trans. William Wilson. Gloucester: P. Smith, 1972.

Doty, W. G. *Letters in Primitive Christianity*. New Testament Series. Philadelphia: Fortress Press, 1973.

Ellingsworth, P. "Colossians 1:15–20 and Its Context," *ExpT* 73 (1962), pp. 252–253.

Francis, F. O., and W. A. Meeks, eds. *Conflict at Colossae*. Society for Biblical Literature. Sources for Biblical Study 4. Missoula: Scholars Press, 1973.

Harrison, P. N. "Onesimus and Philemon," *ATR* 32 (1950), pp. 268–294.

Hengel, M. "Anonymität, Pseudepigraphie, und 'literarische Fälschung' in der jüdisch-hellenistischen Literatur," In K. von Fritz, ed., *Pseudepigrapha* 1, pp. 229–308.

Hobson, D. "The Authorship of Colossians," Diss. Claremont Graduate School and University Center, 1968.

Knox, J. "Philemon and the Authenticity of Colossians," *JR* 18 (1938), pp. 144–160.

Lillie, W. "The Pauline House-tables," *ExpT* 86 (1975), pp. 179–183.

Moule, C. F. D. " 'The New Life' in Colossians," *RevExp* 70 (1973), pp. 481–493.

Neufeld, V. H. *The Earliest Christian Confessions*. Edited by Bruce M. Metzger. New Testament Tools and Studies. Grand Rapids: Eerdmans, 1963.

Polhill, J. B. "The Relationship Between Ephesians and Colossians," *RevExp* 70 (1973), pp. 439–450.

Radford, L. B. *The Epistle to the Colossians and Epistle to Philemon.* WC. London: Methuen, 1931.

Sanders, E. "Literary Dependence in Colossians," *JBL* 85 (1966), pp. 28–45.

Schoeps, H. J. *Paul: The Theology of the Apostle in the Light of Jewish Religious History.* Translated by Harold Knight. Philadelphia: Westminster Press, 1961. Originally appeared as *Paulus: Die Theologie des Apostels im Lichte der jüdischen Religiongeschichte.* Tübingen: J. C. B. Mohr, 1959.

Schroeder, D. "Lists, Ethical," *IDBSup*, 546, 547.

Schütz, J. H. *Paul and the Anatomy of Apostolic Authority.* SNTSMS 26. Cambridge: University Press, 1975.

Schweizer, E. "Christ in the Letter to the Colossians," *RevExp* 70 (1973), pp. 429–514.

Schweizer, E. "Die Weltlichkeit des Neuen Testaments: Die Haustafeln," *Beiträge zur alttestamentlichen Theologie.* Festschrift für Walther Zimmerli zum 70. Geburtstag. Ed. H. Donner, R. Hanhart, R. Smend. Göttingen: Vandenhoeck & Ruprecht, 1977. Pages 397–413.

Schweizer, E. "The Church as the Missionary Body of Christ," *NTS* 8 (1961), pp. 1–11.

Stendahl, K. *Paul Among Jews and Gentiles and Other Essays.* Philadelphia: Fortress Press, 1976.

Synge, F. *Philippians and Colossians.* London: SCM, 1951.

Toussant, C. *L'épître de S. Paul aux Colossiens.* Paris: Emile Nourray, 1921.

Trudinger, L. P. "A Further Brief Note on Colossians 1:24," *EvQ* 45 (1973), pp. 36–38.

Wellburn, A. J. "The Identity of the Archons in the 'Apocryphon Johannis,' " *VC* 32 (1978), pp. 241–254.

Williams, A. L. *The Epistles of Paul the Apostle to the Colossians and to Philemon.* The Cambridge Greek Testament for Schools and Colleges. Cambridge: University Press, 1907.

Introduction

§1 Text and Language

(a) Text

The oldest textual witness of Colossians is the Chester Beatty papyrus (p⁴⁶), dated approximately 200 CE. The oldest parchment codices containing Colossians are the fourth-century Sinaiticus (‭א‬) and Vaticanus (B), as well as Codex Bezae Claromontanus (D, 6th cent.), representing the Western text type. The ninth-century codices K and L (Angelicus) are the oldest witnesses of the so-called Byzantine text type. There are no significant differences in the transmission of the text; only the author's frequent variation between the pronouns "we" and "you" (ἡμεῖς—ὑμεῖς) is typical, generally from the original "you" to the more engaging "we." The most important variants will be discussed in the exegesis of the respective reference. Unless otherwise noted, the translation is based on the third edition of the *Greek New Testament* (UBS³) and on the 26th edition of the Nestle text (Nestle–Aland; see bibliography); the reconstruction of the text is essentially the same in both.

(b) Language

The language of Colossians is the Koine of an individual with a basic training in Greek rhetoric, and it has certain commonalities with the language of the main letters of the apostle Paul, from which it borrows a number of its expressions.[1]

Comparing Colossians with those letters is also the best method of characterizing its language.[2] Several investigations have been con-

---

[1]Sanders, *Dependence*, passim.

[2]Otherwise, in its use of the appositional genitive, Col. may be compared with the language of the historian Diodorus Siculus; Bujard, *Untersuchungen*, p. 72, note 4.

ducted on the language of Colossians; the most significant are those
of Ernst Percy, *Probleme der Kolosser- und Epheserbriefe*, 1946, pp.
16–66, and Walter Bujard, *Stilanalytische Untersuchungen zum
Kolosserbrief*, 1973.

In contrast to the uncontested letters of Paul, in Colossians we encounter longer sentences (e.g., 1:3–8 or 1:9–20); conspicuously frequent relative clauses;[3] clustered epexegetical (explanatory) genitives
("the word of truth of the gospel," 1:5 et al.); numerous instances of
paronomasia (grouping of etymologically related words, e.g., "he
grows the growth"); polysyndeta (2:22, 23; 2:1 et al.), and especially
pleonasms (e.g., 1:22), whose frequency exceeds the Pauline average
by far.[4] Further characteristic of Colossians is the identifying (relative)
ὅ ἐστιν ("which is," "that is"–without regard for the gender of the
correlative).[5] In contrast to the argumentative thought of the apostle
Paul, the style of Colossians may better be characterized as associa-
tive speech.[6] The indicators of Paul's rhetorical directness, however,
are not to be found in Colossians.[7]

From these observations, which already signal the transition to the
statistics of words, I want to point out the copious use of verbs of the
word stem πληρ, which contrasts with the absence of the words utilizing the preposition ὑπέρ, occurring so frequently in Paul.[8] Colossians contains 34 terms otherwise not found in the NT (NT hapax
legomena); 28 expressions not found in Paul elsewhere, 10 that occur
only in Ephesians and Colossians in the framework of the NT, and
15 that in the Pauline corpus are found only in these two letters.[9] On
the average, these numbers are one third higher than those emerging
from a comparison of the uncontested Pauline letters or groups of letters with the entire NT and with the Pauline corpus respectively. Some
of the Pauline concepts are conspicuously absent, such as the singular of ἁμαρτία, δικαιοσύνη or πιστεύειν. Colossians and Ephesians
also lack the address ἀδελφοί μου, which, in the uncontested letters
of Paul (in the Pauline homologoumena), is missing only in the brief
letter to Philemon.[10]

---

[3]V. Spottorno, "The Relative Pronoun in the New Testament. Some Critical Remarks,"
NTS 28 (1982), pp. 132–141.

[4]Bujard, *Untersuchungen*, p. 165.

[5]Percy, *Probleme*, p. 33f.

[6]Schenk, "Christus," p. 139.

[7]Bujard, *Untersuchungen*, pp. 201, 214. This concerns such expressions as, "Now
is the appropriate time!" (2 Cor. 6:2).

[8]Ibid., p. 162f.

[9]On the statistics, consult Holtzmann, *Kritik*, p. 104ff.; Lohse, p. 133f.; cf. Kümmel,
Introduction, p. 299f.

[10]E. Schweizer, "Zur Frage der Echtheit des Kolosser- und des Epheserbriefes," most
recently in idem, *Neotestamentica*, Zürich–Stuttgart, 1963, p. 429.

§2 Question of Authorship and Literary Genre

(a) Authorship problem (I)

The peculiarities mentioned above can be explained in a variety of ways. E. Percy was convinced that the affinities with the language of the apostle Paul (similar word sequence, attribution of prepositions without article placed at the end, etc.) are stronger than the differences and that the analysis of vocabulary and style does not have to be seen as an argument against authenticity.[11] But then, W. Bujard has posited the most comprehensive investigation of the style of Colossians to date and concluded it with a vote in favor of the deuteropauline origin of this letter.[12] The stylistic differences are obvious and do not show up only in the polemic against the heresy, so that we cannot explain it in connection with the new theme[13] or as an adaptation to the rhetoric of the Asian province.[14] They can be seen most conspicuously in the introductory thanksgiving. Although in its solemnity the salutation is Pauline, it would be particularly easy for a disciple to imitate the letters of the teacher at this point. Where new ideas are formulated, it is more difficult to maintain the borrowed style. The argument in defense of authenticity is sometimes pursued by using the influence of the cited older materials.[15] These, however, are able to influence the vocabulary more than the style, which is essentially uniform in the entire epistle.

More important still is the comparison with the main letters in terms of content. The similarity of the argument of Col. 2:12f. with the teaching Paul attacks in 1 Cor. 4:8f. does not permit us to move Colossians close to the first letter to the Corinthians. And the obvious difference between Col. 2:12f. and the analogous sentences in Rom. 6:5f. (see §13) again rules out the possibility of dating it close to Romans.[16]

---

[11]Percy, Probleme, p. 66; so also Lohmeyer, p. 12f. A. di Marco is also inclined to interpret his investigations concerning the chiasm in Paul's writings in favor of the authenticity of Eph. and Col., "Chiasmus," p. 9; cf. pp. 28–30. M. Barth asserts that the differences in style and language are, in fact, an argument for authenticity, "Die Einheit des Galater und Epheserbriefs," TZ 32 (1976), pp. 78–91. According to him a forger would have imitated the Pauline style better (p. 87). For the recipients, however, a clear theological position and the emphasis of apostolic authority were more important than the style, which as hearers they were not able to evaluate very well (Col. 4:16).

[12]Bujard, Untersuchungen, p. 220; Schenk, "Christus," p. 139, refers to a sharp contrast to the argumentative thought of Paul.

[13]Thus Schmid, Zeit und Ort, p. 126, who speaks of the variation in the psychological situation. Similarly Dibelius, p. 53; Kümmel, Introduction, p. 301f.; Houlden, p. 135f.; Caird, p. 156f. et al.

[14]So Reicke, "Setting," p. 438. He has to presuppose the same in 2 Tim., which only escalates the problems. See § 4 (a) and § 12.

[15]Wikenhauser–Schmid, Einleitung, p. 430f.; Kümmel, Introduction, p. 300.

[16]See also Lindemann, "Gemeinde," p. 115f.

Based on the characteristics of style, it is further difficult to place Colossians close to Philippians. We would have to assume that Paul here attempted to alter the style intentionally, whereas in the prescript, as well as in the concluding list of greetings (4:18), he deliberately presents himself as the one who is already known for his apostolic authority from Philippians and Philemon (see §3 [a]). It is unlikely, therefore, that the two letters (Colossians and Philippians) were written during the imprisonment in Caesarea (Acts 24–26) in approximately 56–58 CE.[17] The same concerns also apply to the tradition of the origin of the two letters (including Philem. and Eph.) from the Roman confinement (even according to the postscript in the MSS K, L et al.), approximately 58–60 CE (Acts 28:16, 30f.).[18]

Not all of the arguments in favor of the authenticity of Colossians have thereby come to naught. The language of a writer can change drastically in the course of his or her life. Theoretically it would be possible to separate Colossians and Ephesians temporally from the other Prison Letters (Ephesus-Rome, or two imprisonments in Rome, the second one after the planned trip to Spain; Rom. 15:24; 1 Clem. 5:7); but in practice this is hardly possible because of the relationship between the list of greetings in Colossians with that in Philemon (see §3 [b]). The classic expression of the alternatives was offered by Ernst Käsemann, who wrote concerning the writing of Colossians: "If authentic, as late as possible on account of the style; if not authentic, as early as possible."[19]

Recent scholarship has tied up all of the interpretation of Colossians with the problem of its authenticity.[20] The fact that the likely later author intended to write in a Pauline manner [21] relativizes the problem somewhat, but does not remove it. It merely denotes that there are several exegetical observations which retain their importance regardless of the yet-to-be-addressed question of authorship. If Colossians were authentic, we would have to assume a new phase in Paul's thought and literary style. If it were the case that Colossians is a deuteropauline letter—which is our position, it is necessary, in turn, to

[17]E.g., Lohmeyer, p. 14f.

[18]E.g., Schiwy, p. 373, and, with reservations, Kümmel, Introduction, p. 305f.; Caird, p. 157.

[19]Käsemann, "Kolosserbrief," p. 1728. In favor of a late date in the framework of Paul's life argue e.g., Oltramare, p. 27ff. and Jülicher–Fascher, Einleitung, pp. 134, 142.

[20]For an overview of the discussion, see e.g., Lähnemann, Kolosserbrief, pp. 12–28; cf. Schmauch, p. 44.

[21]Schenk argues that the theology of Colossians cannot be reconciled with the Pauline theology, in spite of the Pauline opening of the letter and of the Pauline expressions. He asserts: "The two viewpoints are worlds apart," "Christus," p. 150; on this see § 13. Bujard, Untersuchungen, p. 129, merely speaks of the difference in the structure of thought in terms of the train of thought.

place it in a certain time frame[22] and in a particular historical and spiritual realm. For this reason, we shall further consider the authorship question in connection with the position of Colossians within the framework of the Pauline letters (§3 [d]) and in terms of a comprehensive evaluation of its deuteropauline character (§4). Our interpretation of Col. 4:7–18 likewise supports a deuteropauline origin.

(b) Literary genre

On the basis of its broader purpose and fundamental importance, Colossians is a type of writing designated as epistle.[23] It was meant to help the recipients in dealing with a spiritual threat. In contrast to the letters to the Corinthians, which address concrete questions asked by the addressees, the issue here is a dangerous, possibly threatening heresy. Similar to Ephesians but unlike Romans, for instance, the fundamental theological themes are not addressed in a clear, logical sequence; instead, the entire epistle tends to be paraenetic.[24] In two instances (1:15–20; 2:14f.) the paraenesis relies theologically on formal expressions having older, liturgical content.

§3 Position in the Framework of the Corpus Paulinum

(a) Prison Letters

Colossians exhibits a variety of strands of relationships with three of the other letters of the Pauline corpus. The first area of similarity pertains to theology. As in Phil. 2:10f., 3:21, and elsewhere, Colossians emphasizes Christ's exaltation and his sovereignty over the entire created order, inclusive of the suprahuman, heavenly powers. The same is true of Ephesians, which, in fact, is connected with Colossians via numerous parallel pericopae (see below, §3 [c]). The remaining commonalities are delineated in *Table 1* on page 6.

Since we argued (§2 [c]) that Colossians and Philippians cannot be dated in one and the same imprisonment, the Prison Letters are related only through the references concerning the apostle's condition and through some theological themes. Philippians was probably written[25] during the Ephesian imprisonment, which is only indirectly at-

---

[22]Even so the dating would not be very remote from the Pauline era; cf. § 4 (a). The late dating in the second century is not realistic; see Kümmel, *Introduction,* p. 298f.

[23]Berger, "Apostelbrief," p. 230f.

[24]Bujard, *Untersuchungen,* p. 129.

[25]Suhl, *Paulus,* p. 342, dates Col. in the Ephesian imprisonment, even prior to the Corinthian letters. In order to explain the stylistic and theological differences, he attributes it to Epaphras (p. 168, note 93); on this cf. § 4 (a).

	Phil.	Phlm.	Col.	Eph.
Exaltation and sovereignty of Jesus Christ emphasized	+	–	+	+
Several parallel segments	–	–	+	+
Similar lists of greetings	–	+	+	–
Writers Paul and Timothy	+	+	+	–

TABLE 1

tested (1 Cor. 15:30ff.; 2 Cor. 11:23);[26] Colossians and Ephesians must have originated at a later time. The hypothesis that Philippians was written after Colossians, because according to Col. 4:10, Mark, whom Paul wants to send to Colossae, is no longer with him in Phil. 2:20,[27] is influenced by the tradition that all the Prison Letters originated during the Roman imprisonment (§2 [a]).[28] Philippians, however, represents the particular strand to which Colossians could be tied within the realm of Paulinism. The problem of the relationship to the letter to Philemon will be examined in a broader framework.

(b) Colossians and Ephesians, Pastoral Letters, and Philemon
There are conspicuous divergences between Colossians and Ephesians on the one hand and with the Pastorals (1, 2 Tim., Tit.) on the other, particularly in terms of style, understanding of office, and especially of eschatology (cf. Col. 2:12f. with 2 Tim. 2:18). Hence at least one of these groups of letters has to be secondary. Most biblical scholars are of the opinion that this is true of the Pastorals. However, if two divergent text groups emerge as late writings of a well-known author, the authenticity of both is thereby subject to question. No disciple of an apostle would contradict the authentic apostolic writings. Yet the theological divergences of the two groups of letters can easily be

[26]An overview of the arguments is offered in Kümmel, *Introduction*, pp. 288–291. Duncan even argues for several imprisonments of the apostle Paul in Ephesus, *Ministry*, p. 145ff.
[27]von Soden, p. 17.
[28]Schmithals, "Composition," argues that, based on the earliest manuscripts and canonical lists, Eph. and Col. formed a minor collection of Prison Letters, p. 253ff. Against this, cf. Schenke–Fischer, *Einleitung*, pp. 233ff., 242ff.; they presuppose that the letters of Paul were not collected until after the apostle's death and after the subsequent crisis of Paulinism. They take Col. to be a deuteropauline writing. So also Sand, "Überlieferung," p. 19ff., who, in contrast to them, presupposes continuity in the collection of the letters of Paul—which is quite plausible.

explained as different interpretations of the Pauline heritage by two groups of disciples (see *Table* 2):

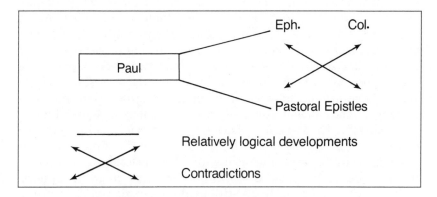

TABLE 2

If Colossians were authentic, or if it had been written on behalf of the apostle by Timothy or by an amanuensis (see §4 [a]), it would mean that both letters had to have been written in quick succession. Colossians would have to have been written after Philemon, since according to Col. 4:9 Onesimus was already a proven coworker of the apostle. In line with part of the tradition, it would also have to be presupposed that the letter to Philemon originated in Rome, since it was written after the main letters.[29] Several scholars presuppose, however, that the letter to Philemon originated in Ephesus.[30] Reasons: According to Philem. 22, Paul wants to visit Philemon, whereas from Rome he wanted to travel to Spain (Rom. 15:24, 28); in addition, it is more plausible that Onesimus fled to Ephesus than that he dared to journey to Rome. One thing is certain: Colossians was written *after* Philemon, and in its interpretation, we shall have to take Philemon into consideration. If Philemon were written during the same imprisonment as Philippians (that is the segment dealing with the imprisonment of the apostle), then Philemon must have been written after Philippians, because, according to Philem. 22, Paul (in contrast to Phil. 1:12–26) anticipates his imminent release (see also §3 [d]).

(c) Relationship to Ephesians
The parallels between these two letters are numerous and obvious. Only the passages of Col. 1:6–8, 15, 17; 2:1–2, 5, 9, 11, 15–18, 20–23; 3:2–4, 7, 11; 4:9–18 have no parallels and analogues in Ephesians. The

[29]Among the authors who consider Col. as deuteropauline, Schenke–Fischer date Philem. in the Roman imprisonment, *Einleitung*, p. 154ff.
[30]Wikenhauser–Schmid, *Einleitung*, p. 477ff.

following passages in Ephesians are without parallel in Colossians: Eph. 1:2–3, 5, 8–9, 11–12, 14; 2:4, 7–11, 17–20, 22; 3:4, 6, 8–12, 14–15; 4:4–5, 7, 9–12, 14, 17, 21, 26–28, 30; 5:1–2, 7, 9, 15, 18, 21, 23–24, 26, 28–29, 31–33; 6:2–3, 10–17, 23–24.[31] Nevertheless, only a few pericopae agree verbatim (except Col. 3:18–4:1 par.); in other words, there is no slavish copying of one letter by the other, but these are two writings from one spiritual workshop, or perhaps two works of one editor.

It is possible to view Colossians as an abridged version of Ephesians; it may also be, however, that Ephesians, which is more general in scope, incorporated some segments of Colossians in a broader framework. E. Th. Mayerhoff has argued for the former option.[32] According to him, Colossians utilized some themes of Ephesians in its polemic against a heresy that he identified as the teaching of the Gnostic Cerinthus. According to tradition, Cerinthus taught in Ephesus (Iren., Adv. haer. III, 4, 4); he attributed the creation of the world to a lesser deity (ibid. I, 26, 1). Consequently Colossians was dated late.[33] Mayerhoff has correctly discovered some gnostic features in the heresy attacked in Col. 2:8, 16–23 (see §12);[34] it is not possible, however, to identify it as a directly verifiable gnostic group. For this reason alone we ought not date Colossians in the second century.

Another argument in favor of the former option is found in the allusions that we encounter in Colossians but that can be understood only with difficulty apart from a knowledge of the corresponding parallels in Ephesians. This applies to Col. 1:20, for instance, which deals with an all-encompassing reconciliation, while in Eph. 2:14–17 reconciliation is more precisely characterized as an ecclesiological-cosmic event.[35] It appears, however, that these are allusions to an older liturgical tradition already familiar to the recipients of Colossians, and to its broader context and Sitz im Leben.[36]

The problems outlined above led H. J. Holtzmann (1872) to the hypothesis of a later (between 100–125 CE) revision of a lost, authentic

---

[31]For a synopsis, see de Wette, Lehrbuch, pp. 313–318; Abbott, p. xxiii; Haupt, pp. 65–68; Percy, Probleme, p. 360f., cf. pp. 362–418 (commentary on the points of contact); an overview is also available in Ernst, pp. 254–257.

[32]Der Brief an die Kolosser, Berlin, 1838, p. 148ff.

[33]Baur has adopted Mayerhoff's argument, Paul, vol. 2, 1–6, 43–44. For him Eph. is the same as the letter to the Laodiceans, as Marcion also claimed.

[34]Schenke–Fischer, Einleitung, pp. 162f., 171.

[35]Ewald, p. 20ff. (however, he also identifies the letter to the Laodiceans with Eph., p. 17ff.); Burger, Schöpfung, pp. 23–25.

[36]Burger allows for this possibility too, Schöpfung, p. 139. van Roon's hypothesis in "Authenticity" has no basis; according to him Eph. and Col. were not adapted to one another until they were read publicly in the course of their worship services; so also M. Barth, "Die Einheit des Galater- und Epheserbriefs," p. 85f. C. L. Mitton, The Epistle to the Ephesians, Oxford, 1951, pp. 247f., 252f., has found numerous references in Eph. which can be understood as combinations of two references in Col. (e.g., Eph. 1:7 and

letter to the Colossians (and of the list of greetings in Rom. 16:1–23) by the author of Ephesians. The result is the extant Colossians. Accordingly, the original Colossians had roughly the following content: Col. 1:1–15; 1:23–2:5; 2:8; 2:11–3:4; 3:5–4:6; conclusion.[37] This hypothesis[38] is able to integrate the arguments for the sequence Eph. → Col., as well as those for the sequence Col. →Eph., but it lacks support in the text of Colossians, which contains no traces of a later revision.[39] What remains after the removal of the most obvious parallels with Ephesians is indeed more in keeping with the style of the remaining Pauline letters than the totality of Colossians. Yet in an altogether non-Pauline manner, it is devoid of any theological argumentation, so that one has to ask why it was written to begin with.[40] In the case of Colossians, therefore, we shall work with an integral text.

In favor of the second option, the priority of Colossians,[41] is the style of Ephesians, which is even more removed from the language of the main letters of Paul than that of Colossians (Eph. 1:3–14, *one* sentence). There are further notable differences in the vocabulary (e.g., διάβολος instead of the Pauline σατανᾶς). Likewise a comparison of the overall character of the two letters favors the priority of Colossians. If Colossians had been written later, it would be difficult to explain why it lacks salvation history statements, as well as the expressions about the unity of the church, which play such a significant part in Ephesians. It is more likely that the epistle, which has stood the test in the polemic against an actual heresy,[42] was used as a source in the formulation of a broader exposition on the unity of the church (Eph.). The polemical sections had to be excised, and some statements that presupposed acquaintance with liturgical tradition were formulated more broadly and more clearly.[43] Thus the Prison Letters

---

Col. 1:14, 20). By contrast Munro, "Evidence," presupposes the priority of Eph. but has to allow for later layers in both letters.

[37]Holtzmann, *Einleitung*, p. 291ff. An overview of the attempts at reconstructing an original letter to the Colossians is found in J. Moffatt, *An Introduction to the Literature of the New Testament*, Edinburgh, 1912[2], 156ff.

[38]It has been adopted e.g., by Schmidt–Holzendorff, p. 793; Ochel, *Annahme*, passim; Masson; R. Knopf, *Einführung in das Neue Testament*, New York, n.d., p. 85f.

[39]Thus correctly by Jülicher–Fascher, *Einleitung*, p. 134.

[40]Caird, p. 157.

[41]In summary form in Merklein, "Theologie," p. 26f., esp. note 10; cf. Schmauch, p. 42f.

[42]Hooker argues against the notion that Col. polemicizes against a concrete heresy, "False Teachers," pp. 317, 327, 329.

[43]Some scholars assume an intermediate stage between Col. and Eph.–the explanations of a Pauline commentator, Burger, *Schöpfung*, p. 157. It is not appropriate to argue for the priority of Eph. on the basis of the sequence within the NT canon, because one of the decisive factors in its determination was not the date of writing but its volume.

were likely written in the following sequence: Philippians (at least 1:1–3:1 and 4:4–23),[44] Philemon, and after a longer period of time Colossians–Ephesians.

(d) Consequences for the question of authorship (II)

Style (§1) and theology (§13) point to Colossians as a deuteropauline writing. As mentioned earlier, if it were an authentic letter of the apostle Paul, it would have to be placed in the vicinity of Philippians and Philemon (especially due to the similarity of the list of greetings in Philemon and Colossians; cf. §4 [a], and →4:7–18)—quite a difficult task, considering the differences in style and theology. It is even more difficult to demonstrate the authenticity of Ephesians. Certain scholars take Ephesians to be deuteropauline, whereas they attribute Colossians to the apostle Paul.[45] Many exegetes, however, consider both epistles to be deuteropauline;[46] some of them argue explicitly for two authors.[47] In favor of this one may point to the shift in the emphasis on the unity of the church, comprised of Jews and Gentiles in Ephesians, whereas combatting a concrete heresy is in the forefront in Colossians. Conversely the unfolding of an older liturgical tradition that is similar but whose verbal agreement is never precise allows for a common author for both epistles.[48] Common to both letters are especially the theme of the sovereignty of Christ, who is exalted over the entire created order, and the emphasis upon the church as his body (→2:19; §14). The problem of one or two authors is diffused somewhat, if we assume that Colossians, like Ephesians, arose from the same circle of Pauline disciples (cf. §4 [a]).

§4 Concerning the Deuteropauline Character of Colossians

(a) Authorship (III), date, and place of writing

The letter to the Colossians was written in the name of the apostle Paul. Paul, a diaspora Jew whose Hebrew name was Saul, hailed from

---

[44]If we assume that Phil. was written in Ephesus, its older and larger part may well have been written prior to 1 Cor.; cf. Vielhauer, Geschichte, p. 168ff.; Schenke–Fischer, Einleitung, p. 129.

[45]E.g., Dibelius, p. 85; E. J. Goodspeed, The Meaning of Ephesians, Chicago, 1933, pp. 3–17, argues similarly to Mitton (Ephesians, see note 36 above) that Eph. is an introduction to the Corpus Paulinum in which Col. belongs as an authentic letter; Bénoit, "Rapports," p. 22 et al.

[46]E.g., Baur, Paul, vol. 2, pp. 11ff., 49, and the majority of the Tübingen school. The more recent discussion is summarized in Lohse, p. 253f. and Ernst, p. 258ff.

[47]See Vielhauer, Geschichte, p. 212; Schenke–Fischer, Einleitung, p. 186; Käsemann, "Epheserbrief," RGG³ II, 517–520, esp. col. 519 et al.

[48]Summarized in Lohse, "Pauline Theology." The argument that Col. avoids the concept of spirit is not pertinent since the expression "in the Spirit," which is typical

Tarsus. Because of an encounter with Jesus (1 Cor. 9:1; 15:8; Gal. 1:15f.; cf. Acts 9:1–19; 22:6–16; 26:12–18) he became a Christian around 35 CE. He understood the gospel as the message of the resurrection and interpreted it within his teaching on justification by faith: If God raised to new life the crucified Jesus whom he rejected according to the stipulations of the Mosaic law, then in Jesus was revealed the higher and decisive intention of God. Specifically, this is the salvation of the sinner from the final judgment (Rom. 2:16), the sinner's justification by grace, which is perceived by faith as trust in God (Gal. 3:6–4:7; Rom. 3:21–26). Even while Paul was still alive, some people viewed his proclamation as an erosion of the pursuit of an ethical betterment of life (Rom. 6:1). In reality, according to Paul, the justification of the sinner is at the same time the most fundamental prerequisite for the new life in this world (Rom. 6:2–11). The issue of the unity of the church especially served as the impetus for the development of the Pauline doctrine of justification. In the church former Jews regarded former Gentiles as second-rate Christians who had not been Jews before their baptism (Acts 15:1; Gal. 2:11f.). In the doctrine of justification Paul wanted to demonstrate that, by their faith, believers are the true descendants and heirs of Abraham (Gal. 3:6ff.; Rom. 4).

Despite the arguments from the Old Testament, his interpretation of the gospel—a new interpretation of the Jewish Bible—created tension with the Jewish-Christian groups, including the leader of the church in Jerusalem (Gal., indirectly Acts 15:1–35; 21:15ff.; cf. 2 Cor. 11:1–6).[49] Among several Christian groups this led to a critique of the Pauline heritage. In the letter to the church in Ephesus in the Apocalypse of John (Rev. 2:1–7), we hear nothing about him, although he labored there for an extended period of time. Instead, it addresses the sect of the Nicolaitans, which may be identical with the adherents of Nicolaus, the Gnostic (Iren., *Adv. haer.* I, 26, 3).[50] At the beginning of the second century, in 2 Pet. 3:15f., we read that some ignorant people twisted the letters of Paul.

---

for Eph., also shows up in Col. 1:12, and since Col. seeks to avoid the concept pneuma because the opponents favored it (→1:12; § 12).

[49]That there was a Jewish-Christian antipauline front has been emphasized by G. Lüdemann, "Antipaulinismus," passim. His attempt to stereotype the opponents of Paul mentioned in the various epistles is as one-sided as the picture which W. Schmithals sketched of the gnostics as Paul's universal opponents (esp. in the collection of essays, *Paul and the Gnostics*, ET by John Steely, Nashville, 1972). There are several points of convergence between Judaism and gnosis, but these do not represent an advancement in the theologically divergent basic disposition. Hence the antipauline front had only few common features.

[50]According to Irenaeus, Nicolaus was identical to the deacon of Acts 6:4.

This does not mean that Paul was forgotten or rejected by the church in general.[51] After the destruction of Jerusalem, when some Pharisees gained control of virtually all Judaism, including the diaspora, and the church separated from Judaism, the Pauline position gained prominence. It was capable of serving as foundation of the independent existence of the church and of rescuing the Bible (the OT) for the church. Hence the church is the true heir of the promises of Israel. In this manner Paul indirectly contributed to the later shaping of the two-partite canon. Nevertheless, he cannot be considered as the second founder (next to Jesus) of Christianity, as some liberals claimed. Paul respected the disseminated Christian confessions and liturgical materials and interpreted them: the confession of faith in 1 Cor. 15:3b–5, the confession of the son in Rom. 1:3f., the Carmen Christi in Phil. 2:6–11; the homology of the Lord in Rom. 10:9 or 1 Cor. 12:3, the confession of the resurrection of Jesus in 1 Thess. 1:10; 1 Cor. 6:14; Rom. 10:9 et al. With the earliest Christian groups he also utilizes the Abba appellation, which in all likelihood originated with Jesus (Rom. 5:15; Gal. 4:6).

Colossians wants to be understood as in line with this Pauline theological tradition, regardless of how the question of authorship is resolved.

Though the topic of justification is missing in Colossians, it also recedes into the background in Philippians and in the Corinthian correspondence (it is mentioned only in 1 Cor. 6:11; 2 Cor. 5:21; Phil. 3:9). Meanwhile the gospel has penetrated into the predominantly Gentile world. In 2 Corinthians, the "for us" concerning the resurrection of Jesus is interpreted more in terms of reconciliation (5:18–21); Philippians underscores the exaltation of Jesus, made possible by the cross and which is the perspective of Christian humility (Phil. 2:9–11; 3:10, 21). This aspect occurs not merely at the apocalyptic cataclysm at the end of this age, as still presupposed in 1 Thess. 1:10 and 1 Cor. 15:23,[52] but immediately upon death (Phil. 1:21–23). At this point, redemption in the present is not yet anticipated as directly as it is presupposed in Col. 2:12f. and 3:1 (§13); nevertheless, the assurance of salvation is already expressed as present citizenship in heaven (Phil. 3:20). It was at this point that Colossians was able to tie in (on reconciliation: Col. 2:19f., 22). Since there are additional commonalities (§3, table 1), we may regard Philippians as a theological link between the main letters of Paul and Colossians. The question of whether Paul himself still made the theological transition from the assurance of the heavenly citizenship to the present participation

---

[51]Emphasized in Lüdemann, *Paulus*, pp. 112ff., 401ff; see in ET *Paul*.
[52]In this regard we do not know the meaning of Rom. 6:5, 8.

in the resurrection of Christ,[53] or whether it was made by one of his disciples,[54] ought to be answered in favor of the second alternative according to our observations thus far. Likewise the results of the preliminary analysis of the theological structure of Colossians (§5 [b]; §6) as well as some further individual observations are more fitting under the assumption that the letter is the effort of a disciple.

Significant for Colossians, for instance, is the normative role that the absent apostle plays in view of the threat of heresy (→1:24; →2:1–5). It is noteworthy that the objective meaning of the concept of faith becomes prominent in the formulations of faith handed down by tradition (1:23; 2:7, cf. Eph. 4:5) and that the apostle considers his task to be that of teaching (διδάσκειν, cf. §6 [c]) rather than proclamation (κηρύσσειν, as in Rom., 1 and 2 Cor., Gal., 1 Thess.). Proclamation is already a matter of the past (1:23).[55] Similar shifts in emphasis can also be observed in the understanding of the church (see §14). It is further significant that Christ is conceived of as the firstborn from the dead (1:18b—the hymn), that is, as the hope for those who have fallen asleep. Paul has reached this conclusion about the gospel in 1 Thess. 4:13–18 and in 1 Cor. 15; in a different way he had to defend it in 2 Cor. 5 as a tenet of faith not to be taken for granted. Here we encounter it as an already accepted hymn that the author interprets in terms of the present assurance of salvation. These are further theological reasons that make it impossible to date Colossians close to the Corinthian letters (cf. §2 [a]; §3 [b]).[56] In addition, a postPauline origin is favored by the fact that Col. 1:6 and 23 stress the worldwide spreading of the gospel, and the practice of reading of the apostolic letters in the community is presupposed (4:16).

Everything that causes us to doubt the authenticity of Colossians does not at all change the fact that we must interpret it as a text that seeks to link up with the thought of the main letters of Paul and that, in this sense, authentically renders the apostolic witness. With all the relative theological continuity, however, the question of authorship is not a matter of indifference, first, for reasons of classifying it in a specific time frame. Based on our evaluations, the scope of the possible dating shrinks to a quarter of a century, roughly the years between 58 and 83 CE. During these years the Jewish War, including the fall of Jerusalem, serves as the line of separation between the various dating options—a factor that is not unimportant in the interpretation of the text.

---

[53]E.g., Lohmeyer, p. 10ff.; Kümmel, Introduction, p. 303; Martin, NCBC, p. 83; Schiwy, p. 384.

[54]Lohse, Schweizer, Gnilka, in loco.

[55]It is virtually identical with the catechetical passing on of doctrine, 1:5, 23.

[56]Against Ollrog, Mitarbeiter, pp. 219ff., 236ff.; in favor, Ernst, p. 151.

The interpretation of Colossians as a writing of a disciple of Paul, however, is contested particularly because we would have to assume a certain falsification in the writing process of this epistle. Therefore, with regards to the theology and the ethics of the false authorial references, we are required to add a few summarizing observations at this point.[57]

(a) The most fundamental reason for writing pseudonymous letters was to defend the authority, and generally also the teaching, of a significant teacher. And that the teaching is threatened is attested in Col. 2:4, 8, 16ff. But problems arise when the teachings of a teacher are defended in the disciples' writings which are disseminated under the teacher's name, even if the teacher is absent or has died.

(b) In some respects it is understandable that a writing is attributed to a famous name. In Israel several Psalms have been connected with David, and the wisdom sayings were accorded to King Solomon, etc. Similarly, the epistle to the Hebrews was classified in the Pauline corpus because of its closeness to the Pauline theology.[58] Yet these associations were generally made later. This applies in the NT especially to writings authored anonymously during the time of the outward loss of authority, after the death of the apostle; these were only later attributed to an individual from the apostolic circle.[59] In the disputed Pauline writings (antilegomena), as well as in the Catholic Letters of the NT we encounter a pseudonymity that, by means of various personal references in the text (in Col. it is especially the list of greetings), from the outset endeavors to create the impression of an authentic writing. According to modern criteria, this is forgery.

(c) A writing under an assumed name may in a sense be understood as an attempt to furnish the teaching advocated there with the authority related to the generation of the alleged author. Christian pseudepigraphy indeed looks for the author's name in the apostolic age, which is sometimes more important in the selection of the pseudonym than the name itself. Thereby Christian pseudepigraphy is differentiated from similar practices in other realms where the cult is derived from a mythical story. In the realm of Christianity it is pre-

[57]The following evaluations have been presented more extensively in "Das theologische Problem der neutestamentlichen Pseudepigraphie," *EvTh* 44 (1984), 486–496.

[58]Origen, *Fragm. Hebr. Homil.* in Euseb., *Hist. eccl.* VI, 25, 11–14; cf. Brox, *Verfasserangaben*, p. 74f. Overall, M. Hengel, "Anonymität, Pseudepigraphie und literarische Fälschung in der jüdisch–hellenistischen Literatur," in *Pseudepigrapha I* (Fondation Hardt. Entretiens sur l'antiquité classique 18), Vandoeuvres–Geneva, 1972, pp. 229–308.

[59]K. Aland, "The Problem of Anonymity and Pseudonymity in Christian Literature of the First Two Centuries," *JTS* n.s. 12 (1, 1961), 39–49, esp. pp. 42ff. Thereby he relativizes the consciousness of intellectual property in antiquity. See also H. R. Balz, "Anonymität und Pseudepigraphie im Urchristentum," *ZThK* 66 (1969), 403–436; K. M. Fischer, "Anmerkungen zur Pseudepigraphie im Neuen Testament," *NTS* 23 (1976–77), 76–81.

supposed that the revelation of God and also the norm of the teaching are bound up with Jesus of Nazareth and with the earliest (apostolic) witnesses. It is an expression of the incarnational faith of the Christian. In this light we also understand that the canonical recognition of some Christian pseudepigraphal writings was especially the result of the theological, dogmatic assessment. For instance, Origen says that while Hebrews was not written in Pauline language, it nevertheless contained Pauline theology. Hence he acknowledged it as Pauline (Euseb., *Hist. eccl.* VI, 25, 11–14). The historical location was contingent upon the dogmatic assessment. On the other hand, the dogmatically unacceptable writings were at the same time also rejected as later fabrications (Tert., *Bapt.* 17, 4).[60]

(d) A significant source of infringement upon acknowledging intellectual property was the awareness of a special task from God which the writer was able to receive through a deep, spiritual experience. A number of faithful coworkers of the apostle emerge in Colossians (1:7; 4:7, 9ff.), among whom Epaphras has a representative function in the service of Christ. In this case the adjective πιστός, in the passive sense, denotes the recognition by God (1 Cor. 7:25 et al.). Others are called "fellow workers for the kingdom of God" (see 4:10f.). Among these one might look for the writer of Colossians.[61] This somewhat mitigates the offensiveness of pseudepigraphy, but fails to remove it completely, for by means of the divine commission one could argue for immediacy, as John the Revelator, for instance, had done (Rev. 1:1, 9f.).

(e) The use of the names of the apostles by the opponents constitutes a significant external impetus for the writing of the canonical pseudepigraphy.[62] Indirectly the extra-canonical Pauline pseudepigraphy is already documented in 2 Thess. 2:2. A letter of this type shook the faith of the recipients not only by way of the false teaching itself, but also through its outward authority, for a letter could replace the personal address of the apostle (2 Thess. 2:15). It is understandable that, with similar methods, they resisted the dangers of fictitious and post-dated apostolic letters. It served as some sort of antidote.[63] For us, however, this continues to be offensive ethically,

---

[60]For this reason, only with reservation can the pseudepigraphal letters of the NT be compared with such letters as Acts 15:23–29 or 23:26–30, both of which derive as "pedagogical" fiction from the illustrative tendency in ancient historiography (E. Güttgemanns, "In welchem Sinne ist Lukas 'Historiker'?" *LB* 54 [1983], 9–26, esp. p. 17f.).

[61]Cf. Gnilka, "Paulusbild," p. 183.

[62]On the designation pseudepigrapha, see § 18 (b) below.

[63]On the topic as a whole, see Brox, *Verfasserangaben*, p. 98f.; Speyer, "Pseudepigraphie," p. 256f.

especially when the claim to the writer's own handwriting is underscored thereby (see 4:18).

(f) In the dictated letters (Rom. 16:22) the author's handwritten greeting expressed the personal relationship of the writer to the recipients[64] and the apostolic authority in the apostolic letters.[65] Only in a very indirect manner did it also confirm the personal identity of the writer, which the one delivering the letter was able to confirm.[66] The author's handwritten part in Gal. 6:11 was intended to authorize the proclamation of the gospel to the uncircumcised; in 1 Cor. 16:21 the signature introduced the apostolic verdict; and in Philem. 19 Paul vouched for the debts of Onesimus via his signature. Only in 2 Thess. 3:17 does the signature clearly have the function of identification over against the false letters of Paul (2 Thess. 2:2). But it is precisely this that causes problems for the immediate Pauline origin of 2 Thessalonians. The written confirmation of the identity was especially necessary in post-dated letters. In Colossians the handwritten signature (4:18) does not have a specifically identifying function. It is especially intended to evoke reminiscences of the apostle. Its specific motive may have been to underscore the exhortation addressed to Archippus. Consequently, Col. 4:18 cannot be used as an argument in support of the authenticity of Colossians, nor can it be used against the latter, as is the case in 2 Thess. 3:17. Theologically the apostolic signature, in all instances, confirms the authority of the respective letter as an authentic witness of the resurrection of Jesus.

(g) Subjectively it was possible to appeal to fiction (ψεῦδος) as an antidote to a problem, as found in Plato (Polit. II, 382C).[67] Origen deals even more extensively with the theory of deception (Contra Cels. IV, 18f.). We have shown, however, that this was only considered as an emergency measure (see [c] above). We need to consider further that the canonical pseudepigrapha succeeded as apostolic letters, and as such they were later included in the canon. Calling into question their authenticity poses a new problem with which we can come to terms only by appealing to the grace of God. By God's grace the legitimate apostolic intention succeeded, despite human failure and

---

[64]E.g., "Fare well" ἔρρωσο (Deissmann, Ancient East, p. 170f.) or opto multos annos (G. Marini, I papiri diplomatici, Rome, 1805, nr. 73, in Roller, Formular, p. 75) were written by hand.

[65]H. Hegermann, "Der religionsgeschichtliche Ort der Pastoralbriefe," in Theologische Versuche, vol. 2, Berlin, 1970, pp. 47–64, esp. p. 54ff., argues that the issue was one of authenticating the theological bent without ethical objection. He underestimates the element of fiction.

[66]Against Roller, Formular, pp. 74, 131–33, 143, 190, who draws his conclusions mainly on the premise of the official letters.

[67]According to Plato only physicians, not commoners, may use the antidote: Resp. III, 389B; see also Brox, Verfasserangaben, p. 82ff.

literary falsification. Thus the biblical canon is made holy, not as a human endeavor, but by the grace of God—this also applies to the evaluation of the historical authenticity of some of its writings (for further information on this, see §18 [b]).

(h) In contrast to what has just been said, the final two observations address only certain parts of the problem. The relative theological continuity of Colossians, as we have established it in relation to the main letters of Paul, does not mean that the author of Colossians, in case it was not Paul, had to have been an extraordinary personality congenial to Paul.[68] Such a perspective does not take into consideration the disciple-teacher relationship of antiquity, as it was shaped by hellenistic philosophical and theological schools.[69] The existence of the Johannine writings with their various strands and layers attests to this.[70] Moreover, because of the Pastoral Letters (§3 [b]), the problem of the deuteropauline writings in the NT cannot be ignored. If, in line with the majority of exegetes, we regard the Pastoral Letters, whose content is also linked up with Paul (e.g., see 1 Tim. 1:15), as products of a school, it is feasible that there were other, even earlier groups of Pauline students in Asia Minor.[71] These developed and defended the fundamental concerns of Pauline theology in a different manner.[72]

(i) Finally, concerning Timothy and the modified hypothesis of an amanuensis as a possible explanation for the authorship issue of Colossians:

Timothy was a significant fellow-worker of the apostle Paul and was with him in Ephesus (1 Cor. 4:17). His father was a Gentile, while his mother was a Jewess who became a Christian (Acts 16:1-3). The two Pastoral epistles in which he emerges as an exemplary functionary of the church are most likely deuteropauline.[73] In any event, they at-

[68]So Percy, *Probleme*, p. 356, cf. p. 136. This argument has already been used in earlier years: Such a genius of a Pauline disciple cannot remain hidden; Beet, p. 8.

[69]W. Bousset, *Jüdisch–christlicher Schulbetrieb in Alexandrien und Rom*, FRLANT 23, Göttingen, 1915, p. 3ff.

[70]On this issue, see R. A. Culpepper, *The Johannine School. An Evaluation of the Johannine–School Hypothesis Based on an Investigation of the Nature of Ancient Schools*, SBLDS 26, Missoula, 1975, who investigates the entire phenomenon of the theological and philosophical schools in antiquity; see esp. pp. 258–60.

[71]We may also attribute Hebrews and 1 Peter to the Pauline disciples. On the other hand, 2 Thessalonians should probably also be considered among the early pseudopauline writings.

[72]On the Pauline school, see Lohse, p. 253f.; Gnilka, p. 21ff. Lindemann, *Paulus*, p. 130, however, argues that Col. and Eph. document the unbroken reputation of Paulinism but that they do not represent products of the school, because of the differences in argumentation (no justification terminology, p. 120; idem, *Aufhebung*, p. 253f.). Yet he admits that they are closely connected with Paul (*Paulus*, p. 117f.). At best one might speak of a "fading" of the Pauline theology in the school (or schools) of Paul; so Müller, *Theologiegeschichte*, p. 86ff.; cf. Sand, "Überlieferung," p. 16ff.

[73]Summary in Vielhauer, *Geschichte*, p. 216f.; Conzelmann–Lindemann, *Interpreting the NT*, pp. 201–207.

test to the fact that Timothy was an important co-worker of the apostle Paul. According to 1 Tim. 1:3 and 4:11f., he was entrusted with the responsibility for the church in Ephesus. Hence it appears that the Pastoral Letters originated in the area of Asia Minor. Their advanced understanding of office indicates that they originated later than Colossians and Ephesians and that they reacted differently (§13) to similar problems (heretical speculation, 1 Tim. 6:20, cf. Col. 2:16–20, 23; §12) in a similar geographical area.

Timothy's status as joint author, the relative continuity with Pauline theology, and the temporal proximity to the main letters of Paul, though reiterating the linguistic difference, have recently led interpreters to the conclusion that Timothy influenced both the style and theology of Colossians as joint author and amanuensis of the apostle Paul.[74] Paul authenticated his writing in Col. 4:18.[75] Whatever the case, the letter remains pseudonymous. In Col. 1:23d–25, 1:29–2:5, and 4:3d–18 Paul speaks in the first person singular. Had he truly verified the letter, he would have discovered that the statements of 2:12f. diverge from those made earlier (§13). Further, since there is no evidence in primitive Christianity for the practice of using substitute authors or amanuenses[76] who formulated not only sentences, but entire sequences of thought,[77] it is hardly conceivable that Paul permitted someone to act as a substitute for him in this manner. This does not rule out that Timothy could have been the author. In this case, however, it would have been a later author who wrote this letter after the apostle's death.

From this we may already draw conclusions regarding the question of time and place of writing: approximately 70 CE or later.[78] The image of the spiritual temple in Ephesians (2:21f.) – developing the brief statement of 1 Cor. 3:16 (cf. 2 Cor. 6:16) – presupposes the ostracization of the Christians from the synagogue some years after the fall of Jerusalem. Colossians must have been written somewhat earlier, from within Asia Minor, because Tychicus (himself from Asia) is said to have been the carrier (4:7; Acts 20:4). Perhaps it originated in the provincial capital Ephesus which, as we may have to assume, was the

[74]Schweizer, p. 26f.; Lähnemann, *Kolosserbrief*, p. 181f., note 82, mentions Epaphras as the possible editor.

[75]Other adherents of this hypothesis are e.g., Schmidt–von Holzendorff, p. 791; in part Thompson, p. 106 and Ollrog, *Mitarbeiter*, p. 226. Ollrog stresses that there are more "we" passages in Col. than in the other Pauline letters, p. 226, note 112.

[76]Concerning the amanuensis hypothesis, see Roller, *Formular*, p. 334f.; against it, see note 71 above. That Col. was formulated by an amanuensis of the apostle Paul is argued, e.g., by Bénoit, "Rapports," p. 21f.

[77]The assumption of Harrison, *Paulines*, p. 65ff., that Col. was edited by Onesimus, has no basis.

[78]So e.g., Gnilka, p. 22f.

center of the Pauline school.[79] The epistle was intended for Christians who had been threatened by a heresy. Later this heresy also reached Ephesus (Rev. 2:1, 7; cf. 3:14ff.). The author remains unknown. If he had the same identity as the author of Ephesians (cf. §3 [d]), he would have had to have been a Jewish Christian because of the exposition of Eph. 2:11–22. He held Epaphras, the missionary of the Lycus Valley, in high esteem[80] and himself belonged to the disciples of Paul.[81]

(b) Colossae and the addressees of Colossians[82]

Colossae was a town in Asia Minor, situated on the Lycus, the tributary of the Meander, and on the route connecting Ephesus and Sardis, the largest cities of the province of Asia, with Tarsus in Cilicia. Nearby were the towns of Laodicea and Hierapolis. Laodicea is mentioned in Col. 2:1; 4:13, 15, 16, as well as in Rev. 1:11 and 3:14ff. (letter); Hierapolis is cited in Col. 4:13. The capital of the province was Ephesus, where Paul labored for more than two years (Acts 19:1, 10). An earthquake destroyed Colossae in 60–61 CE. This can be derived from the following pieces of information: Tacitus records that Laodicea was destroyed by an earthquake (Tac., Ann. 14, 27, 1) and Orosius (early 5th cent.) says that "Laodicea, Hierapolis, Colossae terrae motu conciderunt" (Adv. Paganos 7, 7). This is clearly a late report on the same earthquake. In his description of the Lycus Valley from the seventies of the first century, Pliny does not mention Colossae (Hist. Nat. 5, 105).[83] Laodicea was soon rebuilt (Tac., Ann. 14, 27, 1; Sib. 4, 107; indirectly Rev. 1:11; 3:14, around 95 CE). Colossae, which had been previously pushed back economically by Laodicea, remained an insignificant village among the ruins. The city of Colossae is not attested on coins until the reign of Antoninus Pius (138–161).[84] The

---

[79]See Acts 19:9–10; Westcott, p. 6; Scott, p. 3f.; Masson, p. 85; Hugédé, p. 10; Lohse, p. 254; Ernst, p. 151; Gnilka, p. 22; Schenke–Fischer, Einleitung, pp. 168, 244; Merklein, "Theologie," p. 27f. Following the Marcionite prologues to the letters of Paul, too, Col. originated in Ephesus (Preuschen, Analecta II, p. 87). In the latter, however, the letter's authenticity is assumed.

[80]Suhl, Paulus, p. 168, note 93, supposes that Epaphras was the writer of Col; cf. →4:21f.; cf. Gnilka, "Paulusbild," pp. 181f., 192f.

[81]H. Ludwig, "Der Verfasser des Kolosserbriefes — ein Schüler des Paulus," Diss. Göttingen, 1974, esp. p. 230; Schille, Paulusbild, p. 55f. On the author see also →4:7–17; Gnilka, "Paulusbild," p. 185f.

[82]On the entire subject, see Lohse, pp. 36–38; Gnilka, pp. 1–4; Martin (NCBC), pp. 2–7.

[83]He mentions Colossae only in those instances when he does not report about his own experience and perhaps takes a retrospective glance: 5, 145; 31, 29.

[84]Schweizer, "Zur neueren Forschung," p. 171. In the Middle ages most interpreters had no idea of the geographical location of Colossae and sometimes identified it with Rhodes, where the giant statue of the god Helios, the colossus, was situated. So the famous geographer Vicenzo Coronelli as late as in 1696.

town of Chonos (Greek Χῶναι), south of the former Colossae, originated in the fifth century; its continuity with Colossae is quite indirect.

There were Jews in the Lycus Valley. They were descendants of the
two thousand Jewish families resettled from Babylon to Asia Minor by
Antiochus III as protection along his territorial boundaries.[85] They
were allowed to live according to their traditions (Sabbath observance,
synagogue etc.; Jos., *Ant.* 12, 147–153), but they became very hellen-
ized. According to the Talmud (b. *Shab* 147 b), the wine and the baths
of Phrygia ruined the ten tribes of Israel.[86] We know that heterodox
Jews adopted some of the formal demands of the Mosaic law (e.g., the
sanctity of the Sabbath),[87] but at the same time Judaism was influenced by the hellenistic religions.[88] For us this is significant in
view of the mention of Sabbath observance (Col. 2:16) and circumcision (2:11), both of which the Colossian heretics practiced (§12). This
does not mean that the recipients themselves were Jewish Christians.
The majority of them were uncircumcised Gentile Christians (2:13).[89]
They were, however, influenced by a heresy that adopted the elements
of the syncretistic environment described above.

Some scholars have taken the destruction and fall of Colossae in
61 or 62 CE as an argument in support of the authenticity of Colossians.[90] But this can also be interpreted differently.[91] If everything we
have said concerning the deuteropauline character of Colossians is
correct, addressing a letter, post-dated in the life of the apostle, to a
community that has already disappeared, is theoretically the best
method to promote a letter as authentic. Already the Colossian church
was no longer able to say that it did not remember such an epistle.[92]
Yet the destination of Colossae was not chosen merely because that
city was in ruins at the time the letter was written. In the vicinity
of Colossae there must have been churches (the rebuilt Laodicea, Col.
4:16, and perhaps also Hierapolis, 4:13) that were threatened by the
heresy combatted in Colossians. For this reason, the author was able

[85]We gather from the accusation against the Roman governor of the province of Asia,
Flaccus, who confiscated Jewish funds, that the number of Jews was considerable; they
have been estimated in the thousands; Cicero, *Flacc.* 28, 68.

[86]R. Chelbo around 300 CE; Billerbeck II:270.

[87]Documentation in Nilsson, *Geschichte*, p. 665ff.; J. B. McMinn, "Fusion of the
Gods," *JNES* 15 (1956), pp. 201–213, esp. p. 210ff.

[88]The cults of Hypsistos and of Sabazios could have been attractive for them; cf.
C. Colpe, "Hypsistos," in *Der kleine Pauly* II:1291–92; C. Roberts, Th. C. Skeat, A. D.
Nock, "The Guild of Zeus Hypsistos," *HTR* 29 (1936), pp. 36–88; more circumspect
is S. E. Johnson, "The Present State of Sabazios Research," in ANRW II 17/3, Berlin–New
York, 1984, pp. 1583–1613.

[89]Col. contains no direct quotations of the OT.

[90]Most recently Reicke, "Setting," p. 432.

[91]Cf. Lohse, p. 255.

[92]Lindemann, "Gemeinde," p. 128f.

to link up with the list of greetings of the letter to Philemon,[93] which was obviously sent to Colossae.[94] Hence if Colossians is deutero-pauline, which it most probably is, it was intended for the Christians in the broader region of the province of Asia, but not directly for Colossae.[95] Perhaps Col. 4:16 points out the scope of the destination: The epistle is (also) to be read in Laodicea. This is intended to explain why the letter reached Laodicea belatedly (→4:16). The Laodicean destination finds its support in the references of 2:1 and 4:15. The letter to the Laodiceans which is mentioned in 4:16 as the twin of Colossians[96] either has existed in actuality or is intended to underscore the significance of Laodicea. Paul also wrote a letter to the Laodiceans that, through no fault of his own, has regrettably been lost.[97] Fortunately Paul also addressed their problems in the letter to the Colossians that reached them all the same. The implication of this hypothesis[98] is that the individuals whose authority is supported in Colossians (→1:7; →4:7–17) were also known in the important community of Laodicea (cf. Rev. 3:14–22); in addition, some of them may have also helped organize the church at Laodicea.[99] This is in harmony with the assumption of a deuteropauline origin and a relatively early dating.

§5 Structure and Problem of the Commentary

(a) Problem of exegesis

The structure assists in discovering the inner arrangement of the text. For this reason, some of the older exegetes have already devoted considerable attention to the structure of the text (the Bible of Kralice,[100] Bengel). Structural analysis, that is, the linguistic analysis of

[93]Lohse, p. 254f. Philemon does not surface in the list of greetings in Col. because it was known already prior to its destruction that he no longer lived in the vicinity.

[94]Schenke–Fischer, Einleitung, pp. 155, 167, assume that the writer of Col. identified a certain Epaphras, the missionary of the Lycus Valley, with the Epaphras of Philem. merely in order to accommodate his own letter in the time frame of the remaining letters of Paul. This, however, is less likely, since Philemon would then be included in the list of greetings.

[95]Schenke–Fischer, Einleitung, p. 167, argue that the heresy of Col. already threatened more sizeable segments of the church. Similarly Vielhauer, Geschichte, p. 201; Marxsen, Introduction, p. 184f.

[96]Schlier, Epheser, p. 31f., identifies it, similar to Marcion, as the canonical letter to the Ephesians.

[97]Lindemann, "Gemeinde," p. 122f.

[98]It has been posited by ibid., p. 133f.; see also his commentary, p. 12f.

[99]Ibid., pp. 125–127; Gnilka, "Paulusbild," pp. 182–184.

[100]The commentary of the NT which has been published in conjunction with the new edition of the Czechoslovakian translation of the NT by Jan Blahoslav (published without commentary in 1564) is part of the six volumes of the Czechoslovakian translation of the Bible printed in Kralice (Moravia) in 1593 (1594). It offers a careful structuring

larger text units, therefore, links up with this tradition.[101] There were, and continue to be, several problems associated with its application in exegesis.

At times the linguistic analysis of the text assumed the role of a self-contained philosophy in which the text became its grammatical code of the fundamental powers, functionally related with Platonic ideas.[102] The structure of the text as sign was isolated from its function as witness. In reality linguistic analysis constitutes only one of several dimensions of hermeneutics. The text represents the realities to which the former relate specifically, but it cannot be emancipated from the latter. For this reason its clarity is persistent (even in the third century the church fathers were able to use Colossians as a direct polemic against their contemporary heretics), though not constant. Later it had to be reinterpreted (e.g., allegorically or by means of the various tools of contemporary critical exegesis). This means that we are able to investigate the biblical text as an autosemantic whole for methodological reasons only. The results of such probing may not be divorced from the historical-critical investigation, nor from the inquiry into the history of its impact; in other words, in the exegesis we also need to utilize the information obtained outside of the text. The skill of exegesis is the search for the real relationship between the various methodological approaches to the text. In this manner alone can its complementary nature be reflected and its projection be indicated which the reality attested by it brought about in our understanding.[103] The text has also been interpreted from various vantage points during the Reformation, namely, within the framework of the tradition of confession and faith, as well as of the historical sense.

In terms of the practical organization of the commentary this means that it addresses the structural analysis in its preliminary overview (here, in §5 [b] and §6) in which the text is considered as a whole and from a certain distance. The other observations have to be brought to bear in the successive exegesis. Thus we endeavor to respect the basic structure of the text whose "spatial" dimension (representing clearly the classical form of the scroll) accords with its understand-

---

of the text in its various levels and which is mostly intended for homiletical purposes; Ch. Donner, "Some Elements of Structural Analysis in the Notes of the Bible of Kralice," CV 23 (1980), pp. 57–63.

[101]For a summation of the issue, see R. Kieffer, "Die Bedeutung der modernen Linguistik für die Auslegung biblischer Texte," TZ 30 (1974), pp. 223–233; P. Pokorný, "Das Wesen der exegetischen Arbeit," CV 23 (1980), pp. 167–178.

[102]M. Corvez, Les Structuralistes, Paris, 1969; Berger, Exegese, pp. 66–68.

[103]See note 101 above. W. Schenk, "Was ist ein Kommentar?" BZ NF 24 (1980), pp. 1–20, argues for the possibility of achieving a comprehensive text-linguistic theory of exegesis; cf. W. Richter, Exegese als Literaturwissenschaft, Göttingen, 1971.

ing in time; we thus hope to achieve this by hearing it as it was read — continuously.

We are also led to organize the commentary in this manner by our position concerning the second problem of the structural analysis: the separation of the text from the authorial (redactional) intention. In part, a text is indeed shaped by elements and dimensions of the language that have been applied without reflection and unconsciously. The verbalization of an intention can be compared with a task that can be carried out with a difficult instrument, even though one does not fully understand the construction of the instrument. Only an expert is capable of describing the instrument by analyzing the product which the expert manufactured with its help. The exegete does the same with the text when he or she investigates the structure of its language. Yet the exegete is to undertake that only as a support task which serves to understand better the product and its function: The text contains references to events concerning the broader history; it connects with older witnesses that have been handed down; it contains the personal witness of its author — all of this cannot be isolated from the analysis of the structure of its language. The commentary which seeks to consider all of these dimensions is to be organized (traditionally, in fact) as an interconnected meta-text that pursues the text successively.[104]

(b) Overview of content and structure

Table 3 displays the internal structure of the epistle and at the same time depicts some inner relationships, like the recurring motifs that serve as overlapping compositional devices. The axis is to be followed from top to bottom; one and one-half of a millimeter corresponds to roughly one verse of text. In the following we endeavor to explain the structure in more detail.

1:1–2. As an established part of the letter form, *the opening* is clearly distinct from the corpus of the letter.

Part I: 1:3–23. *The prayer of thanksgiving and intercession — the premise of salvation in Christ*. This concerns a prayer in indirect speech, a notation of the most important topics of prayer (cf. 3:16; 4:2).[105] It is clearly set apart from what follows by a shift from the first person plural to the first person singular (which is all the same anticipated in 1:23c = transition) and by a new theme. In terms of its function in the framework of the letter, it is an expanded introduction that views the condition of the writer and the recipients from

---

[104]On the matter of hermeneutics, see also § 17 (c–e).
[105]In this regard, see O'Brien, *Thanksgivings*, p. 62f.; Aletti, "Colossiens," pp. 11–20.

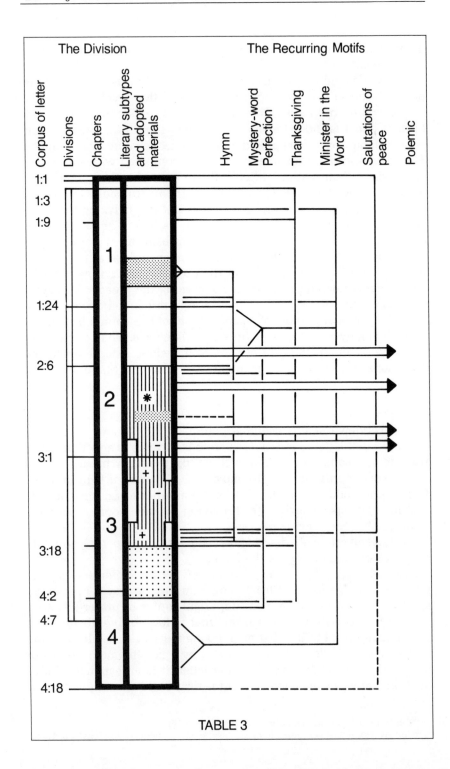

TABLE 3

the perspective of the gospel. For the author, prayer belongs to the basic behavior of humanity from which presuppositions may be derived for the solution of all problems. The hymn (1:15–20) is cited in this context and is of fundamental significance for the subsequent argument regarding the heresy. The whole pericope consists of a chiastically structured prayer of thanksgiving (1:3–8) and intercession (vv. 9–20). Thus there is a marked change between 1:8 and 1:9. But since 1:3–23 is connected via the concept gospel (1:5, 23) and via the loose form of the indirect prayer, we take this part to be a pericope made up of two sub-pericopae. In intercession the apostle prays for the recipients, that they may be able to give thanks (1:12); the hymn is introduced as a paradigm of a prayer of thanksgiving (cf. Table 5). The reconciliation of all things that Christ brought is applied in vv. 21–22 to the recipients, and the pericope concludes with paraenesis, which at the same time serves as a transition to the next pericope.

Part II: 1:24–2:5. *The authority of the apostle — connecting salvation with the apostolic proclamation.* Here the author speaks in the first person singular. Sometimes 2:4–5 is attached to the following pericope;[106] however, these verses are still part of the apostolic authority theme and constitute the transition to the next pericope. In this part the author is introduced as the true mystagogue who initiates into the mystery (μυστήριον) of true salvation and of perfection (1:28) by means of his public proclamation of the gospel. It is emphasized that the solution to the possible crises of the community being addressed is found in the adherence to the apostolic authority. On the detailed structure, see →1:24–2:5.

Part III: 2:6–23. *The thesis (propositio and probatio)*[107] *— true and false appropriation of salvation.* This part contains paraenetic elements and may well be designated as paraenesis. As far as its concrete function is concerned, however, it is related to the so-called major dogmatic segments of the Pauline letters. After emphasizing the danger threatening the recipients (2:8, the negative thesis) follows the thesis (2:12–13) concerning baptism, which becomes the death and resurrection with Jesus Christ by faith (little asterisk in Table 3). It refutes the heresy here characterized by allusions and qualified as heresy. The point of closure of this pericope is a matter of debate. Some interpreters[108] and editors[109] reckon vv. 20–23 to be a negative prelude to the following paraenetic section; but these statements are so closely

---

[106]So e.g., Gnilka.

[107]Some of the elements of the structure of the letters have been adopted from ancient rhetoric; cf. P. L. Schmidt, "Epistolographie," and H. Hommel-K. Ziegler, "Rhetorik," in *Der kleine Pauly*, vols. 2, 4.

[108]Among the more recent ones, e.g., Gnilka.

[109]Especially the Greek New Testament.

related to combatting the heresy that they rather belong to this part than that they form a transition to the paraenesis.

Part IV: 3:1–4:6. *Paraenesis for the new life (exhortatio)*. The paraenetic part is the most extensive one. The imperative has actually already occurred from the beginning of the third pericope because paraenesis was the reason for the entire letter; but the polemic against the heretics does not conclude until the end of chapter two. In its structure, this part divides into three sub-sections. 3:1–17 is the paraenesis deriving directly from the theological argument (*exhortatio generalis*); 3:18–4:1 is the household code; and the conclusion contains exhortations concerning external missionary activity (4:2–6). There is a decisive turning-point between sections one and two. Here ends the argumentation that derived directly from the thesis in 2:12f. and that connects Parts III and IV (cf. §6 [b]). Towards the end of the first subsection some motifs that unite the entire epistle also return (gratitude, perfection, singing hymns, wish for peace; cf. Table 3). Yet some of these (prayer, gratitude, mystery) still occur after the household code. One senses that the author found it difficult to introduce the household code (cf. §17). The writer considered it both a supplement (the arch of several overlapping compositional devices does not extend beyond 3:15–17) and a part of the body of the letter, which concludes in 4:2–6 (Table 3). All of this only confirms the conclusion that the household code, as a literary sub-type, belongs to the totality of Part IV in the framework of the epistle.[110]

4:7–18. *Personal notes and greetings*. The final part (*conclusio*) contains information and greetings that, similar to the opening, support the theological thesis indirectly via the characteristic of the writer's coworker and partly also of the recipients (cf. §6 [b]).[111]

§6 *Structure of the Theological Argument*

(a) *Dispute*

The text's structure is only one of its dimensions. Up to now we have described the surface of the fabric and thereby seek to know how

---

[110]It would do violence to reconstruct a symmetrical structure, as e.g., di Marco, "Chiasmus," p. 29, attempts. Parts II–IV match the format of the letters of antiquity (J. L. White, *The Form and Function of the Body of the Greek Letter*, SBLDS 2, Missoula, 1972); the extensive prayer of thanksgiving and petition (part I) is a unique Pauline feature which contributes to the structure of the entire letter; cf. Table 3 and O'Brien, *Thanksgivings*, p. 19ff.

[111]In the main segments, this structure corresponds with that found in Lähnemann, *Kolosserbrief*, p. 61f. Most exegetes have recognized the parameters of the main segments at least as one of several breaks in the paragraphs. A fundamentally different organization offers Lamarche, *Structure*, p. 453ff.: Main part (Part II) = 1:21–2:15; the polemical part (Part III) = 2:16–4:1.

it "functions."[112] At the outset we endeavored to link the structure with the analysis of the most important codes that divulge something of the inner logic of the theological argument. Most conspicuous among them is the code of conflict and of confrontation (cf. arrows in Table 2). The opposition and warning find their concrete expression in the relationship (the contact) with Jesus Christ as Lord, which the author again offers to the recipients through proclamation and paraenesis. Both polemic and paraenesis find their motivation in the proclamation. The proclamation is focused in the thesis in 2:12f. This thesis distinguishes Colossians and Ephesians from the rest of the Pauline letters (§2 [a]) and at the same time becomes the backbone of the theological argument (§13). It is positioned almost exactly in the arithmetical center of the corpus of the letter. The segments dominated by it are marked with vertical hatching in Table 3. First of all, it is presented, shaped, and developed as the counter-position to the heresy (2:6–15). Then its negative and positive aspects are explained alternatively (Table 3: + and –). Its importance arises from the fact that it has become the overlapping medium in the arrangement of the literary surface: It links Parts III and IV (2:6–3:17); hence its explication also takes on the shape and function of paraenesis.

The thesis is that the Christian has been buried with Christ in baptism (negative aspect) and has been raised (positive aspect). Basically the semantic axis here is life itself (cf. the paraphrase in 2:13), the boundaries of which (in reverse order) express its two poles (burial, death/resurrection, life). Specifically at issue, however, is the death and the new life of Jesus Christ that other human beings also have made their perspective.

Indirectly this thesis is already presented in Part I, the center of which is an older Christian hymn (see [c] below and §9 [d]). The hymn represents the foundational text, which the epistle then explicates. The text then develops the thesis into new dimensions, but is linked with the hymn by means of the prominence of the exaltation of the redeemer and of his victory over death. The Pauline proclamation of the cross, whose soteriological and paraenetic aspect it is to be crucified with Christ, is not itself part of the hymn's concern, but the author presupposes that it is contained implicitly in the hymn (→1:20). As a model of thanksgiving (1:12) the hymn belongs to the tradition of faith handed down (2:7), with which both the author and the recipients are familiar. It contains the gospel (1:23), also described as a mystery (→1:26).[113]

---

[112]We have already indicated some of the results of the following deliberations in the titles of the individual segments (§ 4 [b]).

[113]The origin of the hymn will be examined in § 9 (a–b, d). At this point, a lexical observation will suffice: The title Christ (§ 7) occurs often in Col., namely, roughly

It is possible that Colossians contains still other materials drawn from the older tradition, but these could also be viewed as loose allusions. We encounter a series of traditional expressions in 2:14–15; likewise the household code, at least as a secondary literary type and in some particular exhortations, is connected with older patterns (§17).

(b) Roles

The task of determining the roles in an argument is as important as in a narrative. Only it is essential to be careful to characterize them from the author's perspective and to correlate them in their functions within the ancient church.

According to 1:1 the apostle Paul and Timothy (cf. §4 [a]) are the writers (authors, senders). They speak in the first person plural (1:3 and others); yet in 1:24; 2:1; 4:7, 18 it is only the apostle Paul who speaks. Thus the letter is submitted entirely to his authority. His thesis (2:12f.) is dependent upon the interpretation of baptism in the post-baptismal teaching in Rom. 6:1–11 (§13). Accordingly, baptism is an actualization of the death and resurrection of Jesus. For the baptisand this means participation in Jesus' death and the promise of the resurrection. In Col. →2:12; 3:1 and Eph. 2:5f. baptism is depicted as resurrection (§13). This shift in emphasis is connected with the defense against the heresy (§12), but now it also enables us to define the theological role of the writer. He identifies himself with the apostle Paul but develops Pauline theology at the same time and from it derives the new thesis of the resurrection with Jesus Christ.

The recipients are addressed in the second person plural and described as the "saints in Colossae" (1:2). They represent a larger Christian group (4:13, 15; cf. 2:1; §4 [b]) comprised of house churches (→4:15). Through Epaphras (1:7; 4:12) they are related to the Pauline mission. Others who represent or guarantee the connection with the apostle Paul (middlemen between the writer and the recipients) are listed and characterized in →4:7–14. The writer is afraid that the recipients are not capable of resisting a threatening heresy. The epistle is designed to unmask the heresy as a great threat and to equip the recipients theologically. The backbone of the theological argument is focused on the thesis. Since the thesis represents a new development of Pauline theology, we may designate as recipients those who, unlike the writer, have not been capable of drawing such conclusions from their faith shaped by Paul. From the writer's viewpoint they are

---

in every third verse. It is missing only in the hymn and in the household code, or it occurs only in the combination Christ the Lord (3:24). Hence these are elements which do not show the imprint of the author's mode of expression as much.

"intermediary players" who are affected by two streams of spiritual influence.

The opponents (false teachers) will be described in more detail later (§12). They are heard about in 2:4, 8, 16–19, 20, 23 in the third person singular or plural or only indirectly: "No one" (2:4, 8, 16), or only in the allusions to their doctrine (2:20, 23). They "judge" (2:16), that is, they strip the gospel of any absolutes, an action that is described as a threat to the unity of the church with its Lord (2:19).

The role of the assistants is not played by individuals but by the traditions to which both parties appeal in support of their authority. The writer uses the cited hymn (1:15–20) as his helper. It is introduced via expressions in the first person plural, which encompasses both writer and recipients as early as 1:13. Similarly the segment in 2:14f., which is influenced by older Christian tradition, is also related to "us." The argument of the apostolic writer is supported by the authority of the tradition. In all probability the opponents were also familiar with the hymn.[114] Hence the hymn is able to support a specific position only in terms of a specific interpretation (§9 [a]). The opponents, too, have had their helpers in the traditions (2:8), though they cannot be described in more detail.

The reciprocal relationships of the roles characterized to this point can be depicted as follows (Table 4):

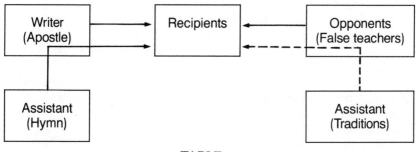

TABLE 4

(c) Functions

We have already made some remarks under (a) concerning the functions of the actors and their roles. In order to gain a better understanding of the spiritual battle, we have to account for other actors who carry out the crucial functions in the theology of Colossians and who are described as the concrete subjects of the whole event (e.g., 1:1; 1:29). The false teachers venerate God and Jesus Christ as well as the supernatural powers. Therefore we are dealing with an event on two

---

[114]Schweizer, "Versöhnung des Alls. Kol 1, 20," in Jesus Christus in Historie und Theologie, FS H. Conzelmann, ed. G. Strecker, Tübingen, 1975, p. 499f.

different levels that, in turn, link the event. The reciprocal relationships, then, which will be sketched briefly below, are concerned with the theological functions within the total purview of the writer.

God — Jesus Christ. God is the decisive "person" whose work is the creation of the universe (1:16). Jesus is one with him as his Son (1:13); he is the image of God (1:15), all things were created through him (1:16), and the fullness of God dwells in him (1:19; 2:9). He brought about reconciliation, which is also worked out in the cosmos (1:20). He rules the kingdom into which God moves the "saints"; the power of God that brings about resurrection and new life is effective through him. For the false teachers, Jesus did not play such an important part. They did not deem him capable of mediating effectively between heaven and earth.

God in Jesus Christ — the supernatural powers (§10). According to the hymn, the "authorities and powers" are God's creation. But they became (as basic principles of this world, 2:8) the object of false teaching, which leads people astray. Yet they are subordinate to Christ (2:10); through the cross he has "disarmed" them (2:15). His exaltation after death on the cross has rendered ineffective their attempt to hinder people from access to God. When the Christian dies with Christ in baptism, that Christian also dies to the supernatural powers (2:20). Thus the writer conceptualizes what the hymn says concerning universal reconciliation.

The false teachers — the supernatural powers. The supernatural powers played a special part in the speculation of the false teachers. They had to be revered and "appeased" in order to gain access to God (§12).

God in Jesus Christ — the writer. The writer introduces himself as the one commissioned by Jesus Christ (1:1). His mission is in accordance with the will of God (1:1) and is described as ministry of the gospel (1:23).

The writer — the recipients. In relation to the recipients, the ministry of the apostle and of his fellow laborers is depicted as instruction (1:28; cf. 1:7), whereas in the earlier letters of Paul it is proclamation (§4 [a]). Through his own suffering the apostle helps the church to persevere in its temporal trials and to fulfill its mission (1:24; cf. 4:13). The relationship of the recipients to the writer is not clear. Although they supported the work of his co-laborer (1:4), we are not told what their present relationship to the writer is.

The writer — the false teachers. The writer condemns the false teachers because they diminish (2:16) and threaten (→2:23) the recipients' salvation. We know nothing at all about the relationship between the false teachers and Paul. Perhaps they considered themselves to be his disciples. This might have led the writer to identify fully with Paul in his polemic against them (cf. §4 [a]).

The false teachers – the recipients. The false teachers could be "deceiving" the recipients (2:4). It is plausible that in the writer's interpretation only some of the house churches among the recipients defended the Pauline theology (→4:15–17 →2:4).

God in Jesus Christ – the recipients. God relates to the recipients through his grace (1:6); through Jesus Christ he effects their salvation (2:12f.). On the recipients' part, their thanksgiving (εὐχαριστία), cf. Table 3) is to match the grace (χάρις) of God.

Based on what has just been stated, one may draw conclusions that may be significant for the commentary itself. First, we note that some roles are virtually constant in the Pauline letters and, hence, that their functions in Colossians correspond with those in the remaining letters of the Pauline corpus. The differences have to do with the varying features of the respective roles. Thus the relation of writer-recipients in 2 Corinthians, for instance, is dominated by criticism; in Colossians this is mostly aimed at the false teachers (opponents).

Further, the sore points (negative communications) have become evident: The supernatural powers want to be emancipated from God. The opponents lead astray the recipients who respond incorrectly to the pressure of the powers (§12). The relationship of the recipients to the false teachers and to the writer is unclear.

Finally, we see that in Colossians the writer's apostolic authority is not emphasized in comparison with the authority of the other apostles, but first and foremost as the fundamental authority of the church.

Exegesis

Opening (Inscriptio), 1:1–2

(1) Paul, an apostle of Christ Jesus by the will of God, and Timothy our brother, (2) To the saints and faithful brethren in Christ at Colossae: Grace to you and peace from God our Father.

The opening contains references concerning the writer and the recipients, as well as the wish of well-being that in Christian letters frequently replaces the greeting at the beginning and end of the letter. In the wish of well-being, faith indeed discovers the most profound dimension of human interrelationships: The common bond between writer and recipients exists because of the grace of God and the common perspective of eschatological peace.

1 The first verse corresponds almost verbatim with 1 Cor. 1:1. As in Gal. 1:1 et al., Paul (see §4 [a]) is identified as an apostle. According to the Pauline understanding, the apostle is a witness of the gospel whose authorization is given directly by God (1 Cor. 15:8–10). Following Acts 1:21f., however, an apostle must have been one of the companions of the earthly Jesus. The Pauline understanding of apostolicity in Colossians is not only assumed, it is also accorded a new development (→1:24).[1]

The reference to the will of God points to the authority of the apostolic office[2] and its origin. In contrast to Col. 1:9 and 4:12 (cf. Mark 3:35 par.), where θέλημα denotes the object of the will of God (cf. Rom. 2:18; 12:2), here it means God's determined will (Gal. 1:4). In its ob-

---

[1]On the origin and problems of the early Christian apostolate, see the summary by H. Riesenfeld, "Apostel," RGG³ I, pp. 497–499; J. A. Bühner, "APOSTOLOS," in EWNT I:342–351; R. Schnackenburg, "Apostel vor und neben Paulus," in Aufsätze und Studien zum NT, ed. idem, Leipzig, 1973, pp. 244–263; cf. Berger, "Apostelbrief," p. 207ff.

[2]Perhaps in contrast to the apostles as the one commissioned by the Christian communities; Phil. 2:25; 2 Cor. 8:23.

jective sense, however, the concept of the "will of God" became pivotal in the Christian teaching of the second Christian generation (Eph., Matt., John, Pastorals); in addition, the commissioning of Paul to apostleship is already understood as part of God's "program" (cf. 1:26f.). In addition to 2 Cor. 1:1, the apostle also introduces himself in essentially the same manner in 2 Tim. 1:1.

Timothy is mentioned as joint writer (§4 [a]) and is characterized as a brother. Paul's spiritual child (1 Cor. 4:17; cf. 1 Tim. 1:2) has become his brother who labors together with the apostle. Likewise the recipients are said to be brothers (1:2).[3] This is not meant to be the designation of an office here,[4] which it might be in the case of "fellow servant," for instance (1:7; 4:7). In 2 Corinthians, Philippians, Philemon, and, together with Silvanus in 1 Thessalonians and 2 Thessalonians, Timothy is still mentioned as joint writer.[5] Usually such mention is intended as a second or third witness of the apostolic statements that regulate and exhort the Christian community, perhaps in the sense of Matt. 18:16 (cf. Deut. 17:6; 19:15).

2 In contrast to 1 Thessalonians (2 Thessalonians), Galatians, 1 Corinthians, and 2 Corinthians, the recipients are not addressed as a community (ἐκκλησία) here, but as saints and as fellow believers. In this instance, ἅγιος is not an adjective, since Paul uses the plural of ἅγιος only substantively (exception: Eph. 3:5). The prescript of Ephesians, which is dependent upon Colossians (§3 [c]), clearly uses it as a substantive. In this sense, "the saints" are not the people who are particularly pious or morally perfect. These are later meanings of the term. Here it has to do primarily with holiness in the nonethical sense of separation from the sphere of the profane and relation to God (cf. 1 QM 10.10); as in the main letters of Paul, so here it has to do specifically with being part of the holy people — holy, because it has been entrusted with the gospel (→1:26).[6] "The saints" represents the oldest self-designation of the church. Thereby it has identified with the true Israel. According to Rom. 15:16 the saints are characterized as an offering for God, purified by baptism and by the Holy Spirit. The address "to the saints" emphasizes that the recipients are part of the one fellowship of all Christians (cf. →1:24).

---

[3]Ellis, "Paul," p. 448f.

[4]Chrysostom, currently e.g., E. E. Ellis, " 'Spiritual' Gifts in the Pauline Community," NTS 20 (1973–74), pp. 128–144, who also takes the recipients to be Paul's coworkers, because of the designation of brothers; against this, Schweizer, p. 30, note 12.

[5]On the matter of joint writers as witnesses in ancient letters, see Roller, Formular, p. 153ff. In Gal. 1:2 all of the local brothers are cited as writers together with Paul. In this case, the entire church serves as witness, as in Matt. 18:17.

[6]Cf. Conzelmann, p. 132: They are declared saints by an act of God; cf. 1 Cor. 1:2 and the designation "holy Gentile people" (גּוֹי קָדוֹשׁ) and 1 Pet. 2:9; Exod. 19:6 (23:22 LXX).

On the human side, holiness has its correspondence in faith (1:4). They are brothers in the faith (Eph. 1:1)[7] "in Christ"—fellow Christians (Gal. 3:16). This self-designation, too, has its prehistory in the OT (Ex. 2:11). "In Christ" (§7) is to be taken adjectivally here, similar to the later adjective "Christian";[8] nevertheless, it still points clearly to God's saving act in Christ (→1:28).

"In Colossae" is the geographical locus (for details see §4 [b]). Regardless of how we answer the question of authorship (§4 [a]), this means that the recipients belong to the Pauline sphere (→1:7; §6 [b]; §4 [b]).[9]

The wish of well-being, which replaces the greeting,[10] is formulated tersely.[11] Peace as greeting is already documented in the hellenistic letters (χαίρειν καὶ εἰρήνη; yet it became characteristic especially in Jewish greetings (cf. Luke 7:40; John 20:19, 21).[12] Peace means well-being in the broadest sense, while Pauline theology places special emphasis on the peace with God, on the ability to stand in God's judgment (Rom. 5:1 et al.).[13] This eschatological concept is understood in Colossians as the deliverance from the pressure of the superhuman powers (→1:20; 3:15). In any case, it is that peace which arises from God's initiative, as the concluding phrase clearly expresses. Grace (χάρις, cf. 1:6; 3:16) is God's grace (cf. the greeting in Rom. 1:7 et al.). Grace is a synonym in 1:6 for the gospel (see 1:5). This wish for grace gains particular significance because it comes from the apostle.[14] Even if we consider it to be from a pseudonymous writer, we must assume that he understood himself to be the mediator of the apostolic blessing (§4 [a]). In addition, the motif of peace as salutation occurs in 3:15, and "grace" is also the concluding wish in 4:18.

The addition "and of the Lord Jesus Christ," attested in several significant manuscripts (ℵ, A, C, etc.), is a harmonization of the salutation in Phil. 1:2 et al.[15]

---

[7]See note 4.

[8]Bultmann, Theology, I:328–329; →1:28.

[9]In the title which has been attached later (The Epistle of the Apostle Paul to the Colossians), several MSS (p[46], B*, A, I, K, et al.) have ἐν Κολασσεῖς—a frequent variation of the name of this city which has also influenced the form in 1:2 in some MSS (I, K, et al).

[10]On the form of the apostolic letter, see Berger, "Apostelbrief," p. 201f.

[11]Only in 1 Thess. 1:1 is it briefer in the Pauline corpus.

[12]One of the few parallels of the salutation "grace to you and peace" in nonbiblical letters can be found in the prescript of the letter of Baruch to the imprisoned brothers (syr Bar Apoc 78:2, transl. by A. F. J. Klijn in Kümmel, Jüdische Schriften V, p. 123ff.); cf. Gnilka, p. 27.

[13]This is emphasized in the phrase "of God our Father." A reference to the giver of the blessing which is formulated in this manner represents a further characteristic of the Christian epistle; Berger, "Apostelbrief," p. 202.

[14]Berger, "Apostelbrief," p. 197.

[15]Cf. Kramer, Christos, p. 153.

§7 Excursus: The Honorific Title Christ[16]

The title Christ (χριστός, מָשִׁיחַ, מְשִׁיחָא) means "the anointed one."
Early Judaism used it as designation for the eschatological king of
Israel, namely, in the compound expressions "the anointed of the
Lord" (respectively, "his anointed") or "the anointed one of Israel"
(Ps. Sol. 17:32; 18:5, 7; 1 Enoch 48:10; 52:4; 1 QSa 2.11–22). Not until
the time of early Christianity did this title also begin to be used in
the absolute sense. As the expression of Jesus' majesty it emerged in
connection with the sayings concerning the salvific significance of
his death (Gal. 3:13; 1 Cor. 8:11; Rom. 5:6, 8 et al.), as well as with
the confessional statements that identify him in this manner, as in
Acts 9:22. The fact that this title prevailed, despite the reticence of
the earthly Jesus with regard to it (Mark 8:29–33), reveals that (a) messianic hopes were associated with Jesus during his lifetime (cf. Mark
15:26, par.), and (b) the early Christian experience of Easter excluded
the expectation of another Messiah, so that, paradoxically, it was precisely the crucified Jesus who, as the Anointed One, was declared to
be Lord.[17] For Paul this title (which to the Gentiles was incompre-
hensible) became a proper name, though the apostle himself is familiar with its significance (2 Cor. 1:19–22, note the play on words
with χριστός – χρίειν) and emphasizes the double name Jesus Christ
when the gospel is threatened (1 Cor. 1:1–10). This double name occurs only three times in Colossians, namely, in the formulaic expressions (1:1, 3, 4). Otherwise the discussion is about Christ. For the writer
the use of the title Christ as a designation for Jesus is typical; this,
however, has nothing to do with the polemic against the false teachers.[18] On "in Christ" see →1:28.

[16]See esp. W. Grundmann, TDNT IX:521–580, esp. 556–560.

[17]The absence of this title in the logia source reflects the awareness that Jesus dis-
tanced himself from it during his earthly life. It is in no wise an argument for a later
origin of this designation for Jesus; against G. Schille, Anfänge der Kirche, Munich,
1966, pp. 191–193.

[18]Documentation in Francis, "Argument," esp. p. 200; cf. § 6, note 113 above.

Part One: Prayer of Thanksgiving and Intercession—The Premise of Salvation in Christ, 1:3–23

1. Prayer of Thanksgiving,[1] 1:3–8

(3) We always thank God, the Father of our Lord Jesus Christ, when we pray for you, (4) because we have heard of your faith in Christ Jesus and of the love which you have for all the saints, (5) because of the hope laid up for you in heaven. Of this you have heard before in the word of the truth, the gospel (6) which has come to you, as indeed in the whole world it is bearing fruit and growing—so among yourselves, from the day you heard and understood the grace of God in truth, (7) as you learned it from Epaphras our beloved fellow servant. He is a faithful minister of Christ on our behalf (8) and has made known to us your love in the Spirit.

Following the apostolic salutation, the letter opens with a prayer in indirect speech (§5 [b]). The first part is a prayer of thanksgiving in a lengthy and involved sentence which we have divided in v. 5 in the translation. Another prayer of thanksgiving is inserted into the following prayer of intercession as a model of thanksgiving (1:12ff.). Thanksgiving to the gods also appears in several letters from the hellenistic and imperial era, especially among the Stoics (cf. Epict., Diss. I, 6, 1ff.).[2] The letter of Apion (2nd cent. CE) may serve as a model of a number of such letters;[3] at the beginning he thanks the god Serapis, whom he calls Lord, for the rescue in distress at sea: "I give thanks (εὐχαριστῶ) to the Lord (τῷ κυρίῳ) Serapis for having saved

---

[1]In general, O'Brien, Thanksgivings, pp. 62–104; T. Y. Mullins, "The Thanksgivings in Philemon and Colossians," NTS 30 (1984), pp. 288–293. Against Lohse he demonstrates that the prayer of thanksgiving is Pauline in structure and is connected with the content of the entire letter. It is in no wise possible to argue against the authenticity of Col. based on the prayer of thanksgiving.

[2]Schubert, Thanksgivings, p. 132f.; Lohse, p. 40f.

[3]Schubert, Thanksgivings, p. 158ff.

me (ἔσωσε) when I was in danger on the sea" (BGU II:423).[4] E. Lohse draws attention to the letter from 2 Macc.: "Having been saved from great danger by God, we are very grateful to him" (εὐχαριστοῦμεν; 1:11). This is a solemn hellenistic manner of expressing gratitude.[5] Here it is intended to affirm that the relationship of writer-recipient is anchored in the grace (χάρις) of God (cf. 1:3; 3:17 with 1:6; 3:16).[6] Elsewhere the combination of thanksgiving with intercession is supported in Phil. 1:3–11 and Philem. 4–6.[7] This is in line with Pauline thought[8] and also prompts the paraenesis as a summons to daily thanksgiving. Thanksgiving obviously quickly gained specific forms in the Christian communities (3:16; §9 [d]).

Philemon 4–7 is the immediate model for this thanksgiving. In both cases the gratitude concerns the faith of the recipients and their love toward other Christians (saints, cf. 1 Thess. 1:3, 7f.). Yet here it refers to the collective recipients and has its own development, given the new situation.[9] Similarly to Philem. 5 and 7, the statement of the recipients' love (ἀγάπη) occurs both at the beginning and the end of the thanksgiving (1:4, 8). In between, the reason for the love is stated: the gospel which they received earlier as a result of the missionary effort.[10] This motif concludes the thanksgiving in 1 Thess. 1:9f. (→1:6).

3 The gratitude is directed to God whom the writer describes as the "Father of our Lord Jesus Christ."

§8 Excursus: God, the Father of our Lord Jesus Christ[11]

Similar to the witnesses of faith in Israel, God is not defined speculatively here; neither is he introduced to the readers (hearers) merely as the ruler of nature; rather he is attested concretely through his revelation in history. Instead of characterizing God as the one who led his people out of Egypt (Exod. 20:2), in the church God is especially the one who raised Jesus Christ from the dead (1 Thess. 1:10; 2 Cor.

---

[4]According to Helbing, Papyri, p. 89ff.

[5]The verb εὐχαριστεῖν does not have a distinct Hebrew equivalent. The shorter thanksgivings in Paul are found in 1 Thess. 1:2ff.; 2:13ff.; 1 Cor. 1:4ff.; Phil. 1:3ff.; Rom. 1:8ff.; Philem. 4.

[6]Stressed by Berger, "Apostelbrief," p. 224, in contrast to Schubert, Thanksgivings, p. 183.

[7]As a liturgical element it also appears in the Prayer of the Eighteen Benedictions; cf. the 18th with the 19th benediction of the Babylonian redaction; Billerbeck IV, 215; see also O'Brien, Thanksgivings, pp. 19–69.

[8]On this issue, see Berger, "Apostelbrief," p. 219ff.

[9]See also Eph. 1:16ff. and in this conjunction Conzelmann, Ephesians, p. 56.

[10]On the chiastic structure, see Dibelius; Lohse.

[11]In general, see P. Pokorný, Der Gottessohn, ThSt 109, Zürich, 1971; M. Hengel, The Son of God, ET by J. Bowden, Philadelphia, 1976; Conzelmann, Outline, pp. 94–103.

4:14; Rom. 4:24; 8:11; see on Col. 2:12; 1 Pet. 1:21 et al.). Instead of presenting him as the God of Abraham and of Isaac (Gen. 28:13; Exod. 3:6 et al.), in the church he is presented as God, the Father of the Lord Jesus Christ (2 Cor. 1:3; Eph. 1:2), or as the God and Father (Rom. 15:6; 1 Pet. 1:3; cf. 1 John 1:3; 2 John 3).[12] This is a prePauline form.

The designation of God as "Father" is typically Christian. It was used in the OT only for the relationship of God to the people of Israel as a whole (Deut. 32:6; Isa. 63:16 et al.) or of God to the king (2 Sam. 7:14 et al.; cf. Ps. 2:7). Jesus expressed his unique relationship to God by addressing him as Father[13] and passed it on to his disciples in the Lord's Prayer. Paul knew it as well and called the believers' attention to the fact that as the true Son of God, Jesus gave them the right to call upon God as "Father" (אַבָּא, even cited in Aramaic; Rom. 8:15; Gal. 4:6). The designation Son of God for Jesus soon prevailed in the early church (Rom. 1:3 et al.). If God raised him from the dead, his unique relationship to God was confirmed thereby.[14] Hence the new Christian designation for God as Father was in response to Jesus' title of Son of God.

Clearly, this is not a matter of a physical relationship (see Ps. 2:7). Even in Luke 1:35 and Matt. 1:18, 20, where the physical conception is already present, the emphasis lies on the divine sending of Jesus. Father is only one of the terms for God. The other was Lord (κύριος), which became common particularly in the public reading of the Bible (Philo, Mut.; §§20f. 23). In Christianity it quickly became a title for Jesus (e.g., Rom. 10:13; 1 Cor. 1:2; cf. §17 [c]), the dissemination of which was fostered by its occurrence in several hellenistic connections. Behind this title is the conception in the Christian sphere that Jesus sits at the right hand of God (e.g., Acts 2:33; Rom. 8:34; Heb. 1:3; 1 Pet. 3:22) and executes God's will (cf. Ps. 110:1 with Matt. 22:44). As Lord, Jesus was distinguished from God (the Father; 1 Cor. 8:6). The title Kyrios and Jesus' sitting at the right hand of God are also used in the theological argumentation in Col. 3:1 and Eph. 1:20. Because the false teachers have relativized the significance of Jesus (§12), these honorific titles of his are emphasized here.

The metaphorical expressions for the deepest relationships are not a primitive means with significance only in religious parlance. The key concepts of human language are metaphorical: Rise, fall, progress, fulfillment, alienation — all these are concepts that merely signal what is meant and do not designate them precisely. They are irreplaceable because reality is grasped not only descriptively. All the more this

---

[12]Here following MSS א, A, et al.
[13]J. Jeremias, "Abba," in Abba, ed. idem, Göttingen, 1966, pp. 15–67.
[14]Pokorný, Gottessohn (see note 11 above), p. 32f.

applies to the eschatological reality and to the relationships anchored in it. In a certain sense the early Christians were aware of this characteristic of language. This can be seen in Colossians in the use of the images of being buried together with Christ and of the resurrection with Christ, or of the cancelling of the debt (2:12–14). Several concepts and images have been used in parallel; they were deemed the highest level of human language used in thanksgiving to God.

Πάντοτε, meaning "always" or "continually," can refer to the thanksgiving (We always give thanks . . . when we pray for you)[15] or to the prayer (We give thanks . . . continually praying for you).[16] The similar statement in Phil. 1:4 (always, in every prayer) confirms that both meanings are in mind here, a factor often noted in commentators' translations. The first meaning is not to limit the giving of thanks (only when we pray, cf. 1:9); the second is not to be understood in terms of a prayer vigilance (cf. →4:2), but it is to express the continuity of thanksgiving (cf. 1 Cor. 1:4).[17]

4–5a According to 1:7f., the writers have heard from Epaphras concerning the spiritual life of the recipients. What they have heard is expressed by means of the triad faith-love-hope, which also occurs in 1 Thess. 1:3; 5:8 and 1 Cor. 13:13 (cf. Pol., Phil. 3:3).[18] Perhaps this is part of the earliest Christian catechetical tradition.[19] Thus for the readers and hearers (4:16), this is not the repetition of an account which Epaphras rendered about them; instead, what they are primarily and vividly shown is the correct Christian lifestyle into which they are to continue to grow (1:10).

For Paul, faith (πίστις) is primarily an event coming from God[20] that brings people into relationship with Jesus Christ (→1:28). It is the other side of the power of God that was at work in the resurrection of Jesus, which "empowers" people (1:11) and which is actualized in baptism (1:14; Gal. 3:25; Eph. 4:5).[21] Here the attention is on Jesus as the ob-

---

[15]RSV, ĒP, EÜ, and most commentaries.

[16]Lohmeyer, TOB.

[17]In some MSS (B, D, G, et al.) the "for you" (περὶ ὑμῶν) is expressed by means of the less common equivalent preposition ὑπέρ (Blass–Debrunner–Funk, Grammar § 229; § 231) which has perhaps been influenced by the analogous rendering in 1:9.

[18]Philem. 5 mentions only love and faith, though "the good" (τὸ ἀγαθόν) as the object of hope is obviously used in the place of hope: H. Riesenfeld, "Faith and Love Promoting Hope. An Interpretation of Philemon v. 6," in Hooker, Paul and Paulinism, pp. 251–257.

[19]Cf. also Gal. 5:5f.; Heb. 6:10–12; 10:22–24; 1 Pet. 1:3–8, 21–22; Eph. 4:2–5; Caird, p. 167. The triad did not only arise in the anti-Gnostic polemic; on this issue, see Lohse, p. 45f.; Bornkamm, "Hoffnung," p. 207; O. Wischmeyer, Der höchste Weg, p. 144ff.

[20]Binder, Glaube, p. 5; D. Lührmann, Glauben im frühen Christentum, Gütersloh, 1976, p. 33ff., emphasizes the roots of the concept of faith in the language of the OT. Over against this, G. Barth, "Pistis in hellenistischer Religiosität," ZNW 73 (1982), pp. 110–126, has drawn attention to the widely known concept of pistis in hellenistic religion.

[21]Lohse, p. 46.

ject and content of faith, as the analogous phrase "love . . . for all the saints" and the parallel in Philem. 5 indicate.[22]

For love the word ἀγάπη was used, and this was not very common in the pagan literature of that time.[23] It describes in the NT mostly turning toward other people, whose destiny is God's salvation (Luke 6:27f., par.; Rom. 12:9, 12, 21). For Paul faith "works" through love (Gal. 5:6). Here it is love shown to other Christians that is praised (Gal. 6:10, cf. 5:13; 1 Thess. 3:12; 4:9; Rom. 12:9f.).[24] In the Johannine circle love for one another already moves to prominence. This development may overshadow a demand that Jesus intended to be absolute. On the other hand, it is designed to make love concrete; for once Christian communities were established, believers experienced a significant part of their life in them. It was not long before love for one another became one of the basic Christian virtues (1 Thess. 4:9; Heb. 13:1); it was considered to be an important aspect of agape (Rom. 12:9-21; 1 Pet. 1:22; 2 Pet. 1:7). Paul gauged faith's effect in love for the saints (1:2) very concretely, if not materially: e.g., in the proceeds of the collection for the poor in Jerusalem (2 Cor. 8:4; 9:1, 12f.; Rom. 15:25) or in the gift to him personally while in prison (Phil. 4:10-20). As an expression of Philemon's love he expected the runaway slave Onesimus (Philem. 5, 7, 16) to be accepted. Here Christians' mutual love is the manner of Christian existence, a sign of the growth of their faith, a noetic means of the knowledge of the mystery of the gospel (2:2f.) and the bond that unites all things for the purpose of perfection (3:14; Eph. 4:24f.).

Hope ἐλπίς is described here as a possession prepared[25] in heaven; it is the premise of love. Grammatically it is possible that the phrase "because of the hope" refers to the apostle's prayer of thanksgiving εὐχαριστοῦμεν; but the hope, held in deposit, the spes quae speratur, is correlated with faith as its object and eschatological goal. This itself provides the reason for both faith[26] and love. Hope is the consequence of faith in Rom. 5:1-5 and Gal. 5:5;[27] here it is positioned at the beginning and "above," kept in heaven. Its basis is the exaltation of the resurrected Christ (1:18b-20; Eph. 1:18-23) who, at the same time, is

---

[22]Conzelmann; Gnilka.

[23]O. Wischmeyer, "Agape in der ausserchristlichen Antike," ZNW 69 (1978), pp. 212-238.

[24]Focusing love upon the neighbor as a fellow brother was common in the OT: Lev. 19:18.

[25]ἀποκεῖσθαι is almost a technical term for something that has been prepared and deposited, cf. 2 Macc. 12:45; on the origin, see Dibelius, p. 6.

[26]Lightfoot, p. 132.

[27]Lindemann, Aufhebung, p. 42, note 90; on hope in Paul, see G. Nebe, "Hoffnung" bei Paulus, StUNT 16, Göttingen, 1983, following the review by H. Hübner in ThLZ 108 (1983), pp. 738-741.

present in the Christian community (1:27).[28] The shift in emphasis is similar to the one observed between Rom. 6:1–11 and Col. 2:12f.; 3:1 (§13). The "spatial" interpretation of Christian hope (cf. the "above" in Col. 3:1) relativizes the dimension of the future fulfillment, which is rarely the case in the main letters of Paul (cf. Tit. 2:13). In place of a future fulfillment we read in 3:4 of a future unveiling of the content of hope (of eschatological praise and of being with Christ).[29] However, the temporal-future (3:4)[30] and the spatial (3:1) dimension of the Christian hope have a related theological function here: they substantiate the paraenesis.[31]

On the other hand, there is the notion of a deposited heavenly treasure found in Jewish apocalyptic (4 Ezra 7:14, cf. v. 77), in the tradition of the sayings of Jesus (Matt. 6:20f., par.; Mark 10:21, par.), and which is not foreign even to the apostle Paul (1 Cor. 2:7).[32] Apocalyptic expectation and the anticipation of salvation, therefore, are not mutually exclusive. Theoretically the emphatic reference to the salvation that awaits could weaken perseverance and patience;[33] yet it is emphasized that faith must grow (2:19), which means both a deeper insight into the mystery of the gospel (2:2; Eph. 1:18) and improved relationships among Christians in the church (3:12–15). The certainty that what is new "already contains the future," may, circumstances permitting, strengthen its support.[34]

For Paul, as well as for all of early Christianity, heaven (οἱ οὐρανοί) is understood in the Jewish sense, namely, as God's creation (Ps. 102:26; 115:15), as the realm high above the (flat) earth (Is. 55:9), and as inaccessible to humanity by its own power. From the human vantage point, it is the place from which God reveals himself (Mark 1:11, par.; Rom. 10:6)[35] and the locus of the eternal life of Christians (2 Cor. 5:1ff.; Phil. 3:20).[36]

5b The second part of this verse draws attention to the past dimension of the gospel. The Christian is able to speak of the eschato-

---

[28]Bornkamm, "Hoffnung," pp. 207, 211.

[29]Emphasis by Schenk, "Christus," p. 150; according to Lindemann, Aufhebung, p. 42, this shift in emphasis is connected with the polemic against the heresy, cf. § 12 and § 13.

[30]On the tracks of futuristic eschatology in Col., see Steinmetz, Heils-Zuversicht, p. 29ff. Against this, Lindemann, Aufhebung, p. 44, argues that the anticipation of the parousia is not an issue in Col.

[31]Cf. Schillebeeckx, E. Christus und die Christen. Freiburg, 1977, p. 182f.

[32]Bornkamm, "Hoffnung," p. 208; Kuhn, Enderwartung, pp. 181–186.

[33]Cf. Ernst, p. 157.

[34]Already in Jesus' proclamation an affinity to this structure of thought can be found. Such expressions as Col. 1:5a may indirectly be influenced by the parable of the treasure (Matt. 13:45f.).

[35]The biblical witnesses were well aware that God, as the creator, is not restricted to heaven (1 Kings 8:27).

[36]It was also regarded as a dimension of the kingdom of God.

logical revelation as that which has already taken place. It is affirmed, not merely promised. In Christian theology apocalyptic eschatology separates into the revelation attested in Jesus Christ and into the fulfillment hoped for. Originally Paul saw this as two phases of the events of the end (1 Thess. 1:9f.); later, however, it developed into two focal points of Christian orientation.[37] The emphasis in v. 5b shifts from salvation anchored in the already realized redemption to its proclamation and its prior appropriation by the recipients (1:13; 1:5, 6, 9; 2:6; Eph. 1:13; cf. 1:25).[38] Thus the bond between the recipients and their Pauline past is underscored.[39]

The message of the gospel, the proclamation of the resurrection of Jesus,[40] is the word of the truth. "Of the gospel" is an appositive paraphrase of what has been said previously (cf. Eph. 1:13). The "word of the truth" can denote a true word, but here the truth is also the content of the proclamation. The Hebrew understanding of truth as that which is reliable (the word stem אמנ)[41] and the Greek conception of truth as that which is revealed (cf. 1:26) both find an echo here. Thus the word of truth is the resurrection of Jesus proclaimed in terms of the grace of God. In contrast, untruth is identical with the denial of the grace of God (→3:9; Eph. 4:25–29). At the same time, the concept of truth emerges as the opposite of the false doctrine of the opponents.[42]

6 The term truth closes the chiastically arranged statement. "In truth" does not describe the kind of understanding, but its content, such as "in which you have heard of the grace of God in its truth." Knowledge of truth means becoming a Christian (1 Tim. 2:4; 2 Tim. 3:7; Tit. 1:1; Heb. 10:26; 2 John 1; cf. Col. 2:2f.).[43] That the gospel has reached the recipients and is among them[44] is part of the worldwide movement. "In the whole world" essentially refers to the Roman Empire (Rom. 1:8) in which the gospel comes to fruition and grows. As far as the actual number of Christians is concerned, that was a bold statement. Christians, who gradually emerged in every large

[37]The systematic discussion of this problem has been treated in depth especially in O. Cullmann, *Christ and Time*, rev. ed., ET by F. V. Filson, Philadelphia, 1964, and later in J. Moltmann, *Theology of Hope*, ET by J. W. Leitch, New York, 1967, p. 172ff. (e.g., "Diskussion über die 'Theologie der Hoffnung,'" Munich, 1967); on the problem of a "double eschatology," see P. Pokorný, "Der Theologe J. B. Souček," *EvTh* 32 (1972), pp. 241–251, esp. p. 246.

[38]In the Pauline homologoumena the past dimension of hearing the word of God (1 Thess. 1:6; 2:13; Rom. 10:14) is emphasized only in Gal. 1:8–11.

[39]Schenke-Fischer, *Einleitung*, p. 168.

[40]Cf. Pokorný, *Christology*, pp. 66–68.

[41]Prov. 22:21, cf. 2 Cor. 1:19 (Rev. 3:14)—Jesus as God's Amen; Jenni–Westermann, *Handwörterbuch* I:203ff.

[42]Schweizer, p. 35.

[43]Ibid., p. 37.

[44]παρεῖναι εἰς is found only here and in 1 Macc. 11:63; Peake.

city, were a minuscule minority in the eyes of their contemporaries. Hence the statement concerning worldwide growth is more an expression of faith than a realistic estimate (cf. →1:24). Similar to the uncontested letters of Paul (1 Thess. 1:8; 1 Cor. 1:2; Rom. 1:8; 15:16), the spreading of the gospel[45] is here understood as the fulfillment of the eschatological praise which the peoples of the earth will render to the Lord (Ps. 67).

The gospel bears fruit and grows. The life of a Christian group is here characterized by two verbs. "Bearing fruit" καρποφορεῖν is used as a means. It is the "dynamic" medium attesting to the internal energy of the gospel.[46] In conjunction with the mission, the image of fruit denotes the faith that the gospel finds (Rom. 1:13; Mark 4:20, 28, par.). The fruit that believers bear signifies their whole life (Rom. 7:4, 5) or their good works (Gal. 5:22; Phil. 1:11; Col. 1:10).[47]

Logically growing should precede fruit bearing, but the author is here thinking first of all of the recipients' specific faith ("among yourselves"); only then does he set it in the larger context of growth as the manner of existence of the whole church (→2:19). Numerical growth is indeed in view (1 Cor. 3:6f.), but since it denotes the metaphysical growth of the church as the body of Christ at the same time (2:19; Eph. 4:15), it is impossible without the growing inner relationship with God (1:10).

7 Epaphras,[48] from whom the recipients learned the gospel, obviously was the missionary of the Lycus Valley (Colossae, Laodicea, Hierapolis; →4:12f.). He is described as the beloved fellow servant who serves Christ together with the apostle. His importance as a disciple of Paul is underscored by the listing of his attributes: Beloved (ἀγαπητός) describes a specific relationship (Is. 42:1; Mark 1:11, par.;

---

[45]The spreading of Christianity was aided by various circumstances: The intelligible and financially commonly accessible preaching ministry; monotheism; the incarnation of Jesus Christ to which every common person had an affinity; the worldwide horizon of faith; the connection with the ancient oriental tradition (OT) which was in late antiquity understood as a reflection of an immediate experience with God, etc. (J. Leipoldt, "Der Sieg des Christentums über die Religionen der Alten Welt," most recently in Von den Mysterien zur Kirche, ed. by J. Leipoldt, Leipzig, 1961, pp. 163–196; A. D. Nock, Conversion, Oxford, 1933, p. 183ff.; O. Gigon, Die antike Kultur und das Christentum Gütersloh, 1966, p. 86ff.; Schweizer, p. 37). The rapid dissemination of Christianity cannot be explained thereby, however. Other traits, as e.g., its exclusiveness or its demanding morality, made the church's competitiveness with other religions (e.g., the Isis cult) more difficult. Hence the lasting effectiveness of the gospel has to do with its content, namely, with the realistic view of human alienation (sin) and with the discovery of the deepest perspective of life in relationship to God which Jesus made accessible and which faith accepts as a gift.

[46]Lightfoot; Haupt; Peake; Bratcher–Nida.

[47]Chrysostom ad 1,9: the works; Theodoret: living in community is praiseworthy (πολιτεῖα).

[48]On the name, see Dibelius, p. 7.

9:7, par.) in which the dignity of the beloved is derived from the one who loves (Mark 12:6, par.). In Paul some fellow workers are described in this way; in Colossians this is also true of Tychicus, Onesimus, and Luke (4:7, 9, 14). A fellow servant is the one who, like the apostle, is a "servant" of Jesus Christ (cf. 4:12); it has almost become a functional designation (of Tychicus in 4:7). The servants of God in Judaism were the patriarchs or prophets to whom God entrusted his hidden secrets (Amos 3:7; 1 QpHab 7.5; Rev. 1:1; 10:7; cf. Col. 1:26ff.; 4:3).[49] As a fellow servant, Epaphras was the administrator of the apostolic mandate (Rom. 1:1; Phil. 1:1; Gal. 1:10), as the phrase "on our behalf" also indicates.[50] Likewise it has to do with the functional designation "servant" (διάκονος, →1:23),[51] which expresses the action of the servants of Christ to those outside (in the proclamation of the gospel, 1:25ff.; Eph. 3:7ff.).[52] In contrast to 1:2, faithful (πιστός) here is construed in the passive and describes the one who is recognized by God as dependable. From reflecting upon this verse two conclusions may be drawn: (a) The epistle is to reinforce the Pauline interpretation of the gospel that Epaphras has represented.[53] At this point it has already become a matter of tradition and doctrine, while the continuity (cf. 1:5) as well as the quality of the revelation (cf. 1:23) of the apostolic proclamation have been accentuated.[54] (b) The apostolic office, therefore, is tied to the gospel.[55] His dignity derives from the bearing of fruit in the proclamation of the gospel, to the foundation of which the apostles bear witness.[56]

8 In keeping with the chiastic structure of the prayer of thanksgiving, the issue of love (→1:4) recurs here. It is that love which expresses itself concretely[57] and which has its source in the Holy Spirit[58] (Rom.

---

[49]Schweizer, p. 37.

[50]The reading ὑπερ ἡμῶν (on our behalf), which Nestle–Aland[26] and UBS[3] take to be secondary (Metzger, 619f.) since it could be influenced by the preceding ἡμῶν, has a claim to priority all the same, in our opinion, because of its excellent attestation (p[46], ℵ*, B) and because ὑπερ ὑμῶν may be influenced by the conspicuous statement in 1:24.

[51]Cf. Ollrog, *Mitarbeiter*, p. 225. Ernst, p. 159, surmises that Paul evangelized the major cities and left the missionary work in the outlying areas to his fellow workers.

[52]If used in the absolute sense, διάκονος described an office in the church already at the time of the apostle Paul, Phil. 1:1; Rom. 16:1; 1 Tim. 3:8ff.

[53]Lindemann, "Gemeinde," p. 127.

[54]Wegenast, *Tradition*, p. 129, note 1; Merklein, *Amt*, pp. 237–240.

[55]Emphasis in Ollrog, *Mitarbeiter*, p. 222.

[56]This also applies to →1:24f., where the suffering of the apostle illustrates the authority of the gospel, while it does not legitimize it; cf. Gnilka, "Paulusbild," p. 192f.; against this, Lohse, p. 110f.

[57]Therefore, the characteristic of that love as *"spiritualis dilectio"* ([Ps-]Oecumenius, Calvin) can lead astray.

[58]The Holy Spirit is mentioned only here and in 2:5 (cf. § 13). Yet the working of the Holy Spirit is assumed in Col.; see J. D. G. Dunn, *Baptism in the Holy Spirit*, London, 1970, ch. 15.

15:30).[59] It follows from v. 9 that the Colossians also demonstrated their love toward the apostle Paul and his fellow workers.[60]

2. Intercession, 1:9–11

(9) And so, from the day we heard of it, we have not ceased to pray for you, asking that you may be filled with the knowledge of his will in all spiritual wisdom and understanding, (10) to lead a life worthy of the Lord, fully pleasing to him, bearing fruit in every good work and increasing in the knowledge of God. (11) May you be strengthened with all power, according to his glorious might, for all endurance and patience with joy,

The combination of thanksgiving and intercession represents a liturgical element.[1] The intercession ushers in a new sub-section; its position in the framework of the first major part is illustrated in *Table 5*.[2]

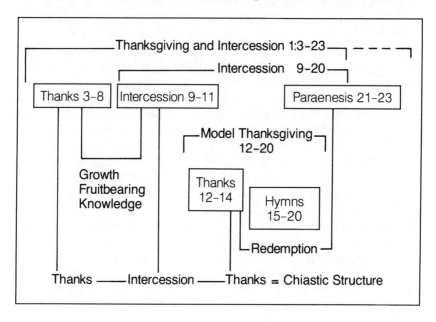

TABLE 5

[59]Gnilka, p. 38, cf. Eph. 2:22; differently in Schweizer, p. 38; see also Schweizer, "Christus," p. 308f.
[60]Haupt.

[1]Cf. note 7 in 1:3–8.
[2]The table shows that Col. 1:9–20 is an intercession, as Eckart, "Beobachtungen," p. 91, has observed correctly; on his argument that this represents an earlier liturgy (p. 99f.), see →1:12 and § 9 (d). The difference in style and vocabulary which Eckart discovers here, applies to Col. as a whole (see also Lohse, p. 65, note 3).

In their intercession[3] the senders are praying that the recipients might be able to thank God in the manner demonstrated in 1:11b-14, because in Christ, God acted as the hymn (1:15-20) depicts it in song. Already in 1:21-23 the recipients are again addressed directly, as in v. 9; in the argumentation, however, v. 21 connects directly with the prayer (καὶ ὑμᾶς). Thus in the background of the chiastic structure of thanksgiving (3ff.)-intercession (9ff.)-thanksgiving (12ff.)[4] there is a deeper structure in which the second thanksgiving is part of the intercession.

The senders represent the apostolic authority as one of God's vehicles for the proclamation of his mystery (1:25; 4:3) as well as for the formation of the church. The apostles and their helpers represent the grace of God (→1:24); they are laboring for the salvation of the recipients (1:28f.)[5]

The Christian community being addressed is to recognize, acknowledge, and confess to all of creation its dependence upon God in Jesus Christ. In this basic attitude the community is able to be one with the senders; from the author's perspective, when the community depends upon the apostolic witness it embodies the later post-apostolic generations.

9 "So" (διὰ τοῦτο) refers to the faith and love of the recipients, as v. 4 makes clear. Hence the intercession is a response to the good news about the growth of the recipients as a Christian community. They need intercession if their growth is to reach its goal and the goal is to be filled[6] with the knowledge of the will of God (πληρωθῆτε τὴν ἐπίγνωσιν = acc. of thing[7]; cf. Phil. 1:9f.).[8] In distinction to 1:1, the will here signifies the content of the decision rather than the decision itself (cf. Rom. 12:2). The content itself is intimated in 1:12ff.[9] From a comparison with 2:2, where we read about the knowledge of the mystery of God, it appears that the will of God is analogous to the mystery of God. In fact, it is the gospel of Jesus Christ (→1:27; 2:2) and is especially thought of in terms of the reconciliation of the world brought about by Jesus Christ (→1:20; Eph. 1:9-11, 17f.). According to Colossians, the process of the progressive discovery of the encom-

[3]A longer petition as an opening of a report in the form of a letter can be found in 2 Macc. 1:2-6.

[4]For a comparison with similar structures in contemporary prayers, see Gnilka, Epheserbrief, p. 27.

[5]Wiles, Prayers, pp. 4, 298ff.

[6]πληροῦν here may be influenced by the term πλήρωμα (fullness), which plays a significant part in 1:19 and 2:9 (§ 9 [b]).

[7]Blass-Debrunner-Funk, § 159.

[8]In his Zürich dissertation, the 17th-cent. Burkhardus took this in support of the Reformation doctrine of the testimonium internum spiritus sancti.

[9]Hence the statement about the will of God is not without context here, as Eckart argues in "Beobachtungen," p. 89; see Schrage, Einzelgebote, p. 168f.

passing grace of God (1:6) is related to the endeavor for a new life. The paraenetic sentences are placed between the reference to the knowledge and to its actual goal (1:10f.). In v. 9b the knowledge is defined more specifically. It is to come to pass "in all wisdom and spiritual understanding." The cluster of the terms knowledge-wisdom-understanding shows up in the OT (Exod. 31:3; Is. 11:2), in Judaism (Sir. 1:19), and in early Christianity (Barn. 2:3; 21:5). The noun "understanding" (σύνεσις; בִּינָה), as well as its corresponding verb, refer to the knowledge of God (Rom. 3:11; 15:21; 2 Cor. 10:12); in Ephesians they refer directly to the knowledge of the "mystery of Christ," namely, of God's plan of salvation (3:4), and to his will (5:17). "Understanding" here may also designate the ability to discover the will of God in the various religious expressions and as indicated by the indirect parallel of Phil. 1:9f. to distinguish them from false doctrine. In any case, this involves an understanding wrought by the Spirit (3:16, cf. Eph. 1:3; 5:18).

The terms discussed here, knowledge (gnōsis; here ἐπίγνωσις) and wisdom σοφία, were prominent in several contexts at that time. For this reason their occurrence cannot be used as evidence of a particular influence. We also read about knowledge as the content of salvation in the Qumran writings (1 QS 10.9, 12; 1 QH 2.18), frequently in conjunction with the goodwill of God (1 QS 11.17b–18). At the same time, however, the Qumran documents emphasize the hiddenness of God's plan of salvation (1 QS 11.18ff.), whereas the entire mystery of God is revealed in Christ, according to Col. 2:2.[10] Knowledge is also the fundamental concept in Gnosticism as a religiophilosophical and theosophical movement (§12; →3:10). In Judaism, wisdom was the mediator of creation (§9 [b]; →2:3), and in some of the second-century gnostic systems (esp. the Valentinian system) it mediated between the material creation and the divine world. Like the Gnostics' understanding, knowledge here is the path of salvation; in contrast to Gnosticism, which is concerned with knowledge of one's own divinity (Iren., Adv. haer. I, 25, 5; Corp. Herm. I, 18), however, its object here is God's love and grace (1:6; Eph. 1:10f.; 2:2f.; 3:9f.). Likewise typical here is the connection of knowledge with references to the social aspects of life — an association virtually unknown in Gnosticism. Hence the statements concerning knowledge must be regarded as an implementation of the authentic witness and the theological reflection of the author.

10 From Table 5 we learn that the knowledge of the mystery, which is expressed especially in the hymn of 1:15–20, creates the conditions for a new lifestyle and is its basis (1:9). Knowledge of God is the in-

[10]On the issue of the knowledge of the mysteries of God, cf. Col. →1:26; 2:2 with 1 QS 3.15f.; 1 QH 12.13.

strument of growth;[11] it is not that which grows.[12] That which grows
is the gospel (1:6). It grows by means of expansion to other people
in missions (1:4–6) and (1:10f.), by means of the effect in the Christians'
life in togetherness.[13] Here, as well as in 2:6 and 4:5, "to lead
a life" (περιπατεῖν) denotes lifestyle. The Christian lifestyle is related
to Christ as Lord (2:6ff.). Similar to the entire Pauline corpus, in Colossians
and Ephesians the title Lord, Kyrios, is the most significant
one and becomes prominent especially in paraenesis (Col. 2:6; 3:22,
24).[14] "Worthy" is an expression from Pauline paraenesis. It refers
to the lifestyle corresponding to the gospel (Phil. 1:27), to God (1 Thess.
2:12), that is, the calling of God (Eph. 4:1). To walk worthy of the Lord
means to live in a manner pleasing to the true heavenly Lord, not
merely pleasing to others (cf. 3:22 – ἀνθρωπάρεσκοι).

As in 1:6, "bearing fruit" is here connected with "growing." In the
former, the reference is to the mission; here it is to good works. Paul's
references to works are mostly negative, namely, the works of the law.
Positively, "the work" refers to the proclamation of the gospel with
its consequences (1 Cor. 9:1; Phil. 1:22); the latter also includes the
works of faith (1 Thess. 1:3), namely, the fruit of faith and of the Spirit
(Gal. 5:22; 6:7–9), which is not unimportant before the judgment seat
of God (2 Cor. 5:10; Rom. 2:7–10).[15] The phrase "in every good work"
is not common in Paul;[16] nevertheless, as in Paul, so here good works
are understood as a consequence of the new life in the grace of God
(3:1ff.; Eph. 4:7ff.).[17]

11 The paronomastic (power–strengthened) and pleonastic (all
power– might) expression (cf. 1:19; Eph. 3:16) once again underscores
that paraenesis is anchored in the power of God with which the church
is linked by faith. "All" (πᾶς) occurs seven times in 1:4–11, twice in
this verse. It is typical of the pleonastic style[18] and is intended to emphasize
that the power of God, which has become evident in the exaltation
of Christ, is fully sufficient for the salvation of humankind
(→1:16).[19] The "glory" (δόξα) belongs to the dimension of the eschaton,
roughly analogous to the heavenly light of the kingdom of God

---

[11]Alford; Gnilka.

[12]As would be the case following the variant readings of the later MSS, see Nestle–Aland[26].

[13]In this sense, the OT uses the verb הָלַךְ, e.g., in Prov. 8:20.

[14]Neugebauer, In Christus, p. 147ff.

[15]L. Mattern, Das Verständnis des Gerichts bei Paulus, AThANT 47, Zürich, 1966, p. 151ff.

[16]Schweizer.

[17]Eph. 2:8–9 emphatically rejects righteousness by works.

[18]Norden, Agnostos Theos, pp. 244–350, has pointed out the affinity of this expression to Stoicism; see also O'Brien, Thanksgivings, p. 83; Bujard, Untersuchungen, p. 159f.

[19]Hooker, "Teachers," p. 321.

(1:12f.; Eph. 1:18f.), and denotes the manner of God's nature and work (cf. כָּבוֹד). From the human perspective it is the perfection of life and the presence of God where God's work manifests itself directly. In this world the glory of God is made manifest in Jesus Christ, the crucified one (1:20; 1 Cor. 1:23–25). This is the great mystery made manifest in him (1:26f.; 2 Cor. 4:6).

Might (κράτος) here means the redeeming power by which God is able to bring about the transformation of the situation of sinful humanity, and it is expressed in terms such as "deliver," "transfer into the kingdom of his Son" (1:13), "reconcile," and "present before him" (1:22). The power (δύναμις) that strengthens (δυναμοῦν) Christians is the power that has been revealed in the resurrection of Jesus (Eph. 1:20) and that is at work in the world through the apostles (Col. 1:29). Both terms (power and might) constitute a certain antipode over against the statements concerning the powers and dominions in 1:13, 16; 2:10, 15 (cf. §10).[20] Sharing in the power of God is the concrete aspect of the knowledge of God, that is, the empowerment that arises from that knowledge. In practical terms, this empowerment works itself out (surprisingly) in the two virtues of endurance and patience/longsuffering.

In some instances in the Pauline corpus, endurance (ὑπομονή) is an eschatological virtue: perseverance in hardship, which draws its strength from the anticipated consummation (Rom. 8:25; 15:4 et al.). Its horizon is God's judgment (1 Thess. 1:2–10; Phil. 1:3–11).[21] Patience/longsuffering (μακροθυμία) was especially held to be one of God's attributes (Ps. 86:15 = LXX 85:15);[22] but here, similar to 3:12 (cf. Eph. 4:2; Gal. 5:22), it is a social virtue that is connected with the church's life as community. Patience/longsuffering and endurance are not merely passive virtues; rather, they are expressions of the power of the Risen One who makes possible the life of the church as life in togetherness within the Christian communities. Endurance is part of the communal life in terms of sociability. Precisely as such it is tied up with the power of God, because only those who have experienced this power acknowledge their own sin and know that their attempt at this new life is not deserved (1:21f.). They realize that, together with other people, they have a common Lord (3:11). For this reason patience/longsuffering is linked with humility (3:12; Eph. 4:2; Gal. 5:22f.).

Only when endurance and patience/longsuffering are combined with joy are they expressions of the power of God (that is of the Holy

---

[20]Schmidt, "Natur- und Geistkräfte," pp. 94f.; 135f.; 142.

[21]Wiles, *Prayers*, ch. 6.

[22]F. Hauck, *TDNT* IV:581–588, esp. p. 586; J. Horst, *TDNT* IV:374–387, esp. p. 384, note 82.

Spirit), cf. Gal. 5:22 (joy . . . patience); Rom. 12:12 (rejoice . . . be patient); 1 Thess. 1:3–6. Joy puts an end to the passive character of both virtues, and thus they become signs of the presence of God and instruments of his working (Phil. 4:4f.).[23]

3. Paradigmatic Prayer of Thanksgiving, 1:12–14

(12) giving thanks to the Father, who has qualified us to share in the inheritance of the saints in light. (13) He has delivered us from the dominion of darkness and transferred us to the kingdom of his beloved Son, (14) in whom we have redemption, the forgiveness of sins.

The second prayer of thanksgiving is part of the intercession (Table 5). For the recipients this segment is a summons to thank God,[1] the reason for the thanksgiving, and the model of the prayer of thanksgiving. The hymn (1:15–20) that follows it unfolds the third aspect, and in 1:21–23 the paraenesis is substantiated by the central concern of the prayer of thanksgiving. The author sees the most profound condition for overcoming the heresy in the posture of gratitude to God. The central concern of the prayer of thanksgiving (1:13f., 22) has the same meaning as the central concern of the entire epistle (2:12f.; 3:1; §14).

The observation that vv. 15–20 are a hymn (see §19 [a, d] below) and that vv. 12–14 also contain liturgical phrases (see below) still does not mean that the author adopted the segment of 1:12 (or 13)–20 as a liturgical unit, as some interpreters argue.[2] Nevertheless, the scholars who take 1:12–20 to be a liturgical unit have made several relevant observations: They have recognized, for instance, the relationship

---

[23]The phrase "with joy" can also be joined with the following phrase "giving thanks to God" (Dibelius; Lohse; Gnilka; O'Brien, Thanksgivings, and several translations and text editions of which the UBS[3] offers an overview in loco). The frequently attested connection between joy and endurance and patience/longsuffering favors our interpretation.

---

[1]Gnilka, p. 44.

[2]So G. Bornkamm, "Das Bekenntnis im Hebräerbrief," most recently in Studien zu Antike und Urchristentum, Ges. Aufs. II (BevTh 28), Munich, 1963[2], pp. 188–203, esp. p. 196f., who regards the entire segment of 1:12–20 as a liturgical prayer of thanksgiving. We have observed, however, that we are more likely dealing with an entity shaped by the author (Table 3 and 5). Similar to Bornkamm argue e.g., also Norden, "Kunstprosa," pp. 250–254; Lohmeyer, p. 40ff. (1:13–20—a unit); Schille, Hymnen, p. 81f.; Zeilinger, Erstgeborene, pp. 38–44, 138f. Käsemann, "Baptismal Liturgy"; Lohse, p. 67; idem, "Christologie"; Vielhauer, Geschichte, pp. 196, 201; cf. O'Neill, "Christology," p. 89, have indeed distinguished between the hymn of 1:15–20 and the context, but they take Col. 1:13–20 to be an older liturgy all the same. Käsemann even considers 1:15–20 to be a pre–Christian text (p. 150ff., cf. § 9 [b]). He has correctly recognized, however, that the entire segment constitutes a condition for the polemic against the heresy (p. 164f.). On this discussion, see O'Brien, Thanksgivings, p. 71ff. Against limiting this segment to 1:13–20 is the argument that 1:12 and 1:13 are joined together via the semantic axis of light/darkness, cf. Gnilka, p. 45.

between the statements in 1:12–14 and the baptismal event. In the argument of 2:12f. the deliverance from death (2:13, cf. 1:12f.) and the forgiveness of sins (2:14, cf. 1:14) are clearly connected with baptism (2:12). The designation "Son of his love" (1:13, cf. Mark 1:11, par.: baptism of Jesus) also points to baptism.[3] Likewise significant are the analogies with 1 Pet. 1:3–5 where the connection with baptism is quite clear (1:3).[4] "Redemption" (ἀπολύτρωσις, 1:14) obviously is a concept characterizing the salvation event actualized in baptism, even before Paul (Rom. 3:24; 1 Cor. 1:30);[5] only here the emphasis is placed more on God.[6]

The similarity of 1:12–14 with the aforementioned argument of 2:12f. speaks against viewing 1:12–20[7] as a pre-shaped unit. In both instances the comparison indicates pre–Pauline conceptions (relationship of the believer with Christ, forgiveness of sins)[8] which have been given a new interpretation, however, and which we rather ought to consider as authorial formulations inspired by the liturgical tradition.[9] The other argument against viewing this segment as pre-shaped is the discovery of the hymn in 1:15–20 (§9[a]), which forms a contextual unit already bearing a Christian imprint (§9 [b]). Therefore, 1:12–14 represents an introduction to the hymn (1:15–20) that the author formulated in dependence upon the liturgical tradition and in which he alludes to the baptism of the recipients.[10]

12 In the Greek text "giving thanks" is a participle that ties the prayer of thanksgiving to the strengthening of the recipients in 1:11. The verb is the same as in 1:3, where it characterized the attitude of the senders. Thus the apostolic model is to leave its imprint upon the recipients.

The conception of the lot or share (κλῆρος, גּוֹרָל) is a common OT expression for salvation (e.g., Deut. 10:9) and is especially connected to the distribution of the promised land after its conquest (e.g., Josh. 13:7; LXX Ps. 15:5). In Judaism this picture is already transferred to

[3]Käsemann, "Baptismal Liturgy," p. 158f.
[4]Deichgräber, Gotteshymnus, p. 77f.
[5]Käsemann, "Baptismal Liturgy," p. 161f.
[6]Sanders, "Dependence," has discovered several expressions from Rom. in Col. 1:12–14; their meaning has changed here, however. This supports the assumption that this represents a deuteropauline work. It is not a mechanical imitation, however, as we shall see especially in the analysis of Col 2:12f. (§ 13).
[7]On the assumption that even 1:9–20 constitutes a pre-shaped unit, see note 2 on 1:9–11.
[8]Lohse, p. 67. Sanders, Hymns, p. 4, takes 1:12–14 to be an independent, brief hymn.
[9]According to Schweizer (p. 46f.), this may be an independent development of an introduction formula to the hymn of 1:15–20.
[10]Summary in O'Brien, Thanksgivings, p. 74f.; Deichgräber, Gotteshymnus, p. 82; Kehl, Christushymnus, p. 28f.; Löwe, "Bekenntnis," p. 306f.; Schweizer, pp. 45ff., 50f. (baptismal terminology is likely but cannot be demonstrated); the issue is seen similarly by Hegermann, Schöpfungsmittler, pp. 89–93; Lähnemann, Kolosserbrief, p. 35.

the eschatological blessing (Dan. 12:13; Wisd. 5:5; 1 QS 2.2; 11.7; 1 QM
13.5; *1 Enoch* 37:4; 39:8;[11] TAbrah. Hs. A XIII). In this sense the pre-
synoptic tradition of the logia of Jesus (Mark 10:17; Matt. 5:5) and Paul
(1 Cor. 6:9f.; 15:50; Gal. 3:29; 5:21) also refers to the share in the inheritance. Colossians 3:24 also speaks of salvation in Jesus Christ as
an inheritance (κληρονομία). Salvation is described pleonastically
in the present reference as participation (μέρις) in the share of the
saints.[12] Perhaps this indicates that the recipients' salvation is part
of the gift available to more people.

The saints (→1:2) are the people under God's protection and are the
possession of the one truly holy God (Exod. 19:6). It is not quite clear
whether this applies to the church at this point (as in 1:2) or to the
angels (as e.g., in 1 Thess. 3:13, cf. Zech. 14:5). In favor of the former
alternative is, e.g., the reference in *1 Enoch* 38:4f., where the saints
are identified as the righteous individuals. The latter is supported,
e.g., in 1 QS 11.7f.; 1 QH 11.11f., where it applies to the angels. At
any rate, in apocalypticism angels were understood to be righteous
people transformed by God (*1 Enoch* 51; Matt. 22:30, cf. 1 QS 4.20–23;
Pol., *Phil.* 12:2),[13] so that fellowship with angels may be the perspective of humans.[14] According to Eph. 2:19, such fellowship is already
part of the present life of the church. This expression favors the interpretation of the fellowship with angels also in this instance (cf. the
parallel of Eph. 1:18).[15]

God has "enabled" (ἱκανοῦν) the recipients[16] to share in the inheritance of the saints. Salvation, then, is an unmerited change of the
human situation and perspective, brought about by God, similar to
the deliverance in v. 13. Only, it is rather the inward transformation
of the pardoned that is emphasized in the concept of enablement. The
power of God[17] that raised Jesus from the dead (→1:11; →2:12), at the
same time touches sinners' hearts and makes possible growth in spir-

---

Cf. also note 85 on 1:15–20 and on § 9–11. Otherwise, T. E. Pollard, "Colossians 1:12–20:
A Reconsideration," NTS 27 (1981), pp. 572–575, who points out the Jewish associations.

[11]Lohse, "Christologie," p. 165.

[12]κλῆρος and μέρις are almost synonyms. In the OT, likewise, they are often cited
side by side: LXX Deut. 10:9, cf. LXX Ps. 15:5; Bénoit, "Άγιοι," p. 84f.

[13]Cf. Lohse, p. 70f.; idem, "Christologie," p. 165ff.; Bénoit, "Άγιοι," p. 93.

[14]Schweizer, "Christus," p. 298.

[15]Dibelius, pp. 8, 64; Schlier, *Epheser*, p. 84; Deichgräber, *Gotteshymnus*, p. 80;
Gnilka, p. 47; Schnackenburg, *Epheser*, p. 74; Barth, *Ephesians*, p. 151f.

[16]"You" (ὑμᾶς), according to the oldest text witnesses; ἡμᾶς is probably an adaptation to 1:13.

[17]It is not impossible that the conception which forms the backdrop of this verse,
together with the conception of deliverance out of darkness (1:13), have been influenced
indirectly by the OT term שַׁדַּי as an epithet of God which, among other suggestions,
has been interpreted "the Sufficient One" (M. Weippert, "שַׁדַּי," in ThWAT, p. 876; G.
Bertram, "'IKANOΣ in den griechischen Übersetzungen des Alten Testaments als Wie-

itual understanding (1:10f.).[18] The enabling of a person begins with conversion and baptism (2:12f.), also characterized as the translation into the realm of light (cf. Acts 26:17f.). The hymn cited (1:15–20) is meant to support this assertion (see §9 [d]; §10). Or, in other words, the central concern of the hymn is paraenetically applied to the threatened community of the recipients, here as well as in 2:12f. (§13). The light is salvation in the presence of God (Is. 60:19f.; Rev. 22:5) – the new life for alienated human beings (Eph. 5:8ff., cf. Col. 1:21). Conversion has also been expressed in similar terms in the Jewish diaspora (Jos. Asen. 15:13),[19] and for Justin (Apol. I, 61:12) baptism is already enlightenment (φωτισμός).[20] That the saints belong to the realm of light, therefore, can be understood neither gnostically as a reference to their divine origin[21] (they need forgiveness, 1:14), nor in the sense of an essential dualism of the Qumran sect (e.g., 1 QM 1.1f.; salvation is offered to everyone, Col. 1:28f.).

13 If the enabling was more akin to inward conversion, then deliverance (ἐρρύσατο),[22] much like being transferred (μετέστησεν)[23] or presented (παραστῆσαι, 1:22),[24] refers to the salvific event (cf. Exod. 14:30; Rom. 7:24) that precedes conversion (Eph. 2:5) and is actualized in it. It is the deliverance from the evil power of sin (1:22) that has been wrought in the resurrection of Jesus (2:12f.). This deliverance makes it possible to resist the evil one (3:1ff.; Eph. 2:2; 6:10–20, cf. 1 Pet. 2:9). Thus deliverance is also associated with a change of ages[25] which, though not visible yet,[26] has nevertheless already been won.

[dergabe von schaddaj," ZAW 70 [1958], pp. 20–31). In the LXX this has been translated as ἱκανός (Job 31:2; 39:32 [40:2]; Ruth 1:20, 21) and in Philo it becomes an expression of the perfection of God in the cosmic context (Philo, Mut. 27ff.).

[18]In 2 Cor. 3:5f. the qualification by God is understood as commission to (apostolic) service. In a similar context Rom. 15:13 (cf. 2 Cor. 3:6) refers to the power of the Holy Spirit. Here the Holy Spirit is not mentioned (cf. Acts 26:18).

[19]Cf. 1 QM 13.9 where the issue is not conversion but the eternal election of the members of the sect.

[20]Cf. H. Conzelmann, TDNT IX:310–358; A. Wlosok, Laktanz und die philosophische Gnosis, AHAW 1960/2, Heidelberg, 1960, p. 249f.

[21]E.g., NHC II/4; 97:13ff. and esp. Ps. Thom. 1:1–3, where the heavenly Father is identical with the light.

[22]The reference is to the final judgment (1:22, cf. ῥύειν in 1 Thess. 1:10, cf. Exod. 14:31 et al.) which follows from the death and resurrection of Jesus. Thus it is already a certainty and it is possible to speak of it in the aorist (cf. →2:12f. and § 13).

[23]Used by Josephus, Ant. 12, 149, with reference to the migration of several thousand Jews to Asia Minor.

[24]The second character trait of the Father, in contrast to the first (the qualification), is expressed in a relative clause.

[25]Zeilinger, Erstgeborene, p. 143.

[26]Col. also knows of a certain eschatological proviso: 1:10, cf. Eph. 4:13ff. (growing); 3:5 (what is being revealed), cf. Eph. 6:13 (the trials to come), cf. § 13; on the contrary, Lindemann, Aufhebung, p. 41ff.

Being transferred into the kingdom of his Son, the condition for the enabling (1:12), is the positive side of the change of ages. The kingdom of the Son is identical with the inheritance of the saints in light. Instead of speaking of the kingdom of God, the text here (and essentially also in Eph. 5:5) renders it the kingdom of the Son, which, in the framework of the Pauline corpus, occurs elsewhere only in 1 Cor. 15:24–28, where the kingdom of the Son represents a preliminary stage of the kingdom of God prior to the ultimate turn of the ages.[27] We are dealing with a development of the motif of the exaltation and enthronement of Jesus at his resurrection (Rom. 1:3f.; 8:34; 2 Pet. 1:17).[28] However, what is viewed as a future consequence of Jesus' assumption of power in 1 Cor. 15 is here seen as its present dimension (cf. 3:1). Entrance into the kingdom of the Son is akin to the resurrection with Christ in baptism (2:12; §13).[29] The connection with baptism is indicated by describing Jesus as the "beloved Son" (Mark 1:11, par.; cf. Mark 9:7). To be loved also means to be chosen for a task. Corresponding to the designation "Son" is that of God as Father in 1:12. The "kingdom of the Son" thus already extends now to where the Son is acclaimed as Lord (cf. Rom. 10:9) and where God is addressed as Father (Rom. 8:15–17; §8).[30]

14 Redemption is paralleled by the forgiveness of sins,[31] that is to say, it is already accomplished in Christ: Eph. 1:7, yet already in 1 Cor. 1:30; Rom. 3:24; 1 Pet. 1:18. Originally the concept of redemption (ἀπολύτρωσις) denoted the freeing of a slave or prisoner through weapons or a ransom, but even the OT speaks of redemption figuratively as the forgiveness of sins (LXX Ps. 129:8f. λύτρωσις). In Christianity this concept had been firmly adopted prior to Paul, specifically, in the interpretation of the substitutionary effect of the Christ event and as actualized especially in the Lord's Supper (Mark 10:45 par.) and in baptism (1 Pet. 1:18, 23). The allusion to baptism, therefore, is contained both here and in Eph. 1:7, 13f.[32]

Among the gnostic Sethians, too, we read of baptism as redemption. In the *Three Steles of Seth* (NHC VII/5) and in the gnostic *Gos-*

---

[27]The advent of the direct reign of God is described in similar terms; Ernst, p. 165; Aletti, *Colossiens*, p. 4.

[28]Cf. Ps. 110:1; Hahn, *Hoheitstitel*, p. 192f.

[29]According to Schenk, "Christus," pp. 149–151, Col. understands Jesus' baptism as his earthly resurrection; in this connection, see § 9 (c), note 84 on 1:15–20, and →1:26.

[30]The Qumran parallels to Col. 1:12–14 are relativized in that the designation of God as Father occurs only in 1 QH 9.35; see J. Jeremias, *The Prayers of Jesus*, London, 1967, pp. 35–43.

[31]This represents a parallelism; "forgiveness of sins" is not a later gloss, as proposed by Burger, *Schöpfung*, p. 70.

[32]The final redemption, which is the object of the Christian hope (Rom. 8:23; Eph. 4:30), is the completion of salvation, actualized (sealed—Gnilka, *Epheserbrief*, p. 85, esp. note 5) in baptism.

pel of the Egyptians (NHC III/2; IV/2), redemption (the Coptic verb nūim) is conceived as deliverance of the perfect generation (VII/5; 121:3 et al.) that has gone astray in the world (III/2; 63:8f.) and now possesses divine understanding (VII/5; 125:13f.; III/2; 66:5–7, cf. Col. 1:10). This, then, is the redemption intended for those who are worthy of it (VII/5; 121:14; III/2; 55:15f.; 66:2—Coptic ímpša, cf. ἱκανοῦν in Col. 1:12). Gnostic baptism[33] is also addressed (III/2; 66:4f.). Consequently, no later than at the beginning of the second century[34] did the Gnostics express their doctrine of redemption in terms similar to Colossians and Ephesians. While these Gnostics were Christian, and it is likely that the *Gospel of the Egyptians* is associated with Colossians (→ 2:14),[35] on the whole these Sethian writings clearly have their basis in certain older hellenistic, Judeo-Christian conceptions also known to the author of Colossians (cf. §12) and that, among other things, are reflected in the hymn of 1:15–20.[36] In Col. 1:9–14 this tradition is adapted, with a polemical shift in emphasis, against the heretics; it is substantially different, therefore, from its gnostic form. The alienation of the perfect generation is not its fate here, but its guilt; those who are worthy of redemption here are not human beings who share their essence with deity, but they are those who are "qualified" (1:12), whose sins God has forgiven in Jesus Christ. Regardless of whether this represents a liturgical unit or an ad hoc formulation, the forgiveness of sins as a typical trait of Christian proclamation (Luke 24:47; John 20:23, cf. Mark 2:9f., par.) is emphasized as a counterweight to the doctrine of the heretics.[37]

In both parts of the Bible the forgiveness of sins is proclaimed as the only true way to renew the relationship between God and humanity (e.g., Jer. 31:33f., cited in Heb. 10:16ff.). The initiative in this is taken by God, that is, by his delegate (e.g., Mark 2:9f.). The forgiveness[38] itself effects the sinner's healing and return to God (cf. Luke 15:11–32, confession of sins after the forgiveness). It places the sinner into the new realm in which God is encountered as heavenly Father. Christian forgiveness of sins is anchored in the death and resurrection of Jesus Christ (1 Cor. 15:3b–5, cf. Col. 2:12f.).[39] Here the

---

[33]The gnostic baptism is not yet spiritualized here; Böhlig–Wisse, *Nag Hammadi*, p. 37f.

[34]Both writings contain early material.

[35]Böhlig–Wisse, *Nag Hammadi*, p. 37.

[36]In NHC VII/5; 121:9f., the redeemer is characterized as the one pointing above, to heaven.

[37]Cf. Schnackenburg, "Aufnahme," pp. 42–46.

[38]For John the Baptist forgiveness of sins made possible the renewing of life which was to be lived in strict adherence to the law, however. The threat of judgment was the means to overcome future sins (negation of the negation): Matt. 3:7–10; Luke 3:7–9.

[39]Cf. H. Thyen, *Studien zur Sündenvergebung*, FRLANT 96, Göttingen, 1970, p. 152ff.

last statement of the following hymn is anticipated interpretively (1:20) through the message of the forgiveness of sins.[40]

4. Hymn, 1:15–20

(15) He is the image of the invisible God,
the first–born of all creation;
(16) for in him all things were created,
in heaven and on earth,
visible and invisible,
whether thrones or dominions
or principalities or authorities —
all things were created through him and for him.
(17) He is before all things,
and in him all things hold together.
(18) He is the head of the body, the church;
he is the beginning,
the first–born from the dead,
that in everything he might be pre-eminent.
(19) For in him all the fulness of God was pleased to dwell,
(20) and through him to reconcile to himself all things,
whether on earth or in heaven,
making peace by the blood of his cross.

Bibliography: (a) All the commentaries, in loco, cited in the major bibliography; (b) of the monographs and essays cited in the major bibliography esp.: Aletti, *Colossiens*, passim; Bornkamm, "Bekenntnis" (note 2 on 1:12–14), p. 196ff.; Burger, *Schöpfung*, pp. 3–114; Deichgräber, *Gotteshymnus*, p. 143ff.; Eckart, "Beobachtungen," p. 100ff.; Ernst, *Pleroma*, passim; Harder, *Paulus*, p. 46ff.; Hegermann, *Schöpfungsmittler*, p. 88ff.; Käsemann, "Baptismal Liturgy," passim; Lähnemann, *Kolosserbrief*, p. 38ff.; Maurer, "Begründung," passim; O'Brien, *Thanksgivings*, p. 71ff.; O'Neill, "Christology," passim; Schenk, "Christus," pp. 140–151; Schenke, "Erlöser," p. 221ff.; Schille, *Hymnen*, p. 81f.; Schmauch, pp. 42–59; Schnackenburg, "Aufnahme," passim; Schweizer, "Kirche," p. 293ff.; Steinmetz, *Heils-Zuversicht*, p. 69ff.; Wengst, *Formeln*, p. 170ff.; Zeilinger, *Erstgeborene*, p. 39ff.

(c) Other works: Bammel, E. "Versuch (zu) Col. 1:15–20," ZNW 52 (1961), pp. 88–95; Beasley–Murray, P. "Colossians 1:15–20: An Early Christian Hymn Celebrating the Lordship of Christ," in (FS F. F. Bruce), pp. 169–183; Burney, C. "Christ as the 'APXH of Creation (Prov. 8:22; Col. 1:15–18; Rev. 3:14)," JTS 27 (1926), pp. 160–177; Charlesworth, J. H. "The Odes of Solomon—Not Gnostic," CBQ 31 (1969), pp. 357–369; Craddox, F. B. " 'All Things to Him': A Critical Note on Col. 1:15–20," NTS 12 (1965–66), pp. 78–80; Ellingsworth, P. "Colossians 1:15–20 and its Context," ExpT 73 (1961–62), pp. 252–253; Feuillet, A. "La Création de l'univers "dans le Christ" d'après l'Epître aux Colossiens (I. 16a)," NTS 12 (1965–66), pp. 1–9; Gabathuler, H.–J. *Jesus Christus. Haupt der Kirche—Haupt der Welt*, AThANT 45, Zürich/Stuttgart, 1965; Glas-

---

[40]This expression is not common in Paul, though he is familiar with the intended event (Rom. 3:24–26); H. Leroy, EWNT, p. 440; Souček, in loco; § 4 (a).

son, T. F. "Col. I:15, 18 and Sir. XXIV," *NovT* 11 (1969), pp. 154–156; Hengel, M. *The Son of God*, ET by J. Bowden, Philadelphia, 1976; Hockel, A. *Christus der Erstgeborene. Zur Geschichte der Exegese von Kol. 1:15*, Düsseldorf, 1965; Hofius, A. "Erwägungen zur Gestalt und Herkunft des paulinischen Versöhnungsgedankens," *ZThK* 77 (1980), pp. 186–199; Kasting, H. *Die Anfänge der urchristlichen Mission*, BevTh 55, Munich, 1969; Kehl N. *Der Christushymnus Kol. 1:12–20*, SBM 1, Stuttgart, 1967; Lohse, E. "Imago Dei bei Paulus," in *Libertas Christiana* (FS F. Delekat), BevTh 26, Munich, 1957, pp. 122–135; Lyonnet, S. "L'Hymne christologique de l'Epître aux Colossiens et la fête juive de Nouvel An," *RSR* 48 (1960), pp. 93–100; Merklein, H. "Zur Entstehung der urchristlichen Aussage vom präexistenten Sohn Gottes," in *Zur Geschichte des Urchristentums* (FS R. Schnackenburg), QD 87, Freiburg i. B., 1979, pp. 33–62; Montagnini, F. "Linee di converquenze fra la sapienza veterotestamentaria e l'inno christologico di Col. 1," in *La Cristologia in Sao Paolo*, (Atti della XXIII settimana Biblica), pp. 37–56; Münderlein, G. "Die Erwählung durch Pleroma. Bemerkungen zu Kol. 1:19," *NTS* 8 (1961–62), pp. 264–276; Pöhlmann, W. "Die hymnischen All-Prädikationen in Kol. 1:15–20," *ZNW* 64 (1973), pp. 53–74; Robinson, J. M. "A Formal Analysis of Colossians 1:15–20," *JBL* 76 (1957), pp. 270–287; Sanders, J. T. *The New Testament Christological Hymns*, NTSMS 15, Cambridge, 1971; Schenke, H. M. "Der Widerstreit gnostischer und christlicher Christologie im Spiegel des Kolosserbriefes," *ZThK* 61 (1964), pp. 391–403; Schnackenburg, R. "Die Aufnahme des Christushymnus durch den Verfasser des Kolosserbriefes," in *EKK–Vorarbeiten* I, Zürich–Neukirchen 1969, pp. 33–50; Schneider, G. "Präexistenz Christi," in *Neues Testament und Kirche* (FS R. Schnackenburg), Freiburg, 1974, pp. 399–412; Schneider, G. "Christologische Präexistenzaussagen im Neuen Testament," *Internationale katholische Zeitschrift* 6 (1977), pp. 21–30; Schüssler-Fiorenza, E. "Mythology and the Christological Hymns of the New Testament," in *Aspects of Religious Propaganda in Judaism and Early Christianity*, ed. R. Wilken, Notre Dame, 1975, pp. 17–41; Schweizer, E. "Kolosser 1:15–20," in *EKK–Vorarbeiten* I, Zürich–Neukirchen, 1969, pp. 7–31 (reprinted in E. Schweizer, *Beiträge zur Theologie des Neuen Testaments*, Zürich, 1970, pp. 113–145); Schweizer, E. "Versöhnung des Alls. Kol. 1:20," in *Jesus Christus in Historie und Theologie* (FS H. Conzelmann), Tübingen, 1975, pp. 487–501; Talbert, C. H. "The Myth of a Descending–Ascending Redeemer in Mediterranean Antiquity," *NTS* 22 (1975–76), pp. 418–443; Vawter, F. B. "The Colossian Hymn and the Principle of Redaction," *CBQ* 33 (1971), pp. 62–81; Vischer, W. "Der Hymnus der Weisheit in den Sprüchen Salomons 8:22–31," *EvTh* 22 (1962), pp. 309–326.

§9 Interpreting the Hymn

(a) Structure

The majority of scholars acknowledges the hymnic character of Col. 1:15–20, or of 1:12(13)–20, respectively.[1] Yet the problem is whether it represents an expression of the author[2] or whether he has adopted

---

[1]Some misgivings about the designation of hymn are voiced in O'Neill, "Christology," p. 87 and Schenk, "Christus," p. 144; see § 9 (d).

[2]As in the more recent scholarship, especially Dibelius, p. 10ff.; Moule, pp. 60–62; Caird, p. 174; Hooker, "False teachers," p. 316f.; with modifications, Kehl, *Christus-*

an older liturgical tradition.[3] Most of the more recent scholars presuppose the latter,[4] even if the parameters are not uniform (→ 1:12–
14). Most interpreters assume, however, that the older hymn is to be
found in Col. 1:15–20. Vv. 12–14 also contain older liturgical elements
that divulge something about the *Sitz im Leben* of the following hymn
(cf. [d] below), but the hymn is set in relief as a unit of material in
which Christ is extolled, while the praise refers to God the Father in
1:12–14.[5] A further argument in favor of viewing this as adopted material is the analysis of its functions within the epistle (§6), which
indicates that the text of the hymn supports the argumentation of the
writer only indirectly.[6] In terms of form, the hymn is distinguished
from the context by the frequency of concepts and word combinations
rarely occurring in Paul. They are linguistic elements common in hellenistic thought, especially in rhetoric (image, firstborn [2x], beginning, heaven and earth [2x], visible and invisible, all things, the listing
of the heavenly powers, the prepositions in–through–to: ἐν–διὰ–εἰς
[2x] and the "he" predicates). The hymn is structured symmetrically.
Each stanza begins with a nominal sentence, namely, with "He (Gk.
uses the relative pron.) is,"[7] which is then defined more specifically
by means of "the firstborn" in the second part (1:15a and 18b). This
is followed by a sentence beginning with "for in him," in which εἴτε[8]

---

hymnus, p. 163f. For Kehl, in its original form the hymn was written by Paul and was
expanded later. O'Neill, "Christology," p. 87ff., presupposes that the author of Col.
adapted only individual liturgical expressions in 1:9–23 and that there is no such thing
as an earlier unit.

[3]On the history of investigation, see Aletti, *Colossiens*, p. 20ff.; Gabathuler, *Jesus
Christus*, p. 11ff.; Kehl, *Christushymnus*, p. 29ff. The assumption of Ch. Massons (pp.
97–107) that vv. 18b–20 were added later by the "author of Eph." (cf. the structuring
of the text in Nestle–Aland[26]) has been refuted by P. Ellingsworth; cf. Schweizer,
"Forschung," p. 184f.

[4]E. Norden has become the pioneer of this discovery; he also distinguished between
the two stanzas (*Agnostos Theos*, p. 253). This division is also respected by those scholars
who have chosen a different venue of interpretation than the main stream which we
are describing in more detail, as e.g., in Bammel, "Versuch," or Lähnemann,   *Kolosserbrief*, p. 38.

[5]Aletti, *Colossiens*, p. 15ff.; on Col. 1:15–20 as a literary unit, ibid., p. 139f.

[6]Caird, p. 174f., asserts full agreement of the hymn's expressions with the concern
of Col. as a whole. The analysis of Sanders, "Dependence," p. 35f., whereby Col. 1:15–16
contains sentences and word combinations from 2 Cor. 4:4; Rom. 1:20; 1 Cor. 8:5f.,
and Rom. 11:36, does not have to lead to the conclusion that the author formulated
those two verses in dependence upon Paul. We notice that the agreements refer to the
phrases widely used in hellenistic language, such as the sentence with the accumulation of prepositions in →1:16, for instance.

[7]A christological expression in the form of a sentence with a pronoun as subject and
the subsequent predicate occurs four times here: 1:15, 17, 18 (2x); Francis, "Argument,"
p. 198. The phrase "He has delivered us" in 1:13 is a direct analogy to this; cf. also
Heb. 1:3.

[8]In English roughly translated "whether . . . or."

occurs two to four times and which uses the prepositions "through" and "to."

If we do not include the middle sentences with the "he" predicates, all of which begin with "and" (vv. 17–18a), we observe that the two stanzas have analogous structures with roughly the same scope (Table 6). The middle part would then be an intermediate stanza, an intermezzo.[9]

The key statements of both stanzas have a partial parallel in Rev. 3:14b and 1:5a.

	Verse			
	15	He is . . .		In Greek
		the first-born		
	16	for in him . . .		87 Syllables
		. . . . . .		
A		. . . . . .		
		. . . . . .		
		. . . . . .		
		. . . through him and for him		
	17	And he is . . .	8 Syllables	
O		And . . .	11 Syllables	37 Syllables
	18	And he is . . .	18 Syllables	
		He is		
		the first-born		
	19	for in him		
B	20	. . . through him and for him		97 Syllables
		. . . through him		
		. . . . . .		

TABLE 6

The Table emphasizes the characteristics of the hymn's symmetry, but it also points to certain irregularities. This may mean that the author adapted the hymn to his argument, not only by means of a liturgical introduction (1:12–14), but also via some commentarylike supplements.

As early as 1949 Ernst Käsemann made some observations of lasting significance in this connection. He examined the epexegetical

[9]Maurer, "Begründung," p. 83f.; Schweizer, "Kirche," p. 295, but less clear in his commentary; Gabathuler, Jesus Christus, pp. 125–131; Kehl, Christushymnus, p. 42; Sanders, Hymns, p. 12; Lähnemann, Kolosserbrief, p. 38; Martin, NCBC, p. 64f.; Gnilka, pp. 58f., 66ff.; Zeilinger, Erstgeborene, p. 42f.; he considers v. 20b to be an Abgesang, namely, the latter part of a stanza.

genitive "of the church" in v. 18. Not only is this verse longer than the others in this brief intermediate stanza, but even more so, in its context the notion of the church does not fit the content. The first stanza speaks of Christ as the agent of creation and of his cosmic lordship; v. 18 sums up the first stanza (see under [c]). Likewise salvation, which is the concern of the second stanza, is presented in a cosmic dimension, so that the notion of the church may be an interpretive gloss.[10] If, on the one hand, it stands in contrast to the older hymn, it, on the other hand, conforms conspicuously with the explanations in ch. 2 (2:19 et al.), as well as with the picture drawn within the same theological framework of Christ–church–world in Eph. 1:22f. As Lord of the world, Christ is at the same time the head and savior of the church.

Käsemann also characterized the phrase "by the blood of his cross" in v. 20 as an insertion.[11] Already the subsequent "through him," which has the effect of an awkward addition, points to the unevenness. For this reason, some MSS omit it (B, D* et al.) As far as the overall text-critical evaluation is concerned, it is part of the text. The sentence becomes smoother if we omit "by the blood of his cross." The message of the cross was significant for Paul (1 Cor. 1:17f. et al.); and he, as well as his disciples, knew the Lord's Supper tradition from which the phrase "in the blood" (Rom. 5:9; Eph. 2:13 et al.) is derived (cf. 1 Cor. 10:16; 11:25 par., 27). Grammatically only the participle "making peace" is awkward; in Greek it is masculine, whereas the subject of the sentence is neuter—τὸ πλήρωμα, the fulness. Various attempts have been made to solve the rather obvious problem of the structure of the hymn.

(1) To begin with, εὐδοκεῖν (delight in, determine) can be understood and translated transitively: "For in him it pleased God to have all the fulness dwell."[12] This conveys a correct material correlation; nevertheless it contradicts the immediate context. The author alludes to this verse in Col. 2:9 and understands "to dwell" as an intransitive verb, and the writer interprets the fulness to be the fulness of God, the fulness "of deity." Hence "fulness" is the subject. Incidentally, the last occurrence of God as the grammatical subject is in v. 13.[13]

---

[10]Käsemann, "Baptismal Liturgy," p. 150f. Already Lohmeyer clearly speaks of an addition, p. 61, note 2. The reconstruction attempts are noted with fundamental reluctance by Aletti (Colossiens, p. 24ff.), though his linguistic analysis underscores precisely this feature (ibid., p. 184).

[11]Käsemann, "Baptismal Liturgy," p. 152; Lohse, p. 82; Deichgräber, Gotteshymnus, p. 149f.; Vawter, "Hymn," p. 70; Lindemann, p. 25; similarly Hegermann, Schöpfungsmittler, p. 92f., who also omits the last line.

[12]So e.g., the following translations: Luth., Cral., Zür., Jer., NEB, TOB; among the interpreters e.g., Haupt, Lohmeyer, Ernst.

[13]For a summary of the arguments, see Münderlein, "Erwählung," p. 266.

(2) The remaining proposed solutions consist of deletions. Apart from the two glosses, some scholars also delete the second "through him" (v. 20b),[14] which has already been addressed and which could not have come about until a later transcription. In this case, the subject of "making peace" could be Christ, who is being discussed. Regardless of the textcritical difficulties related to a solution like this, it would be an incongruent change of the subject, which is not customary in a hymn.

(3) For the above reason, some interpreters also omit "making peace." The passage would then read as follows: "and through him and to himself to reconcile all things, whether on earth or in heaven."[15] Thus a meaningful and grammatically smooth sentence emerges. In an attempt to achieve symmetry between both stanzas, that is, to eliminate the intermediate stanza, several scholars have suggested further deletions.[16] It is an understandable endeavor that has yielded useful secondary results (discovery of new symmetrical features, more specific determination of the intermediate stanza). The disadvantage, however, is the hypothetical nature of the results. If one deletes entirely the second to the last line in which the seams of an addition are found, one has to presuppose at least two revisions of the original hymn, for which we have no evidence. Thus we end up in hypotheses that are inevitable in scholarship, but whose divergence attests to their provisional character.

Relatively many scholars omit the listing of the heavenly powers in v. 16 ("thrones . . . authorities") and the final clause in v. 18 ("that in everything he might be pre-eminent"). In terms of formal considerations, the more recent attempt by Christoph Burger attains virtual perfection. His reconstruction,[17] according to my translation, is as follows:

> He is the image,
> the first-born of all creation,
> for in him everything was created,
> visible and invisible.
> He is the beginning,

[14]Schweizer, Gnilka, in part also Schille, Hymnen, p. 81, and Schiwy, who retains the phrase "by the blood of his cross."

[15]So Harder, Paulus, p. 46ff., as the pioneer in researching this hymn (with further strictures); Schweizer, "Kirche," 294ff.; Schweizer, "Col. 1:15–20," p. 10 (in the commentary he retains "making peace"); Sanders, Hymns, p. 12; Martin, Reconciliation, p. 114; including other strictures, Gabathuler, Jesus Christus, p. 131; Kehl, Christushymnus, p. 37; retaining the second "through him": Conzelmann; Wilckens, p. 716, note 2.

[16]Next to those cited in notes 11 and 15, also Ernst, p. 175f.; Robinson, "Formal Analysis," p. 286, who also presupposes transpositions, et al.

[17]Burger, Schöpfung, p. 38. Schenk, "Christus," p. 147ff., also starts with his reconstruction.

the first-born from the dead,
for in him the fulness *has come to dwell*,
things on earth and in heaven.

Burger dared to forego the symmetry of the verses using εἴτε (lit. "if
. . . " or "whether . . . or") in the first and second stanza and thereby
achieved a composite and rhythmic structure. The content of the second stanza becomes a problem, however. As soon as the saying concerning the reconciliation of all things is omitted, the meaning of the
second stanza becomes very obscure. The praise of Jesus as the beginning of the eschatological resurrection assumes the conception of
his exaltation above all creation. If this expression in a hymn is combined with conceptions of preexistence of a later development, a certain tension may surface.[18] From the beginning Christ was "equal with
God"; later he is exalted in order to receive the divine majesty. The
second expression has its sole meaning in the restoration of a disturbed
relationship, here understood as the reinstatement of Christ's key position in the cosmos (the notion of the cosmic peace; →1:20). The
severance is emphasized in the hymns: Phil. 2:8 (death on the cross);
Heb. 1:3 (purification for sins);[19] Eph. 2:14–18 (. . . he has reconciled both).[20] This is also indicated in Col. 1:20. As soon as one omits
both "making peace" and "to reconcile," that which points to the
deep disorder disappears, both stanzas express the same thing, and
the saying concerning the dead becomes a foreign particle. I do not
mean hereby to reject the attempts at reconstructing the original form
of the hymn. The only conclusion from what has been said is that,
at this juncture, we need to maintain that the hymn, including the
minor deletions, is the older copy of Col. 1:15–20, as affirmed by most
scholars. This refers to the two deletions suggested by E. Käsemann,[21]
and probably also the phrase "that in everything he might be pre-
eminent" in v. 18b, which disrupts the symmetry of the expression
in comparison to the first stanza.

The problem of the masculine participle "making peace" in v. 20
is best solved via a *constructio ad sensum*, in which the logical subject would be the (divine) fulness (v. 19; i.e., God[22]).[23] In contrast to
a change of subject, this is quite feasible in hymnic speech.

---

[18]Hegermann, *Schöpfungsmittler*, pp. 106, 123f.
[19]Cf. Wengst, *Formeln*, p. 166ff.
[20]Wengst, *Formeln*, p. 181ff.; Burger, *Schöpfung*, p. 177ff. Burger argues that the author of Col. augmented the hymn of Col. 1:15–20 with several elements from Eph. 2:14–18
(p. 139, cf. p. 24).
[21]See note 11.
[22]Schweizer, "Kolosser 1:15–20," p. 21.
[23]E.g., RSV, Ewald, Abbott, Souček, p. 26; Masson, Käsemann, "Baptismal Liturgy,"
p. 158f., Lohse, p. 98; Merklein (*Amt*, p. 34); Martin, NCBC, p. 60f.

(b) History of religions background
The hymn extols Christ in the third person and does not mention him directly. If we remove the glosses (church, blood of the cross), it is easily assumed that this originally was a pre–Christian hymn.[24] If we took only the first stanza to be the original hymn, this would certainly be possible.[25] However, the observations concerning the revision of the second stanza by the author of Colossians, which we submitted under (a), militate against this. And in the second stanza we hear of the "firstborn from the dead" (v. 18b)—an expression difficult to conceive of outside of Christianity.[26] The new, true life is the theme of the gospel as Easter message (1 Thess. 1:10; 1 Cor. 15:3b–5 = the content of *pistis*; Rom. 1:3–4 et al.) and later of the gospel's soteriological and paraenetic developments (1 Cor. 15:12ff., the interpretation of the content of *pistis*; Rom. 6:11 = the interpretation of the *pistis* content in the postbaptismal teaching; Luke 15:24, 32 = an interpretation of the *pistis* content via Jesus' parable in conjunction with a dispute about the Lord's Supper). The phrase "the firstborn from the dead" also occurs as a predicate for Jesus in Rev. 1:5, obviously in conjunction with baptism (cf. Col. 1:12–14). It may still have originated in the post–Easter, apocalyptic, imminent expectation that conceived of the new presence of Jesus as the beginning of the eschatological, collective resurrection to judgment or to new life respectively (among others, cf. Dan. 12:2f., 1 *Enoch* 51:1f.; 4 Ezra 7:29ff.; *TBenj.* 10). But whenever this concept is retained in a Christian context, it describes or implicates Christ as the one who makes possible hope in death (Rev. 1:5f.; Heb. 12:23[27] = the assembly of the firstborn[28]). But the oldest extant explanation of the relationship between the resurrection of Jesus and humanity's hope in death, comes from the apostle Paul (1 Thess. 4:13–18). That was after the year 50 CE, and even some time later it was not clear to all the Christians in Corinth (cf. 1 Cor. 15). Likewise Rom. 8 explains how the relationship with Jesus Christ as the firstborn son of God (8:29), which is obtained through the Spirit and by faith (8:15ff.), also makes possible hope in death (8:38). In the hymn, however, this is already assumed. Already the combination with the agency of creation and with the image of reconciliation affirms that the second stanza is to be understood so-

---

[24]So Käsemann, "Baptismal Liturgy," p. 150ff.
[25]On the hypothesis of the later formulation of the second stanza, see note 3 above.
[26]So Hegermann, *Schöpfungsmittler*, pp. 102, 109; Gabathuler, *Jesus Christus*, p. 52; Lohse, "Christologie und Ethik," p. 102; Lohse, pp. 83, 97; Lähnemann, *Kolosserbrief*, p. 39; Burger, *Schöpfung*, pp. 7, 41f., 52.
[27]The probable meaning is that this refers to Christians who have already died; see O. Michel, *Der Brief an die Hebräer*, KEK 13, Göttingen, 1966[12], in loco.
[28]Cf. the picture of Israel as the first-born son in Exod. 4:22f.; Sir. 36:17.

teriologically and not as thoroughgoing apocalyptic. Only during the phase of reflecting upon their faith did Christians draw these conclusions from the message of the resurrection; as far as the agency in creation is concerned, the earliest evidence is found in 1 Cor. 8:6 (cf. John 1:1ff.). There Paul applies the tripartite formula, which he cites in Rom. 11:36, for instance, in an abridged form to Christ as the agent of creation and as savior. The already common phrase, "through the Lord Jesus Christ" (1 Thess. 5:9 et al.), supported this theological and linguistic development.[29] The hymn of Col. 1:15–20 presupposes such expressions, similar to the notions of preexistence that are alluded to in the mission formula (Gal. 4:4 et al.) and that take on thematic character, e.g., in Phil. 2:6–11.[30] Therefore the hymn originated later than the major letters of the apostle Paul, probably in the realm of Greek-speaking Jewish Christianity. Both the author of Colossians and the recipients were familiar with it. This also has ramifications relative to the dating of Colossians (§3). In any case, we may deem the hymn to be a Christian liturgical tradition,[31] the glossing and commenting of which, in the framework of Colossians, does not serve a Christianizing purpose, but merely denotes a shift in emphasis.

In this connection we have to deal with still another interpretation of the hymn which presupposes that it has been influenced by Gnosticism.[32] In this case we are dealing with a Gnosticism that is already Christianized;[33] but the idea of uniting the fulness, the pleroma, with a human being (the verb κατοικεῖν) is derived from Gnosticism in this interpretation. Hence the influence of the Gnostics would be combatted in Colossians by means of a radical gnostic interpretation of the Pauline theological heritage, namely, in the sense of a realized eschatology.[34]

It is not impossible that the indwelling of the divine within humanity was already then a common conception for some Gnostics.[35]

---

[29]Schneider, "Präexistenz," pp. 403–405; on the soteriological interpretation of the formula in 1 Cor. 8:6, see W. Thüsing, *Per Christum in Deum*, Münster, 1965, p. 225ff.

[30]Schneider, "Präexistenz," p. 409f.; Schneider, "Präexistenzaussagen," p. 28f.

[31]The scholars who express misgivings concerning the existence of literary forms in early Christianity, as E. A. Judge, "Die frühen Christen als scholastische Gemeinschaft," in Meeks, *Sociology*, pp. 131–164, have underestimated some facts which I cite in § 9 (d).

[32]Schenke, "Widerstreit," passim; idem, "Erlöser," p. 221f.; Schenke–Fischer, *Einleitung*, p. 162.

[33]Schenke, "Erlöser," p. 222.

[34]Idem, "Widerstreit," p. 403.

[35]Documented for instance in the account on Cerinthus, in Iren., *Adv. haer.* I, 26, 1; in *Gos. Truth*, NHC I/3; 31:4f. et al., or in the account on the Ophites and Sethians, in Iren., *Adv. haer.* I, 30, 12–14.

For the beginnings of Gnosticism outside of Christianity,[36] which have a similar time frame to Colossians, however, it was not characteristic.[37] When it surfaces in the Jewish tradition, it is not associated with the docetic tendency, as was the case in Gnosticism. This is especially true in the case of Jewish wisdom speculation, where wisdom dwells (cf. →1:19; Ezek. 37:27) in the people of God (Sir. 24:8) or in the prophets (Wisd. 7:27).[38] Christian theology, including Colossians and Ephesians, joined in these ideas (Rom. 8:11; Col. 3:16; Eph. 3:17; Did. 10:2 et al.). The emphasis rests upon the presence of the one dwelling in his realm; hence this represents a distinction of the "dwelling place" and not a docetic endeavor to relativize,[39] as it did for the Gnostics, for instance, who later interpreted such expressions in their favor.

The pleroma in Col. 1:19 is indeed already hypostatic, but it does not yet describe the fulness of the aeons, as the later gnostic pleroma did, or the universe (which is yet to be reconciled), as in the Stoic sense.[40] Instead, it describes the fulness of God (2:9), his will, or his acts; it surpasses all superhuman beings mentioned in 1:16f., and gives them their meaning (→1:19). The pleroma is the authority and power of God, working through its bearer in whom it is focused.[41] If all the fulness dwells in Christ, he mediates God himself, while the Christian, "in whose heart dwells the word of Christ" (Col. 3:16), in turn represents God in his or her environment (cf. 1:27f.). This is the venue of the "filling" from God through Christ to the world. In this manner, the author of Colossians also emphasizes the role of the church (→1:18a; 2:9f., cf. Eph. 1:23; 4:33). Thus the pleroma here is neither the filling (content[42]) nor that which is being filled or completed but, as we have already mentioned, the fulness of the will and work of God,[43] the

---

[36]On the pre- or nonchristian origin of Gnosticism, see e.g., H. J. W. Drijvers, "Die Ursprünge des Gnostizismus als religionsgeschichtliches Problem," most recently in K. Rudolph, ed., Gnosis und Gnostizismus, WF 262, Darmstadt, 1975, pp. 798–841. See also E. M. Yamauchi, Pre-Christian Gnosticism, Grand Rapids, 1983[2].

[37]E.g., for the ancient gnostic systems of the Naassene sermon, Hippol., Phil. V, 7, 3–9, 9, or of Poimandres, Corp. Herm. I, 1–32.

[38]According to Wisd. 7:28, God loves only the one who "dwells with wisdom."

[39]Only in Shep. Herm., Man. 10, 2, 5 is there a warning that the Holy Spirit is also able to depart from the believer. This is not a christological statement, however.

[40]Documentation in Wohlenberg, p. 64; Ernst, Pleroma, p. 9ff.

[41]God is also able to fill someone with wisdom: Exod. 35:35; cf. the prayer of Jacob, in K. Preisendanz, ed., Papyri graecae magicae II, Leipzig–Berlin, 1931, p. 149.

[42]So Moule, p. 59.

[43]According to Philo, Mut. 27f., the creator was "filled with himself" since before the creation of the world. "To be filled" is a picture of his creative contentiveness. While this is not the pleroma in its cosmic significance, it is perfection in its cosmic effect.

perfection[44] that radiates outwardly (Eph. 1:23; 4:10).[45] By faith humanity is able to experience this power.[46]

If the second stanza is to be given a gnostic interpretation, it has to be isolated from the first stanza, which views the relationship of the redeemer to the creator quite positively. This is not the case in the gnostic texts that address the indwelling of the divine in Jesus (cf. Gos. Truth, NHC I/3; 17:14–20, where the visible world is described as a distortion). Otherwise it would be necessary to assume that the hymn was the product of a gnostic group which relativized the contradiction between the visible and the invisible world and emphasized its connection through various emanations.[47] In this regard, the first stanza of the Sethian tractate on the Trimorphic Protennoia from Nag Hammadi (NHC XIII/1; 35:1–50, 24) could serve as a startling parallel. Accordingly the Protennoia is the first-begotten (35:4f.) through whom the universe was shaped (38:12) and who mediates (to aeons and humans) the image of God (47:11ff.).[48] Still, this parallel does not yet substantiate the gnostic character of the hymn. It is a non-Christian example indeed, whose basic conceptions quite possibly already existed towards the end of the first Christian century; however, the parallel references to our hymn are not themselves typically gnostic. More likely they were drawn from Jewish wisdom speculation and from the logos teaching. That which is typically gnostic (salvation through remembrance of the spiritual aeon rather than through reconciliation, salvation's focus upon that which is heavenly), as proclaimed in Trimorphic Protennoia, is of little help in the interpretation of Col. 1:15–20. The conception of the firstborn from the dead is foreign to that tractate. Hence the author of Colossians was acquainted with the basic gnostic conceptions, or with related ideas, but he did not acknowledge them (§12). In some instances the hymn he cites could be understood gnostically, and the Colossian heretics could have interpreted it in their favor, but it is not determined by Gnosticism. Its ci-

---

[44]Cf. the perfection in Odes Sol. 17:7.

[45]Hegermann, Schöpfungsmittler, pp. 96, 106f.; Kehl, Christushymnus, p. 123; Ernst, Pleroma, p. 119f.; cf. the Hermetic tractate Ogd. Enn., NHC VI/6; 60:12 (the heart which is filled with immortal life) with Col. 1:9 (the Christians who are filled with the knowledge of God). This is not far removed from the conception that Christ exists or dwells (Eph. 3:17, 19) in or among (ἐν – 2 Cor. 13:5) Christians.

[46]The speculations about the gnostic's "filling" in Ep. Jac., NHC I/2; 2:28–4:22 date from the 2nd/3rd cent. and show Christian influence. Likewise the pleroma concept in Auth. Log., NHC VI/3 is dependent upon the NT; cf. 25:33f. with 1 Cor. 15:24 (ἀρχή, ἐξουσία, δύναμις) and with Col. 1:16; see Parrott, Nag Hammadi, p. 268.

[47]Schenke, "Erlöser," p. 222. Marcion omits Col. 1:15b–16: A. v. Harnack, Marcion – das Evangelium vom fremden Gott, TU 45, Leipzig, 1924², p. 51.

[48]C. Colpe has collected the parallels of this writing to John 1:1–18: "Heidnische, jüdische und christliche Überlieferung in den Schriften aus Nag Hammadi III," Jb. f. Antike und Christentum 17 (1974), pp. 109–125.

tation is no *captatio benevolentiae* of the "philosophers" (2:8) or of the recipients who were influenced by their philosophy. The author in fact brings this text on stage as his aid and witness (§6 [b]) to support him in the polemic against the heresy.[49] Gnosticism is part of the hymn's environment and of its history of influence.[50] The scholars who reconstruct the original hymn similar to Ch. Burger (see [a] above), frequently take it to be an expression of emanationistic thought.[51] This is correct in the sense that the image (εἰκών) here is not merely a reflection of God as in Gen. 1:26f. (→1:15) but is, at the same time, the origin of creation, a seal in the active sense, the divine agent in the shaping of the chaos (Philo, *Leg. All.* III, 96).[52] At the same time, however, it remains the reflection of the invisible God (Philo, *Conf. Ling.* 62f.)[53] which is identical to the Logos and the "beginning" (ἀρχή), according to Philo (*Conf. Ling.* 146f.; *Somn.* I, 239).[54] In the hymn we encounter the cosmological speculation in a form having affinities with Philonic teaching and aspiring to interpret the OT at the same time. Furthermore, even before the writing of Colossians, Christian cosmological speculation was used in the Christian proclamation of the resurrection and in the declarations of faith concerning the exaltation and preexistence of Jesus.

This brings us to the positive response to the question of the history-of-religions classification of the hymn. Since the hymn is also related to some of the Hermetic writings[55] as far as terminology and conceptions are concerned, it must have shared some intellectual background with Hermeticism and with early Gnosticism. All three realms were familiar with Jewish wisdom speculation, which we have discussed above. In the latter we encounter the notion of the preexistence

[49]Schweizer, "Kolosser 1:15–20," p. 9. Aletti, *Colossiens*, p. 185, resists a "gnostic" interpretation of the hymn. Yet he does not investigate more closely the possibility that the opponents might have been close to gnosticism.

[50]This also applies to the parallels from the gnostic *Gos. Eg.*, NHC III/2 and IV/2 where the judgment of the heavenly powers ushers in the reconciliation of the world and opens up the possibility of incorporation into the spiritual body. This is said to be the mystery: III/2; 63:4–64:3. This is followed immediately with an allusion to Col. 2:14f.; cf. Böhlig–Wisse, *Nag Hammadi*, p. 192. A direct quotation of Col. 2:9 is found among the Perates, see Hippol., *Phil.* V, 12, 5. On the remaining gnostic parallels, see Jervell, *Imago*, p. 136ff.

[51]In a heightened form in Schenk, "Christus," pp. 143, 149.

[52]See Hegermann, *Schöpfungsmittler*, p. 97; Burger, *Schöpfung*, p. 31.

[53]The more specific designation of "the invisible God," therefore, does not have to be viewed as an addition by the author (so Schenk, "Christus," p. 149), see Hegermann, *Schöpfungsmittler*, p. 98.

[54]See Hegermann, *Schöpfungsmittler*, p. 97; Früchtel, "Vorstellungen," p. 14ff. On the Philonic references which are important for the interpretation of the hymn, see the overview in Sanders, *Hymns*, p. 84f. On wisdom as the reflection of God in Philo, see e.g., also *Leg. All.* I, 43 and cf. with Wisd. 7:17–26.

[55]On the parallels between Col. 1:15–20 and *Corp. Herm.* XI, see the overview in Sanders, *Hymns*, p. 84f.; cf. Lähnemann, *Kolosserbrief*, p. 39.

of wisdom (Prov. 8:22ff.; Sir. 1:1ff.),[56] which knows the beginning and goal of the cosmos, which is the image of the goodness of God (Wisd. 7:15–30),[57] and which indwells the prophets (Wisd. 7:27) or all of the people of God (Sir. 24:3–8).[58] The tradition of the proverbial sayings of Jesus is evidence for this conception in the service of Christology (Matt. 11:25–27 par., according to which Jesus mediates to human-kind the knowledge of God; Matt. 11:19 par., where Jesus and the wis-dom of God are identical; Matt. 12:42 par., where he is superior to the wisdom of Solomon). This represents an early christological tra-dition that influenced the Synoptic tradition, Paulinism, and the Jo-hannine circle.[59] The conceptions of wisdom speculations have been used in Col. 1:15–20 to develop the statement concerning the exalta-tion of Jesus (cf. Rom. 1:3f.; Mark 12:36f.).[60] At the same time an al-lusion is made to the LXX text of Gen. 1, where the concepts "beginning" and "image" (vv. 1, 26) occur. Philo of Alexandria, too, makes the connection with Gen. 1 when he speaks of the logos which, for him, is sometimes identical to wisdom (*Leg. All.* I, 65).[61]

The background to the hymn, then, may be sought in the intellec-tual continuum leading from earlier Jewish wisdom speculation, via the Alexandrian school culminating in Philo,[62] to the Odes of Solo-mon[63] and to some of the Hermetic tractates. In Alexandria this in-tellectual current also benefitted from Platonic elements[64] that played a significant part in Gnosticism. For the Gnostic, separation from the visible world becomes the condition for salvation. The correlations in the history of ideas are presented in Table 7, albeit in a very ten-tative fashion. We notice that there are several christological hymns

[56]Burney, "Christ"; Aletti, *Colossiens*, p. 141ff.; Montagnini, "Linee," pp. 51–56.

[57]On the wisdom-oriented background of the hymn, see Schweizer, "Kirche," p. 295ff.; Moule, p. 58ff. Most scholars point out the connection between the hymn and speculative wisdom.

[58]Glasson, "Colossiens"; Mack, *Logos*, p. 21ff. Aletti limits himself to wisdom speculation as the history-of-religions background of the hymn. But many of the lin-guistic codes which, according to him, connect these domains (the one mediator: the whole creation, pre-existence: the dependence, the hiddenness: the revelation and others; *Colossiens*, pp. 180–182) also occur in the Philonic Logos teaching.

[59]H. Köster–J. M. Robinson, *Trajectories Through Early Christianity*, Philadelphia, 1971, p. 207ff.; cf. Schüssler-Fiorenza, "Wisdom," p. 17ff.

[60]P. Hoffmann, "Jesusverkündigung in der Logienquelle," in *Jesus in den Evange-lien*, SBS 45, Stuttgart, 1970, pp. 50–70, esp. p. 59.

[61]On the relationship of logos/sophia in Philo, see Früchtel, "Vorstellungen," p. 177f.; Mack, *Logos*, pp. 96f., 133ff.

[62]For N. Kehl the hymn is derived directly from Jewish wisdom speculation, *Chris-tushymnus*, p. 64.

[63]In the Odes of Solomon the creator is called "Lord" and is worshipped: e.g., 4:15; 16:8–20; cf. Charlesworth, "Odes," pp. 366–368 and 360f.

[64]On the hypostatic beginning (ἀρχή) cf. Plato, *Phaedr.* 245, and on the picture's function, *Tim.* 92.

in the NT emphasizing the preexistence of Christ[65] (Phil. 2:6–11; Heb. 1:3f.; John 1:1ff.) or at least presupposing it (1 Tim. 3:16).[66] In Phil. 2:10, Heb. 1:4f., and 1 Tim. 3:16 the dignity of the redeemer is expressed by means of a comparison with angels.[67] Besides highlighting the terrestrial creation, Col. 1:16f., 20 also focus on the heavenly powers.[68] This is a development of the conception of the exaltation,[69] which is closely connected with the kerygma of the resurrection. This background also explains why in the second stanza the redeemer is able to bring about cosmic reconciliation.[70] Since the statement about reconciliation is connected with that concerning Christ as the first-born from the dead (see [c] below), it is evident that the given conceptions in the second stanza are furnished with a new correlation. The history-of-religions background, therefore, is restructured into a new statement in the hymn. The parallels that are placed above the line of dashes in the table, are not immediate ancestors of Col. 1:15–20, and we cannot assume an early redeemer myth behind them, especially because they lack a unified language.[71]

(c) Theological intentions

The hymn extols the key position of Jesus (a) as the agent of creation and (b) as the agent of reconciliation and the giver of new life. These are grand statements that do not use titles of majesty sparingly. This is astounding, considering that all of this refers to an impoverished Jew who ministered about thirty to fifty years earlier as a prophet and teacher in a Roman province and who was executed as one of the less significant mischief-makers.[72]

Compared to other, related hymns (Table 7), it appears that this hymn bypasses the incarnation almost entirely.[73] In regard to the latter, only the hymn of Heb. 1:3f. can be adduced as a parallel. In it the incarnation is only indirectly alluded to through the saying concerning

---

[65]The prominence of pre-existence is what distinguishes the Philonic logos concept and the redeemer of Col. 1:15–20 from the Stoics' conception of the logos (Craddox, "All Things"). For this reason we shall use the Stoic hymns only in the interpretation of individual motifs, but not as a parallel from the history of religions.

[66]On their commonalities, see Vischer, "Hymnus," p. 318; Schnackenburg, "Aufnahme," p. 33ff.

[67]Summary in Hengel, Son of God, p. 86ff.

[68]Details in Bammel, "Versuch," p. 90.

[69]Summary in Merklein, "Entstehung," p. 41ff.

[70]In Philo this is only a marginal idea and outside the logos speculation (Spec. Leg. II, 192; III, 131); contra Lyonnet, "Hymne."

[71]Contra Talbert, "Myth." He has merely collected individual motifs and conceptions. We are more inclined to agree with Schüssler-Fiorenza, "Wisdom," p. 38, for whom the early Christian statements of exaltation and pre-existence use the "language and elements of various myths and mythologies."

[72]This is roughly the formulation of Moule, p. 58f.

[73]On the incarnation in the other hymns, see Vischer, "Hymnus," p. 319.

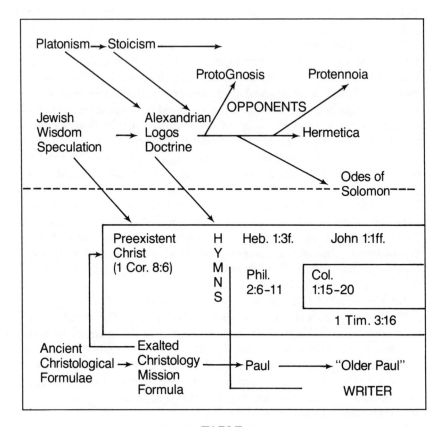

TABLE 7

the exaltation of Jesus at the right hand of God, which took place after
he had purified people from their sin.[74] Exaltation presupposes de-
basement. In Col. 1:15–20 it is even less clear (see [a] above) that the
agent of creation and the firstborn from the dead are identical to the
incarnate one—the earthly Jesus who died for sinners. The gospel as
oral proclamation of the resurrection of Jesus has indeed focused from
the outset on the majesty of Jesus and was soon also interpreted as
his exaltation; in this hymn, however, the severance caused by human sin appears to be ignored. This contradiction can only be avoided
if we relate the first stanza to the eschatological new creation; [75] this
contradicts, however, the common Jewish and Christian catechetical
structure of creationsalvation also contained in this hymn. First Jesus
is described as the agent of creation, then the focus turns to the new

---

[74]Cf. Michel, Der Brief an die Hebräer, p. 96f.
[75]Zeilinger, Erstgeborene, e.g., p. 188.

life in death and to the reconciliation.[76] We also encounter a trace of this tradition in Rev. 1:5 and 3:14. Its wording is closer to our hymn than Heb. 1:3f., but it is preserved only in fragmentary form. In Rev. 1:5, similar to Acts 26:23, Jesus is called "the firstborn of the dead and the ruler of kings on earth." In expressions like these the resurrection is presupposed as an exaltation (cf. [b] above).[77] The gospel of Easter is further developed in the hymn, namely, as influenced by the Jewish concept of wisdom. Such conceptions have been applied to Jesus even prior to Paul.[78] In the hymn the reconciliation of all things appears to be an objective change in the supernatural spheres of power, a result of the exaltation of Jesus.[79] Hence the superiority of Jesus is emphasized in order to show that the supernatural powers do not determine the fate of human life (→1:20). The redeemed are able to recognize Jesus Christ as the agent of creation, that is, as the one who reveals the meaning of creation as a whole, and who thus is able to overcome the separation between the creator and the sinful creation. The incarnation is merely implied in vv. 18b and 20 of the hymn, and the sinful disruption of the pristine harmony can only be inferred from the expression concerning reconciliation. Perhaps the reverse order of "on earth or in heaven" (1:20, in contrast to 1:16 where the issue is creation) is intended to indicate that the cosmic reconciliation is anchored in the reconciliation that occurred in the human arena in the life of Jesus.[80] These, however, are indirect pointers at best.

Only by means of the authorial additions (see [a] above) have the cross of Jesus (1:20) and the role of the church with its witness been emphasized. The originally cosmic body (the organism of the world) is understood in v. 18 as the body of the church. The church is the body of the head, to whom the entire universe is subject (→1:18); in other words: The church is the realm in which Jesus is fully acknowledged and confessed as the agent of creation and the reconciler whose authority extends to all of creation (→1:20). Thereby the Christian is freed and commissioned to cooperate in the shaping of the new life "in Christ." This also becomes the new background for the household code in Col. 3:18–4:1 and for the view found in Ephesians, according to which the Christian life is a battle with the rebelling heavenly powers (Eph. 6).[81] Ephesians 1:22f. (cf. 4:13, 15) offers a substantiation for the older expressions in terms Jesus' twofold authority.

[76]Hegermann, Schöpfungsmittler, p. 106.
[77]Conzelmann, p. 137f.; Hegermann, Schöpfungsmittler, p. 123.
[78]See (b) above; Merklein, "Entstehung," pp. 42f., 48ff.
[79]Burger, Schöpfung, p. 52f.
[80]Differently in Kasting, Anfänge, p. 139.
[81]The more recent understanding of the political responsibility of Christians also received its impetus here: Schillebeeckx, Christus, pp. 180f.; 193ff.; 205ff.

Among other things, the reconciliation of all things is demonstrated by life in fellowship within the community (Col. 1:21f. and esp. Eph. 2:14–21). It has been questioned whether this view is indeed found in Colossians, since the body can be understood in a cosmic sense, according to Col. 2:17 and 19.[82] However, since the conception of the church as a supra-individual body is already found in Paul (§14), since the body is referring to the church in Col. 1:18, 24, and 3:15, since this view is developed in Ephesians, and since both references mentioned above can also refer to the church (→2:19), most interpreters assume that the author of Colossians applied the soma concept consistently to the church.[83] It is true that in Colossians this notion serves the direct polemic against heresy, while in Ephesians the unity of the church, comprised of Jews and Gentiles, is predicated upon it. Nevertheless, both instances emphasize that, in the church, the human race is able to participate in the authority of Christ through baptism and faith. This is closely associated with the argument of Colossians (2:12f.). The ecclesiological view of the soma concept in Colossians is supported by the allusions to baptism that we have detected in 1:12–14.[84]

(d) Sitz im Leben

What kind of Sitz im Leben could the original hymn have had in the Christian community of Asia Minor? What does it mean that this is a hymn? Recently some concerns have been voiced regarding the literary genre of the hymn.[85] This is indeed a very comprehensive genre whose classical examples outside of the NT can be found in Greek religions and later in developed Christian hymn-writing (e.g.,

[82]So Dibelius, p. 36; Burger, Schöpfung, p. 76f.

[83]So Souček, p. 31; Schweizer, p. 91; Schweizer, "Kolosser 1:15–20," pp. 25–31; Conzelmann, p. 138; Gabathuler, Jesus Christus, p. 147; Ernst, p. 170; Gnilka, p. 152; Löwe, "Bekenntnis," p. 310f.

[84]Schenk, "Christus," p. 149f., was correct in pointing out that motifs from the tradition of the baptism of Jesus also come to light in the hymn (cf. →1:19). From this he concluded that the author of Col. understood the baptism of Jesus as his earthly resurrection, since the saying of the cross (v. 20) only occurs after the saying about the resurrection (v. 18b), "Christus," p. 150. This, for Schenk, is the mystery addressed in 2:2 ("Christus," p. 151). For him the Gospel of Mark has a similar conception of mystery (see Mark 4:11 in connection with 1:11). But this cannot be substantiated. For Mark the gospel is focused on the message of Easter (Mark 16:6f., cf. Pokorný, "Der Anfang des Evangeliums," in Die Kirche des Anfangs, FS H. Schürmann, Leipzig, 1978, pp. 115–132); the sequence death–resurrection in Col. 2:12, 13 affirms that this has to do with the resurrection after death, which is addressed in Col. 1:20, 22. The conception that Jesus' baptism was his infilling with the Spirit which is influenced by the Christian experience of the Spirit, in no wise denotes a shift of the resurrection into the life of Jesus (cf. also § 13). On the understanding of the mystery in Col. and Eph., see the works of Penna and Caragounis (→1:26).

[85]Schenk, "Christus," pp. 144–146 (and further sources there). For him the hymn is an "undefined remaining category," (p. 144).

Ambrose). And yet, even if we use this designation for thanksgivings having symmetrical features and formulated in elevated language, this is justified to the extent that such thanksgivings, however diverse they were, fulfilled a similar function in the Christian congregations: Gratitude to God and mutual edification. This is true of most of the hymns of the NT listed in Table 7. Following Col. 1:12, Col. 1:15–20 is the example of a eucharistic hymn (cf. Table 5), serving the purpose of exhortation and instruction (3:16; Eph. 5:19f., cf. Heb. 13:15). Thus the hymn is placed between prayer and proclamation.[86] Since hymns and odes like this are sung "in the spirit," it is possible to detect in them predecessors of the eucharist of the Christian prophets; this is discussed in conjunction with the Lord's Supper in *Did.* 10:7.[87] The function of hymns in public worship as developments of the homologia is clearly expressed in Phil. 2:10f. Since the hymns noted in Table 7 are also related contentwise, it is conceivable that they also "functioned" similarly in the church.[88] The inclusion of the hymnic elements in the heavenly liturgy of the Apocalypse of John also discloses something about the role of hymns in public worship.[89] Thus Col. 1:15–20 represents a hymn[90] or an ode.[91] Related in terms of content are, among others, the Odes of Solomon with their mystical — not gnostic — piety.[92] The singing of hymns in Col. 3:16 is a sign that the word (λόγος) of Christ has come to dwell in the believers (ἐνοικεῖν, 3:16a, cf. κατοικεῖν in 1:19 and in [b] above). There is little likelihood, therefore, that the hymn was bound up with the baptismal rite, though it presupposes baptism and is introduced by the reference to the baptism of the recipients (→1:13). Rather, this only means that the author of Colossians quite obviously understood baptism as the common sign of all Christians, so that his argument in →2:12f. also alludes to baptism.

If the hymn is described as thanksgiving (→1:12), it does not denote a direct formula of faith[93] which would have had its *Sitz im Leben* in the catechism. The hymns have a different form and a dif-

[86]Deichgräber, *Gotteshymnus*, p. 23.
[87]Cf. Bornkamm, "Bekenntnis," (see above, note 2 on 1:12–14), p. 196f.
[88]Cf. Sanders, *Hymns*, pp. 1–5.
[89]Summary in K. P. Jörns, *Das hymnische Evangelium*, StNT 5, Gütersloh, 1971, pp. 161f., 180ff.; cf. Aletti, *Colossiens*, p. 4f.
[90]Likewise W. Bujard, who is cautious in the use of the adjective "hymnic," designates Col. 1:15–20 as hymn: *Untersuchungen*, pp. 88, 99.
[91]A list of typical hymns from the world of the NT is provided in J. H. Charlesworth, "A Prolegomenon to a New Study of the Jewish Background of the Hymns and Prayers in the New Testament," *JJS* 33 (1982), pp. 265–285.
[92]E.g., Odes Sol. 16:8–20, where the logos is said to be the agent of creation, cf. Charlesworth, *Odes*, p. 365ff.
[93]Deichgräber, *Gotteshymnus*, p. 145f.

ferent function in the life of the community, though contentwise they
are related to the confessions and formulas of faith.

One of the hymnic elements, 1 Tim. 3:16, is described as the communication of the "mystery" (μυστήριον, v. 16a). In several instances
in the NT "mystery" denotes the gospel of the resurrection, that is,
of the exaltation (1:5) as fulfillment of the eternal, all-encompassing
intention of God (→1:26).[94] In this sense, then, as revelation of the
most profound intention of God, the Logia source (Q) likewise understood Jesus' declaration of joy (Matt. 11:25–27, par.),[95] which has been
mentioned in connection with the wisdom of God. In terms of conception, the mystery ties into apocalyptic thought (→1:26), though
what is decisive here is that the true mystery is no longer hidden in
the secret writings but can and should now be expressed in hymns,
for instance. In the midst of this world it is a faith venture to praise
Christ as the one already exalted.[96] Behind this hymn is the view of
Christian worship as proclamation of the Lordship of Christ in the
face of all powers that influence humanity and seek to determine its
destiny. It is a liturgical proclamation, different from preaching[97] and
confession, which appeal directly to people and aim at their conversion. The praise of the Lord Jesus Christ as the agent of creation and
as the one who reconciles is at the same time the declaration in public worship of the creatureliness of the superhuman powers, the denial of their deification, and a real break in their fateful activity.

The hymn functions in the argumentation as the author's assistant, and we have to assume that the opponents (heretics) were also
acquainted with it (§12).

15 To begin with, the dignity of the redeemer is expressed by determining his relationship to God: He is[98] the image (εἰκών) of the
invisible God. The allusion is to Gen. 1:26f. (Priestly source) where
humankind was the image (צֶלֶם) of God. Humanity was the reflection of God by representing God in the rest of the created order (Gen.
1:28). It is with this background in mind that the redeemer's designation as the firstborn of all creation is to be understood (v. 15b).[99]

[94]Caragounis, *Mysterion*, e.g., p. 140.

[95]Christ, *Jesus Sophia*, p. 81ff. On this aspect T. Arvedson points out correctly, too,
that the hymnic formulation of the mystery of Christ is to be seen here: *Mysterium Christi.
Eine Studie zu Matth.* 11:25–30, ASNU 7, Uppsala–Leipzig, 1937, pp. 123, 150. Perhaps
the Gospel of Mark, too, viewed Jesus' proclamation of the kingdom of God from the
post–Easter perspective in the same manner, cf. Mark 4:11f., par. What the emphasis
on the revelation, associated with the mystery of God, is intended to mean to the Gentiles in Col. and Eph., is expressed, in Mark, from a different viewpoint by means of
the saying about the hardness of heart of "those outside," namely, the Jews.

[96]In contrast to Rom. 11:36 and 1 Cor. 8:6, the emphasis in the hymn shifts from God
the Father to Jesus. The connecting link is found in 1 Cor. 15:26–28.

[97]Cf. →1:20 and Aletti, *Colossiens*, p. 129; Schweizer, p. 294f.

[98]On the translation of the introductory phrase, see note 111.

[99]Cf. Lohse, "Imago," p. 124f.

The function of the image of God was expanded in hellenistic Judaism. As a reflection of God it is at once also the original image of the rest of creation (evidence in [b] above); as the Logos it is also called the firstborn (Philo, *Conf. Ling.* 63). This is also what Paul has in mind in 2 Cor. 4:4. Jesus Christ presents God not merely through his Lordship within the rest of creation, but especially through his insight into the will and mystery of God. Most of the time this image is identical to wisdom (§9 [b]), which God grants to exceptional individuals (Wisd. 7:15–30). Hence in Col. 1:15 the "image of God" (in contrast to Phil. 2:6) is already an independent designation, the bearer of which has close affinities to the Philonic Logos (cf. Philo, *Conf. Ling.* 62f.; 145f.).

God's intention in creation is focused and incarnate in Christ. For this reason, the discussion moves swiftly to his relationship to the rest of creation.[100] His precedence as the firstborn consists not only of his temporal priority. The firstborn here is a mark of honor (cf. Heb. 1:6)[101] expressing especially the privileges of the firstborn (cf. Gen. 27, esp. v. 29). Practically speaking, this means that, from the siblings' vantage point, the firstborn is on the side of the father.

When the hymn originated, the dogmatic distinction between the begotten Son of God and the created order that was in vogue during the Arian controversy was not yet formulated. The title "firstborn" emphasizes the priority of the redeemer here[102] and is not intended to obliterate the boundaries between him and other human beings. The question posed by the early interpreters of when and how Jesus became the image of God, namely, whether he was already revealed as the preexistent one or only as the incarnate God,[103] represents a secondary and later problem connected with metaphysical thought. The specification "of the invisible God" characterizes the image especially as a reflection. At issue is not an external reflection, but the revelation and realization of the will of God, which culminates in the incarnation. Otherwise "the image of the invisible" would be a logical aporia. Since the context (1:6–17) speaks of the image as the agent of creation (i.e., of the original image), some scholars see an internal contradiction and omit the specification as an addition.[104] They find another reason for this in the different meaning of the adjective "invisible" here and in v. 16. The formulations "invisible God" (cf. 1 Tim. 1:7) and "the visible and invisible" (cf. Ign., *Trall.* 5:2; Ign., *Rom.* 5:3) are fixed, however, and are used linguistically as entities.

---

[100]Wohlenberg, p. 65; Burger, *Schöpfung*, p. 43.

[101]So Hockel, *Erstgeborene*, p. 126f.; on the documentation see in loco.

[102]On the dogmatic ramifications, see Calvin, in loco.

[103]Thus e.g., Oltramare I:135.

[104]Burger, *Schöpfung*, p. 30; Schenk, "Christus," p. 149; others, such as Ernst (p. 175), eliminate it on stylistic grounds.

More significant is the theological tension discernible in a "semantic aporia."[105] But the hymn has a congruent structure: (1) The image genuinely has a revelatory quality.[106] Wisdom of Solomon 7:26, for instance, speaks of wisdom as the image of God's goodness that mediates the creation of the world (Wisd. 7:21) and the defeat of evil, as well as the communion with God (Wisd. 7:27, 30). (2) The predicate "image of God" likely describes primarily the experience with the human and resurrected Jesus Christ (2 Cor. 4:4–6),[107] but precisely in the perspective of faith, the glory of God can also be discovered in creation, for creation and resurrection are the works of the same God (2 Cor. 4:6). Hence "the image of the invisible God" is the redeemer in his comprehensive function as mediator between God and creation. (3) This development of the proclamation of the resurrection is described in terms of its inner logic in Col. 1:15–20. In Judaism, for instance, the experience of the exodus was also formulated earlier than the belief in the creator; yet the creation account is placed at the beginning of the Bible, and the belief in the creator initiated the catechetical tradition.[108] Thus the sequence of agent of creation–redeemer also became traditional for Christianity. Since the resurrection of Jesus is significant for the entire creation, his work is anchored "protologically" here.[109] The redemption, which is the theme of the second stanza, is actually viewed as a restoration and a more profound development of the preexistent situation.

Verse 15 not only expresses the dignity of Jesus, therefore, but emphasizes at the same time that it is[110] precisely he[111] who represents God in his authority and grace and who provides access to him.[112]

---

[105]Schenk, "Christus," p. 144.

[106]Jervell, Imago, p. 220; Aletti, Colossiens, p. 85.

[107]Cf. Schweizer, p. 64, note 18.

[108]Summarized in K. Beyschlag, Grundriss der Dogmengeschichte I, Grundrisse 2, Darmstadt, 1982, p. 59f., cf. p. 70ff. The general spreading of that sequence also militates against interpreting the first stanza in terms of the eschatological, new creation, as e.g., in Zeilinger, Erstgeborene, e.g., p. 188.

[109]Internally the first stanza of the hymn is structured similarly to the statement in John 1:18 where Jesus is viewed as a heavenly mediator, while presupposing at the same time that he is the Word which became flesh (John 1:14) as well as the son of Joseph (6:42). In Gos. Truth, too, Jesus is both the revealer of the invisible Father (NHC I/3; 19:14–25) and the crucified one (18:24).

[110]Steinmetz, Heils-Zuversicht, p. 72.

[111]O'Neill, "Christology," p. 90, insists that this is also expressed by the "he is . . ." (ὅς ἐστιν), which he translates "He it is who is the image. . . . " In this case the subsequent titles (the image, the beginning) would probably have no article in Gk. Objectively the emphases on the dignity of Jesus and on the centrality of Jesus can be distinguished, cf. Aletti, Colossiens, p. 46f.

[112]Schweizer, "Kirche," p. 296; idem, "Kolosser 1:15–20," p. 18f.: "Conversely, the community of the hymn of Colossians knows that there is no authentic image of God which is not identical to Jesus Christ to begin with." Cf. Feuillet, "Création," p. 4.

16 This verse characterizes the function of Jesus more precisely as the agent of creation. It is introduced by a causal ὅτι, similar to v. 19.[113] The verse is arranged chiastically: . . . all things were created (Gk. aor.) . . . (listing) . . . all things were created (Gk. perf.) . . . .[114] In the OT the accumulation of predicates using "all" emphasizes the dignity of the only God (Neh. 9:6; LXX 2 Ezra 19:6). "All things" (τὰ πάντα, in vv. 17b and 20 translated as "the universe") is a designation here for the totality of creation,[115] to which the invisible heavenly beings also belonged, which stands in contrast to the contemporary understanding of the cosmos.

It is difficult to determine which of the beings listed are visible and which are invisible. Based on the symmetry, the thrones and dominions could be the visible ones,[116] but in TLevi 3:7f. the thrones, together with the authorities, are designations for the classifications of angels.[117] Ephesians 1:20f. (cf. Jude 8; 2 Pet. 2:10) and later 1 Enoch 61:10 confirm this as far as the "dominions" are concerned. Both terms have their origin in the political arena but were then also transferred to heavenly beings, similar to the principalities (ἀρχαί) and authorities (ἐξουσίαι). This second doublet occurs as a fixed combination as early as Plato[118] and designates the invisible, cosmic powers (Col. 2:15; Eph. 6:12). As far as the context is concerned, these concepts also describe the heavenly beings here (cf. Col. 2:9f., 15; Eph. 1:21f.; 6:12). The sixth and seventh line of the first stanza, therefore, list only what is invisible.

In terms of origin, the conception of the supernatural, invisible powers[119] may be a residue of early polytheism.[120] Judaism placed such powers alongside angels, that is, alongside the fallen angels of

---

[113]In actuality ὅτι is only intended to develop in more detail the preceding sentence; Alford.

[114]On this structure, see Pöhlmann, "All-Prädikationen," p. 59f.; v. 17, which is shorter, is structured similarly. The difference in tense (aor. and perf.) corresponds with the internal structure of the stanza, namely, from the one-time act of creation to the expression of 1:17b.

[115]On τὰ πάντα as universe, see e.g., Corp. Herm. XIII, 17; Orph. Fragm. 168 (Kern).

[116]So Lindemann, Aufhebung, p. 209; Bammel, "Versuch," p. 92ff., includes the thrones and dominions among the earthly beings, according to the chiastic schema of X–Y–Y–X.

[117]Further documentation in O. Schmitz, TDNT III:160–167, on p. 167.

[118]K. Weiss, TDNT I:338–392, on p. 390.

[119]M. Dibelius, Die Geisterwelt im Glauben des Paulus, Göttingen, 1909; K. L. Schmidt, "Die Natur- und Geisteskräfte im paulinischen Erkennen und Glauben," in Eranos-Jb. 1946, Zürich, 1947, pp. 87–143; G. H. C. Macgregor, "Principalities and Powers. The Cosmic Background of Paul's Thought," NTS 1 (1954–55), pp. 17–28; G. B. Caird, Principalities and Powers, Oxford, 1956; Schlier, Principalities, p. 11ff., has a catalogue of the names of the heavenly powers; P. Pokorný, "Kirche und Mächte," CV 2 (1959), pp. 71–82; W. Carr, Angels and Principalities, NTSMS 42, Cambridge, 1981; Schillebeeckx, Christus, p. 490ff.

[120]Caird, Principalities, p. 14ff. (see note 119 above).

Gen. 6. In determining their role, it is important that they move between heaven and earth, between humankind and God (1 Cor. 8:5).[121]
They are able to separate humanity from God (Rom. 8:38f.), but God
will strip them of their power at the end of time (1 Cor. 15:24); and
the church, therefore, is able to and ought to resist them (Eph. 6:12).
Because the concrete effect of those powers was so negative, many bib-
licists have considered them to be something essentially evil, hence,
as explicit expressions of the devil's power.[122] Against this Col. 1:16
points out that they, too, are God's creation originating in Christ, that
is, whose innermost destiny it is to serve him. Their negative effect
is to be derived from their misuse[123] – which is connected with sin –
from their overestimation and deification, and from the exchange of
creature and creator (Rom. 1:23–25). For this reason Paul underscores
in Rom. 8:39 that the previously listed powers are God's creation and
that they are not able to separate humanity from the love of God, if
humanity acknowledges Jesus as Lord. The exaltation of Jesus and the
respective Christian confession signify a de-mystification of the mis-
used, superhuman powers. While their positive destiny is emphasized
only in Colossians and Ephesians, it is already presupposed in Paul
(Rom. 8:22ff.). 1 Corinthians 8:6 may be the immediate ancestor of
Col. 1:16: "yet for us there is one God, the Father, from (ἐξ) whom
are all things and for (εἰς) whom we exist, and one Lord, Jesus Christ,
through (δι') whom are all things and through whom we exist."[124]
This is a confession-like formula[125] that describes in good Jewish fashion the one God as the only creator, but who, from the Christian perspective, created everything through Jesus Christ. The purpose of the
accumulation of prepositions, which is elsewhere documented as a
linguistic phenomenon accompanying Stoic pantheism,[126] is to emphasize creation's total dependence upon the creator, whose purpose
Jesus Christ represents.[127] Since God the Father is the initiator of creation, the preposition "from" is not used here. Otherwise it is difficult to distinguish the functions of the various prepositions from one

---

[121]According to Philo they surround God, though they are subservient to him: *Conf.
Ling.* 171.

[122]E.g., Schlier, *Principalities*, p. 17f.

[123]Cf. Carr, *Angels* (see note 119 above), p. 52: They are essentially neutral entities.

[124]Translation of Ch. Wolff, *1. Korinther*, p. 4.

[125]Deichgräber, *Gotteshymnus*, p. 116.

[126]E.g., Marc. Aurel. IV, 23; additional documentation in Norden, *Agnostos Theos*,
pp. 247–250; Feuillet, "Création," p. 1f. Cf. also Rom. 11:36 and 1 Cor. 15:28 with the
Platonic–Stoic writing of PsArist., *De mundo* VI, 397b; →1:20. Zeilinger, *Erstgeborene*,
p. 192, points out Ps. 8:7 (LXX) as a parallel manner of speaking.

[127]M. D. Hooker ("False Teachers," p. 331) has compared the role of Christ which
is assumed here, with that of the Torah in Judaism which was also regarded as agent
of creation; documentation in Billerbeck II (1965⁴), p. 356f. This idea is probably little
more than a background echo.

another. They, as a whole, are to have a cumulative effect. "In" (instrumental ἐν) and "through" mean almost the same thing; only the phrase "for him" is capable of pointing to the eschatological goal of creation (cf. Rom. 11:36).

The proclamation in the worship service of the key role of Jesus is the true beginning of the eschatological reality, a rerealization of the triumphal procession mentioned in Col. 2:15.[128]

§10 Excursus: Significance of the Heavenly Principalities and Authorities

Do the beings listed in Col. 1:16 conform to something real or is this merely a distorted reflection of the mindset of the "composers" of such hymns, or of the collective subconscious of the communities reciting them? With all the problems of the theory of knowledge and of language associated with it, we must affirm that there is a reality behind the discussion about the superhuman powers.

These realities are today described via more neutral and objective concepts. One speaks of the influence of cultural traditions, positive and negative biases, of the order of nature, of the laws of society or of the tendencies of its development.[129] In a certain sense, reality is described more precisely by means of such concepts—more precisely in the sense that they are more directly verifiable. But as far as their effect upon the human subject is concerned, they are more superficial and one-sided. For instance, aging and dying is a biological process that can be described as such, yet humans often experience it, in a very real way, as a hostile pressure with which they must deal on their own by utilizing their inner strength. A rumor can be defined as erroneous information, but it quickly gains its own existence and can be perceived as a personal enemy of the victim. The initiator may retract the slander and apologize to the victim, but the rumor has already been emancipated and has become a superhuman power. There is nothing evil in aging as such, yet when one aspires to be one's own lord and therefore is wrapped up in one's own possibilities, the reduction of one's focused perspective is experienced as one's "last enemy" (1 Cor. 15:26). The value of information is also indispensable for life, but as soon as the information is false, it becomes a life-threatening force. Idealistic thought has the tendency to under-

[128]A similar proclamation of the victory and authority of Jesus is likely in mind in 1 Pet. 3:18–22: W. Bieder, Die Vorstellung von der Höllenfahrt Jesu Christi, AThANT 19, Zürich, 1949, pp. 114–117; J. B. Souček, "Das Gegenüber von Gemeinde und Welt nach dem ersten Petrusbrief," CV 3 (1960), pp. 5–13.

[129]Cf. M. Barth, The Broken Wall: A Study on the Epistle of the Ephesians, Chicago–Philadelphia–Los Angeles, 1959, p. 90.

estimate these superhuman realities, and positivism has not taken seriously their effect upon the human subject. Only the materialistic dialectic has again begun to pay attention to its role. The biblical presentation has not become redundant thereby, however, because it emphasizes the deepest anthropological level of personal conduct upon which redemption is projected.

The NT expressions cannot be distilled into a doctrine of the heavenly powers. The designation and the particular function of these beings vary in different contexts. Nevertheless we are able to observe some common tendencies: The principalities and authorities, similar to the angels, stand between God and humanity (→1:16; Heb. 1:4). When they emerge in conjunction with sin or with the devil, as beings emancipated from the will of God (e.g., Eph. 6:11), they become those evil powers that separate humanity from God, instead of bringing to mind God's goodness. In this case the victory of Christ is sometimes interpreted as their subjection and sometimes as their dissolution.[130] Similarly the worldly authorities are also capable of oscillating between both poles, even though it is especially their positive role that is emphasized in Pauline thought (Rom. 13:1–7; 1 Tim. 2:2; Tit. 3:1; 1 Pet. 2:13f.). The argument of Günther Dehn made its connection at this juncture; according to him those heavenly powers are behind the principalities in terms of the worldly authorities.[131] As a relativizing of the Pauline understanding of authorities, this was particularly helpful in the time of the German Kirchenkampf.[132] This argument is unfit to provide access to the respective statements of the NT, though a certain parallelism of the position between God and humanity on the part of both phenomena cannot be denied, and the ambiguity of many expressions (thrones, dominions, principalities, authorities) is most likely not an accident. In Rev. 1:5 the beginning of the related hymnic fragment is referring to earthly authority, and the entire Apocalypse of John focuses upon its dissolution. Again, 1 Cor. 2:6–8 may be understood by regarding the heavenly rulers of this world as participants in the crucifixion of Jesus. In both cases the principalities and authorities are a reality that faith needs to take very seriously, though they are not ultimate reality. Colossians 1:16 correctly warns against rendering diabolical superhuman, heavenly powers, as Rom.

[130]Cf. also Col. 1:29 with 2:15. In contrast to Schenke ("Widerstreit," p. 402), I do not consider these as poles in juxtaposition; →2:15; see also J. V. Lee, "Interpreting the Demonic Powers in Pauline Thought," NovT 12 (1970), pp. 54–69, esp. p. 66.

[131]G. Dehn, "Engel und Obrigkeit," Theologische Aufsätze Karl Barth zum 50. Geburtstag, Munich, 1936, pp. 90–109, esp. 100f., cf. Dibelius, Die Geisterwelt (see note 119 above), p. 200, and here § 18 (c–d).

[132]In our context we shall not address this issue. For a summary see Cullmann, Christ and Time, p. 169ff.; and J. V. Picca, "Romans 13:1–7," Biblioteca di Scienze Religiose 34, Rome, 1981, pp. 74–80.

13 similarly prevents, in principle, the authorities from being diabolical. Objectivizing evil leads to fatalism indeed, viz., to gloating over
against the world, and this obscures the power of the grace of God.
This is precisely the power Colossians emphasizes as the main argument (2:13); it is assumed in 2:20ff. as well as in the paraenesis
(cf. 1:20; 2:8 and §13).

17 This verse is part one of the intermediate stanza and, as its re-
frain, roughly summarizes the first stanza. The phrase "and he is,"
repeated twice, corresponds to the style of a revelatory speech, similar
to the introductory phrases of both stanzas.[133] The first line corresponds to "He is . . . the firstborn of all creation," and the second
one to "all things were created through him and for him."[134] The parallelism of these two expressions is even clearer in the intermediate
stanza. In the first one, Jesus' position is expressed in terms of his
preexistence (cf. John 8:58);[135] the second stresses that the universe
was not only created by him but it has its existence in him (cf. Rom.
11:36; 1 Cor. 8:6; Col. 1:20). Similar aspects of God are found in Sir.
43:26 and in the pseudoaristotelian writing *Concerning the World.*[136]
The manner in which the cosmos exists in Christ is indicated in the
last line of the intermediate stanza (v. 18a; cf. *Corp. Herm.* XI, 4; Philo,
Fug. 112).

18a If we take the saying about the church to be an addition (§9
[a]), Christ is here extolled as the head[137] (§14) of the body,[138] which
is identical to the cosmos of v. 17. Therefore, the fact that he is the
head of the cosmic body signifies that "in him all things hold together" (v. 17b).

§11 *Excursus: Body of Christ (I)*

According also to the above-mentioned pseudoaristotelian writings,
God is for the cosmos what the helmsman is for the ship or the law
for the state.[139] All of these are variants of the conception of the cosmos as an animated organism, as emphasized for instance in the

---

[133]Documentation in Norden, *Agnostos Theos*, pp. 187ff., 204ff.

[134]"Endure, exist" (συνίσταναι) in the perf. ind. occurs only here in the NT, which
serves as one of the arguments in favor of the hymn's existence as an independent entity.

[135]Contra Hugédé, who maintains that πρό is merely a designation of rank; on the
other hand, Ernst, Gnilka, cf. →1:18a.

[136]VI, 397b. On the nature of that treatment, see Nilsson, *Geschichte*, p. 297f.

[137]In contrast to the titles "image" and "beginning" (vv. 15 and 18b), the Gk. for
"the head" has the definite article here. The likely reason for this is that the more
specific designation of "the first-born who . . . " is not used here. On the OT background, see Schmauch, p. 57.

[138]Body = σῶμα; I translate σάρξ as "flesh," "fleshly" or "corpus," "corporeal"
or "personal."

[139]PsArist., *De mundo* VI, 399b.

Orphic fragment no. 176 (Kern) and in the Leidener magic papyrus no. V[140] (cf. Plat., Tim. 30B; Epict., Diss. I, 14, 2; Philo, Spec. Leg. 96; Diog. Laert. VII:142f. et al.). In the magic papyrus the cosmic spirit is described as the lord who causes all things to grow[141] (cf. Col. 2:19). The conception of the macroanthropos and its members, or of a supra-individual head, has also found entrance in Gnosticism and in Christianity, e.g., Thunder, Perfect Mind [sic Nebront Ger.], NHC VI/2; 17:15–24; Gos. Truth, NHC I/3; 18:29–40 (cf. Hippol., Phil. V, 7:6ff., the Naassene sermon); Ign., Trall. 11:2; Acts John 99ff.; Odes Sol. 17:4–16.[142] But this was merely a conception, not a comprehensive concept or an all-encompassing myth.[143] In Col. 2:19 this conception is applied to the church (cf. →1:18b and 3:15). Its occurrence in the pagan world and in Gnosticism leads us to the assumptions that the polemic against "philosophy" in Colossians and later the founding of the unity of the church in Ephesians are to be construed, to a large extent, as a discussion on the correct application of this conception (Col. 1:24; 2:9b–10, 17, 19; 3:15; Eph. 1:22f.; 2:16; 4:4, 12, 15f., 25; 5:23, 30, cf. §14; §16). In the interpretation of Colossians it is important to know, therefore, how this conception is modified. In the hymn it emphasizes the key position of the redeemer, hence it is subservient to a larger concept of thought that is characteristic for the entire series of similar texts and that connects with the wisdom and logos doctrine (§9 [b]).[144] On the question of how the author of Colossians adapted this conception for his theological intention, see §14, as well as the remaining observations on 1:18a.

The author of Colossians has modified the portrait of the redeemer as the exalted one and as the supra-individual head by augmenting it with "the church" (§9 [a]). Accordingly, the agent of creation is recognized as Lord only in a certain realm, namely, the church, to which the recipients belong.[145]

At the same time, this particular group of people is described here as the body which is joined with the head by the grace of God and by faith. And because it is the body of the Lord of the "principalities and authorities," the result, within that framework, is a unique op-

[140]The text is given in Reitzenstein, Studien, p. 99 (as well as further documentation of this conception) and the translation in Fischer, Absicht, p. 73.

[141]Reitzenstein, elsewhere.

[142]Further documentation in Käsemann, Leib, p. 69f.; Pokorný, Epheserbrief, pp. 50–69; Schwanz, Imago, pp. 24–42; Fischer, Absicht, pp. 58–67.

[143]Colpe, "Leib-Christi-Vorstellung," p. 182; Colpe, Die religionsgeschichtliche Schule, p. 180ff.; on the emanationistic understanding of the macro-anthropos conception, see § 9 (b) above.

[144]Schweizer, "Kirche," pp. 293f., 313f.

[145]Zeilinger, Erstgeborene, p. 203; Weiss, "Gnostische Motive," p. 322; R. S. Barbour, "Salvation and Cosmology: The Setting of the Epistle to the Colossians," SJT 20 (1967), pp. 257–271.

portunity to overcome the fateful pressure of these powers (Eph. 1:22f. and §§14 [b] and 15).[146]

The knowledge of God, which for Philo can be attained through contemplation of the creation (*Leg. All.* III, 97–100) — Paul mentions this as an unrealized potential (Rom. 1:20) — is in the hymn bound up with Christ.[147] The author of Colossians adds: It is bound up with Christ as proclaimed and working in the church.

18b Verse 18b begins the second stanza, whose form is symmetrical to the first (Table 6). In terms of content we have described the second stanza as "soteriological" (§9 [a–b]).

The redeemer's main predicate here is "the beginning" (ἀρχή),[148] a concept that, similar to "the image," occurs in Gen. 1 and that was also used by hellenistic Judaism (e.g., Philo, *Conf. Ling.* 146f.; §9 [b]).[149] In our case, this predicate belongs to the one who, from the perspective of mortals, opened up the way to new life. Hence this is the beginning of the new creation, the new humanity (3:10).[150] This emerges in the second line which speaks of the "firstborn from the dead." The term "beginning" is not merely used in the temporal sense here. In a somewhat parallel statement in Rev. 1:5, the firstborn of David is made equivalent to the ruler among the kings of earth. This is an allusion to Ps. 89:28 where the LXX (Ps. 88) calls the highest among the kings the firstborn. Revelation 21:6 and 22:13 speak of the beginning in conjunction with the beginning and end, the Alpha and Omega (cf. Rev. 1:8). Likewise here, "the beginning" is a description of authority and lordship.[151] While the intermediate stanza alluded to this position via the saying concerning the head,[152] it is only in the second stanza that we find its substantiation (in line two). "He is the beginning" means that he also was exalted above the last enemy, death, which was considered to be one of those superhuman powers in antiquity (cf. 1 Cor. 15:26; Rom. 8:38). In this sense it denotes the new humanity. Creation and resurrection from the dead as new creation are also linked in Rom. 4:17, and in the hymn of Heb. 1:2f. we

---

[146]Schweizer, *TDNT* VII:1074, cf. Gaugler, *Epheserbrief*, p. 79; Lindemann, *Aufhebung*, p. 212.

[147]Kehl, *Christushymnus*, pp. 70–81.

[148]The identical term occurs in the plural in the first stanza, meaning "principalities." On the seeming incongruency which O'Neill, "Christology," p. 87ff., has pointed out, what has been said relative to the adj. "visible" →1:15, also applies here.

[149]Montagnini, "Linee," p. 45f. The use of "the beginning" (incl. def. art.) in some MSS (p[46], B et al.) may be an allusion to the beginning of Gen. 1:1.

[150]Cf. Burney, "Christ," p. 170ff.; Houlden, p. 169f.

[151]T. Holtz, *EWNT* I:155f.

[152]That the Hebrew term for "beginning," רֵאשִׁית derived from the word stem ראשׁ with the basic meaning of head (רֹאשׁ), does not yet mean that the hymn was originally written in Hebrew or Aramaic. In contexts such as this both terms are synonymous in several languages.

encounter the redeemer as the agent of creation and the exalted one (cf. §9 [c]).

The saying about the firstborn from[153] the dead has served as key to the new, deeper significance of the first line of this stanza. Its original intent was apocalyptic in that the resurrection of Jesus was regarded as the beginning of the imminent, general resurrection (cf. Rev. 1:5 or Acts 26:23 where this meaning still finds an echo). However, already in Rom. 8 Paul concludes from the Easter message (8:1) that the resurrection of Jesus also makes the new life available to those who die prior to the new age (8:38f.). While he also makes a case for this as early as 1 Thess. 4:13ff.,[154] in Rom. 8 he argues that Jesus is the firstborn among many brothers (8:29, cf. 1 Cor. 15:20;[155] Heb. 12:23). Romans 8:29 also points out that the designation of God as Father and Jesus' title of "Son of God" resonate with the notion of the firstborn. It is but a small step to the notion of Christians as adopted sons and daughters of God (Rom. 8:15ff.), who are dependent upon the firstborn.[156] Within the framework of the hymn, therefore, the "firstborn from the dead" has a key position.[157]

The added final clause, "that in everything he might be preeminent," is an augment, as already indicated (§9 [a]). It combines the doubly key position of the redeemer. It gives meaning to all of creation, or as we might express it today: to this history and to the universe; furthermore, the alienation within creation was overcome through him (1:20). He has become the beginning of the new creation.

19 In the LXX as well as in the NT the verb "pleased" denotes the purpose of God (e.g., Ps. 149:4; Gal. 1:15; 1 Cor. 1:21).[158] It was linked in the Christian tradition with the confession of Jesus as Son (§8) and points to his one-time and unique mission from God (Mark 1:11, par.; 2 Pet. 1:17). It was consistent, therefore, with Jesus' introduction as God's "beloved Son" in 1:13f. In that tradition, "pleased" is a free

---

[153]MSS p⁴⁶, ℵ (first hand), and others omit ἐκ = from. The sentence reads the same way in Rev. 1:5. The meaning is not altered thereby.

[154]Cf. also 1 Cor. 6:14; Rom. 6:11; 8:29.

[155]Here Christ is described as the firstfruit of those who have fallen asleep, cf. 1 Clem. 24:1; cf. Zeilinger, *Erstgeborene*, p. 181f.; cf. § 9 (b).

[156]On the conception of the first-born as the one who, in the perspective of others, holds the key position, see also e.g., the Naassene poem Hippol. *Phil.* V, 10, 2. In this context (Easter, exaltation, pre-existence) the predicate "the first-born" is used earlier with reference to Jesus in early Christian writings (already in Paul, Rom. 8:29), than in the sense of a physical first birth, namely, as Mary's first child (cf. Luke 2:7, cf. Matt. 1:25).

[157]Zeilinger, *Erstgeborene*, pp. 184–190; Lähnemann, *Kolosserbrief*, p. 41. On the assumption of W. Schenk ("Christus," p. 149f.) that "the first-born from the dead," in the view of the author of Col., refers to the baptism of Jesus as his earthly resurrection (cf. 1:13), see note 84 above and 1:26.

[158]Cf. also e.g., 1 QS 8.6 for the Essenes.

rendering of Is. 42:1.[159] The emphasis in the latter rests on the subject (the servant of God, here Jesus) described in this manner, whereas his earlier position is not addressed. The phrase "was pleased" is not to be understood in terms of later adoptionism. Its relationship with the baptism of Jesus in which God voices his pleasure in his beloved son, as well as with the Christian baptismal confession (cf. 2 Cor. 1:19–22),[160] is also reflected in 1:12–14 (→1:13) and attests to the fact that the language of the hymn was influenced by earlier Christian liturgical terminology and by the language of the LXX and not by gnosticism.[161]

The concept of "fulness" (the pleroma, cf. §9 [b]) is not used in the sense of the totality of creation here, since the cosmos was reconciled out of the initiative of this fulness. The pleroma signifies the consistency of the will of God as well as the intensity of his work, which is given added emphasis through the term $\pi \tilde{\alpha} v$. That the reference is to the fulness of God arises from 2:9, where it is also apparent that the fulness is the subject of the event.[162] The affinity with the tradition of the baptism of Jesus indicates that the pleroma, in a certain sense, is here understood as the Holy Spirit.[163] Accordingly, the Spirit of God in his fulness indwelt Jesus (on this, see §9 [b]); God has destined him to fulfill his deepest and ultimate purpose for the totality of creation.

The author of Colossians who added the phrase concerning the church in v. 18 was convinced that the fulness was made manifest in the church (2:9ff., cf. with §9 [a]; →1:18).[164]

The fulness of God has come to dwell in Jesus Christ. The fact that God, specifically one of his hypostatic qualities, is able to indwell human beings is an ancient Jewish conception. God dwells upon Mt. Zion (Ps. 68 [LXX 67]:17; Jub. 1:17 et al.), among his people (Lev. 26:12), among those faithful to the law (TDan 5:1),[165] or in the new Jerusalem (Rev. 21:3). This is also true of the wisdom of God (§9 [b]) or of the word of Christ (Col. 3:16). Christians frequently used this metaphor to express the work of the Holy Spirit (Rom. 8:11; 1 Cor. 3:16; 6:19).

The question of when the pleroma came to dwell in Christ is not raised here. As we have stated already, this sentence may be influenced

---

[159]There the verb רָצָה is used, see Münderlein, "Erwählung," p. 267.

[160]Münderlein, "Erwählung," p. 271. On the assumption that the baptism of Jesus is understood mythically in Col., see note 84 above.

[161]The concept of satisfaction plays a significant part in Gnosticism: G. Schrenk, TDNT II:748.

[162]Details in § 9 (a).

[163]According to Rom. 8:11 the life-giving Holy Spirit dwells in believers; cf. Münderlein, "Erwählung," p. 272f.

[164]Ernst, Pleroma, pp. 92f., 100ff.; Merklein, Amt, pp. 95f., 120.

[165]Gnilka, p. 71.

by the account of the baptism of Jesus (Mark 1:9–11, par.), in which Jesus' status as Son of God and his endowment by the Spirit are actualized at the outset of his public ministry.[166]

The statements of Col. 1:19–20 substantiate the proclamation of v. 18b (causal ὅτι, as in v. 16a). The Risen One discloses the way into the new creation because he was one with the Father and has overcome the cosmic threat through his cross.[167]

20 The fulness of the Godhead has been made effective through Jesus Christ; through him the entire creation was saved and was brought to its destination. Only the statement in v. 18b hinders us from construing the hymn (as we reconstructed it [§9 {a}]) as a song of praise of cosmic harmony (§9 [b]). But since the gospel is presupposed as the message of the resurrection (cf. §9 [c]), we have to examine what is meant by the reconciliation of all things: "to reconcile . . . all things, whether on earth or in heaven."

The cosmic interpretation of salvation was not common in earlier Christian texts. In order to comprehend what the hymn seeks to emphasize in this manner, we shall endeavor to outline step by step the assumptions of this new theological phase and thereby to interpret the remaining lines of the hymn.

(a) The words dealing with cosmic reconciliation and with the making of peace are meant to interpret the Easter message (§9 [c]) that Jesus announced in advance in the proclamation of the kingdom of God. Hence the "cosmic" expressions are meant to comment on the hope given to humanity (cf. →1:18b).

(b) Even the singing of the hymn itself was an event between heaven and earth (§9 [d]). For instance the hymn of Phil. 2:6ff., too, was a demonstration of the subjection of all authorities to the authority of Christ, which was also demonstrated in the bowing of the knee in the Christian community's worship (2:10f.).[168] Thus it is a liturgical actualization of the eschatological peace that is effectively breaking into this world through the power of the exalted Christ (1 Cor. 2:7–16; Eph. 3:10).[169]

(c) Our deliberations regarding the principalities and authorities (1:16; §10) now assist us in comprehending the relationship between the gospel, proclaimed in the Christian sermon and mission, and the exaltation and authority of Christ, made manifest in the liturgy (cf.

[166]Cf. F. Lentzen-Deis, *Die Taufe Jesu nach den Synoptikern*, FrankfThSt 4, Frankfurt, 1970, p. 277ff.

[167]On the implications which W. Schenk ("Christus," p. 150) has drawn from the sequence "resurrection – baptism of Jesus – cross," see note 84 above and →1:26.

[168]The related hymn of 1 Tim. 3:16 also reckons with the demonstration of the victory of Jesus in the face of the heavenly powers.

[169]Elsewhere in Eph. the cosmic reconciliation also has its future dimension, Eph. 1:10, cf. Col. 3:4; on this also see § 13.

§9 [d]; Eph. 1:20–23). When Jesus, crucified in this world, is present as the Resurrected One, it is also revealed that the superhuman powers ruling this world possess no ultimate authority; they are no longer the last unconquerable enemies (1 Cor. 15:26, cf. 1:18b).[170] This interpretation of the gospel rapidly spread in early Christianity and is already firmly in place in Paul (1 Cor. 15:27).

In the popular worldviews of antiquity, most of which bore a Stoic–Platonic imprint, the material world was considered to be one of the "filthy" realms, removed from God and governed by lesser powers. The tractate *Concerning the World*, which we have mentioned already, emphasizes that "everything has its existence from God and through God" (ἐκ . . . διὰ . . . συνέστηκεν; Ps.Arist., *De mundo* VI:397b); at the same time it focuses upon the distance of the earth from the divine center (ibid.,[171] cf. Plat., *Phadr.* 248A).[172] The earth is situated at the boundary between harmony and disorder (ταραχή). The Orphic hymn of Zeus is cited at the conclusion of the tractate (following Kern, Fragm. 168) where Zeus is celebrated in song as the cosmic father and the head of the cosmos (*De mundo* VII:401a–b), but in the remote spheres his rule is perceived as fate (*De mundo* VII:401b). According to some Stoic writings, the material person is separated from God (e.g., *Corp. Herm.* I, 11, 15) by the elements of the world (στοιχεῖα, cf. →2:8). While human beings originate from the spiritual realm, they are held in prison, as it were, in the sphere of nature (*Corp. Herm.* I, 14). This notion, however, is already associated with the nature of Gnosticism.[173] But even if we remain within the Stoic–Platonic mindset of the late hellenistic and early imperial era, it is comprehensible that the proclamation of the gospel could be perceived as an effective overcoming of the supra-individual pressure.

(d) Why then is this new condition that we have just described called reconciliation (ἀποκαταλλάσσειν) and making peace (εἰρηνοποιεῖν)? The second verb is better suited for what has been said to this point. Liberation from the fear of superhuman powers may be compared with peace. In connection with the New Year celebration Philo, for instance, says that through the grace of peace-making (εἰρηνοποιοῦν) God removed not only the battles among the nations but also the battle in nature (φύσις; *Spec. Leg.* II, 190;[174] 192, cf. §9 [d]). So likewise in Eph. 2:14–18 (cf. 4:3) the formation of the church is described as cosmic

---

[170]On the characteristics of this pacification, see Martin (Exeter), p. 41ff.

[171]Nilsson, *Geschichte*, p. 296f.

[172]Further documentation in E. Schweizer, *Lordship and Discipleship*, SBT 28, London, 1960.

[173]Gnosticism also knows the conception of the battle among the inferior aeons, e.g., *Orig. World*, NHC II/5; 125:32ff.

[174]Lyonnet, "Hymne," p. 97ff.; Schweizer, "Versöhnung," p. 490.

peace-making and the Christian mission as battle for such peace (Eph. 6:15), reflecting Christ's peace with God (cf. Rom. 5:1). The concrete result of the cosmic peace to come is the victory over the power of death, which is the "last enemy," as far as the unreconciled are concerned (1 Cor. 15:26, 54–57), so that for humanity death already loses its inimical power in the present (Phil. 1:21). The language of these expressions may be influenced by Is. 57:19.

The formulation of the description of salvation as cosmic reconciliation was not common, either in hellenistic Judaism or in the contemporary pagan religions.[175] It does play a significant role in the theology of Paul, however, for whom reconciliation is a certain equivalent of justification by the grace of God (2 Cor. 5:18–21; Rom. 5:10f.). The initiative of reconciliation comes from God.[176] By means of reconciliation God changes humanity's position so thoroughly that, in many cases, the disposition is also changed. As a believer he or she is "filled" with God's love. Paul likewise speaks of the reconciliation of the world (2 Cor. 5:9), but there the cosmos is only the sum total of humankind, as e.g., in John 3:16. The church is to advance reconciliation ever farther. In this context Col. 1:20 clearly speaks of cosmic reconciliation; the church is present only as the confessing singer of the hymn. This singing declares something that has significance for the entire creation (cf. Rom. 8:19ff.). In contrast to Paul, however, the emphasis has shifted here. The concluding statement of this hymn creates the impression that the reconciliation consists of a new supernatural order, with Christ as the cultic Lord at the head (E. Käsemann).[177] Only by referring to the liturgical character of this hymn is it possible to relativize this critical portrait. A hymn does not embody the entire theology of the community reciting it. This hymn proclaims the liberation from the fateful cosmic pressure, and for precisely this purpose the writer uses the term "reconciliation," which already played an important part in the language of Christian soteriology earlier. In fact, this denotes the restoration of the original function of the cosmic powers (Eph. 1:10; 2:10–23). For Christians they cease to be the "last enemies" (§10). Yet this is not to say that the entire creation is in the eschatological state of salvation. Against this militates the saying about the resurrection as the beginning of the new creation (1:18b). Hence cosmic reconciliation is not the same thing as recon-

---

[175]F. Büchsel, *TDNT* I:254.

[176]Ibid., *TDNT* I:255–259, esp. p. 255: (In the reconciliation [transl.]) "The supremacy of God over man is maintained in every respect." Similarly Käsemann, "Erwägungen," p. 51f.

[177]Käsemann, "Erwägungen," p. 58. On the derivation of historical events from astral powers, a well-known piece of documentation can be found in Virg., *Eclogae* IV. On this issue, cf. note 109 above.

ciliation between God and humanity, or as reconciliation between human beings. In essence, reconciliation here is a metaphor (cf. the par. Eph. 2:14–17). In addition, the two supplements by the author of Colossians have brought the hymn closer to Pauline theology and to the center of the NT.[178]

The hymn originated only after the apostle Paul's stay in Ephesus (§3; §9 [b]). Since statements about reconciliation, intended to interpret the gospel, are found both in the hymn and in Paul, the hymn may be influenced by Pauline theology. Yet, in Paul as well as in the hymn, such expressions are linked to the older formulas concerning reconciliation (Rom. 5:11; 2 Cor. 5:19a). Whether or not they have been influenced by the idea of atonement or by the Servant Songs of Second Isaiah (Is. 53:10–12; 2 Macc. 7:30–38, where καταλλάσσειν is also used; 7:33) can no longer be determined with certainty. Conspicuous is that, in the Servant Songs, we also read of the worldwide peace in the presence of God (Is. 52:6–10).[179] This idea was taken up by an early christological tradition which influenced not only the formulas of prayer and blessing and paraenesis, but also the reconciliation Christology that links Pauline theology with the theology of the hymn.[180] The objectivizing tendencies found in the hymn[181] remained protected against their worst misuse as long as they were linked with these older traditions. In this connection, the fundamental significance of reconciliation is the averting of the wrath of God in the final judgment (Rom. 1:15; 5:9–11; 2 Cor. 5:10–20) and the opening up of the way to God.[182]

With the author's insertion of the phrase "by the blood of his cross" in v. 20 (§9 [a]), he also mentions the Pauline theology of the cross, again tying into the tradition of the Lord's Supper and baptism (cf. Rom. 3:24f.; Rev. 1:5). In Rom. 5:9 the statement concerning reconciliation is related directly to the reference to the blood of Christ, and in Col. 2:14 the author uses a picture of the forgiveness through the

[178]Otherwise in Schenk, "Christus," p. 148ff.

[179]Hofius, "Erwägungen," p. 194ff.; cf. P. Stuhlmacher, Vom Verstehen des Neuen Testaments. Eine Hermeneutik, rev. ed. NTDErg. 6, Göttingen, 1986, pp. 231–234; against this, C. Breytenbach, Versöhnung, Neukirchen, 1987.

[180]Käsemann, "Erwägungen," p. 52ff.

[181]The sentences about the reconciliation of the cosmos in Gos. Eg., NHC III/2; 63:16 are already dependent on Col. 1:20, cf. Böhlig–Wisse, Nag Hammadi, p. 37.

[182]Finally I want to mention N. Kehl's hypothesis according to which ἀποκαταλλάσσειν in Col. 1:20 means the restitution of the human sin of confusing the creator with the creation, as Paul described it in Rom. 1:23 (ἀλλάσσειν), 25, 26 (μεταλλάσσειν, Christushymnus, p. 159ff.). This is theologically correct and almost ingenious in its formulation, but it is debatable whether the choice of expression in Col. 1:20 is connected with the allusion to the stem mentioned. Semantically the basic stem and the compounds were far removed from one another. One would have to assume etymological speculations in the background of the hymn, as commonly found in Philo, for instance.

cross of Jesus (2:13; →2:14f.), which he adopted from the tradition. The reason for the insertion, therefore, was the Pauline interpretation of the cruel death of Jesus as the means of reconciliation. The inner motive for the addition was closely associated with the motive that led to the addition of the term "the church" in v. 18a: God's reconciliation is affirmed by the church that confesses the crucified Christ as the heavenly Lord, as delineated in Eph. 2:11-21.[183] In the framework of Colossians, the reconciliation of all things is construed as that reconciliation which reaches people through the Christian mission (i.e., through proclamation) and thus liberates them—not merely in liturgical form—from both sin (2:13) and the anxiety of the world (cf. 1:23). Through the entire explanation of this section (esp. §9 [b]) we have shown that the author of Colossians considers the hymn, including all of these differences, as his theological assistant and treats it as his ally.

5. Application of the Hymn, 1:21-23

(21) And you, who once were estranged and hostile in mind, doing evil deeds, (22) he has now reconciled in his body of flesh by his death, in order to present you holy and blameless and irreproachable before him, (23) provided that you continue in the faith, stable and steadfast, not shifting from the hope of the gospel which you heard, which has been preached to every creature under heaven, and of which I, Paul, became a minister.

With the addition of verses 21-23 the author applies the hymn to the recipients. Similar to his glosses (→1:18; →1:20), he interprets the cosmic, objectivizing conception of redemption in historical and personal categories. The perspective that Christ has made available is presented as the perspective for people, for the recipients. The correlation has been made possible via the concept of reconciliation (→1:20), which is used again in its original intent as a designation for the relationship between two person-like subjects, as God–humanity here (1:22). Roughly the same thing is expressed in 1:14 as redemption and forgiveness of sins. Hence the hymn is encompassed by two similar interpretive statements. However, 1:21-22 are direct allusions to the statements of the hymn. Both segments, as commentaries, refer to the recipients' baptism. In it Christians have received their reason for hope,

---

[183]If Eph. 2:14–18 also represents an earlier hymn, the author of Eph. has reworked it more thoroughly. Schweizer's interpretations point in this direction as follows: Schweizer, p. 83f.; idem, "Kirche," p. 314; idem, "The Church as the missionary body of Christ," most recently in *Neotestamentica*, 1963, pp. 317–329; Lohse, p. 103; idem, "Christusherrschaft," p. 205; Kasting, *Anfänge*, p. 140f.; Weiss, "Gnostische Motive," p. 322f.; Martin (NCBC), p. 61.

and it is the constant incentive for the renewal of the mind on the part of the Christian community. The final verse links the prayer of thanksgiving and intercession (1:3–23) with the next major section.

21 The Greek καὶ here has adverbial connotations and means "also." The emphasis focuses on the fact that the statement of the hymn has direct implications for the hope and the life of the recipients. The exaltation of Christ overcomes the breach which threatened their life. The acting subject is again Christ, the redeemer (1:22). The previous condition of the recipients is described by a twofold predicate in the form of two expressions associated with the verb "to be" (participle and adjective). What emerges is a rhetorically forceful sentence.[1] Initially they are estranged, reminiscent of contemporary philosophical categories. Here, however, the reference is to being distant in relation to God, to life outside of his covenant and of his promises (Eph. 2:12; 4:18), to life forfeited to judgment, to the "wrath" of God (Col. 3:5–7), to life described as being dead in 2:13. At the same time it is an allusion to the pagan descent of the recipients (cf. 1:27). Then the recipients' previous disposition is characterized as "hostile," that is, once more, hostile in relation to God, which is underscored by the more specific designation "in mind" (Eph. 4:18).[2] It is the opposite of love toward God "with one's whole mind" (Gesinnung, Luther: Gemüt). Mark 12:30 (par. Luke 19:27) describes as enemies those who refuse to acknowledge God as their Lord (cf. LXX Ps. 36:20).[3] Their wrongheaded action is but a result of their inward attitude (Matt. 7:17 par.; Luke 6:44f.). This negative statement is linked in 1:23 to the word concerning the faith that ushers in the new life. Hence the "evil deeds" are those which do not arise out of gratitude to God (3:17). For Paul these were generally the outward works of legal righteousness (Rom. 3:20 et al.); here their content is listed in 3:8 and includes everything that may be interpreted as actual blasphemy of God (cf. Rom. 3:13ff.).

22 "Now" refers to the time after Easter; it is the "now" of the beginning new age (2 Cor. 6:2) in which all things become new by the grace of God. For the recipients this is being actualized since they have become Christians, that is since the arrival of Epaphras (1:7) and since the mystery of the gospel has been communicated (2:2). This means that they have become incorporated thereby into the now of the time after the resurrection of the redeemer (2:12f.; §13). Already in the OT reconciliation[4] made access to God possible (→1:20). Thus

---

[1]Blass–Debrunner–Funk, § 352.

[2]τῇ διανοίᾳ – dat. of relationship.

[3]According to Phil. 3:18 the "enemies of the cross of Christ" are those whose God is their belly.

[4]The combination of δέ with ἀποκατήλλαξεν is not common linguistically, though it is possible (documentation in Alford); for this reason some MSS have tried to modify

it overcomes the estrangement and hostility. For Paul (Rom. 5:10) the surrender of Jesus as the Son sent by God is the true representation of the love of God and the realization of reconciliation brought about by the true and final atoning sacrifice. Accordingly, it states in this connection that the redeemer accomplished reconciliation by the will of God, by means of the "body (σῶμα) of his flesh (σάρξ),"[5] that is, through the sacrifice of his body.[6] Consequently the cosmic reconciliation has to do especially with those people (1:27) who are given the new life (2:12f.) as the only valid hope (1:23, cf. 2 Cor. 5:18-21; Rom. 5:10f.). For this reason they can be assured that they will pass God's judgment.

The instrumental "by his death" explains how reconciliation came about. This is to be viewed as a parallelism, for it is clear that the reconciliation through the body of Jesus was the reconciliation by the death of Jesus.

In keeping with the references to the atoning sacrifice, cultic terminology is used to present the results of reconciliation: Humanity is made "holy" (→1:2) and "blameless" (Eph. 5:27), like the sacrifice acceptable to God (Heb. 9:14; 1 Pet. 1:19). The meaning of this cultic designation (Rev. 14:5) is similar to the forensic "irreproachable" (cf. Phil. 2:15; Eph. 5:27). The redeemer will present[7] the recipients of the letter (through the ministry of the apostle →1:28) in this manner in the judgment of God ("before him" refers to God the Father, see 1:12;[8] on the issue as a whole, cf. 2 Cor. 5:21).

23 In 1:20-22 reconciliation is characterized as an event not dependent on human beings, yet at the same time as an event that affects the human being as subject, as a person. One's changed position is also worked out in one's disposition. The individual may be called upon to persevere. This is indeed primarily an invitation, since the condition refers only to the final clause in 1:22b:[9] You too will per-

---

the text. A semitic model is assumed here by O'Neill, "Christology," p. 93; he takes the reading of D* to be original.

[5]This distinguishes the earthly, mortal body of Jesus from the body of the church (1:18, 24). Σάρξ here does not mean the sinful body, as in Paul, but a substance, namely, humanness (Conzelmann, p. 131). The documentation for the respective Hebrew term from Judaism (גְּוִיָּה; e.g., 1 QpHab 9.2, cf. Sir. 23:17) also stress that this refers to the concrete "natural" human body. These have not influenced the use of that word combination in this instance: Braun, Qumran I:227. On the translation, see note 138 on 1:15-20.

[6]Otherwise reference is made to the blood in conjunction with reconciliation: 1:20; Eph. 1:7; 2:13, cf. Rom. 3:25; 5:9. On reconciliation, see →1:20 and § 9 (d).

[7]Schweizer: "to present;" cf. 1:28; Jude 24. O'Neill, "Christology," p. 90, takes παραστῆσαι imperativally.

[8]So most interpreters; κατενώπιον αὐτοῦ is translated differently (namely, "before himself") by EÜ. Wilckens, Gnilka.

[9]Introduced by παραστῆσαι—the inf. of purpose.

sonally stand irreproachable before God, if . . . , or, formulated even more freely: Everything God has offered you by his grace will also reach its goal in you, if. . . .[10] The proclamation of reconciliation is also connected to an appeal in 2 Cor. 5:18–21. The emphasis in our reference is to "abide." This is to be linked with the "faith," since ἐπιμένειν is not used in the absolute sense in the NT.[11] This concept often implies a terminus ad quem, that is, it expresses perseverance in terms of a period whose parameters are set by the judgment of God (1:22) and by the eschatological revelation of Christ (3:4). Its fulfillment is not expected imminently, rather it is placed at the goal of the existence of the entire community (cf. 4:5). That in which the recipients are to remain is already reality in the present. This is a specific feature of the theology of the letters to the Colossians and to the Ephesians (§13). The recipients have the basis of hope; only they are not to forsake it. The reference to the faith indicates, however, that this is not an antithesis to the theology of the major Pauline epistles. While in Eph. 4:5 faith is understood as the content of faith handed down, elsewhere in Colossians and Ephesians it means primarily the fides qua creditur (Col. 1:4; 2:5, 12). Both meanings are involved here. Hence the subordinate clause expresses (a) that the completion of salvation is yet to happen (cf. 2:12f.; §13) and is not yet present "visibly" (3:3, cf. 2 Cor. 5:7) and (b) that it is possible to "abide" and that this summons is not unreasonable.

Three images illustrate what it means to remain in the faith. The first two (foundation, firmness, cf. 2:7) are associated with building construction (cf. 1 Cor. 3:10f., 17 et al.)[12] and are linked with Is. 28:16, similar to Eph. 2:20.[13] The third expression (not to be deterred, or not to shift) negates a relationship that may be disturbed by external influences (1 Cor. 15:58). The foundation on which the life of the believing community is built and which is not to be forsaken is the hope of the gospel (subjective gen.). The gospel was the issue even at the beginning of the letter and there, too, it was associated with hope (→1:5). Here the gospel is the message of the resurrection, as found in the second stanza of the hymn. It is nothing other than what the recipients had heard and received earlier (1:5; §9 [a]), namely, the living Christian tradition (cf. 2:6, 8).[14]

---

[10]The condition is expressed by εἴ γε, as e.g., also in 2 Cor. 5:3 (Alford).

[11]Haupt.

[12]Lohse, p. 109, note 2, adduces evidence from Qumran.

[13]Is. 28:16 was a common christological testimony in early Christianity (Rom. 9:33; 11:11; 1 Pet. 2:6), cf. C. H. Dodd, *According to the Scriptures*, London, 1952, p. 41ff. Hence it does not mean that this is an allusion to Eph. 2:20, as argued by Coutts, "Relationship."

[14]Merklein, "Theologie," pp. 31–32.

The counterpart to the introductory thanksgiving extends to the end of v. 23. As in 1:6, the subject here is the worldwide mission, though it also depends upon the hymn, as the concepts "creature" and "heaven" indicate. The mission is the result of the reconciliation of all things (→1:20). Factually the assertion that the gospel has been preached to every creature would be an exaggeration, but at issue here is a statement which underscores the authority and scope of the Christian mission. Whatever takes place in mission applies to the whole world; its concern is the whole creation (→1:26); §9 [d]). God is the true subject of the mission (→4:3), and the apostle is his servant.[15] The believers, then, take a key position in the framework of the entire cosmos.[16] The reference to heaven is intended to emphasize the objectivity of the hope founded in God (→1:5).

As in 1:7f., so here the discussion is about the servant of the gospel. The former mentions Epaphras who brought the gospel to the Lycus Valley as a representative of the apostle ("on our behalf"); here Paul is cited directly as the servant of the gospel (cf. Eph. 3:1ff.). He is the apostolic guarantor of the true teaching (→1:7). This announces the theme of Part II in which Paul, and his teaching, in contrast to the opponents, is introduced as the true servant of the church.

[15]See esp. Gnilka, p. 92.
[16]Lähnemann, *Kolosserbrief*, p. 44.

Part Two: The Authority of the Apostle—Connecting Salvation with the Apostolic Proclamation, 1:24–2:5

In a certain sense, this section is a digression because 2:6 connects both with 2:5 and with 1:23. The part in between is written in the first person singular. Since the entire epistle wants to defend the Pauline witness (§ 4 [a]), this segment gains special significance. We consider it as Part II of the letter (see § 5 [b]). It demonstrates the dependence of the community addressed—and actually the whole church—upon the apostle Paul and the tradition of teaching issuing from him: "The community is bound not only to its confession of faith, but, at the same time, to the apostolic office as guardian of the truth."[1] On the structure of this section, see →2:5.

1. Apostle and Church, 1:24–29

(24) Now I rejoice in my sufferings for your sake, and in my flesh I complete what is lacking in Christ's afflictions for the sake of his body, that is, the church, (25) of which I became a minister according to the divine office which was given to me for you, to make the word of God fully known, (26) the mystery hidden for ages and generations but now made manifest to his saints. (27) To them God chose to make known how great among the Gentiles are the riches of the glory of this mystery, which is Christ in you, the hope of glory. (28) Him we proclaim, warning every man and teaching every man in all wisdom, that we may present every man mature in Christ. (29) For this I toil, striving with all the energy which he mightily inspires within me.

[1]Käsemann, "Baptismal Liturgy," p. 166; cf. Marxsen, *Introduction*, p. 180f.

In the first segment of Part II, the author speaks, as the apostle Paul, of his mandate in general. Thus his mandate is closely associated with God's entire plan of redemption.

24 For interpreters this verse is a puzzle, for it seems to be saying something that relativizes the Pauline witness concerning the sufficiency of redemption in Jesus Christ. For Paul (e.g., Rom. 3:24), access to God and salvation has been opened up conclusively for humankind through the passion and death of Jesus Christ. Through the resurrection God has declared his allegiance with humanity. Likewise the author of Colossians has indicated in his gloss in 1:20 that he wants to take his stand in this Pauline heritage. According to 1:24, the apostle is to be accorded some of the vicarious labor as well.

The attempts at interpretation can be organized into several main groups,[2] whose nuances are sometimes rather fluid, so that we shall only focus on the typical features of the respective tendencies of interpretation. Actually they all agree that ὑστέρημα does not denote need and deficiency as much as what is lacking or remaining.[3] We have translated it by using the verb "to lack."

(a) There are interpreters who confirm the first impression mentioned above, understanding the sufferings of Christ as a subjective genitive; for them Paul is presented as the one who consummates the redemptive work of Christ after him. Soteriologically, however, Paul's suffering is only the secondary suffering of Christ's servants[4] who endure everything that Christ took upon himself in his willingness to be sacrificed and everything that for external reasons he was unable to take upon himself as the incarnate one and as an individual (Chrys., Homil. IV, 2; MPG 62:327[5]). This has to do with a mindset that understands the substitutionary suffering quantitatively.

(b) The main argument against interpretations of this kind is that in the NT the term affliction (θλῖψις, mostly plural) is never used as a designation for the suffering of Jesus Christ.[6] It expresses the outward exigencies of people and especially their persecution and oppression on account of their faith.[7] In this connection the genitive

---

[2]A detailed history of investigation is offered in Kremer, *Leiden*, pp. 5–154; see also Schmauch, pp. 60–63.

[3]Percy, *Probleme*, pp. 129–136, and idem, "Zu den Problemen des Kolosser- und Epheserbriefes," *ZNW* 43 (1950–51), pp. 178–194, esp. p. 190, asserts that ὑστέρημα denotes only the lack of something already given. Against this, Kremer, *Leiden*, p. 167, who appeals to LXX Judg. 19:19, among others; cf. 1 Thess. 3:10 and Phil. 2:30.

[4]Not only the apostle.

[5]Among the more recent exegetes, the following are inclined to follow this interpretation: Haupt, Schweitzer, *Mysticism*, p. 141ff.; Windisch, *Paulus*, p. 244f.; Kremer, *Leiden*, pp. 189–191; cf. Zeilinger, *Erstgeborene*, pp. 89f., 92.

[6]Soden, p. 37; Ewald, p. 343; Peake, p. 515; Martin (NCBC); G. Delling, *TDNT* VI:305.

[7]This is particularly clear in 2 Cor. 1:4, 8; 2:4 etc.; cf. Kremer, *Leiden*, p. 171f. In Paul the term πάθημα (suffering) occurs only in Phil. 3:10, as a designation of the suf-

τοῦ Χριστοῦ is rather to be taken as a genitivus auctoris[8] or as an objective genitive, as seen e.g., in the "sufferings of Christ" in 2 Cor. 1:5, or in the "death of Jesus" in 2 Cor. 4:10 (cf. 4:11 and Heb. 11:26).[9] The result is that the phrase "for the church" has to be applied to the suffering of the apostle. In his life Paul fulfills the afflictions of the church. Thus it is intended to mean neither that he fulfills those afflictions that Christ took upon himself for the sake of the church[10] nor that this refers to a double representation (for Christ and for the church;[11] cf. Eph. 3:13).

(c) Against this interpretation (b) one may argue with Jacob Kremer that it is scarcely possible to "fulfill" the distress coming from the outside. For this reason some interpreters have translated this as "the remainder of the afflictions of Christ in the domain of my body," and have understood it to be the totality[12] of suffering that every believer is to endure on account of the faith.[13] In that case, however, the phrase "for the church" is virtually inexplicable.[14] As far as some parts of its implications are concerned, this suggestion may be useful only as contrast against the first interpretive tendency (a). It indicates that the suffering of the apostle is something other than the substitutionary (satisfactory, expiatory) suffering of the Lord Jesus Christ.[15] For this reason one sometimes uses the term edificatory suffering, of which suffering for Christ's sake is also part. It is a joyful suffering because the sufferer knows that Christ has already accomplished salvation (2 Cor. 6:10; Phil. 2:17; Rom. 5:3, cf. Matt. 5:11, par.; 1 Pet. 4:14 et al.). As we have already pointed out, this interpretive tendency misconstrues the specific role of the apostle, who represents in Colossians the gospel concerning the authority of the resurrected Jesus Christ above all powers and authorities. In this sense, as the servant of the

---

fering of Christ. In 2 Cor. 1:5 the παθήματα τοῦ Χριστοῦ are clearly the sufferings for Christ's sake: Gnilka, p. 95, note 10.

[8]Clearly presented in M. Carrez, *De la souffrance à la gloire. De la δόξα dans la pensée paulinienne*, Biblioth. théol., Neuchâtel, 1964, p. 126: "les 'douleurs' qui viennent du Christ." Concerning the older interpreters who take it as a genitivus auctoris, see Oltramare, p. 235.

[9]Hence the translation "afflictions of Christ" or "distresses of Christ" (Schweizer).

[10]Thus understood, e.g., by the RSV, NEB; cf. Bratcher–Nida, p. 37.

[11]Thus Windisch, *Paulus*, p. 244.

[12]Thus also the interpretation in Kralice.

[13]Ewald, p. 344; Peake, Wohlenberg, E. Hoskyns and N. Davey, *The Riddle of the New Testament*, London, 1931, p. 226f.; W. F. Flemington, "On the Interpretation of Colossians 1:24," in W. Hornbury and B. McNeil, eds., *Suffering and Martyrdom in the New Testament*, Cambridge, 1981, pp. 84–90.

[14]Though Carrez, *Souffrance* (see note 8 above), p. 126, also links the phrase "of Christ" with "in my flesh," he understands it as apostolic suffering which benefits the church, therefore; cf. idem, "Souffrance et gloire dans les épîtres pauliniennes," *RHPR* 31 (1951), pp. 343–353, esp. p. 352f.

[15]Lightfoot, Ewald, Moule et al., in loco.

gospel (1:23) the apostle is at the same time the servant of the church
(1:25) to which he not only belongs but against which he also contrasts his mandate (cf. 2:1; Eph. 3:1, 13). Because he is not present,
it is likely that this statement is meant to explain the absence of the
apostle (who is perhaps no longer alive) and to support his authority
at the same time.

(d) This has been expressed by that interpretive tendency which
understands the afflictions of Christ as the measure of suffering that
God has destined for the church.[16] In that case it is comprehensible
that the apostle's suffering can benefit the church (Eph. 3:13). Among
this group are also some interpreters who take the genitive τοῦ Χριστοῦ
as a subjective genitive, namely, those who consider Christ to be
equivalent with the church as his mystical body (Aug., *Enarr. Ps.* 61;
MPL 36:703f.; similarly in *Ps.* 142; Oecumenius, Lombard, Calvin),[17]
or who take the suffering of the church to be a subsequent suffering
of Christ, since it happens "in Christ" (→2:18).[18] In this framework
a relatively substitutionary service[19] (cf. Gal. 6:2; Luc., *Toxaris* 40)
on the part of an individual for the benefit of the church is possible.
In this context one generally thinks of a measure of suffering or
"effort,"[20] determined by apocalyptic boundaries, which is supported
by the apocalyptic expressions in 1:25ff. (office = οἰκονομία, mystery, ages, reveal).[21] As far as the context is concerned,[22] then, those
afflictions still lacking are the sufferings that belong to the yet-to-
be-expected mission of the church. This interpretation has its weakness as well. Whereas the conception of an apocalyptic measure of
suffering can be documented (see e.g., Mark 13:7f., 9, 13, 19f.; 1 *Enoch*
47:2; on the shortening of the period, 2 *Bar.* 20:1ff.),[23] this does not

[16]Documented comprehensively by J. Schneider, *Die Passionsmystik des Paulus*, Untersuchungen zum NT 14, Leipzig, 1929, p. 55f. and by R. Stuhlmann, *Das eschato-
logische Mass im Neuen Testament*, FRLANT 132, Göttingen, 1983, passim.

[17]Lightfoot, Alford, Oltramare, pp. 236, 241; Schlatter, (Carrez), Caird; cf. Gnilka, p.
96f.

[18]A. Deissmann, *Die neutestamentliche Formel "in Christo Jesu,"* Marburg, 1892,
p. 80ff., who refers to a sphere influenced by Christ, in which the suffering of the church
takes place.

[19]Kremer, *Leiden*, p. 193.

[20]In a certain sense, the measure of suffering is linked to the measure of ministry,
cf. Kremer, *Leiden*, p. 172f.

[21]Calvin, in loco: " . . . *hoc modo implentur passiones, quas Pater illius corpori
suo decreto destinavit.*" Bengel, in loco: "*Fixa est mensura passionum, quas tota
exantlare ebet ecclesia, quo plus igitur Paulus exhausit, eo minus et ipsi posthac et
ceteris relinquitur.*" So also Kralice; Dibelius, p. 23; Lohmeyer; Souček, p. 39f.; Thompson; idem, "Ephesians 3:13 and 2 Timothy 2:10 in the Light of Colossians 1:24," *ET*
71 (1959–60), pp. 187–189; Mussner, *Christus*, p. 140f.; Caird, Lohse, Martin (NCBC).

[22]Grammatically and lexicographically there are several interpretive options, see
point (a) above.

[23]The documentation is given by Stuhlmann (note 16 above), p. 91ff.; Lohse, p. 115f.
For the Talmudic documentation on the travail of the messianic era, see Billerbeck I, 950f.

explain in what sense it might be utilized here.[24] In Colossians the apocalyptic thought structures are altogether in the background, of course (§ 13).[25] Hence the conception of the God-given period has to be redirected here.

As far as the context is concerned, the specific mandate the church is to carry out on behalf of Christ is clearly the mission in the full sense of the term.[26] The eschatological goal which constitutes the boundary of "completing" is to "present [to God] every person mature in Christ" (1:28, cf. 2 Tim. 2:10), that is, to bring about the appropriation of the redemption that has already been accomplished, in order that those addressed may stand in the last judgment (cf. →1:22). The completion of what is lacking in Christ's afflictions (1:24) is essentially synonymous with making fully known the word of God (1:25). In other words, the apostle's struggle linked with suffering, which is to become the struggle of the church as a whole, means to lead people to the "knowledge of God's mystery of Christ" (2:2). The final revelation of the glory of Christ (3:4) will confirm Christian proclamation as the decisive word of truth (1:5; 4:3). Therefore apostolic suffering is not a struggle for Christ in the form of the church as his spiritual body, but a struggle for the church in the power of Christ. This explains the tension between the Pauline witness concerning salvation that is already complete and this expression, i.e., the tension between the exaltation of Jesus and the reconciliation of all things (1:20) and that which is still "lacking." The apostle struggles and suffers in order that people may "realize" that their salvation in Jesus Christ is already completed, in order that, by faith, they may share in the already completed reconciliation.[27] The opponents endeavored to convince the recipients that there are obstacles other than their own in the structure of the cosmic powers that separate them from God and impede reconciliation (§ 10; § 12). The absent apostle struggles and suffers for the recipients so they may recognize that nothing is able to separate them from the love of God in Jesus Christ; by faith, they already have resurrection and the new life (1:27b; →2:12f., cf. →1:13). What is still "lacking" is the appropriation of the already com-

[24]This is the objection raised by Conzelmann, Ernst, p. 185; Schweizer, p. 105 et al.; against this, see Stuhlmann (note 16 above), p. 100.

[25]Through his suffering the apostle shortens the time before the parousia all the same, according to Lohse, p. 116; Stuhlmann (see note 16 above), p. 101.

[26]Chrys. Homil. IV,2; MPG 62, 327; Severian v. Gabala (4th–5th cent.; Staab, Pauluskommentare, p. 321); Oltramare, p. 241; Soden, p. 37; Dibelius, Masson, TOB (Ed. intégr., in loco), Schweizer, p. 105f.; Gnilka, p. 97f.; cf. Zeilinger, Erstgeborene, p. 90ff. In his sermon on suffering and the cross, Luther interprets it in terms of the call to renewal of all of Christendom (WA 32:29).

[27]Photius of Constantinople emphasizes both the sufficiency of Christ's suffering and the analogy of the fate of the master and the disciple (Matt. 10:24, par.); Staab, Pauluskommentare, p. 631ff.

plete salvation. And the afflictions of Christ represent the suffering linked with the apostolic proclamation of salvation. It is no simple struggle, for sinful humanity is reluctant to admit a dependence upon a gift from the outside. The argument of the letter (2:12f.) stresses that in Christ the believer is able to participate in the fulness of God (2:12f.; 1:19). The word of God is being "fulfilled" (1:25); nevertheless, the apostle pays a price for it in his labor, as he "fulfills" his missionary mandate (1:24., cf. 4:17).[28] And yet it is a joyful kind of suffering, for salvation is already a reality, and through the apostolic ministry God is raising up his church made up of sinners and Gentiles (1:27, 29). The highlighting of such "completing" may have influenced the use of the concept of ὑστέρημα (that which is still lacking).

Though the church as a whole is called to be a witness of the faith (3:12–17), the apostle, as an original witness, fulfills a specific mission. By means of his mortal existence ("in his flesh") he demonstrates the crucified Christ[29] (e.g., Gal. 6:17; Phil. 3:10; 2 Cor. 4:10f.). Furthermore he underscores and verifies his proclamation of the gospel by his joy in suffering.[30] By referring to his suffering, Paul defended himself against the accusations of the opponents in 2 Cor. 10–13; here the authentication of his witness is also important. A message proclaimed in this manner cannot be fraudulent.[31] According to 1:29 Christ himself works through the apostle (cf. Phil. 4:13). The apostle is distinguished from other Christians by means of the specific mandate of the original witness (1:1, 23; Eph. 3:5, cf. Gal. 1:12). According to Eph. 2:20 he is part of the foundation of the church; he fulfills his apostolic mandate for others (1:25; 2:1).[32] The com-

[28]The many derivatives of the stem πληρ- (cf. also 2:9f.), which distinguish Col. from the Pauline homologoumena (§ 1 [b]), are used by the author, perhaps influenced by the opponents as well, in whose teaching the pleroma may have played a significant role (→1:19); so Kremer, Leiden, p. 162; Lähnemann, Kolosserbrief, p. 46; Flemington, "Interpretation" (see note 13 above), p. 86f.

[29]E. Güttgemanns, Der leidende Apostel und sein Herr, FRLANT 90, Göttingen, 1966, pp. 98–125; Schille, Paulusbild, p. 59f.

[30]In early Christian thought the suffering of Christ had its precursors (OT prophecy) and effects (the suffering of the apostles and martyrs)—so E. Kamlah, "Wie beurteilt Paulus sein Leiden?" ZNW 54 (1963), pp. 217–232. In this derived sense the author of Col. is able to draw a parallel between his work and the work of Christ and to appeal to some christological predicates, esp. the substitutionary suffering (Is. 52:13–53:12, cf. Mark 10:45); see also Ernst, p. 187; Wilckens. The interpreter who emphasizes this concern in isolation from the rest fraternizes with the interpretation described under point (a) (e.g., Windisch, Paulus, p. 245f.). Kremer, Leiden, p. 162f., resists the apostle's overestimation by relating the possibility of relatively substitutionary suffering to all Christians in principle (against this, E. Käsemann, Review in ThLZ 82 [1957], pp. 694–695). For a summary on this issue, see T. Holtz, "Zum Selbstverständnis des Apostels Paulus," ThLZ 91 (1966), pp. 321–330.

[31]E. Käsemann, "Die Legitimität des Apostels," ZNW 41 (1942), pp. 33–71, esp. pp. 56, 70f.; cf. Wiles, Prayers, p. 4ff.

[32]Lähnemann, Kolosserbrief, p. 45.

munity addressed is not to engage in mission directly. It is to praise God and take seriously its salvation (3:1ff.), and it is to (and may) remain united with the apostle and his witness even in his absence.

Yet serving the church (1:23, 25) is not the task of the apostles alone. There are also "servants of servants" (1:7; 4:7) who carry out a task assigned by the Lord (4:17) and who represent the apostle (4:12) in his absence (4:18).[33] They represent in the present what is apostolic, and they are able to protect the church from heresy. The prominence of the apostle here functions as protection and "grounding" of the Christian proclamation which is to guard them against the "vagabonding currents" of debilitation and falsification.

The necessary institutional control is implemented in the form of a concrete tradition of the apostolic teaching (→4:7–14).[34]

25 As a witness of Christ, it is the apostle's ministry to lead every person to faith (1:28). This is a strenuous ministry executed by the apostle for the entire church (→1:24).[35] Since the church has a vital role to play in God's redemptive plan (cf. οἰκονομία in Eph. 1:10), the apostolic office (οἰκονομία) has to be viewed as an integral part of the eschatological movement which God himself[36] called into existence.[37] In 1:25b–27 the ministry of the apostle is depicted as proclamation of the mystery of God (→1:26); the entire letter is indeed dedicated to the interpretation of the latter.[38] First of all, the mystery is described more specifically as the word of God — as expression of the will of God which is to be made known to humankind by revelation.[39] The tendency to bring to fruition is inherent in the word of God as the creator's word (Is. 55:10f.). At times it was considered as a hypostasis, as an entity that is dependent upon God, yet relatively independent (Is. 9:7). Later some Christian groups identified the word of God with Jesus Christ (1:27, cf. John 1:1ff.). This is the beginning point of that very important development in the history of dogma. According to 1:27 the content of the mystery is identical to "Christ in you," and in 1:5, 23

[33]Gnilka, "Paulusbild," p. 192f.; cf. Ollrog, *Mitarbeiter*, p. 222ff.

[34]Elsewhere Ollrog fails to take into account that the coworkers could also represent the apostle in this manner in the second generation (after his death).

[35]"For you" refers to the office of the apostle, not to the fulfillment of the word, which does not take place until salvation is consciously appropriated; contra Chrysostom et al., Schweizer et al.

[36]Note the divine passive in the phrase "which was given to me."

[37]J. Reumann, "OIKONOMIA — Term in Paul in Comparison with Lucan Heilsgeschichte," NTS 13 (1966–67), pp. 147–167. For Lindemann, on the other hand, the oikonomia of the apostle, here as well as in Eph., consists of the "proclamation of the (accomplished!) redemptive event in Christ" (*Aufhebung*, p. 78) and its goal is located outside the history of this world (pp. 80, 94f.). We have shown (in 1:24, point [d]), however, that the proclamation of salvation itself belongs to God's plan of redemption, since it has its goal in the eschatological epiphany of Christ (Col. 3:3f.).

[38]Zeilinger, *Erstgeborene*, pp. 45f., 48.

[39]In the OT e.g., in Deut. 5:5; Ps. 119:16.

Christian proclamation is called gospel. The common denominator
of the word of God and the gospel is their verbalization. Hence by
means of a human message the mystery of God may be signalled as
good news. On "fulfilling," see →1:24, cf. Rom. 15:19.

26 The mystery (μυστήριον – cf. § 9 [d]; →1:9, 27; 2:2; 4:3; see esp.
the parallel in Eph. 3:9) is the key term of the entire second part of
Colossians (see Table 3). It is a religious concept[40] that in the Septuagint occurs as a technical term for the mystery religions (Wisd.
14:15, 23, cf. 3 Macc. 2:30). In this sense it denotes something about
which it is important to keep silent.[41] The order of silence regarding
the content of the Eleusian mysteries is the most common in antiquity.[42] In Judaism, however, the other dimension of the concept mysterion gains prominence, which also had its echoes in the non-biblical
world.[43] Not only does it designate the secrecy (thus far) of the de-
crees of God, but also its inward depth and fulness which, in its in-
exhaustibility, becomes distinct as mystery precisely after revelation
and which maintains the advantage over against human thought (e.g.,
1 QS 11.5f.; 1 QM 14.14).[44] In apocalypticism the revelation of the
mystery of God does not occur until the eschatological cataclysm
(1 Enoch 104:11–13). In this age the mysteries are known only to the
wise (4 Ezra 14:26).[45] The Christian proclamation has reshaped the
apocalyptic schema of revelation in favor of the gospel. The eschatological cataclysm, therefore, is already here in the exaltation and new
presence of the crucified one. The new age breaks into our age, and
the mystery which has been hidden from eternity past is now being proclaimed: 4:3; Eph. 3:4–7, 8–11, cf. 1 Cor. 2:6–10; Rom. 16:25f.; 2 Tim.
1:9–11; Tit. 1:2f.; 1 Pet. 1:17–21; Acts Thom. 47; Gos. Truth, NHC I/3;
18:14f. et al.).[46] In this context the meaning of the gospel is expressed
via the codes of time (formerly – now) and of gnosis (hidden –
revealed).[47] The mystery was revealed to "all the saints" (→1:2),[48] to

---

[40]Documentation in Zeilinger, Erstgeborene, p. 94ff.; Caragounis, Mysterion, pp. 3–32;
Penna, Mysterion, p. 17ff.

[41]Caragounis, Mysterion, p. 1ff.

[42]Ibid., p. 13.

[43]Ibid., p. 11.

[44]See the relationship of the paragraph from 1 QS with Col. 1:12; Penna, Mysterion,
p. 67; cf. →Col. 1:9.

[45]Rabbinic documentation in Billerbeck III, 319f.

[46]Dahl, "Beobachtungen," p. 4f.; Penna, Mysterion, pp. 34f., 53f., 63–67; D. Lührmann, TDNT IX:5; Merklein, Amt, pp. 164–170.

[47]Penna, Mysterion, p. 87 et al.; Aletti, Colossiens, p. 136. The time code is relativized by Steinmetz, Heils-Zuversicht, p. 107; Lindemann, Aufhebung, pp. 74ff., 227.

[48]Gnilka, "Paulusbild," p. 186; against the curtailment of this universality of grace,
see Ewald (saints = apostles) or Hugédé (saints = the mature), cf. Penna, Mysterion,
p. 30f.

the entire church.[49] In order to emphasize the role of the apostles, the parallel in Eph. 3:5 (cf. Eph. 3:3) added that the apostles and prophets were the recipients of this revelation. It is part of their "office," however, to proclaim the mystery to all people.[50] "Now" indicates that the generations are to be understood temporally;[51] precisely this aspect places emphasis on the presentness of the character of revelation. In Colossians and Ephesians mystery is a comprehensive concept which views the gospel within the broader framework of the will of God (→1:9), which itself encompasses the entire created order (1:20; Eph. 1:10, 23).[52] In an indirect polemic with the opponents, the present proclamation of the gospel is characterized as the ultimate revelation, which is bound up with Christ.[53]

27 The correlation of the mystery with Jesus Christ is confirmed explicitly in v. 27: It is "Christ in you, the hope of glory." The phrase "in you" means "among you," as indicated by the parallel phrase "among the Gentiles," which refers to the recipients.[54] Consequently the recipients are "born from the dead" (1:18b),[55] in keeping with the argument of the letter (→2:12f.).

The statements about the riches of glory and the hope of glory (→1:11; Rom. 5:2) declare that they refer to the knowledge of the complete salvation and of its appropriation as personal perspective. The entire saying may be influenced by the reminiscence of Rom. 9:23.[56]

---

[49]The unity of the church, made up of Jews and Gentiles, as a result of the apostolic proclamation, is the specific concern of Eph.; cf. Rom. 11:25 and the par. to this reference in Eph. 3:5f. (6:11); Caragounis, Mysterion, pp. 139–142.

[50]Lührmann, Offenbarungsverständnis, p. 119ff. In apocalypticism seers and prophets communicate the mysteries to the community (1 Enoch 1:1ff.), cf. Penna, Mysterion, pp. 29, 79ff.

[51]The personified conception of aeons occurs in 1 Cor. 2:6f.

[52]Penna, Mysterion, p. 57ff. In Eph. it was developed as concept of the anakephalaiosis (recapitulatio; Eph. 1:10; Merklein, "Theologie," p. 28ff. In Col. and Eph. the future has only relative significance; Penna, Mysterion, p. 76ff.; emphasized by Lindemann, Aufhebung, p. 41.

[53]Zeilinger, Erstgeborene, p. 106ff. The term mystery refers to the gospel in several instances in the NT: Rom. 16:25, but also Mark 4:10–12ff.; on this see G. Haufe, "Erwägungen zum Ursprung der sog. Parabeltheorie Markus 4:11–12," EvTh 32 (1972), pp. 413–421. The mystery is construed differently by Schenk, "Christus," p. 147, who understands the revelation schema in Col. and Eph. to be in juxtaposition to the Pauline proclamation of Christ.

[54]Penna, Mysterion, p. 79f. W. P. Bowers' translation: " . . . to his saints, whom God willed to make known how rich the splendor of this mystery among the Gentiles" (in this case οἷς would have to be an accusative attracted to the dative of its antecedent) in "A Note on Colossians 1:27A," in Current Issues in Biblical and Patristic Interpretation, FS M. C. Tenney, ed. by G. F. Hawthorne, 1975, 110–114, founders on the circumstance that for Paul (and Col.) the community never is the immediate missionary.

[55]The Gk. aorist of "to make known" is hardly an aorist belonging to the style of the letter. The writer assumes that the mystery is a construct of the Pauline gospel which has already been preached, as is evident from 1:4–7; cf. note 53 above.

[56]Sanders, "Dependence," p. 39f.

Perhaps the elaborate style[57] is meant to express the riches of hope.[58]

28 There are conspicuous parallels for Col. 1:27–28 in Eph. 1:9, 18; 3:8, 9, 16, 17. What was expressed in the framework of intercession in 1:9 is here presented as apostolic function. Through his proclamation the apostle is to save others from the final judgment. Similar to 1:22, "to present" expresses the presentation before the judgment seat of God (cf. Rom. 14:10).[59] The apostolic witnesses again speak in the first person plural.[60] "In all wisdom" (on wisdom, see →1:9) refers to the manner of apostolic exhortation and instruction and not to their content.[61] Wisdom is the disposition in which one "fears God" (Ps. 111:10), inculcates God's judgment, and takes God's mystery to heart as the gospel (1:26; 2:3).

The frequency of expressions of communication (cf. 2:2) is perhaps intended as deliberate emphasis that the time of obscurity and silence[62] has passed. Everything focuses upon the climax of the gospel, upon the resurrection of Jesus, and upon reconciliation. Similar to the hymn in 1:15–20, the universality of salvation also corresponds with the universality of creation. The resultant discussion focuses upon the "mature (τέλειος) man." This is the "new man" (3:10) who lives with Christ (1:27) and who is able to stand in the final judgment (1:22; Eph. 6:18). Hence this adjective has been used in the early Christian paraenesis (Rom. 12:2; Jas. 1:4, 25; 3:2; Matt. 5:48 et al.). Love is the bond of perfection according to 3:14. Expressed differently, the mature person is the believer (cf. 4:12 with 1:23) for whom the integrity of lifestyle, including the confession of sins (2:13), is decisive. This, then, does not deal with ethical perfectionism. It is not impossible that the notion of "mature" played a part in the philosophy of the opponents.[63]

"In Christ" (cf. § 7) again points to the salvation procured by Christ ("Christ in you," 1:27), the scope (1:20) of which encompasses all of humanity[64] and is taken seriously in the church (1:27; 2:12; § 14).[65]

---

[57]"Riches" plus two genitives, "glory"–twice. For this reason p[46] omits the first "of the glory."

[58]A certain parallel to the emphasis of the riches (not to the style) is found in Rom. 11:33.

[59]Lohmeyer.

[60]Perhaps "we" also refers to the other coworkers here: →4:7–14: Gnilka.

[61]In this case a simple accusative would be more obvious; Peake et al.

[62]Cf. e.g., Mark 8:30; 9:30.

[63]Dibelius, on this cf. § 12 below.

[64]Cf. Neugebauer, In Christus, p. 148. H. L. Parisius, "Über die forensische Deutungsmöglichkeit des paulinischen ἐν Χριστῷ," ZNW 49 (1958), pp. 285–288, interprets it forensically in this instance, following the context; hence it is only by appropriating the apostolic teaching that passing God's judgment can be attained.

[65]Cf. Weiss, "Motive," p. 312f.; Usami, Comprehension, pp. 91–104.

29 This subsection is closed chiastically with a repeated presentation of the apostle's role. In contrast to 1:24 the work of the apostle here is depicted actively as labor (toil, 1 Thess. 2:9; 1 Cor. 4:12; 2 Thess. 3:8) and as struggle (or competition, cf. 2:1).[66] The sentence has a ring of modesty; it is Christ (v. 27) who works in Paul (again the writer speaks in the first person singular). But it is also an authoritative statement from the one who represents Christ (→1:24; Phil. 4:13f.).[67] The energy here is the power and authority of the resurrected Christ in which God's power of creation is reflected (→2:12, cf. Eph. 1:11; 3:7). It finds its expression in acknowledging and confessing him as Lord and in gaining new subjects through missions. Objectively he is the Lord of creation, which God will judge in reference to their relationship to him. The entire letter of Colossians underscores this with the deliberate use of Lord as title (→1:10f.).

2. Apostle and Recipients, 2:1–5

(1) For I want you to know how greatly I strive for you, and for those at Laodicea, and for all who have not seen my face, (2) that their hearts may be encouraged as they are knit together in love, to have all the riches of assured understanding and the knowledge of God's mystery, of Christ, (3) in whom are hid all the treasures of wisdom and knowledge. (4) I say this in order that no one may delude you with beguiling speech. (5) For though I am absent in body, yet I am with you in spirit, rejoicing to see your good order and the firmness of your faith in Christ.

This subsection also deals with the apostle who is striving, and equally prominent is the mystery that has been revealed and that is sufficiently worthy to be the goal of all wisdom and knowledge. New emphases are added, however. That which applies to the entire church is now brought to bear upon the recipients,[1] whose threat by the opponents is indicated for the first time in 2:4. Both opening and closure (thus again in chiastic form, as in 1:24–29) are concerned with the apostle. His striving (2:1, cf. 1:28; 1:24) also applies to those who do not know him personally (2:1, 5). Colossians 2:5 is a behavioral norm for the endangered Christian community.[2] Both the repeated ex-

---

[66]There is only an indirect reference to martyrdom in the words about the struggle; the same is said concerning Epaphras (4:12f.). Only through prayer is the community able to strive alongside, according to Rom. 15:30, cf. Phil. 1:27f. On the issue of the struggle in suffering, see Pfitzner, *Paul*, p. 110f.

[67]If anything similar can be said of the believers at all, God is described as the subject of the action, not Christ specifically: Phil. 2:13, cf. Col. 2:12.

---

[1]Consequently there are no explicit parallels in Eph. on this.

[2]Otherwise Hooker, "False Teachers," p. 325ff., who argues that the complete sufficiency of salvation in Jesus Christ is emphasized by means of merely theoretical alternatives.

planation of the apostle's struggle—which benefits the recipients—
and that of his presence in spirit—which his absence in person
(bodily, lit. "in the flesh") is not able to prevent—may signify that
the witness, the intellectual heritage of the apostle, is always in vogue
and leads to the goal of faith. Thus the epistle can also be read as
a testament of Paul, which becomes easier to explain if its deuteropauline origin is assumed. Otherwise it would be necessary to ask
why the communities living in the orderliness and stability of faith
are presented with a passionate polemic against a heresy, and how
it is possible that such people could be deceived by the false teachers
simply through the art of persuasion (cf. § 4 [a] and § 12).[3]

1 The apostle's struggle (→1:29)[4] concretely benefits the recipients
as well (→1:24). Those addressed are the Colossians, though the Laodiceans are also mentioned explicitly (on the issue of the recipients,
see § 4 [b]).[5] Whereas they do not know the apostle personally (lit.
by face[6]), Epaphras has already presented his spiritual countenance
to them (1:7), and it is also represented throughout this letter.

2 παρακαλεῖν means both "to exhort" and "to comfort." In this case
the notion of "comfort" or "encourage" is more likely in mind (cf.
4:8). In the OT the heart (לֵב) was the organ of the posture of the will
(see the "new heart," Ezek. 18:31) and of personhood (Ps. 22:27). The
Stoic conception was closely related to this.[7] The love (→1:4)[8] that
unites the recipients[9] is concretely their mutual love, as indicated in
3:14 where love is described as the bond of perfection. It is assumed
that this love has its premise in God's love for humanity (3:12). The
unity in love and the deeper knowledge of the gospel as the mystery
of God (→1:26) are closely associated with one another. While the recipients were already familiar with the gospel, because of the heresy
they are to understand God's riches, his fulness[10] (→1:9). This is possible only within the framework of the church in terms of community and in terms of the church as a whole (§ 14; cf. Rom. 12:3–8).[11]

---

[3]The section, therefore, has the features of a *vaticinium ex eventu*. See also Lindemann, "Paulusbild," p. 38ff.

[4]Striving characterizes the apostolic missionary work as a whole, cf. 1:29; 4:12; Pfitzner, *Agon*, p. 109f.

[5]Some of the later MSS add Hierapolis, obviously on the basis of Col. 4:13.

[6]ἐν σαρκί refers to the face, not to "having seen," cf. v. 5: τῇ σαρκὶ = personally
(in body).

[7]According to the Stoics, the logos arises from the heart—Diog. Laert. VII, 159.

[8]For a summary on the concept of agape, see G. Outka, *Agape*, New Haven/London,
1972.

[9]Sometimes συμβιβάζειν also denotes "to explain" (as Dibelius translates it here);
against this, see G. Delling, TDNT VII:763–765.

[10]πληροφορία actually means "full assurance," e.g., Heb. 6:11.

[11]Cf. E. Käsemann, "Ministry and Community in the New Testament," in *Essays on
New Testament Themes*, ET by W. J. Montague, London, 1964, pp. 63–94, esp. pp. 68ff.

The mystery, which is identical with the word of God according to 1:25f., is here given the rather awkward designation of the "mystery of God, of Christ."[12] The second genitive is appositive to "the mystery of God." The mystery of God (subj. gen., cf. 1:25) is Christ himself in the ultimate significance of his being and work (of Christ = obj. gen.), including his agency in creation and the "Christ in you" (1:27).[13]

3 Perhaps the concepts of understanding, knowledge, and wisdom (on this, see 1:9; 3:10) were significant for the opponents, since the author continually seeks to determine their content contextually. Wisdom (§ 9 [b, d]; →1:28) was preexistent in Greek-speaking Judaism (Prov. 8:22–31; Sir. 24; Wisd. 8:4); wisdom consists of being with God spiritually (Wisd. 8:3) and is concerned with salvation (Wisd. 9:18).[14] It was not long before some Christian groups applied the wisdom predicates to the resurrected Christ (Matt. 11:19b, par.). As "children" they praised God for revealing to them his mystery that remained hidden to the wise (Matt. 11:25f., par.).[15] Paul, too, maintains that Christian wisdom is different from the wisdom that the world knows. It is the salvific intention of God which comes to pass in the guise of the cross and of suffering (1 Cor. 2:7).[16] Similar to the logia source[17] and to hellenistic Judaism, Paul viewed the role of wisdom within the framework of the apocalyptic conception of revelation (→1:26; 1 Cor. 2:6–8); yet he emphasized an adherence to the witness of faith in this world at the same time. He stresses that the Resurrected One experienced human life and suffering, including the cross.

We encounter in Colossians a more synthetic perspective of wisdom. In the revelation of the wisdom of God, which begins with the proclamation of the gospel and culminates in baptism, the Christian already participates directly in the resurrection of Jesus (2:12f.; § 13). As a servant of Christ the apostle is at the same time a mystagogue who is able to initiate others into this mystery of the new life.[18]

The treasures, here, are the same as the true riches in v. 2, namely, that which is able to secure life,[19] the heavenly treasures guaranteed by God (cf. Matt. 6:19–21, par.).[20] For Jesus it was the kingdom of God

[12]Thus the oldest text witnesses p[46] and B. All the other readings can be explained as attempts to smooth out the older text (Metzger).

[13]Merklein, *Amt*, p. 211.

[14]U. Wilckens, *TDNT* VII:465–529, esp. 500f.

[15]Christ, *Jesus Sophia*, p. 83f.

[16]G. Sellin, "Das 'Geheimnis' der Weisheit und das Rätsel der 'Christuspartei,' (zu 1. Kor. 1–4)," *ZNW* 73 (1982), pp. 69–96.

[17]According to Matt. 11:16ff. Jesus is the wisdom of God; Christ, *Jesus Sophia*, p. 66.

[18]Schenk, "Christus," p. 147ff., has emphasized the contrast to Paul.

[19]It may be an allusion to Is. 45:3 (cf. Prov. 2:3).

[20]Perishable treasures of people are the opposite: Luke 12:13–21; *Gos. Thom.*, log. 63.

(Matt. 13:44), for Paul the gospel (2 Cor. 4:4–7), while in Colossians it is the gospel as hope that has been laid up (→1:5).[21] The hiddenness of the treasures means that there is no access to the mystery apart from faith. What is emphasized in 1:26 (cf. 2:2) as making manifest the mystery is here expressed in another way: That which is hidden can only be attained in Jesus Christ.[22]

4 The warning against seduction via the art of persuasion or rhetoric (πιθανολογία, cf. →2:8) is contrasted with the content of 2:2–3. The riches of knowledge and the inexhaustible treasures are juxtaposed by beguiling speech. This contrast intends to underscore just how foolish and fatal it could be to allow oneself to be persuaded (1 Cor. 2:4f.; Rom. 16:18).[23]

5 Concerning the role of the absent apostle who "sees" the community that is addressed, consult the introductory paragraph to this section. Steadfastness of faith plus order constitutes the ideal condition of the Pauline community, which is in accordance with the will of the apostolic patron. "Order" (τάξις), primarily a military term,[24] makes possible community, as well as resistance against heresy (cf. 1 Cor. 14:40; 1 Clem. 40–44).

The spirit through which the absent apostle is joined with the community is likely the Holy Spirit, not merely the person's inner self (cf. 1 Cor. 5:3).[25] The Spirit of God does indeed unite the church as the body of Christ (cf. 1:8; 1 Cor. 12:13).

The joy of the apostle serves as a chiastically constructed frame for segment 1:24–2:5, whose focal points are the statements concerning his suffering (1:29 and 2:1).[26] Thus this part of the letter also reflects — and anticipates — the argument of 2:12f. regarding the death and resurrection with Jesus Christ.

Now we are able to articulate how the author conceives of being with Christ in the post–Easter era: It consists of receiving the gospel by faith, of being integrated into the Christian community and its order (cf. 2:19), and of obeying the apostolic teaching passed on by his representatives. Since the argument of the letter (2:12f.) is a bold reformulation of the gospel as the mystery of God, its linking to the apostolic office and heritage must be emphasized.

---

[21]On understanding the treasures as wisdom, see Prov. 3:13ff.

[22]In conjunction with a similar revelatory schema, we read in 1 Pet. 1:12 that the revelation of Jesus Christ was also hidden from the angels.

[23]The numerous warnings against rhetoric indicate that this was a topic of the Christian paraenesis prior to Paul already.

[24]Documentation in Lohse.

[25]Contra Peake, Schweizer, Gnilka et al.; pro Dibelius, Schiwy, Lohse (the personal self which is linked up with the Holy Spirit, p. 131), Houlden et al.

[26]See Aletti, *Colossiens*, p. 19.

Part Three: Debate with the Opponents (Propositio and Probatio)—True and False Appropriation of Salvation, 2:6–23*

1. The Christian is Joined with the Risen Christ (Argument), 2:6–15

(6) As therefore you received Christ Jesus the Lord, so live in him, (7) rooted and built up in him and established in the faith, just as you were taught, abounding in thanksgiving.

(8) See to it that no one makes a prey of you by philosophy and empty deceit, according to human tradition, according to the elemental spirits of the universe, and not according to Christ. (9) For in him the whole fulness of deity dwells bodily, (10) and you have come to fulness of life in him, who is the head of all rule and authority. (11) In him also you were circumcised with a circumcision made without hands, by putting off the body of flesh in the circumcision of Christ; (12) and you were buried with him in baptism, in which you were also raised with him through faith in the working of God, who raised him from the dead. (13) And you, who were dead in trespasses and the uncircumcision of your flesh, God made alive together with him, having forgiven us all our trespasses, (14) having canceled the bond which stood against us with its legal demands; this he set aside, nailing it to the cross. (15) He disarmed the principalities and powers and made a public example of them, triumphing over them in him.

*On the parameters and status of Col. 2:6–23 in the framework of Colossians, see § 5 (b).

Bibliography: See esp. the respective sections in the commentaries and in the following works: Bandstra, Law; Bornkamm, "Heresy"; Hooker, "Teachers"; Lähnemann, Kolosserbrief; Reicke, "Setting"; Schenk, "Christus"; Schenke, "Christologie"; Schenke—Fischer, Einleitung; Schillebeeckx, Christus (full data in main bibliography). Otherwise (apart from the works cited in the notes to § 13) esp.: Beasley-Murray, G. R., "The Second Chapter of Colossians," RevExp 70 (1973), pp. 469–479; Betz, H. D., "Ein seltsames mysterientheologisches System bei Plutarch," in *Ex orbe religionum* I, FS G. Widengren, Studies in the History of Relig. Supp. to Numen 21, Leiden, 1972, pp. 347–354; Bieder, W., *Die Kolossische Irrlehre und die Kirche von heute*, ThSt 33, Zürich, 1952; Delling, G., *TDNT* VII:666–687; Dibelius, M., "The Isis Initiation in Apuleius and Related Initiatory Rites," ET in *Conflict at Colossae*, ed. F. O. Francis and W. A. Meeks, Missoula, 1975, pp. 30–79; Evans, C. A., "The Colossian Mystics," *Bib* 63 (1982), pp. 188–205; Francis, F. O. and W. A. Meeks, *Conflict at Colossae*, Sources for Biblical Study 4, Missoula, 1973; Francis, F. O., "Humility and Angelic Worship" (1962), most recently in Francis–Meeks, *Conflict* (see above), pp. 163–195; Grant R. M., "Les êtres intermediaires dans le judaisme tardif," in U. Bianchi, ed., *Origini dello Gnosticismo*, Leiden, 1967, pp. 141–154; Haardt, R., "Gnosis und Neues Testament," in J. Sint, ed., *Bibel und zeitgemässer Glaube*, Klosterneuburg, 1967, pp. 131–158; Kehl, N., "Erniedrigung und Erhöhung in Qumran und Kolossä," ZKTh 91 (1969), pp. 364–394; Lyonnet, S., "Paul's Adversaries in Colossae" (1956), most recently in Francis–Meeks, *Conflict* (see above), pp. 147–161; Nagel, P., ed., *Menschenbild in Gnosis und Manichäismus*, M. Luther Univ. Wiss. Beitr. 1979/39, Halle, 1979; Schenke, H. M., "Der Widerstreit gnostischer und kirchlicher Christologie im Spiegel des Kolosserbriefes," ZThK 61 (1964), pp. 391–403; Schweizer, E., "Die "Elemente der Welt" Gal. 4:3, 9; Kol. 2:8–20," most recently in E. Schweizer, *Beiträge zur Theologie des Neuen Testaments*, Zürich, 1970, pp. 147–163; Schmithals, W. *Neues Testament und Gnosis*, Darmstadt: Wissenschaftliche Buchgesellschaft, 1984; Szabó, A., "Die Engelvorstellungen vom Alten Testament bis zur Gnosis," in K. W. Tröger, ed., *Altes Testament – Frühjudentum – Gnosis*, Berlin and Gütersloh, 1980, pp. 143–152.

Only the key-phrase "steadfastness of faith" has been carried over from Part II; this also allows for the correlation with Part I (1:23), to which this pivotal section is linked in matters of content. The assumption is that Jesus Christ has the central position both in the entire created order and from the standpoint of human hope. The crux is how people relate to this, that is, how seriously Christians take their baptism. In 1:23 steadfastness of faith is discussed in the form of a conditional clause, here in terms of the summons (2:7). The entire third part has paraenetic features, framing the witness for the true faith and the argument against the heresy.

God himself is the initiator of salvation (cf. 1:3ff.), even though God does not emerge as the grammatical subject until 2:13, as the one who raised Jesus from the dead (2:12). He works through Jesus Christ; "in him" the fulness of God encounters men and women and establishes their new life (→2:11).

6 "Receive" (παραλαμβάνειν), which in a certain sense conforms to ל-ב-ק in the Rabbinic tradition (cf. 1 Cor. 11:23; 15:3),[1] refers to the Christian tradition which has taken on some established forms (cf.

---

[1]On the idea of tradition in Paul, see Wegenast, *Tradition*, p. 34f.; cf. Gnilka, p. 115f.

1:7).[2] In comparison to Gal. 5:25 (let us walk by the Spirit), this represents a shift in emphasis. It is possible that the Christian tradition is accented here as being in contrast to the tradition of the opponents (2:8).[3] The center of the Christian tradition in mind here is the acclamation "Jesus—the Lord"[4] (1 Cor. 12:3; Rom. 10:9), which is used in an expanded form here.[5] The title "Lord" (Kyrios) denotes that the exalted Jesus executes the authority of God (cf. Ps. 110:1 and Col. 3:1) and makes possible the new mode of life[6] in the sphere in which he rules (1:10).[7] The notion of passing on the individual regulations of the new life in the sense of paraenesis (3:5ff.) is hardly in mind here. Since the title Lord is linked with the exhortation in both instances (here and 1:10), we have to consider its paraenetic function in broader Christian circles.[8] Christian tradition as a whole is juxtaposed to the "human tradition" (2:8).

7 As a metaphor of the Christian community,[9] the building and the act of building were common in Paul (see οἰκοδομεῖν in 1 Thess. 5:11; 2 Cor. 10:8) and likely also for his enthusiastic opponents in Corinth.[10] This also applies to Colossians and Ephesians, where the discussion revolves especially around building on a given foundation (cf. 1 Cor. 3:10ff.) or around the continual connection with an existing building (→Col. 1:23; Eph. 2:20f.; 4:12, 16).[11] The image of growth is found frequently in both letters as well (Col. 1:6, 10; 2:19; Eph. 2:21; 4:13, 16). The beginning, the foundation, antedates the present phase of endurance and development. The foundation and "being rooted" correspond to being built up and to fruit-bearing in the present (1:6, 10). For the recipients the beginning is identical to their initial Christian instruction ("as you learned it," →1:7; 2:6) and is made acces-

---

[2]O'Brien, Thanksgivings, p. 101, points out that the introductory thanksgiving (1:1–8) signals several motifs which are developed further in the epistle (cf. e.g., 1:8 with 3:14).

[3]Schweizer, "Christus und Geist," p. 302; against this, Wegenast, Tradition, p. 128.

[4]Lohmeyer, p. 96f.

[5]Cf. the allusion in Phil. 2:11 or 2 Cor. 4:5; Eph. 3:4 where the title Christ is already augmented: Kramer, Christos, p. 217f.; contra Wegenast, Tradition, p. 126ff. The possible allusions to a catechetical schema of salvation history that we encounter in 3:1–4 support the assumption that the author was familiar with a broader tradition of the tradition of faith. On this, see Seeberg, Katechismus, p. 58ff.; against this, cf. the introduction by F. Hahn, p. xixff.

[6]On "leading a life worthy of the Lord" see →1:10, cf. the role of the title Kyrios in the paraenesis in 3:12–4:1; on the "in Christ," see →1:28.

[7]Wegenast, Tradition, p. 128, has recognized this motif correctly. This does not rule out, however, that it was linked with the tradition of the Kyrios acclamation.

[8]On the paraenetic context of the title Kyrios in Paul (1 Thess. 4:1; 5:12; Philem. 15f.), see Neugebauer, In Christus, p. 131ff. and § 16.

[9]Regarding "house" of Israel, see e.g., 1 QS 8.5 or 1 Enoch 53:6; re. "house of wisdom," see Prov. 9:1.

[10]1 Cor. 8:1; O. Michel, TDNT V:119–159, esp. p. 140.

[11]This may be an argument for the later origin of both letters; cf. Ph. Vielhauer, Oikodome, Karlsruhe, 1940, p. 102f.

sible by faith (instrumental dat.).[12] The instruction on steadfastness in faith refers to the tradition of Pauline theology (1:7; →4:7–14).

The summons to gratitude is apparently superfluous. For Paul the full measure (περισσεύειν) is a sign of the era of salvation made available in Christ.[13] When the author speaks of abounding in thanksgiving, he indicates (a) that the recipients may already take part in this era of salvation, according to the argument of 1:12f., but also (b) that their new life depends upon superabounding grace (2:13; Eph. 2:5f.), which has its counterpart, therefore, in the basic human disposition of thankfulness: →1:3; →1:12–14; 3:17; 4:2. This is part of the fundamental theological concerns of Colossians.[14] The opponents perhaps underestimated particularly this dimension of the Christian existence.[15]

8 A new paragraph begins here, commencing the polemic proper against the opponents. Formally it is one single pericope which extends to 2:15. What unfolds is a negative contrast to the ideal, thankful church community which is summarized in 2:5b.

"See to it" (βλέπετε) frequently introduces polemical arguments (in Paul e.g., Gal. 5:15; 1 Cor. 8:9; 10:12, 18; Phil. 3:2; otherwise e.g., Mark 13:5). The opponents are only indirectly referenced ("no one," μή τις); they are characterized by their teaching and their activity, which is compared to capturing and dragging away of prey (συλαγωγεῖν). This is identical to the deception and art of persuasion of 2:4 and to the description of the heresy as "empty deceit" (cf. Eph. 5:6),[16] which has the "appearance of truth" (2:23).

Otherwise the teaching of the opponents is described as philosophy (φιλοσοφία). This description has also been attached to religious persuasions and groups which were linked by means of common teaching or cultic practice (initiation). The Jewish faith, too, was described as philosophy (4 Macc. 5:4; Philo, Mut. 223, φιλοσοφεῖν). In Hermeticism philosophy was identical to the revealed teaching and was associated with magic (Exc. Stob. 23:68). Neither is this yet a negative label in Colossians; philosophy is only disqualified by its characteristics (capturing and empty deceit).[17] This reference cannot serve

---

[12]The analogous statement in 1:23 favors the interpretation as an instrumental dative (so e.g., Lightfoot, Schweizer); arguing in favor of the dative of respect and the understanding of faith as fides quae creditur, e.g., Peake and Gnilka.

[13]Gnilka, p. 117.

[14]Cf. Table 3. In the Pauline homologoumena only 2 Cor. 4:15 and 9:12 speak of abounding thanksgiving.

[15]The reading "abounding in it (i.e. in faith) in thanksgiving," attested in B and in some witnesses of the Western and Byzantine tradition, is influenced by the text of Col. 4:2 (Metzger).

[16]In Eph. 4:22 ἀπάτη more likely denotes self-deception in which sinful man lives, cf. Heb. 3:13.

[17]O. Michel, TDNT IX:172–188, esp. p. 185ff.

as evidence for the Christian tendency against methodological thought, although we cannot rule out that the negative characteristics of the opponents' teaching were influenced by the widespread disregard, at that time, for teachers of popular philosophical rhetoric. Their influence upon Paul and his disciples was only indirect;[18] they were aware of the potential misuse of philosophical rhetoric. From the comments about the opponents' teaching in 2:4 and 8 we are able to learn only that the opponents were probably trained in rhetoric. In order to determine the type of false teaching, we shall now attempt to evaluate the data of 2:8b, together with the polemic of 2:16–23, in a preliminary deliberation.

§12 Excursus: The Colossian "Philosophy"[19]

The polemic against the philosophy threatening the recipients is found in 2:4, 8, 16–23, while the section of Col. 2:9–15, which is presented positively, is also formulated with an indirect consideration of the heresy, as indicated by "for" (ὅτι) in 2:9 and by "therefore" (οὖν) in 2:16.

According to 2:8 the opposing teaching was derived from the elements of the world (στοιχεῖα τοῦ κοσμοῦ, also in 2:20). "Stoicheion" (basic meaning: that which belongs to a series) in the plural can denote elemental substances, fundamental principles,[20] the elements (often conceived of as living beings), or constellations, that is, heavenly bodies.[21] In Galatians, however, this designation is used not only for the pagan deities (Gal. 4:9) but also for the Jewish law with its stipulations (4:3f.).[22] This has led several interpreters to the hypothesis that the Colossian heretics were Jews or Judaizers.[23] In favor of this view is the mention of the sabbaths the opponents keep (2:16) and, indirectly, also the emphasis on a circumcision that is not external, in 2:1. While the veneration of angels (2:18) excludes an identifica-

---

[18]Bujard, Untersuchungen, p. 135f.; Reicke, "Setting," p. 438.

[19]On the supposition that they were no actual false teachers, see →2:1–5. Regarding bibliography for § 12, see notes on 2:6–23.

[20]In Heb. 5:12 stoicheia means basic doctrine or initial confession. Clement of Alexandria, Strom. VI, 62:3 gives the term this meaning in our reference as well. Thereby he endeavors to show the propaedeutic function of Greek philosophy.

[21]According to Delling, TDNT VII:675, 686f., the reference here is not to the heavenly beings because this meaning for stoicheia is not documented before the end of the first cent. CE.

[22]In Mark 7:9 the term tradition is used to denote the Jewish law.

[23]Alford, p. 38; Peake, p. 484; Percy, Probleme, p. 141; Masson; Lyonnet, "Adversaries," p. 151ff.; Houlden, pp. 128, 195; Zeilinger, Erstgeborene, pp. 26, 116ff. That this was a movement related to the Essenes, is argued by Kehl, "Erniedrigung," p. 392ff., and Evans, "Mystics," p. 204; so already Lightfoot, pp. 83–99, 384ff.

tion with the orthodox Jews, it could be interpreted in the sense of the visions of angels that were known to have occurred among the Essenes (1 QM 10.10f.). The Qumran texts also contain evidence of secret instruction concerning holy sabbaths and festivals which remain hidden to the rest of Israel (CD 3.14; 1 QS 9.26–10.8).[24] The opponents cannot be equated with the Essenes, however, since the Essenes followed a solar calendar,[25] which contradicts the reference to the new moons in 2:16.[26]

The heresy, then, must have been a syncretistic movement, whose description must begin with the data in Colossians.[27] We cannot demonstrate that "stoicheia"—elements of the world—was an expression used by the opponents themselves.[28] The author of Colossians may have characterized the opponents' piety thereby. The fact that Colossians is probably deuteropauline leads to the supposition that the choice of this expression (see also 2:20) was influenced by Gal. 4:3f., 9.[29] While "stoicheia" here does not refer to the Jewish law as in Gal. 4:3f., it does refer to realities or beings that, from the Christian perspective, stand between God and humanity, like the Jewish law, according to Gal. 3:19, and like the pagan deities (cf. Gal. 4:8f.; 1 Cor. 8:5f.). This is the common denominator of the elements of the world in Galatians and Colossians.[30] These designations are used functionally. This corresponds to the emphasis on the authority of the resurrected Christ over the heavenly principalities and powers in Col.

---

[24]On the parallels from Qumran, see Braun, p. 231f.

[25]Specifics in H. Braun, *Qumran und das Neue Testament* II, Tübingen, 1966, p. 47f.

[26]Caird, p. 162.

[27]On the method of reconstruction of the heresy, see Scott, pp. 7–9; Ernst, p. 218; Caird, p. 164; Martin (NCBC), p. 8. Schmithals presupposes that Colossians in its present form polemicizes against Gnosis and that the anti-Jewish overtones belong to an authentic Pauline layer (*Neues Testament und Gnosis*).

[28]On the interpretive possibilities, see Beasley-Murray, "Second Chapter," p. 471ff.; Ernst, p. 196f.

[29]Schenke–Fischer, *Einleitung* I, p. 160ff. This relativizes the argument of E. Schweizer, for whom stoicheia here denotes the four elements of the world (earth, water, air, fire), as venerated by the neo-Pythagoreans (on their characteristics, see M. Hengel, *Judaism and Hellenism*, ET J. Bowden, Philadelphia, 1981, p. 210f.); their teaching on the stoicheia is reflected in fragment 58B 1a of Diogenes (Diels I, p. 448f.; Schweizer, p. 132; idem, "Elemente," p. 160f.; idem, "Forschung," p. 178ff.; Delling, TDNT VII:684). Virgil also writes about the purification of the sinful souls in the netherworld, by water, air, and fire (*Aeneid* VI, 739–742, 747), as pointed out by T. F. Glasson, "Water, Wind and Fire (Luke 3:16) and Orphic Initiation," NTS 3 (1956–57), pp. 69–71. Schweizer (pp. 130–132) also points to the role of the elements of the world in the priestly prayers of Philo (*Spec. Leg.*, I, 97) and in the teaching on the elements sees the common background of the false teachers and of the hymn in Col. 1:15–20. Schweizer's argument is the most significant alternative to the interpretation of the history-of-religions background of Col. presented here.

[30]Cf. Ewald, p. 368; Haupt, p. 78; Weiss, "Law," p. 296f.; on the issue, see also Bandstra, *Law*, pp. 40, 69f.

2:8, 15 (cf. 1:16, 20; § 10).[31] The warning against angel worship (2:18) also fits this depiction. The phrase θρησκεία τῶν ἀγγέλων could point to a subjective genitive, and it might be concerned with the participation in the heavenly worship (cf. Rev. 4:4–11; 5:8–14; 11:16–19; Phil. 2:10f.; § 9 [d]);[32] but it is precisely the concern of Colossians to demonstrate that by faith the Christian already shares in the heavenly world, and in 2:18 the writer states explicitly that the believer is not obligated to serve angels (cf. 1:16; 2:15).

The false teachers would in all likelihood not say that they venerated angels. Neither is there any indication that they polemicized against faith in Christ, but they probably relativized it, and they surely considered their philosophy to be a higher venue to God. We hear that they seek to "disqualify" others and that they are puffed up (2:18). The recipients considered it possible to believe in Jesus Christ and adopt the "philosophy" at the same time. For this reason they are primarily exhorted to draw the correct conclusions from their faith (2:6, 16, 20; 3:1). We have to assume that the false teachers influenced a number, if not most house churches in the region addressed (→4:17).[33] Thus the false teachers did not (a) engage themselves as the Christians' opponents; they (b) considered their philosophy as a higher teaching that did not exclude faith in Christ; and their teaching (c) was associated with a cultic communication with superhuman beings that the writer describes as elements of the world, as intermediate authorities between God and the world.[34] The false teachers perhaps termed these heavenly powers (2:10; § 10).

In terms of the history of religions, Martin Dibelius located the Colossian heresy in the vicinity of the mystery religions, especially of the initiation of Isis (cf. Apul., Metam. XI).[35] The term "taking one's stand" (ἐμβατεύειν, 2:18) serves as starting point for this kind of interpretation; this term, among other things, can denote entering the sanctuary when an oracle is received or when a mystery initiation occurs[36] (Apul., Metam. XI, 23:5ff.). Apuleius also reports about the ascetic preparation for initiation (XI, 15:5; 19:1–3; 23:2, cf. →Col.

---

[31]Staab.

[32]Meyer, p. 318; Francis, "Humility," p. 179; idem, "Argument," p. 203f., with reference to 1 QSb 4.25ff.; Corp. Herm. I, 26 et al.

[33]On the related problem in the Johannine realm, see A. J. Malherbe, "The Inhospitality of Diotrephes," in J. Jervell and W. A. Meeks, eds., God's Christ and His People, FS N. A. Dahl, Oslo/Bergen/Tromsö, 1981, pp. 222–233.

[34]So e.g., already Soen, p. 45 and Haupt, p. 15.

[35]Dibelius, "Isis Initiation," passim; so also Hegermann, Schöpfungsmittler, pp. 163–165; Lohse, p. 189; Gnilka, p. 168; cf. Martin (NCBC), p. 5.

[36]Dibelius–Greeven, p. 35; Dibelius, "Isis Initiation," p. 63f. The evidence stems from the inscriptions of the Apollo sanctuary of Klaros, as e.g., παραλ[αβ]ὼν τὰ μυστήρι[α] ἐνεβάτευσεν, Th. Macridy, Jahreshefte des österr. arch. Inst. 15 (1912), p. 36ff., nr. 2, as cited by Dibelius, "Isis Initiation," p. 63.

2:18, 23; Plut., *Is. et Os.* 3, 352Aff.) and about the encounter with the gods of the netherworld and of heaven[37] in the framework of the cultic drama (XI, 23:8). The initiation culminates in voluntary death (cf. Col. 2:12f.) and in a rescue granted by grace (*precaria salus*, XI, 21:6, cf. XI, 23:8). The mystic is united with Osiris thereby, according to Plutarch (*Is. et Os.* 3, 352B).[38] These observations confirm the commonalities of the Colossian heresy with the conceptual world of the hellenistic mysteries[39] and of their endeavor to overcome the syncretistic crisis (cf. Apul., *Metam.* XI, 5).[40]

Yet these commonalities are still not sufficient to identify that philosophy with a mystery religion. Apart from ἐμβατεύειν, τέλειος, τελειότης (mature, perfection),[41] there are no specific terms from the language of the mysteries in Colossians, and even "taking one's stand" is not consistently linked with the mysteries in the documents mentioned.[42] In the polemic against a mystery community one would expect an attack against the deity of the mystery or at least an allusion to its name. This also applies to the identification of the heresy with heterodox Jewish groups which might revere Zeus Sabazios or Hypsistos (§ 4 [b]).[43] The mystery piety would be mingled with the observance of some commandments of the Mosaic law and the veneration of angels would not be ruled out.[44] There is no evidence for asceticism and fasting in that context, however (§ 4 [b]).[45]

[37]The initiate has passed through "all the elements" (XI, 23:8), see also the designation of Isis as "*elementorum domina*," XI, 5:1.

[38]Betz, "System," p. 352.

[39]Even though the apex of the Isis cult in the northern Mediterranean region does not come until the Imperial era, it was already known there in the hellenistic era: L. Vidman, *Isis und Sarapis bei den Griechen und Römern*, RGVV 29, Berlin, 1970, p. 48f.

[40]The heresy originated in the syncretistic environment in which, e.g., the heterodox Jews also participated in the mysteries, as might have been the case in the Lycus Valley (§ 4). This is emphasized correctly by Lähnemann, *Kolosserbrief*, p. 102f. However, it cannot be identified with the milieu in which it originated: Schweizer, "Forschung," p. 175; cf. Pokorný, *Epheserbrief*, p. 82ff.

[41]And that only in the writer's argumentation: 1:28; 3:14; 4:12. Besides, it is also an important concept in gnosticism.

[42]F. O. Francis, "The Background of ἐμβατεύω (Col 2:18) in Legal Papyri and Oracle Inscription," in Francis–Meeks, *Conflict*, pp. 197–207, stresses that it was used in the context of oracles. On the other hand, S. Lyonnet, "L'Epître aux Colossiens (Col 2:18) et les mystères d'Apollon Clarien," *Biblica* 43 (1962), pp. 417–435, argues that this concept from the language of the mysteries is used figuratively here. On the broad religious context of this concept, see S. Eitrem, "'EMBATEYΩ– Note sur Col. 2:18," *Studia theologica* 2 (1948), pp. 90–94.

[43]Nilsson, *Geschichte* II, pp. 657–667. As far as the Jewish part is concerned, Johnson, "Present State of Sabazios Research," pp. 1583–1613, see esp. p. 1608, is much more reticent.

[44]Bousset–Gressmann, *Religion*, p. 330f.

[45]If we take the opponents to be an apocalyptic group (see note 23 above), we have to understand the concepts from the realm of the mysteries in a figurative sense.

Elements of mystery piety and of Jewish conceptions are also combined in Gnosticism,[46] which is not unequivocally attested until the beginning of the second century, however, but which must have had its roots a few decades prior to the first documented evidence. The gnosis against which 1 Tim. 6:20 warns is obviously an earlier phase of the movement that later came to be known as Gnosticism.[47] For this reason several scholars have reconstructed the Colossian heresy with the aid of gnostic models.[48] Gnosticism not only contains elements of the otherwise opposite spheres of religion in late antiquity, but already links them with overlapping structures of thought in which the designation that describes the highest divine principle is relatively unimportant.[49] It appears from Col. 2:23 that the opponents understood their teaching as wisdom. The gnostics have adopted several ideas from the mysteries,[50] but their notion of the invisible, highest God ties into Jewish thought at the same time. From the OT the gnostics have borrowed some stories as well, but the creator was often identified with a lower emanation of the highest deity. Sometimes they also ascribe the creation of the visible world to an angel.[51] The gnostics treasured traditions which contained a mystery (Iren., Adv. haer. I, 25, 5; Hippol., Phil. V, 10, 2; NHC VI/6; 52:7); they also practiced ascetic abstinence (Iren., Adv. haer. I, 24, 2; Corp. Herm. I, 22). All of this would fit well with the data of Col. 1:26; 2:18, 23.[52] Formerly E. Th. Mayerhoff and F. C. Baur identified the Colossian heretics with the gnostics.[53] Despite their angelology,[54] however, we are not able

---

[46]Clearly arranged by K. W. Tröger, "Gnosis im Judentum," in K. W. Tröger, ed., Altes Testament—Frühjudentum—Gnosis, Berlin, 1980, pp. 155–168. We do not consider the question of origin.

[47]N. Brox, Die Pastoralbriefe, Regensburger NT 7/2, Lic. ed. (of the 4th ed.), Leipzig, 1975, p. 33f.

[48]Bornkamm, "Heresy," p. 130; Lohmeyer, p. 8; Souček, p. 8; Bieder, Irrlehre, p. 14ff., 56ff.; Kümmel, Introduction, p. 339; Pokorný, Epheserbrief, pp. 47, 82ff., 114; in part Lindemann, p. 84; cf. Mayerhoff, Colosser, p. 148ff.

[49]H. Jonas, Gnosis und spätantiker Geist I, Göttingen, 1954², p. 92ff.

[50]E.g., Epoptia as gnosis: Plut., de Iside 77, 382C (Betz, "System," pp. 347–352).

[51]E.g., Iren., Adv. haer. III, 2, 1ff.; Trac. Trip., NHC I/5; 112:35f.; Szabó, "Engelvorstellungen," p. 151. A detailed treatment of the origin of angels, demons and nature out of the will of the demiurge is given e.g., in the Ap. John, NHC II/1; 10:19–19:33; 29:16ff., cf. Gos. Eg., NHC III/2; 56:22ff.; see also Grant, "Les êtres," p. 145ff.

[52]The knowledge terminology (1:9f.; 2:2f.; 3:10) is influenced by Paul (e.g., 1 Cor. 8:1ff.) and is probably merely highlighted in the dispute with the heresy.

[53]Mayerhoff, Colosser, p. 148ff. (he thought of Cerinthus); Baur, Paul, p. 21ff.; H. Chadwick, " 'All Things to all Men,' " NTS 1 (1954–55), pp. 261–275, identifies the opponents with proto-Valentinianism. Besides, Gnosticism also adopted Pythagorean motifs: e.g., Hippol., Phil. IV 51, 9, 14 (Simon and Valentinus); B. Aland, "Gnosis und Philosophie," in Proceedings of the International Colloquium on Gnosticism, 1973, Stockholm/Leiden, 1977, pp. 34–75, on p. 42.

[54]Szabó, "Engelvorstellungen," p. 148ff.

to demonstrate that the gnostics esteemed and venerated angels.[55] In Jude 8 (cf. 2 Pet. 2:10) the heretics with gnostic taint[56] are accused of reviling the heavenly powers. This finds its correspondence in what we read in the *Second Treatise of the Great Seth* (NHC VII/2), in the framework of the gnostic critique of Christianity: Accordingly, the OT represents "teaching given by angels which was (merely) concerned with the observance of food (regulations)" (64:1–3).[57] According to these statements the writer of Colossians would be in closer proximity to the gnostics than the false teachers he is attacking. If we said, however, that the opponents felt superior to the recipients and that the veneration of angels, for them, was probably only an intermediate stage en route to salvation, "angels" could have had a negative function as well for them. They are obviously identical to the principalities and powers (§ 10), alienated from their mission (2:10, 15, cf. Eph. 6:12), which later gnostic texts identify as archons. They are creator and ruler of the visible world and enslave humanity. According to *Hypostasis of the Archons* (NHC II, 4) 92:29–32, Norea was forced into service by the archon-demiurge,[58] although she knew that there was a "holy God" above him.[59] Wisdom (cf. Col. 2:23), in the form of a benevolent angel, assists her in obtaining liberation. Hence the gnostics learned how to "disguise" oneself from the archons, that is, to participate in their cult and thus to avert their wrath.[60] According to Origen (*Comm. on Proverb.* II, 16; MPG 13:28f.), the worship of the demiurge, for the gnostics, was an intermediate stage on the way from the pagan veneration of idols to the unification with the highest deity, which was already linked with the rejection of the OT.[61] In this pursuit the observance of various regulations and the practice of asceticism facilitated the spiritual penetration of the spheres of the archons to the highest deity (cf. →Col. 2:16–23). The gnostic was thus able to prove his or her relationship with the highest deity in the presence of the archons (1 *Apoc. Jas.*, NHC V, 3; 33:2–34:20; *Asclepius*, NHC

[55]Haardt, "Gnosis und NT," p. 144. If the *Apoc. Adam*, NHC V/5; 65:20f., speaks of service rendered to the demiurge, for instance, it refers to man's enslavement to the power of the lower deity (Haardt, "Gnosis," p. 142).

[56]Vielhauer, *Geschichte*, p. 591.

[57]Translated by H.-G. Bethge and the Berlin team: *ThLZ* 100 (1975), pp. 97–110.

[58]See also NHC II/5; 112:33ff. and VII/2; 53:14–16.

[59]Schenke, "Widerstreit," (Bibliography on 1:15–20), p. 396f. Summary in Schenke–Fischer, *Einleitung* I, pp. 159–165. So also Käsemann, "Kolosserbrief," p. 1728.

[60]Schenke, "Widerstreit," p. 397.

[61]K. Koschorke, *Die Polemik der Gnostiker gegen das kirchliche Christentum*, N. H. Stud. 12, Leiden, 1978, p. 224. It is not impossible that the humility in Col. 2:18, too, had in mind the gnostic imitation of the temporary humiliation of the redeemer in the incarnation (Phil. 2:8); see the writing the gnostics used, *Teachings of Silvanus*, according to which Christ overcame the tyrannical superhuman powers by his humility; NHC VII/4; 110:24–111:4 (Schenke, "Christologie," p. 218ff.). It cannot be demonstrated, however, that these conceptions influenced the Colossian heretics.

VI, 8; 76:21–77:12; Iren., *Adv. haer.* I, 21, 5; Orig., *Contra Cels.* VI, 31, cf. *Gos. Thom.*, Log. 50).[62] Colossians, which emphasizes the perfection of salvation in Jesus Christ, calls this concern with the archons veneration of angels. It is to lead to the most sublime initiation. Essentially, however, this is a circumvention, and the opponents, therefore, are "puffed up without reason" (2:18). Pauline theology works itself out in this disposition relative to the association with intermediate beings; it has also experienced faith in Christ as liberation from the speculations about the heavenly beings (cf. 1 Cor. 8:5f.).

The background of the "veneration of angels" may also be found in the gnostic teaching of the aeons as spiritual reflections of the highest deity, whose light may also be reflected in the visible images within this creation (§ 10 [b], cf. 2 Cor. 4:6). Its reflection is only indirect and is thus only visible to the gnostics who are able to recognize that light even behind the mask of the material world (→2:21): Iren., *Adv. haer.* II, 14:3f. (cf. *Ps. Thom.* 1:10); *Gos. Thom.*, Log. 5, 22, 83, 84; *Trim. Prot.*, NHC XIII,1; 49:8–20 (accordingly the protennoia exists in disguise in all powers and angels). These conceptions cannot be demonstrated in all of the gnostic layers of tradition; all the evidence comes from a later time.[63] But in light of the speculations about the archons that are present in all the gnostic groups,[64] it is comprehensible how the gnostic attitude, viewed from the outside and critically, could be characterized as veneration of intermediate beings.

Thus the opponents did not attack faith in Jesus Christ,[65] rather they set it within the larger frame of their teaching. The polemic, therefore, focuses upon the consequences of faith, especially upon the understanding of baptism (2:11–13), the church (2:19ff.), and Christian lifestyle (3:1ff.). According to all this, the opponents considered Christ to be an intermediate being, which, though good in contrast to the other archons, was as a visible individual being only an indirect reflection of the divine principle. Only after the liberation from the body did he reach the higher life. A related model of liberation is found in the gnostic tomb inscription of Flavia Sophe (2nd cent. CE):

> . . . if you hasten to see the divine countenance
> of the aeons,

---

[62]Schenke, ("Widerstreit," p. 398) points to the Elchasaites who also revered evil days in order to attain true freedom (Hippol. *Phil.* IX, 16, 2f.), cf. also H. G. Bethge, "Anthropologie und Soteriologie im 2. *Log Seth* (NHC VII/2)," in Nagel, *Menschenbild*, pp. 161–171, esp. p. 166f. On the Mandaean ascent of the soul through the "watch houses" of the planets, see K. Rudolph, *Gnosis*, ET ed. by R. McL. Wilson, San Francisco, 1987, p. 187f.

[63]Cf. Weiss, "Motive," p. 313f.

[64]In the *Corp. Herm.* I, 11, 14f. it is the stoicheia that separate humans from the deity.

[65]Francis, "Argument," p. 203.

the great angel of the full council,[66]
the true son;
you came to the bridal chamber and, immortal,
you ascended
into the bosom of the Father.[67]

The gnostics prepare for such an ascent via asceticism and observance of the taboo regulations; for the sake of their perfection, the mystery of which they "beheld" during their initiation, they concern themselves with the superhuman archons.

On the whole we may depict the opponents as a movement that felt and grasped the basic problems of human existence in nature and history (using our contemporary terminology)—they were not superficial individuals, consumers, or intellectual consumers in the sense of the cultured hedonism of the Epicureans. They sensed and articulated the pressure of the superhuman powers (§ 10) as alienation. They searched for hope and were convinced that there was an invisible God in whom the contradictions of this world are abolished. This God was remote, however, and dwelt on high; only through mystical knowledge, asceticism, and fleeing from this world could he be reached. All of these movements weaken the relationship of their adherents to the world around them and lead to skepticism combined with an exclusive conviction of mission. Colossians combats this with its thesis, according to which the Christian attains the new life in baptism with Christ; no power is able to take it away (2:12ff.; § 13). The completion of salvation is anticipated in the social character of love within the concrete Christian community[68] (2:19; 3:12–15).

It follows from the model of the heresy just sketched that the alternative to the elements of the world as formulated in 2:8, namely, Christ, corresponds only with the opinion of the writer and not that of the opponents. It is a good Pauline alternative, however. Human tradition (cf. 2:22; Tit. 1:14) emphasizes the intermediate beings, combatting or pacifying them. Hence it focuses upon creation, upon that which is "human," upon the world, as the author of Colossians describes it.[69] The true faith is able to live freely (2:16) and to act objectively (3:12ff.), because it is linked with the resurrected Christ as reconciler and agent of creation. In contrast to Paul, Colossians here emphasizes that passing on the gospel (→2:6; →1:23) also has the shape of tradition.

[66]I.e., the redeemer.
[67]G. Quispel, "L'inscription de Flavia Sophé," in *Mélanges Jos. de Ghellinck* I, Museum Lessianum—hist. 13, Gembloux, 1951, pp. 201–214; translation by R. Haardt, *Die Gnosis*, Salzburg, 1967, p. 138; facsimile also in Rudolph, *Gnosis*, p. 212.
[68]Cf. Bieder, *Irrlehre*, p. 56f.; Weiss, "Motive," p. 314.
[69]Francis, "Argument," note 43.

The pericope of 2:9–15 contains several rhythmic and symmetrically constructed sentences (2:9–10, 12, 13, 14b–15) because there are allusions to the hymn and because the author adopts some older liturgical or catechetical word combinations (2:12, 13) or sentences (2:14f.).[70]

9 The reason for the alternative formulated in v. 8 is found in the following verse. Christian faith renders the speculations about the intermediate beings superfluous, because faith leads directly to the divine fulness.[71] The implication of taking the angels and principalities as seriously as the false teachers is to not take seriously God, the Father of Jesus (cf. the argumentation in Gal. 5:2). Colossians 2:9, therefore, is a paraphrase of 1:19, which is directed against the heretics. Since the *pleroma* per se [72] in 1:9 already denotes the divine fulness, the augment "of deity" (τῆς θεότητος) obviously is an epexegetical genitive,[73] which may allude polemically to the designation of the highest deity on the part of the opponents. Accordingly, the Christian is linked with the goal of a journey begun in baptism.[74]

The oneness of Christ with the fulness was dealt with in the past tense in 1:19, whereas the present tense is used here. The more specific designation "bodily" as reference to the incarnation would be more fitting if the aorist were used in the hymn.[75] Christ's present "bodiliness" is a problem. The author may well (a) have had the incarnation in mind. The question of "when" the unification occurred is not posed here; the Risen One remains identified with the temporal;[76] the incarnation as an event is part of the revelation of God as well.[77] These notions may be echoing here, for it is clear that certain expressions occur, both in 1:13 and 1:19, that are related to the language of the pericope of the baptism of Jesus (Mark 1:9–11, par.)

[70]Schille, *Hymnen*, pp. 31, 43, suspects a hymn here which consists of vv. 9, 10b, 11b, 14, 15. But vv. 9 and 10 are dependent upon the hymn of 1:15–20.

[71]That fullness was one of the opponents' concepts of God (so Lähnemann, *Kolosserbrief*, p. 46, note 78) cannot be demonstrated, because this concept is not borrowed from the opponents in this instance but is carried over from the hymn; Burger, *Schöpfung*, p. 112f.

[72]Since the term pleroma in 1:19 is used without further addition, it is clear that even the term itself is capable of designating the "fullness of God." It does not have to be the pleroma in terms of the later gnostic teachings with which we are familiar (e.g., Iren., *Adv. haer.* III, 11, 1—Cerinthus; I, 2, 5f.—Valentinus).

[73]Ernst, *Pleroma*, p. 100; Hugédé, p. 119; against this, P. D. Overfield, "Pleroma: A Study in Content and Context," NTS 25 (1978–79), pp. 384–396, esp. p. 392.

[74]Schweizer. It is not impossible that the opponents viewed Jesus Christ as merely a partial revelation of God, cf. Lähnemann, *Kolosserbrief*, p. 117.

[75]That this was a term the opponents used (so Lähnemann, *Kolosserbrief*, p. 117) cannot be demonstrated.

[76]Lightfoot, Souček, Moule, Houlden, Bratcher–Nida, Martin, Gnilka (in part).

[77]Schweizer, p. 138, cf. A. Anwander, "Zu Kol. 2:9," BZ 9 (NF) (1965), pp. 278–280.

in which the Holy Spirit was united with the earthly Jesus.[78] Here, however, the emphasis is on the current bodiliness. (b) For this reason several interpreters think of the spiritual resurrection body as that part of the new creation of which Paul speaks (1 Cor. 15:44; Phil. 3:21).[79] They have recognized correctly that it is not the objective physicality that is emphasized, but the person of Jesus; σωματικῶς may also mean "personal."[80] But the importance of Jesus is already emphasized in the hymn (1:19), and "bodily" is likely intended to say more than that. (c) Analogous to the addition in →1:18, where the body is described more specifically as the church, it may also point to the attainability of God in the body of the church (→1:24; 2:19; § 15), whose head rules the new creation (→2:10b).[81] This is a significant relationship that emerges clearly in the following verse and that may also have influenced the choice of the term "bodily" in this verse; yet the adverb does not refer to the church directly, since Christ is here described as head and not as body (2:10).[82] (d) The concept *soma* has a further meaning that comes to light especially in →2:17. *Soma* is also the archetype (→1:15), the reality in contrast to the shadow and copy.[83] This is the most probable meaning here, given the framework of the interpretation of 2:19. In Christ one encounters the true, authentic fulness of God, over against which all other conceptions of God, speculations, and experiences are secondary. The application of the term *soma* in its differing meanings is to demonstrate the consequences of this expression in the following discussion (putting off the old body of flesh, 2:11; Christ as the head of the body, the church). The manner in which the significance of Christ is expressed may indeed be described as metaphysical, though in its effect it has closer ties to the Pauline interpretation of the gospel as the message of justification or reconciliation (§ 4 [a]): Through Christ,

[78]Münderlein, "Erwählung," (Biblio. on 1:15–20); Aletti, *Colossiens*, pp. 105, 133f.; on the exegesis, see Burger, *Schöpfung*, p. 87f. According to Luke 3:22 it came to pass by the Holy Spirit taking on the "bodily" form of a dove. The hypothesis of W. Schenk, according to which Jesus was already exalted in his baptism, so that his resurrection was merely the unveiling of his earlier state ("Christus," p. 150f.), is weakened by the indirectness of the argumentation. In keeping with the argument (→2:12f.), the baptism of believers, as "being baptized along with," is not only described as being raised with, but as death and resurrection with Christ.

[79]Meyer; Alford; Ernst, p. 200; Schweizer. In this case the "body of flesh" (1:22; 2:11) would be in juxtaposition to the bodily divinity.

[80]Oltramare; cf. K. Grobel, "Σῶμα as 'Self, Person' in the Septuagint," in *Neutestamentliche Studien für R. Bultmann*, BZNW 21, Berlin, 1954, pp. 52–59.

[81]Peake; Bornkamm, "Heresy," pp. 129ff.; Lohmeyer, cf. Käsemann, "Baptismal Liturgy," p. 158f.; TOB; Gnilka; on the history of this interpretation, see Schweizer, p. 273.

[82]Jervell, *Imago*, p. 223; cf. Burger, *Schöpfung*, p. 88f.

[83]Jervell, *Imago*, p. 224. Elsewhere too, σωματικῶς often denotes "real." So Kralice, Haupt; Dibelius–Greeven; Neugebauer, *In Christus*, p. 178; Lohse; Caird.

salvation and completion of the human life (2:10a) are thereby directly linked to God as creator and reason for being.[84]

10 The climax of the statement in 2:9 comes in this verse: The encounter with Christ signifies that one attains the goal of human life and striving. Through Christ ("in him . . .") the Christian community (the plural refers to the recipients; →1:12; 4:16) is filled (πληροῦν is a play on words with πλήρωμα, 2:9) with the gifts of God (cf. Rom. 15:13).[85] This does not mean, however, that the community or individual Christian lives are also one with the fulness.[86] They reach their completion when they are submitted as community to Christ as their head. Then they are not lacking in anything, for he is able to bring their life to its destination.[87] That which is formulated as a desire in Paul (Rom. 15:13; Phil. 1:10f.; 4:19) is here proclaimed[88] as reality[89] (cf. 2:12f.).

The divine dignity of Jesus Christ denotes that he is superior to the superhuman principalities and powers (→1:16, 18—the reference is again to the hymn).[90] In contrast to the original disposition of the hymn (§ 9 [a]), the writer reckons with two kinds of authority of Christ. He is the head (in terms of "Lord") of the principalities and authorities that are subject to him as the bearer of their original destiny and as their judge (2:10, cf. Phil. 2:10f.), and he is the head of the church that serves him as his body and professes him (→2:19; →1:18a; § 14).[91] The conception of the twofold authority plays a significant role in Eph. 1:20–23.

Colossians 2:11 begins a subsection that continues to 2:15, where the witness concerning the true appropriation of salvation culminates in it. There we also find the argument of the entire letter (2:12f.). We receive a more detailed explanation of what it means for a Christian to be "filled" with Christ (2:10a) and of what the foundation is upon which one is able to build hope in the face of the threat of the supraindividual powers.[92]

11 It is assumed in 1:12 that the recipients are already baptized, but that they obviously did not draw the correct conclusions from their baptism is mentioned explicitly in 2:12. The opponents were probably also baptized, but they did not treasure it as much as they did their special initiation (→2:18; § 12).

[84]See Lohmeyer, p. 106.
[85]Bujard, *Untersuchungen*, p. 188.
[86]So Chrysostom (MPG 62, 339f.); in this case the text would have to say: "Through it you are filled in him" (Alford), or at least "you too are filled in him" (Haupt).
[87]Haupt.
[88]On this, cf. Schweizer.
[89]The context disallows us taking ἐστὲ imperatively.
[90]On the superior position of the head in general, see e.g., 1 Cor. 11:3.
[91]Zeilinger, *Erstgeborene*, pp. 174f., 202f.
[92]Cf. Burger, *Schöpfung*, p. 91f.

To begin with, the writer explains that baptism is the true circumcision. That was not self-evident. Baptism was not introduced as a
replacement for circumcision, and it is not common in the NT to com-
pare it with circumcision. The alternative of circumcision or faith in
Christ, which Paul formulated in Gal. 5:2, was only relevant to Gentile Christians. On the other hand, at the time of writing Colossians,
baptism as an initiation rite de facto replaced Jewish circumcision.[93]
We do not know whether the references to circumcision are pointing
to the practice of the opponents. Circumcision was not typical for the
gnostics, yet there were judaizing gnostic groups (Iren., *Adv. haer.*
I, 26, 2, cf. §§ 4 [b] and 12),[94] and it would conform with the other
Jewish elements of the heresy (2:16). The primary intent of the statement concerning the spiritual circumcision, however, is the prophetic
proclamation of the eschatological situation, of the new age, in which
the circumcision that is "not external," literally "not made by hand"
(cf. ἀχειροποίητος in Mark 14:58; 2 Cor. 5:1; by contrast χειροποίητος
e.g., in Eph. 2:11, concerning the pagan idols, LXX Lev. 26:1; Judg. 8:18
et al.)—the circumcision of the heart—is a sign of belonging to the
people of God (Ezek. 44:7, 9; Jub. 1:23; Odes Sol. 11:1-3).[95] In Rom.
2:27-29 and Phil. 3:3 Paul writes about the spiritual circumcision, and
in the *Gospel of Thomas* a logion of Jesus concerning spiritual circumcision is handed down (Log. 53).[96] Its authenticity is question-
able, but it does attest to the dissemination of that conception. The
distribution or expectation of the gift of the Spirit has been associated with baptism from the beginning (1 Cor. 6:11; 12:13; Eph. 1:13;
4:5, cf. Ezek. 36:25f.). The Johannine call for a rebirth of water and
the Spirit (John 3:5f.), then, is meant to renew, in a certain sense, the
original significance of baptism. Baptism is interpreted in Col. 2:11f.
as spiritual circumcision that signifies participation in the new age.
In view of this, the "circumcision of Christ" should not be taken as
an objective genitive, that is as an allusion to the circumcision of Jesus
following his birth (Luke 2:21) or, in a transferred sense, as an allusion to the suffering placed upon him or to his death.[97] All of this
is presupposed in spiritual circumcision; yet the death of Jesus has

[93]Only very indirectly is this an argument for infant baptism, cf. Dibelius–Greeven.
The reference to the circumcision in 3:11 which appears to support the presence of
Jewish Christians among the recipients is general in its tenor; it is an echo of Pauline
statements such as Gal. 5:6; 6:15.

[94]Lohse, p. 153, note 1; Lindemann, p. 41; Burger, *Schöpfung*, p. 93ff.; further evidence is offered in Klijn–Reinink, *Sects*, see "circumcision" in index.

[95]On the spiritual uncircumcision, see 1 QS 5.5.

[96]Cf. Philo, *Spec. Leg.* I, 8ff., where outward circumcision effects the knowledge of
one's own impotence before God.

[97]So Moule, Masson; Lohmeyer, p. 109; Lähnemann, *Kolosserbrief*, p. 122; Burger,
Schöpfung, p. 94f.

never been understood as circumcision, though the notion of participation in the fate of Jesus, on the part of the baptized, is in the background in 2:12f.[98] The "circumcision of Christ" is a genitive of
quality,[99] because Christ is the new Lord of the person baptized in
his name. The circumcision of Christ as the putting off of the earthly
body (of the "body of flesh" →1:22)[100] is identical with the forgiveness of sins (2:13); for humanity it denotes the change of mastery
(1:12f.). The "circumcision of Christ" surpasses physical circumcision, which removes only a minute part of the body.[101] Because Christ
reconciled humankind with God through the death of his earthly body
(1:22), they may receive the spiritual circumcision, which brings about
the condition of the new life in the midst of this mortal life.[102] This
new life is already prepared "in heaven" (1:5; 2:12f.; 3:3f.). At this
juncture the relationship between the three meanings of the term sōma
becomes evident: Because Christ is to be attained as the true
("bodily") fulness of God (2:10, 17) in the body of the church (2:19),
it is possible for one to take off[103] the mortal "body of flesh" (cf. Rom.
6:6; flesh used negatively in Col. 2:18; Eph. 2:3).[104] The result of it
is "living in Jesus Christ" (2:6). The fact that the foundation is "in
him," that is, "in Christ," is repeated in this section (2:6, 9, 10, 11,
15). According to Colossians the fulness of God is focused in Christ,
to whom the superhuman powers are subject (2:15); so is the salvation
of human beings (2:10–13), as well as the new destinies of their lives
(2:6).[105]

[98]In the mysteries participation in the fate of the deity was characteristic. In the Isis
mysteries the myste also had to change clothes ritually (Apul., Metam. XI, 23f.). Here,
as well as already in Rom. 6, this conception may be used, perhaps in polemic consideration of the faith of the mysteries. The mystical initiation as abandoning the physical
body and as aligning with the logos is described in Corp. Herm. XIII, 3ff.

[99]Ewald; Gnilka, p. 132, esp. note 70.

[100]The body of flesh of the godless priests is given this meaning in 1 QpHab 9.2.
There is no correlation with circumcision, however.

[101]Beasley-Murray, "Second Chapter," (Biblio. on § 12), p. 474.

[102]So Beare; Souček; Hugédé; Lohse, p. 154f.; Ernst; Caird; Schweizer; Burger,
Schöpfung, pp. 91–93; Gnilka, p. 131f.

[103]Cf. 3:9. In the back of it there is the notion that the body is also associated with
the eschatological being as the realm of human identity and of a person's communication with others (sight, address, encounter): 1 Cor. 15:33ff.; 2 Cor. 5:1ff., cf.
P. Pokorný, Die Hoffnung auf das ewige Leben im Spätjudentum und Urchristentum,
AVThR 70, Berlin, 1978, pp. 26–30. On the image of putting off clothes, see →3:8.

[104]τοῦ σώματος τῆς σαρκός – p[46], ℵ*, A, B, C, D* et al.; after σώματος the majority
text adds essentially correctly τῶν ἁμαρτιῶν; cf. →3:5ff.; →3:9.

[105]Putting off the body of flesh, therefore, is not an escape from the social context
of the world which Jesus allegedly realized, according to some later Christian-gnostic
view points (e.g., Iren., Adv. haer. I, 24, 4). The more detailed specification (of flesh,
see note 103 above), the endeavor to make concrete in 3:5ff. and the par. in Eph. 4:20–32
render it impossible that the gnostic meaning had been intended (see note 98 above);
for a different view, see Schenke, "Christologie," p. 222f., and a critical response e.g.,
by Caird, p. 193.

2:12–13 The following two verses, in our opinion, contain the argument of the entire epistle (§ 5 [b]) that dominates the argumentation up to 3:17 (see Table 3) and that is anticipated by the discussion about the "elements of the world" in 2:6–11. Actually the argument is a new formulation of the mystery which is the same as the gospel (→1:26). It is noteworthy that the gospel occurs in its foundational structure as the message of the resurrection at precisely this point. The argument is formulated in two distinct, theologically nuanced forms:

2:12 (old life, then death) — burial — resurrection

2:13 (old life as) being dead — forgiveness as new life (cf. 3:1, 3 and Eph. 2:1–6)

Externally Col. 2:12f. may be viewed as a compilation of Rom. 6:4; 4:24 (Col. 2:12) and Gal. 1:1; Rom. 6:11; 8:32 (Col. 2:13).[106] However, the author himself formulated the phrases "you . . . were raised" and "you . . . were . . . made alive" and thereby shifted the emphasis to salvation as being present. In this manner he sought to emphasize the sufficiency of salvation in Jesus Christ and to free the recipients from the fear that the superhuman powers might one day block the way to salvation for them.[107] We are dealing with a new development of the Pauline heritage, but it is a legitimate development, not merely a superficial dependence.[108] This, however, has to be demonstrated from the history of religions, as well as theologically.

§13 The Argument of this Letter (2:12–13)[109]

The Pauline text upon which the argument appears most to depend is Rom. 6:3–9. Twice in Rom. 6:4f. (2 Tim. 2:11) we encounter a two-part statement in which the resurrection of Jesus is linked with his death and burial. The similar structure of the statement in Col. 2:12 and the verb ἐγείρειν (raise up), occurring only here and in Eph. 1:20 in Colossians and Ephesians, reveal that the argument does indeed contain the kerygma of the resurrection, namely, in a form also found in the faith formula in 1 Cor. 15:3b–5; cf. Rom. 8:34; 1 Thess. 4:14; Rom. 14:9, the short form which does not mention the burial.

Likewise the notion that baptism points to the death and resurrection of Jesus (1 Cor. 15:29;[110] 1 Pet. 3:18–20; Eph. 5:14) is older than

---

[106]Sanders, "Dependence," p. 40f.

[107]Schweizer.

[108]That it is merely an external association is argued e.g., by Schenk, "Christus," p. 138f.

[109]On this issue, see esp. Merklein, "Theologie," pp. 40–53.

[110]More details in Wagner, Röm. 6, p. 269ff. In this connection it is important for us that baptism there is associated with the resurrection.

Rom. 6.[111] It is unlikely, however, that Paul was the first one to interpret this understanding by means of "with Christ."[112] He also refers to dying and to the new life to come with Jesus Christ outside the baptismal context: Rom. 7:4; 2 Cor. 4:14f., cf. 5:14f.; Gal. 2:19; 5:24; 6:14; Phil. 3:10f.[113] In contrast to "in Christ" or "in the Lord"–expressions used with reference to the present faith or in the paraenesis (→1:28, cf. →2:6)–"with Christ" generally refers to the eschatological completion of salvation.[114] By means of this expression Paul articulated the soteriological importance of the history of Jesus (cf. 2 Cor. 5:14).[115] According to Rom. 6, dying with Christ has two ramifications: (a) It provides the reason for the endeavor regarding new life in this world (Rom. 6:4, 6, 11, 13) and (b) it substantiates the hope of the future resurrection of believers (Rom. 6:5, 8; 10:9). The former ramification is already established e.g., in Gal. 2:20; Rom. 7:4b; 2 Cor. 5:15, cf. 1 Pet. 1:3–5. Hence the resurrection of Jesus Christ already in the present makes possible the potential for new life within this world.[116] It may be that Rom. 6 et al. are formulated with reference to some of the mysteries, surpassing and correcting these, but the main concern is defending the Pauline teaching of justification (§ 4 [a]). The liberation from the superhuman powers that takes place in baptism also signifies freedom from the fateful destiny caused by sin and by its consequence, death. In Rom. 6 the death of Jesus is not a mythical model

---

[111]Siber, Mit Christus, p. 191ff.; J. A. T. Robinson, "The One Baptism," most recently in J. A. T. Robinson, Twelve New Testament Studies, SBT 34, London, 1962, pp. 158–175, argues that the death of Jesus was perceived as the all-inclusive baptism for all humanity, in which the individual participates through baptism. The occasional description of the death of Jesus as baptism (Mark 10:38, par.), however, is not relevant for the understanding of baptism. Baptism is the actualization and in some sense also the appropriation of salvation, but not salvation itself.

[112]So Siber, Mit Christus, pp. 197f., 204f.; F. Hahn, "Die Taufe im Neuen Testament," in Calwer Predigthilfen: Taufe, Stuttgart, 1976, pp. 9–28, esp. pp. 17–19; Wagner, Röm. 6, p. 304; Frankemölle, Taufverständnis, pp. 26–30, 40. The phrase "with the Messiah" has been taken from apocalyptic thought (1 Enoch 62:14; 1 Thess. 4:14, 17; E. Schweizer, " 'Mystik,' " pp. 183f., 190–192.

[113]Siber, Mit Christus, p. 222.

[114]Dibelius–Greeven, p. 40.

[115]E. Schweizer, " 'Mystik,' " p. 195.

[116]A direct polemic against a mystery of the dying and rising deity (so H. Braun, "Das 'Stirb und werde' in der Antike und im Neuen Testament," most recently in idem, Gesammelte Studien zum Neuen Testament und seiner Umwelt, Tübingen, 1967², pp. 136–158, esp. p. 152ff.) is not to be expected in Rom. 6 (Wagner, Röm. 6, p. 271ff.; B. M. Metzger, "Consideration of Methodology in the Study of the Mystery Religions and Early Christianity," most recently in idem, Historical and Literary Studies, NTTS 9, Leiden, 1968, pp. 1–24); we do not find an explicit belief in the resurrection in the mysteries nevertheless the nucleus of the belief in immortality is already contained in the hope derived from the union with the dying deity (e.g., Ovid, Fasti V, 225ff.). Dying may denote the dénouement in a higher principle, cf. Pokorný, Epheserbrief, pp. 84f., 96f.

of the fate of the initiates.[117] The subject of the event is not an immanent force but God ("you were raised with him . . . you . . . God made alive together with him").[118] It is an event with substitutionary significance (→2:11);[119] the with-Christ statements are anchored in the interpretation of his death as substitutionary. Jesus' obedience as the Son of God and as the new Adam culminates in his death, and by means of his reinstatement in the resurrection the condition of all people changes (cf. 2 Cor. 5:15).[120] Now everyone is able personally to appropriate salvation by faith[121] and to begin a new life in light of the righteousness of God (Rom. 6:17–7:6). Through baptism the believer is drawn into God's eschatological act of redemption.[122] Romans 6, then, interprets the soteriological "for us" of the older formulations of dying and surrendering (Rom. 5:6, 8; 1 Pet. 2:21; 1 John 3:16 et al.). Paul underscored humanity's dying and being raised with Christ only in order to point out the inclusiveness of the "for us."[123] Hence the twofold consequence of the substitutionary death of Christ: The certainty of the believers' future resurrection and the call to faithfulness which is applicable to all of their earthly life.

In Colossians the second ramification corresponds with the appeal in 3:1b–2, but the first ramification is modified conspicuously in 2:12f.

[117]Differently in M. D. Hooker, "Interchange and Suffering," in W. Horburg and B. McNeil, eds., *Suffering and Martyrdom in the New Testament*, Cambridge, 1981, pp. 70–83, esp. p. 77; against this, see →1:24.

[118]Ernst, p. 203f.; cf. Tannehill, *Dying*, p. 71ff.

[119]Frankemölle, *Taufverständnis*, p. 107.

[120]Schweizer, " 'Mystik,' " p. 197ff. In his later short commentary on Romans, Karl Barth explained the manner of the Christian's participation in the death and resurrection of Christ as follows: "This means that we have a death behind us, our own death inasmuch as our life has been our life in . . . sin. And we have a life before us which will in any case no longer be that life depleted by death. Man lives in this present . . . and this is his sanctification. But what kind of present is that? Paul replies that it is the present life of the man who has been baptized in the name of Jesus Christ. His past, his origin is simply that (as his baptism testifies) he has been received into fellowship with Jesus Christ. And therefore all that which happened in Jesus Christ once and for all for all mankind now also applies to him, now also profits him," *A Shorter Commentary on Romans*, ET by D. H. van Daalen, London, 1963², p. 68.

[121]So Paul. G. Delling, *Die Zueignung des Heils in der Taufe*, Berlin, 1961, esp. p. 97, argues that this was part of the essence of baptism from the start, cf. Tannehill, *Dying*, pp. 73f., 125; K.-A. Bauer, *Leiblichkeit das Ende aller Werke Gottes. Bedeutung der Leiblichkeit des Menschen bei Paulus*, StNT 4, Gütersloh, 1971, p. 150: "In baptism the death of Christ in its universal effect enters the individual life on a specific date."

[122]Wagner, *Röm. 6*, p. 303; cf. already Bornkamm, "Baptism," p. 74ff. Being "drawn in" is depicted in the baptismal rite (immersion—ascent from the water). The baptisand is able to join in this experience (A. Nygren, *Commentary on Romans*, ET by C. Rasmussen, Philadelphia, 1967⁹, p. 233f.), but the crucial aspect is the history of Jesus as the foundation. In Mark 16:6, par., the young man in the white garment of a neophyte who proclaims the resurrection at the empty tomb is directly affected by the whole event but has had no part in the execution of the event because he is the messenger.

[123]Cf. E. Jüngel, "Das Geheimnis der Stellvertretung," ZdZ 37 (1983), pp. 16–23, esp. p. 22.

(3:1a; Eph. 2:1–6; see also § 3), when compared with Rom. 6:[124] "You were buried with him in baptism, in which you were also raised with him . . . you were dead . . . made alive." The eschatological proviso is cancelled or at least diminished,[125] salvation is moved into the present, the significance of death is relativized.[126] With this the writer ties into the hymn: The fulness of God dwells in Christ (1:19; 2:9), and Christians, therefore, are already "filled" (2:10; 1:24); they have redemption "in him" (1:14). Paul defends himself against the charge that his teaching of justification leads to ethical libertinism in Rom. 6 (6:1). The emphasis of the eschatological proviso serves to substantiate more adequately the new ethical orientation of Christians (6:15ff.): We have not arrived at our destination yet. In order to ward off the heretics, however, Colossians emphasizes the sufficiency of salvation in Jesus Christ, the significance of which the heretics relativized (2:18; § 12).[127] We have discovered a similar shift in emphasis in the conception of hope over against the Pauline homologoumena (→1:3f.; Tit. 2:13). An interpretation of the gospel of this type not only modifies the anticipation of the eschatological resurrection still prominent in Paul in 1 Thess. 4,[128] it also relativizes physical death on the whole. In earliest Christian theology, however, they were not fragmented. In John 5:24f. (cf. 11, 16) genuine Christian faith is characterized as overcoming death and as making a transition into the new life. This corresponds with the conception of baptism as rebirth (John 3:3, 5). In the Gospel of Luke, despite the framework of salvation history, we also encounter the conception of becoming a Christian in terms of a resurrection within present existence (Luke 15:24, 32). In both of these Gospels Christians ventured a new interpretation of the kerygma of the resurrection. Likewise the author of Colossians has had predecessors in his milieu who conceived of faith as a later fulfillment of the resurrection of Jesus Christ. As far as the history of religions is concerned, this is inconsistent because the resurrection, as the ul-

[124]It was linked to the understanding of baptism as an actualized salvation event. It cannot be demonstrated that that understanding was already behind the "with Christ" formula and that Paul deliberately modified it in Rom. 6; so also e.g., E. Käsemann, *Romans*, ET and ed. by G. Bromiley, Grand Rapids, 1980, p. 159ff.

[125]Lindemann, *Paulus*, p. 116f.

[126]So e.g., Dibelius–Greeven, p. 31: "in essence . . . what takes place is a shift in emphasis;" Lohse, p. 156; Zeilinger, *Erstgeborene*, p. 176: "realized turn of the aeons;" Weiss, "Taufe," p. 56; Merklein, *Theologie*, p. 48f. The shift in emphasis is relativized esp. by Masson, Moule, Houlden, Caird, Martin and, in part, by Ernst.

[127]Zeilinger, *Erstgeborene*, p. 146f.; Wengst, "Versöhnung," p. 14ff., cf. Grässer, "Kolosser 3," p. 136: "In the past Ananke had to be broken! And that for ever!" and idem, p. 141: "Christ takes the place of Heimarmene."

[128]For this reason Severian v. Gabala emphasizes that, according to the NT, there is a preliminary resurrection of the believers before the end of this aeon (Staab, *Paulus-kommentare*, p. 322f.).

timate hope, must be the resurrection from the dead (cf. 1 Cor. 15:12),[129] but this is not to deny the existence of such conceptions. It is not infrequently that a certain tendency, such as the present hope here, persists by means of an adopted conceptuality, such as the Christian proclamation of the resurrection.[130] Ephesians 5:14 cites a call to resurrection which undoubtedly appeared prior to the writing of Colossians, independent of Paul, and which perhaps found its application precisely in baptism.[131] A call like this is found in the Christian context in Acts Thom. 110 (hymn of pearls) and in Odes Sol. 8:3f. Since similar calls are also documented outside the Christian realm (*Corp. Herm.* I, 27; VII, 1f.; *Ap. John*, NHC II/1; 31:5f.; Turfan, *Fragm.* M 7,[132] cf. Aristoph., *Ranae* 340ff.[133]), and since they are to be interpreted as forms expressing a mythical understanding of the unity of humankind with the dying and revived deity (originally generally associated with nature),[134] it is conceivable that such interpretations of the kerygma of the resurrection were considered to be a dangerous theologoumenon, foreign to Pauline theology.[135] This was also characteristic of Christian Gnostics; the *Gospel of Philip* states: "Those who assert: 'One dies first and is (then) raised,' are wrong. If the resurrection is not received first, while still alive, there is nothing to be received upon death" (NHC II/3; 73:1–5;[136] similarly *Ex. An.*, NHC II/6; 134:6–15; Iren., *Adv. haer.* II, 31, 2, et al.[137]).[138]

Menander, the gnostic, is supposed to have taught explicitly that baptism is identical to the resurrection (Iren., *Adv. haer.* I, 23, 5). The polemical statement in 2 Tim. 2:18 (cf. 2 Tim. 2:11) is directed against enthusiasts of a similar kind, with an obviously gnostic taint, who

---

[129]Thus argued by Sellin, "Auferstehung," p. 223.

[130]E. Käsemann, "On the Subject of Primitive Christian Apocalyptic," most recently in idem, *New Testament Questions of Today*, London, 1969, 107–137, esp. p. 124f., cf. Lic. ed. (of 1st ed. "Zum Thema der urchristlichen Apokalyptik," in *Exegetische Versuche und Besinnungen* II, Göttingen, 1965², pp. 105–131), Berlin, 1968, pp. 193–219, esp. p. 208f.

[131]Pokorný, *Epheserbrief*, pp. 94f., 119f.; Siber, *Mit Christus*, p. 200f.; Gnilka, *Epheserbrief*, p. 262; Schnackenburg, *Epheser*, p. 233; Schenke–Fischer, *Einleitung*, p. 176.

[132]According to Dibelius–Greeven, p. 91.

[133]Additional documentation in Schlier, *Epheser*, in loco. It cannot be demonstrated, however, that the wording of Col. 2:12f. is also dependent upon this tradition; so e.g., Siber, *Mit Christus*, p. 202f.

[134]Cf. Apul., *Metam.* XI, 21 (*voluntaria mors* – *precaria salus* at the initiation) and cf. § 12.

[135]Lindemann, *Aufhebung*, p. 141, cf. p. 251f. This suspicion was reinforced by the occurrence of several sayings of Jesus with a similar disposition, in the *Gospel of Thomas* (Log. 52, 111), which are to be attributed to the gnostic redaction: R. Kasser, *L'Evangile selon Thomas*, Neuchâtel, 1961, in loco.

[136]Translated by H. M. Schenke, *ThLZ* 84 (1959), pp. 1–26.

[137]We are bound to presuppose familiarity with the NT in Ep. Rheg., NHC I/4; 45:25–28, cf. 49:15f.; Steles Seth, NHC VII/5; 124:9–13; 125:10–17; Ex. An., NHC II/6; 134:6–15.

[138]Concerning the present experience of salvation in Gnosticism, see Kippenberg, "Vergleich," pp. 751ff., 765f.

also practiced asceticism;[139] in this case those who assert that the resurrection has already occurred have departed from the truth. Strictly speaking, this also represents a charge against the soteriology of Colossians.[140] In this case Colossians and Ephesians would bear a gnostic imprint[141] or would be formulated favoring the potential understanding of recipients with hellenistic training and a gnostic taint.[142] The interpretation of the resurrection sketched there is in tension with the anti-enthusiastic statements of the Pastorals and essentially also of the apostle Paul (§ 4 [a]).[143] In 1 Cor. 4:8f.[144] Paul polemicizes against the enthusiasts who argue that they are already reigning with Christ in the kingdom of God. This tension within Paulinism does not yet prove that, e.g., Col. 2:12f. on the one hand, and 1 Cor. 4:8f. with 2 Tim. 2:18 on the other hand, represent two concrete theological alternatives. Rather it is a secondary contrast of two types of expressions that have been formulated on the premise of similar internal assumptions, under different circumstances, and at different theological battle lines.[145] The warning of 2 Tim. 2:18 does not affect Colossians directly, nor is that its probable intent (cf. Table 2).

In part the present character of salvation is already expressed in Rom. 6:6; 8:29f.;[146] and in Phil. 1:21–23 it is placed in bold relief, even though the eschatological proviso is heard in Phil. 3:10f., for instance.[147] The common denominator is faith by which one is able to anticipate his or her part in the resurrection (Rom. 6:8) and by which one belongs to the new pre-eschatological existence. In Colossians and Ephesians faith fulfills a similar function as a link between the present and the eschatological future, although there we note a certain objectification of its meaning (→1:4, 23). There we also read that the present resurrection with Christ occurs through faith (Col. 2:12) and that faith is the opposite of spiritual death in trespasses (2:13).[148]

---

[139]D. Aune, *The Cultic Setting of Realized Eschatology in Early Christianity*, NovTSup 28, Leiden, 1972, pp. 216–219; asceticism as accommodation to the eschatological condition.

[140]Schenk, "Christus," p. 150, speaks of fulfillment eschatology in Col.

[141]Schenke, "Widerstreit," p. 402.

[142]Grässer, "Kolosser 3," p. 137f.

[143]Summary in Schenke–Fischer, *Einleitung*, p. 218f.

[144]Note the context of the entire chapter.

[145]Caird; Steinmetz, *Heils-Zuversicht*, p. 144; Weiss, "Paulus," p. 124f.; Ernst, p. 203; A. Oepke, "Urchristentum und Kindertaufe," ZNW 29 (1930), pp. 104–111: He considers Col. 2:12 as a direct commentary of Rom. 6.

[146]Cf. already the statements about the new creation in Gal. 6:15, upon which Col. 3:10f. seems to depend.

[147]Cf. Frankemölle, *Taufverständnis*, p. 112f.

[148]Oecumenius; Chrysostom (MPG 62:340); Peake; Souček. Hence this does not deal with a mere imitation of Pauline terminology: Bornkamm, "Baptism," p. 78f.; Grässer, "Kolosser 3," p. 137f.; L. Fazekaš, "Taufe als Tod in Röm. 6:3ff.," TZ 22 (1966), pp. 305–318, esp. p. 315f.; Lohse, p. 158f.; Schnackenburg, *Epheser*, p. 94.

The *sola fide* corresponds theologically with the *solus Christus*.[149] This had already been the concern of the hymn, thus Col. 2:12f. actually is the soteriological application of its statement about the cosmic reconciliation. Several interpreters have also drawn attention to the elements of the future eschatology in Colossians and Ephesians. According to Col. 3:3f., the full revelation of the new life lies in the future (cf. 3:24; Eph. 4:30; 6:13),[150] but the distinction over against Pauline theology remains clear. The future revelation is more an unveiling than a completion of salvation;[151] salvation is already laid up "above" (→1:5; 3:1), and in substantiating the appeals to the new life, the "not yet" does not play a decisive part. The eschatological time of salvation is not, at this time, set in a chronological tension as much as in an ontological one.[152] On the other hand, however, we must point out that an ontological tension is also intrinsic to a futuristic eschatology, or else it would not be an eschatology. For Colossians the eschaton is where the resurrected Christ is present, and the eschaton breaks into the present in the confession and in the proclamation of the gospel (2:6; 1:25f.). The combination of the presence of Christ with faith and proclamation functions similarly to the eschatological proviso in the main Pauline letters; it motivates the paraenesis and the toilsome mission (3:1ff.; 1:24f.). In contrast to the main letters, thankfulness (3:17, cf. Table 2) and the ecclesiological frame (2:19; 3:16f.)[153] become prominent in the substantiation of the paraenesis.

While it is not the apostle Paul of the main letters who speaks theologically, it is nevertheless Paulinism which does. In the polemic against a religious speculation of the gnostic kind, the emphasis upon salvation that is already laid up "above" is the isotope of the doctrine of justification. Instead of a remote God, the proclamation deals with the God who, in his grace, was brought close to humanity in Jesus Christ. The concrete social expression of participation in the resurrection of Jesus is membership in the church as the body of Christ (§ 14), which thus has a soteriological function.[154] All of this makes it legitimate for us to interpret the argument of Colossians (death and life with Jesus Christ) in analogy with the axis of sin–grace of God (cf. Col. 2:13), which is of paramount importance in the main letters

---

[149]H. F. Weiss, "Motive," p. 321; Grässer, "Kolosser 3," p. 137.

[150]Vawter, "Hymn" (Bibliography on 1:15–20), pp. 76–78; Schillebeeckx, *Christus*, p. 183.

[151]Stegemann, "Alt und Neu," pp. 515, 529; Schenk, "Christus," p. 150.

[152]Sellin, "Auferstehung," p. 222.

[153]Weiss, "Motive," p. 322.

[154]Merklein, "Theologie," p. 49ff. In this case, however, the church is construed primarily as the fellowship of believers which is dependent upon Jesus Christ as its head, cf. P. Bonnard, "Mourir et vivre avec Jésus-Christ selon Saint Paul," *RHPR* 36 (1956), pp. 101–112; Weiss, "Taufe," p. 62f.

of Paul. Second Timothy 2:18 combats a religious enthusiasm by emphasizing the time that separates humankind from the eschatological completion; Col. 2:12f. reinterprets a religious speculation by emphasizing the grace of God, the union with Christ, and the fellowship of the church.

Sociologically a one-sided eschatological understanding of existence could lead to isolation.[155] In Colossians, however, it is to motivate the recipients to concretely separate from the false teachers.

On the argument of the letter, see also § 15.

12 Semantically the entire verse is determined by the contrast of "buried with"–"raised with." In the confession formula of 1 Cor. 15:4a, the burial served as confirmation of Jesus' death. To be buried together means that the baptisand participates in the actual, substitutionary death of Jesus,[156] without having to carry it out physically (Rom. 6:4). Hence in the first phase (submersing) baptism, as rite,[157] imitates the burial (cf. Matt. 12:40). Clearly, this is the common denominator of Rom. 6:4 and Col. 2:12, which are anchored in the baptismal tradition.[158]

The second part speaks of being raised with Jesus Christ in baptism (§ 13). To be sure, for some interpreters ἐν ᾧ refers to Jesus ("in him"), analogous to the same expression in 2:11a.[159] In this instance, however, the immediate grammatical context which refers to baptism is decisive.[160] Fundamentally all of this occurs "in Christ"—as the phrase "in him" in 2:10, 11 indicates—and is recognized "by faith" (§ 13). Here faith is determined by its object; it is faith in God's power as creator (Eph. 1:20)—in God who raised Jesus Christ from the dead (§ 8)—which is once more a traditional designation for God.[161] The conceptual frame changes, however: That which is received "through faith" is that which is already accomplished (→1:5; 3:1f., cf. Eph. 2:5ff.). According to Gal. 5:6 the power of God works (ἐνεργεῖν) through the faith of Christians,[162] while the power (ἐνεργεία) of God here is the object of faith[163] (Col. 1:23). The difference here is not a

---

[155]Meeks, "Body," p. 213ff.

[156]Hence baptism is not merely a cleansing as in the immersion baths of the Essenes: e.g., 1 QS 3.4ff.

[157]The less common term βαπτισμός (p[46], B, D*) is likely the more original one in this case.

[158]Schweizer, esp. p. 144, note 30; P. Pokorný, "Christologie et baptême à l'époque du christianisme primitif," NTS 27 (1980–81), pp. 368–380, esp. p. 376f.

[159]Chrysostom, Meyer, Haupt, Lohmeyer, Dibelius-Greeven, Lohse, TOB, Gnilka.

[160]Calvin, Oltramare, Alford, Peake, Abbott, v. Soden, Haupt, Souček, RSV, (Martin, Caird), Houlden, Ernst, Bratcher-Nida, Schweizer.

[161]In 2 Cor. 1:9 it is already generalized: "God who raises the dead," cf. 2 Kings 5:7.

[162]For this reason several interpreters have also understood the "power of God" in this instance in apposition to faith ("through faith, i.e. through the power of God"): Chrysostom; Calvin; Bengel: fides est (opus) operationis divinae; so also Binder, Der Glaube bei Paulus, Berlin, 1968, p. 55.

[163]Alford, Haupt, TOB.

fundamental one, however, for we read in Col. 1:29 that the power of the resurrected Christ works "through the apostle."[164]

13 This verse is intended to summarize 2:11–12. This is supported by the "and you" (see 1:21).[165] It almost has a disturbing effect because the author used the second person plural earlier.[166] Since he also used some traditional images and terms earlier in 2:11f., there are certain tensions existing between the two analogous formulations of the argument. Prominent in this verse is the contrast "dead/made alive," which is firmly anchored in the Christian tradition (John 5:25; Luke 15:24, 32; Eph. 5:14; § 13). If taken literally, those who have been dead for a long time (2:13) would have to be buried (2:12) with Christ. But this is merely a tension between the two pictures. At issue here is being dead in trespasses, which is to be understood both as moral death and as death in terms of alienation from God (1:21). Transgressions are the cause for being dead (causal dative, so א*, B, L et al.), or they describe being dead per se (ἐν, "in trespasses," so p[46], A, C, D).[167] Already the confession formula of 1 Cor. 15:3b–5 (cf. Rom. 4:24f.; 8:34; 1 Pet. 1:18–21) has explained the death and resurrection of Christ as individuals' liberation[168] from sin. How sin alienates people from God is indicated in Col. 3:5ff. Vices are identical to idolatry which calls for the wrath of God. Fornication, covetousness, etc. are instruments of the powers (§ 12) which separate men and women from God (Eph. 2:1–3). The "uncircumcision of the flesh" is the pagan past of the recipients (Eph. 2:11f.),[169] but more commonly it is also the condition prior to the about-face[170] and prior to baptism, which is tantamount to "putting off the flesh."[171] It is the condition in which the "puffed up" opponents are still caught because they

---

[164]We need to keep in mind, however, that here the apostle is already an authority of the past (→2:1–5).

[165]Most of all the second person plural is to indicate that on account of their faith the recipients are incorporated in the world-encompassing movement of the grace of God (cf. καὶ ὑμεῖς in Eph. 1:13), Usami, *Comprehension*, p. 104ff., esp. p. 108 ("theological change"); Abbott: reiterated for the sake of emphasis; Burger, *Schöpfung*, p. 97.

[166]According to p[46], B, and others, the clause about making alive uses the first person plural once again; א*, A, C, Byz, and essentially also D (without pronoun), use "you."

[167]So Dibelius–Greeven, p. 31; Conzelmann; Lähnemann, *Kolosser*, p. 123; Burger, *Schöpfung*, pp. 98–100. Schweizer, p.147, note 38, ponders the possibility that the omission of death in v. 12 is intentional, in order to make the two verses congruent: In this case v. 12 would refer to someone who has been dead for a long time. The traditional terminology of v. 12 renders this unlikely.

[168]ζωοποιεῖν here is synonymous with ἐγείρειν in 2:12.

[169]Lohmeyer, p. 114; Martin.

[170]Haupt, p. 90.

[171]On baptism as spiritual circumcision, see →1:11, cf. Rom. 2:27–29; 4:9f.; Souček; Moule, p. 97; Caird; Ernst; Schweizer, p. 147; Gnilka, p. 136.

serve the superhuman powers (2:8; 3:6).[172] In the background is the conception of the spiritual circumcision of 2:11 which is understood positively. The decisive issue is that the new life is "in Christ" and enables life in togetherness with Christ within the framework of the entire Christian community (→2:19; § 16).[173]

Since this life is characterized by its freedom from having been determined by sin, it may, on account of the "creation terminology"[174] (make alive), be qualified as truly new life. God, who was the point of issue already in the preceding verse (→2:12), is its subject. The recipients are addressed in the second person plural; thereby the author emphasizes that this also applies to those who underestimate the work of Jesus. At the conclusion of the verse he identifies with all the sinners again and shifts to the first person plural.[175] Since 2:12c, God has been the subject of all that transpires. In the appended participial clause[176] spiritual circumcision, which is at least afforded a specific opportunity in Christian water baptism, is described as the appropriation of the grace of God. The cosmic reconciliation (→1:20; § 9 [c]), depicted as the removal of the alienating pressure of the superhuman powers (§ 10), is again applied to the recipients here (→1:21f.) and is interpreted as the great scope of the grace of God.[177]

2:14–15 or 2:9–15 The final two verses of this section contain six expressions that occur only here in the Pauline corpus (ἐξαλείφειν, χειρόγραφον, ὑπεναντίον, προσηλοῦν, ἀπεκδύεσθαι, δειγματίζειν); "to triumph" (to lead in triumphal procession, θριαμβεύειν) occurs only here and in 2 Cor. 2:14. Four times the respective sentences are introduced by participles (in Gk. the following are expressed participially: "having cancelled," "nailing," "disarmed," "triumphing." The analogous structure, the unusual terms, and the transition to the first person plural in 2:13c reveal that this represents a formal statement with modified older elements. Since "having forgiven" in 2:13 is also a participle[178] and the final subordinate clause in v. 13 also fits the context of the two subsequent verses in terms of content as well as style, some interpreters also include it in the solemn paragraph which they consider to be traditional material. Some have discerned the older

---

[172]Wengst, "Versöhnung," p. 20.

[173]Lohse, p. 153; Burger, Schöpfung, p. 97ff., and others assume that the opponents practiced circumcision, →2:11.

[174]Zeilinger, Erstgeborene, p. 168; the aorist here emphasizes primarily the completion of salvation; Usami, Comprehension, p. 108ff.

[175]Bujard, Untersuchungen, p. 84, against Coutss, "Relationship," p. 204, who derives the change in 2:13 from Eph. 2:1–6, and against all those who identify the change in person with the boundary of adopted material.

[176]Typical for Col.; Bujard, Untersuchungen, p. 60.

[177]Cf. Wengst, "Versöhnung," p. 26.

[178]And also because pardon is a concept that differs from forgiveness in 1:14.

liturgical text already in 2:9–15.[179] Ch. Burger, who dealt with these verses in depth, reconstructed the modified liturgical patchwork [180] as follows:

> He cancelled the bond
> by nailing it to the cross.
> He made a public example of the principalities and powers
> by leading them in triumphal procession.[181]

He correctly focused on vv. 14–15. Colossians 2:9–10 refers to the hymn of 1:15–20, and in 2:12f. we have discovered older common phrases that have been handed down as independent units. The participle of 2:13c (χαρισάμενος; translated "having forgiven") is likewise typical of the author's style. At the same time, the statement concerning forgiveness corresponds with the proclamation pattern of "death and resurrection of Christ—forgiveness of sins," linking it with the rest of v. 13 and perhaps being a contributing influence upon the structure of the paragraph (death–grace; 2:12–14).[182] With the shift to the first person plural in 2:13 the author introduced the following section (2:14f.). In the framework of this segment, then, Col. 2:14–15 represents a new complete unit.

In our opinion, however, the peculiarities in style and content in these two verses are no indication of an adopted older text fragment. There indeed are some traditional phrases and unusual images, but the conspicuous divergence of the attempts at reconstructing an older entity attests to their hypothetical character. We have to take into account that the author formulated Col. 2:14–15 (in contrast to the hymn in 1:15–20) as a solemn confirmation of his argument.[183] The subject change was begun in v. 13 and cannot be considered as argument in favor of a traditional unit (→ 2:13). The parallels in the *Gospel of Truth* (NHC I/3; 24–28) and in the gnostic *Gospel of the Egyptians* (NHC III/2; 64:3f.; 65:18f.)[184] have been influenced by the NT.[185]

[179]Overview of the attempts at reconstruction:
Lohmeyer: 2:13b ("made alive . . . ")–15 (p. 101f.; he attributes the hymn to Paul, however); Schille: 2:9, 10b, 11b, 13b ("made alive . . . ")–15 (*Hymnen*, p. 31ff., cf. Burger, *Schöpfung*, p. 83); Lohse: 2:13b ("having forgiven us . . . ")–15 (pp. 141, 160–168; idem, "Bekenntnis;" so also TOB); Wengst: 2:13–15 (*Formeln*, p. 186f.; Schenke: 2:14–15 ("Christologie," p. 222f.).

[180]For Lohse and Burger, *Schöpfung*, p. 108, this refers to a fragment.

[181]Burger, *Schöpfung*, p. 108 and appendix. The Gk. text of the last line has ἐν παρρησίᾳ θριαμβεύσας—author's translation.

[182]Ibid., p. 99f. For a critique of other reconstructions, see idem, p. 102ff.

[183]So also Schweizer and Gnilka. More reticent in their evaluations of the reconstructions are also Deichgräber, *Gotteshymnus*, pp. 167–169; Ernst, p. 206; Lähnemann, *Kolosserbrief*, pp. 126–129; according to him the hapax legomena could also be taken from the language of the opponents.

[184]Cf. Schenke, "Christologie," p. 222f.

[185]Ménard, *Ev. Verit.*, p. 100; Böhlig–Wisse, NHC III/2, 196. The picture of the plan of redemption as a (vivid) letter from Odes Sol. 23:5–9 again is not a true parallel.

The attempts to reconstruct an older unit have nevertheless contributed to the theological and literary characteristic of the segment under discussion. According to E. Lohmeyer this represents a kerygmatic confession in hymnic form;[186] for G. Schille it is a redeemer hymn in the form of the cross–triumph hymn, as e.g., in Odes Sol. 22.[187] Since the author added a clause regarding the cross in the hymn (→1:20; § 9 [a]), it is probable that, via the traditional statement about the cross, he endeavors (a) to substantiate his argument of 2:12f. and (b) to provide once more a Pauline interpretation of the cosmic reconciliation expressed in the hymn.

14 The last two verses of this segment are actually intended to explain in what manner trespasses were forgiven. The two participles describe the event that has already taken place in Christ (aorist). To begin with, he uses the image of the cancellation of a document, thus abrogating it.[188] The reference is to a bond issued against humanity, the cancellation of which the cross of Christ played a decisive part. This much can be said with certainty. The meaning of some expressions and the conceptions associated with them, however, is not altogether clear.

The Greek term for the document in question is χειρόγραφον, which designated a handwritten document.[189] It may denote a bond,[190] a contract, or an ordinance. In our case, the first option would mean that the sinners themselves wrote that document as their admission of guilt.[191] In this case the phrase "with its legal demands" would be the dative of reference (*Dativus respectus*), meaning something like: ". . . bond (which we surrendered) in view of (certain) stipulations. . . ."[192] This is rather complicated grammatically. The reference is rather to a document written from the opposite point of view, for instance, an ordinance in the light of which people were to feel guilty.[193] We are led to this sort of conclusion in the understanding of this reference in Eph. 2:14f. There the "legal demands" are the

---

[186]Lohmeyer, p. 102; on hymn as a genre, see § 9 (d).

[187]Schille, Hymnen, pp. 31–37, 43.

[188]Cf. ἐξαλείφειν in Acts 3:19; Rev. 3:5, additional evidence in Lohmeyer, p. 117, note 2. It is hardly emphasized that the relationship with its religious intent was annulled by secular legal action; so Lähnemann, Kolosserbrief, p. 128.

[189]Only here in the NT, elsewhere in Tob. 5:3; 9:2, 5; see E. Lohse, TDNT IX:424f.

[190]See Philem. 19.

[191]The inscription of Sardis contains an example of the publicly written confession of guilt before the god Men, cited by W. Carr, "Two Notes on Colossians," JTS 24 (1973), pp. 492–500, on p. 494. However, the term χειρόγραφον does not occur there.

[192]So N. Walter, "Die "Handschrift in Satzungen," Kol. 2:14," ZNW 70 (1979), pp. 115–118, on p. 118.

[193]This is not a pact between human beings and the devil, however. There is no reference to the devil here at all, and the disposition of the heavenly powers is ambiguous (§ 10); against Chrysostom, MPG 62, 341; Bieder and Lohmeyer, p. 116.

stipulations of the Mosaic law regarded by Ephesians as the dividing wall between Jews and Gentiles. Some interpreters understand the document in the same way here.[194] The essential analogy to Gal. 3:24f. and Rom. 3:21ff. supports this view. This obviously was the meaning of this image in the older Christian tradition. The false teachers of Colossae, however, were not teachers of the law (§ 12),[195] and the image is more likely imported to depict a charge against the false teachers in the light of their ascetic orientations and their interpretation of the will of God. Against this the author asserts that the sacrifice of Christ secured complete forgiveness for humanity.[196]

The image of forgiveness as the cancellation of a bond may have been familiar to him from Judaism.[197] In the background was perhaps the conception of the heavenly lists of the guilty (cf. Rev. 20:12).[198] In Judaism the conditions under which forgiveness took place were different than in Paul and here, but the image has a relatively independent function and here refers to overcoming the opposition's accusations.

How the dative τοῖς δόγμασι (with its legal demands) should be understood is problematic.[199] The legal demands (Gk. δόγμα; also "decree," e.g., Luke 2:1; Acts 16:4; later "dogma"), according to some older interpreters, are the Christian statements of faith (dogmas), through which humanity's debt was cancelled.[200] Already the parallel in Eph. 2:15 and the negative connotation of the corresponding verb δογματίζειν (to prescribe stipulations) render this unlikely.

The only remaining interpretation of the legal demands, then, is the negative one, either by combining it with the preceding τὸ καθ' ἡμῶν (in our translation "which stood against us"),[201] or by linking it with the following relative clause, translating it roughly as "and which was against us on account of the legal demands."[202] We under-

---

[194]Calvin; Ewald; v. Soden; Dibelius–Greeven; J. Schneider, *TDNT* VII:572–584, esp. p. 577.

[195]In Eph. and Col. the term law occurs only in Eph. 2:15; cf. Schweizer, p. 150.

[196]That does not mean, however, that Jesus himself was the bond, as O. A. Blanchette, "Does the Cheirographon of Col. 2:14 Represent Christ Himself?" *CBQ* 23 (1961), pp. 306–312, argues on the basis of e.g., Gal. 3:13, Odes Sol. 23; similarly Bandstra, *Law*, p. 160ff. Substitution in terms of the later doctrine of satisfaction was only one of several pictures for the redemptive event in Paul.

[197]Cf. the prayer Abinu Malkenu which was already known at the beginning of the second cent. CE: "Our Father, our King, by your great mercy blot out all our bonds;" Billerbeck III, 628.

[198]Documentation in Billerbeck; Lohse, *TDNT* IX (see note 189 above).

[199]A presentation of the solutions is offered by Hugédé.

[200]An instrumental dative which would refer to "cancelled": Chrysostom, Oecumenius (*decreta gratiae*), Masson.

[201]Oltramare, Peake, Dibelius–Greeven and others; Haupt and others link it directly to the bond and add "written."

[202]Ewald, Souček, Houlden, TOB.

stand the phrase ὃ ἦν ὑπεναντίον ἡμῖν to mean more likely "which stood against us," "which confronted us."[203] This hardly changes the meaning; in either case the sentence is somewhat awkward in Greek. As we have already stated, by "legal demands" the author means the teachings and ascetic regulations of the opponents.[204] "With its legal demands" is the author's clarification[205] for the purpose of actualizing the adopted image.[206] It intends to express that where the crucified and resurrected Christ is now present by faith no regulation, no "element" (2:20), no religious system (2:8) can bar the way to life's destination (→2:12).[207]

The image continues in 2:14b. Besides cancellation, another metaphor is used for the abrogation, namely, that of removal, literally "putting away from among" (cf. 1 Cor. 5:2).[208] "Nailing"[209] is an allusion to the early Christian confession of the death of Jesus on the cross (1:20, 22), which is substitutionary, that is to say, which also opens up the way to new life for the rest of humanity: 1 Cor. 15:3; 2 Cor. 5:21; Gal. 3:13, cf. 6:14.[210] Here it indicates the superiority of those who confess the crucified one and puts to shame those addressed by the document.[211] It cannot be demonstrated, however, that the cross here is an explicit sign of triumph (tropaion),[212] for the positive conception of the cross was tied to the resurrection (2:11, →15). It is more likely an aftereffect of the remembrance of the tradition about the inscription on the cross of Jesus that indicated the charge against

[203]Cf. Walter, "Handschrift" (see note 192 above). Otherwise v. 14a would be tautological.

[204]Cf. Weiss, "Law," p. 304; it hardly refers to a detailed self-accusation, so Carr, "Notes" (see note 191 above), p. 496.

[205]According to P. W. Schmiedel (following Nestle–Aland) this is a later gloss, yet only MS 1881 omits it. Burger, Schöpfung, pp. 107, 111, entertains the notion of a commentator of the text which is not yet canonized. Those ascribing Col. to the author of Eph. may attribute it to the latter (cf. § 3).

[206]It is viewed as a supplement to the adopted hymn by Lohse, p. 164; Wengst, Formeln, p. 190, and others who presuppose an older hymn in 2:14f.

[207]Wengst, "Versöhnung," pp. 16, 20.

[208]αἴρειν belongs to the language of the early Christian confessions: John 1:29; 1 John 3:5; cf. 1 Pet. 2:24.

[209]A hapax legomenon in the NT which means "to nail," "to nail fast"; documentation in BAGD.

[210]Lohse, p. 164. See also note 196.

[211]According to the original hymn (→2:14f.) as reconstructed by Ch. Burger, nailing would be a means of legal annulment; so Deissmann, Light, p. 332ff. Deissmann has also expressed the view that the conception of the annulment of a document by crossing it out is in mind here as well, which would correlate with 2:14a. However, the two metaphors (cancel, nail) focus upon the significance of Jesus' death by crucifixion, in the light of his resurrection, and otherwise may derive from very diverse realms: Lohse, p. 165, note 4; Gnilka, p. 139.

[212]So F. J. Dölger, Die Sonne der Gerechtigkeit und der Schwarze, Liturgiegeschichtliche Forschungen 2, Münster, 1918, pp. 128–141; against this, Dibelius–Greeven.

him (Mark 15:26, par.).[213] Through the resurrection the accusation against the crucified one is transformed into his exaltation and becomes instead the indictment against the opponents. This inversion of the image of the sentence accompanies the entire tradition of the history of the passion.

15 Another picture unfolds here, namely, that of the redemptive event which culminated in Christ—the image of the triumphal procession, which stands over against the image of nailing.[214] It is a figure with several dimensions, all of which work together.

(a) More than anything else, it signifies a victory celebration. The triumphal procession is a metaphor of the resurrection of Jesus, which was also understood as his exaltation.[215] The celebration of victory with a triumphal procession was a common Roman institution, to which already 2 Cor. 2:14 alludes. But there it is the Christians themselves who, as voluntary slaves of Christ, demonstrate the power of their Lord in his triumphal procession.[216] There the triumphant one is Jesus Christ, whereas here it is God[217] through Jesus Christ. This is clearly the meaning of "in him,"[218] which has the effect of a gloss.[219] In both cases Christ has the key position for the entire world, including the superhuman powers (Eph. 1:21). They[220] are led along in the triumphal procession as his captives (cf. Eph. 4:8).

The powers were "disarmed." ἀπεκδύεσθαι means "to put off one's clothes," and figuratively "to disarm oneself" but, like other verbs in Koiné Greek, it was also used with an active meaning.[221] Only a

---

[213]Dibelius–Greeven, p. 31; Ernst, p. 205; Lohse, p. 165, note 7; cf. Schweizer, p. 149. The use of a title on the cross was not common; it has to refer primarily to the tradition of the passion account.

[214]Bujard, *Untersuchungen*, p. 85.

[215]Such pictures were already used prior to the writing of Col (see the hymn in 1 Tim. 3:16). But the metaphorical use of the verb θριαμβεύειν is not documented prior to 2 Cor. 2:14: P. Marshall, "A Metaphor of Social Shame ΘΡΙΑΜΒΕΥΕΙΝ," *NovT* 25 (1983), pp. 302–317.

[216]At the same time the recipients were to be shamed in their self-confidence, see Marshall, "Metaphor" (see note 215 above), p. 315ff.

[217]Only a few interpreters take Jesus Christ to be the direct subject: Lightfoot, Moule, GNB, and as one of the possibilities: Caird.

[218]In its intention it refers to Jesus Christ, not to the cross (so Calvin, Meyer, Abbott, Peake, Haupt) nor to the bond (so v. Soden); cf. the clause "who raised him from the dead" (2:12). The following apply it to Jesus: Alford, Lohmeyer, Dibelius–Greeven, Lohse, Beare, Houlden, Ernst, Schweizer, Gnilka, and others. The Vulgate presupposes the reflexive ἑαυτῷ and relates it to God.

[219]Burger, *Schöpfung*, p. 105, explains it as a later correction which moves the hymn in which Jesus Christ was the subject, closer to the original intent. However, the theocentric thought is characteristic for Col. and Eph.: 1:12f., 27; Eph. 1:17–23; 3:11f., 14–19.

[220]The text has αὐτούς instead of αὐτάς = *constructio ad sensum*; Haupt, p. 99. Perhaps the author thought of the thrones (1:16), Burger, *Schöpfung*, p. 105 (though he regards it as a later addition).

[221]Blass–Debrunner–Funk, § 316, 1. Here it may also be influenced by the obviously active meaning of ἀπέκδυσις in →2:11.

few interpreters take it to be middle (as in Col. 3:9) in this instance, namely, that Christ put off the powers like a garment and thus was freed from them.[222] Others take it to be active, though intransitively: On the cross Christ "put off," namely, his human body with its capability of being tempted.[223] The picture of the triumphal procession is more suitable for the active and transitive notion of "unclothed the powers" (their dignity and lordship)[224] or "disarmed the powers."[225] Both images cohere, and since Eph. 4:8 (= Ps. 67:19 LXX) depicts the victory procession of Christ as the capture of the enemies, we preferred the second option. God did not dissolve, but rather disarmed (§ 10) the superhuman realities that influence life in this world. First Corinthians 15:55 anticipates a disarmament like this, namely, of death as a real superhuman power. According to 1 Cor. 15:56, sin, which takes its power from the law, is the weapon of death. Since we have already shown several times that the author practices a Pauline theology, he very likely links it with that statement here. The disarming is identical to the forgiveness of trespasses in Col. 2:13. Hence a moralistic activism is foreign to the gospel, and, in similar fashion, so is every illusionary escape from the world. The "principalities and powers" are here and belong to the created order (1:16, cf. § 9 [c]); they tend to emancipate themselves from God, but they are not able to separate humanity from the love of God (cf. Rom. 8:31–39).

(c) The triumphal procession is also to demonstrate publicly the power of the triumphant one and the subjection of those defeated (δειγματίζειν, to make public, display publicly, expose [Matt. 1:19], also in the meaning of παραδειγματίζειν = to denounce).[226] It is the powers which are the object of "making public."[227] This can be derived from the context; it is stated[228] that the powers were made a public (ἐν παρρησία) example, which parallels the statement concerning the triumphal procession.[229] Parrēsia was a political term from the tradition of the ancient democracy. It describes the freedom of public

---

[222]Lightfoot, Moule, TEV; details in Lohmeyer, p. 119, note 2. In this case the powers would be the cosmic body of Christ, analogous to the hymn (→1:16–18). But there the picture of the cosmic body is used in the positive sense.

[223]So e.g., Chrysostom, Hippolytus of Rome (Phil. VIII, 10, 7) and Robinson, Body, p. 41, among the contemporary authors. Correspondingly, some Syriac and Gothic MSS read ΤΗΝΣΑΡΚΑ instead of ΤΑΣΑΡΧΑΣ (following Lightfoot, Lohmeyer, p. 119, note 2); an overview of the grammatical options is found in Bratcher–Nida.

[224]Zeilinger, Erstgeborene, p. 172.

[225]Bieder, Die Vorstellung von der Höllenfahrt Christi, p. 78ff.

[226]"He clarified the weakness (of the powers) to all men," Theodoret, cited by Haupt, p. 99.

[227]Cf. note 220 above.

[228]From this Burger, Schöpfung, pp. 106–109, concludes that, influenced by 2:11, the author added ἀπεκδυσάμενος to the older hymn (2:14f.).

[229]Gnilka, p. 142.

speech and address (in the NT e.g., 2 Cor. 3:12; Eph. 3:12; Heb. 10:19; John 7:26; 1 John 2:28) and the boldness associated with it (Eph. 6:19), and later the public nature in general (Phil. 1:20). The public aspect is emphasized because Christian mission is the concrete form of the triumphal procession of Christ (as in 2 Cor. 2:14): 1:25, 28; 4:3, cf. the parallel, liturgically shaped interpretation of the gospel in 1 Tim. 3:16. By means of missions the key position of Christ is asserted;[230] the intended condition of God's creation is restored consciously. Thereby we do not wish to gloss over the tension that exists between the image of the superhuman powers as a part of the creation of God which is good (→1:16; § 9 [c]) and the picture of the powers as defeated opponents and instruments of sin (cf. Eph. 4:9; 6:12ff.; § 10). The theology of Colossians is not a systematic work. Two theological traditions have been adopted, of which the tradition of the exaltation of Christ and the subjection of the powers through the forgiveness of God in the cross of Christ is the primary one for the author. The conception of the agent of creation as the head of the powers (the hymn) serves to point out their significance (2:10, cf. Phil. 2:9–11; Heb. 1:9–14) and the importance of the argument.[231] In terms of relationship with the resurrected Jesus Christ, Christian faith signifies the fellowship with the Lord over the insubordinate principalities and powers which oppress humankind. His Lordship is tantamount to the intention of the creator. The goal of creation, shrouded in mystery, is redemption.

2. Freedom from the External Demands (Polemic), 2:16–23

(16) Therefore let no one pass judgment on you in questions of food and drink or with regard to a festival or a new moon or a sabbath. (17) These are only a shadow of what is to come; but the substance belongs to Christ. (18) Let no one disqualify you, insisting on self-abasement and worship of angels, taking his stand on visions, puffed up without reason by his sensuous mind, (19) and not holding fast to the Head, from whom the whole body, nourished and knit together through its joints and ligaments, grows with a growth that is from God.

(20) If with Christ you died to the elemental spirits of the universe, why do you live as if you still belonged to the world? Why do you submit to regulations, (21) "Do not taste, Do not touch" (22) (referring to things which all perish as they are used), according to human precepts and doctrines? (23) These have indeed an appearance of wisdom in promoting rigor of devotion and self-abasement and severity to the body, but they are of no value in checking the indulgence of the flesh.

---

[230] According to Eph. 3:8–10 the mission even is the means to subject and disarm the powers, cf. Eph. 4:8–16.
[231] Cf. § 18, esp. note 38.

Only now, after the presentation of salvation in Jesus Christ, does the actual polemic against the Colossian "philosophy" occur, against which the writer already warned in 2:8.[1] In view of the allegedly intellectual conception of the supreme deity among the opponents (§ 12), their teaching is here conveyed with a dose of demagogy of human origin (2:22f., cf. 2:8). Since several concepts that played a significant part in the heresy are obviously taken up here, the translation of 2:18f., 22f. is difficult and never altogether clear. The emphasis of the common growth in the church (2:19; § 14) prepares for the paraenetic section (§ 5 [b]).

16 The warning refers to the piety of the false teachers and to the respective demands that they also wanted to impose upon other house churches in the vicinity of the recipients (§ 12).

The "matter" (ἐν μέρει) in question here and for which 2:21 contains an analogy, is the festivals, new moon, and sabbath (Jub. 6:34–38; Just., *Dial.* 8:4),[2] including their cultic significance (Num. 28:9–15; Ezek. 45:17).[3] The false teachers must have borrowed them from Diaspora Jews and then further combined them with the ascetic demands (drink and food). The latter were to serve the purpose of chastising the body (2:23). Perhaps they also were to facilitate the ascent through the spheres of the heavenly powers into the divine realm (→2:9; § 12). Other Christians were considered inferior by the false teachers (2:18), because these regarded their own special initiation (→2:18) as a sign of their superiority. The piety of the Pauline groups (cf. § 4 [a]), which focused upon the cross and the resurrection of Jesus, was too particular for them, compared with their alleged higher wisdom (2:23); perhaps they viewed Pauline Christianity as a possible prelude to the spiritual initiation proper.[4] Since this constituted a threat to the gospel, the writer here categorically rejects food regulations, in a manner similar to Paul's rejection of circumcision in Gal. 5:2–12. This was altogether different from the tolerant attitude toward the "weak" in Rom. 14.

After the warning one is told what to guard against, and only then follows the substantiation, the critique of the opponents' position (2:17).[5] The critique's point of departure is the sufficiency of salva-

---

[1]Hence Col. 2:16–3:4 has no explicit parallel in Eph.

[2]It cannot be demonstrated that only the cultic practices (sacrifices), but not e.g., the Sabbath and the festivals themselves are targeted, as P. Giem, "Sabbatōn in Col. 2:16," *Andrews Univ. Seminary Studies* 9 (1981), pp. 195–210, suggests. In my estimation he arbitrarily separated the evidence of the sacrifices on festival days, new moons, and Sabbaths from the other references to these points in time. On the observance of the Sabbath even among uncircumcized Christians, see Ign., *Phld.* 6:1, and among Gentiles, see Suet., *Tiber.* 32.

[3]Further documentation in Giem, "Sabbatōn," p. 198ff.

[4]Cf. e.g., Apul., *Metam.* XI, 28.

[5]Cf. Zeilinger, *Erstgeborene*, p. 56.

tion in Christ. That position is already implied in the warning against judging.[6] Warnings such as this are likely connected with a tradition derived from Jesus himself (Matt. 7:1, par., cf. Jas. 4:11). Because the individual receives salvation as a gift, that person is not allowed to judge others (cf. 1 Cor. 4:5ff.). True wisdom (Col. 4:5f.) has its human behavior counterpart in forgiveness (3:13f.). The opponents of the writer probably did not consider themselves as false teachers, nor their religious counsel as judging. It is part of the defense against their philosophy, however, to have them unmasked as self-appointed judges.

17 As reason for the warning it is adduced that all[7] the rules and regulations cited in 2:16 are but a shadow of what is to come. That which is to come (τὰ μέλλοντα) is the designation for the future age, for the eschatological completion of salvation (in the framework of the same picture, Heb. 10:1; in apocalyptic e.g., 2 Bar. 4). Both the writer and the opponents were concerned with this reality. Thus the first part of the sentence contains no criticism yet. The opponents, too, viewed their regulations as a shadow of the redemptive reality. In metaphorical language, "shadow" indeed was no derogatory designation.[8] The important issue is to what the shadow points. Shadow and reality are two poles of a semantic axis influenced in antiquity by Platonism[9] and described as σκία and εἰκών (shadow and archetype) but sometimes also as shadow and body.[10] The contemporary reader has to remember that the reference is to an image and that the shadow has an objective and concrete form, while the archetype, as the true reality, was an idea.[11] In the hellenistic environment Jewish conceptions were also interpreted in this manner (cf. Philo, *Conf. Ling.* 190; Heb. 8:5), and the false teachers evidently also viewed their religion as a way into the spiritual world. By contrast, when the author sees the archetype, which is to reflect the respective regulations, in the "body" which belongs to Jesus Christ (possessive genitive), for him the most profound reality and salvation are bound up with Jesus; it is the reconciliation with God which Jesus Christ mediated, and it is the new life with him (3:1–4, cf. 1:20; 2:12f.).

When the emphasis is upon Jesus Christ, it does not yet signify that Colossians stresses the human Jesus. In the hymn of 1:15–20 he bears

[6]Cf. Rom. 14:3ff. In the same chapter Paul rejects the understanding of the kingdom of God as food or drink (v. 17).

[7]Greek ἅ ἐστιν as in 2:22. The reading of B, G, et al. is an adaptation to the more common ὅ ἐστιν (1:24; 3:14), see Lohse, p. 171, note 4.

[8]Bornkamm, "Heresy," p. 129f.

[9]On this cf. Plato, *Resp.* 514A–518A (ch. VII).

[10]E.g., Philo, *Migr. Abrah.* 12; *Conf. Ling.* 190 (σκία—σῶμα/μίμημα—ἀρχέτυπος, or ἰδέα); →2:9; Heb. 10:1.

[11]The interpretations which allegorize these metaphors (shadow—darkness, obscure practices; the body as that which stands in front of the shadow) do not align with the function of the language used here. For an overview of them, see Alford, p. 224f.

several features of a cosmic figure. But beyond this the author of Colossians is acquainted with a tradition regarding the cruel death of Jesus on the cross (1:20), as well as with a catechetical–paraenetic tradition associated with Jesus Christ as Lord (2:6). In the latter the unity and fellowship of the believers played a major role (2:8ff.; 3:11, 14, 17), and within this framework the author develops the notion of the church as body of Christ (2:19). It is likely, therefore, that this understanding of the concept of soma is also included here.[12] The ultimate reality is to be attained in the concrete social milieu of the church in which Jesus Christ is acknowledged as the head. The prominence here is accorded to Jesus Christ and to the church that confesses him, rather than to a supreme idea. In the milieu of the church, faith's archetype is to be attained directly; the way of understanding the reality of God by its shadow (i.e., by adhering to the ritual law) no longer applies in the church.[13]

18 This verse, which is difficult to translate, begins a new warning in parallel to the one of vv. 16 and 17. The reasoning presupposes what has been said previously (2:18b–19a). Because reality (perfection, fulness, salvation) is tied to Jesus Christ and may be attained without observing secondary regulations, faith in Jesus Christ cannot disparage or "disqualify" anyone. The Greek verb καταβραβεύειν (to rob of a prize) denotes an unfavorable or unfair decision—originally as a statement of the referee in the world of sports.[14] Essentially it is the same thing as "judging" in 2:16 (§ 12).

The following term, θέλων, which we prefer to translate "finding pleasure in" (RSV: "insisting"), poses linguistic problems. It is the participial form of a verb with the basic meaning of "wish, desire." It can also refer to the verb "rob of a prize," namely: "No one may rob you wilfully of the prize. . . ."[15] But this is unlikely not only because of the postpositive position of the participle, but also because of the content. That the opponents wanted to rob the recipients of their

---

[12]v. Soden; Masson; Schmidt, *Leib*, p. 192 (he goes to the extent of assuming a shortened form for τὸ δὲ σῶμα τὸ σῶμα τοῦ Χριστοῦ); Lohmeyer (like Schmidt); Hugédé; Moule; Dibelius–Greeven, p. 34 (like Schmidt); Zeilinger, *Erstgeborene*, p. 161; Houlden; Lohse, p. 172f.; Lähnemann, *Kolosserbrief*, pp. 135–137 (who also sees a polemic against the asceticism of the false teachers here); TOB; Ernst (like Lähnemann); in part also Gnilka, p. 148, cf. Martin; Schweizer; against this, Haupt, p. 102; Best, *Body*, p. 121f.; see also →1:19.

[13]Martin (NCBC).

[14]The "prize in a contest" (βραβεῖον) is also discussed in 1 Cor. 9:24 and Phil. 3:14; cf. βραβεύειν (decide, determine, figuratively: rule, in Col. 3:15). On the meaning of καταβραβεύειν, see Blass–Debrunner–Funk, § 150.

[15]Calvin (*volens id facere*); Abbott; Peake; Dibelius–Greeven; Beare; cf. v. Soden, p. 53; Blass–Debrunner–Funk, § 418, 5; documentation in A. Fridrichsen, "θέλων Col. 2:18," *ZNW* 21 (1922), pp. 135–137: e.g., Epict., *Diss.* II, 19:16: καὶ σύ θέλων παίζεις = roughly: and you delight in jesting (when we are about to die).

prize is the opinion of the writer and not the opponents' intention, whose desire it was to help the recipients to attain what they considered to be the true prize. For this reason most interpreters tend to give it the meaning of "wish," "find pleasure in," which is primarily influenced by the language of the Greek Bible where θέλειν often renders the Hebrew verb חָפֵץ (find pleasure; cf. LXX 1 Sam. 18:22; Ps. 146:10).[16]

That in which the opponents find pleasure, namely, humility and worship of angels, are religious attitudes to be attained through obeying food regulations and festival days (2:16). This arises from the analogous structure of 2:16-17 and 2:18-19. Humility and veneration (cultic) are also discussed in 2:23. Hence, in terms of outward appearance, the opponents' worship of angels (re. content, see § 12) likely had the shape of an another cult,[17] especially in the sense of voluntary extra efforts in the area of asceticism, called "humility" by the opponents;[18] cf. Shep. Herm. Vis. 3, 10, 6; Sim. 5, 3, 7, where ταπεινοφροσύνη means fasting (the Heb. stem ענה unites both meanings),[19] and Col. 2:23, where humility parallels severity to the body.[20] Perhaps asceticism was to facilitate access to the supreme deity (§ 12) or to prepare for the reception of the higher revelation during the initiation.[21]

It is difficult to interpret the relative clause, "taking his stand on visions," linguistically, in terms of the history of religions, as well as theologically. It does refer to humility and the worship of angels. The false teachers "saw" all of this. The reference is likely to visions (cf. ὁρᾶν in Rev. 1:2 or ὅραμα in Matt. 17:9; Acts 7:31 et al.)[22] to which the opponents appealed. Literally they saw visions while "setting foot upon" (Gk. participle of ἐμβατεύειν), referring to entering into a confined area, and during the hellenistic period also referring to the *telesterion* of the initiation of the mysteries.[23] The combination with the

[16]See esp. Lightfoot; Haupt; Lohmeyer; Souček; Lohse; Houlden; TOB; Schweizer; Gnilka; on the translation, see Blass–Debrunner–Funk, § 148, 2; documentation in G. Schrenk, TDNT III:44–62, esp. p. 45, note 13.

[17]θέλω . . . ἐν θρησκείᾳ (2:18) and ἐθελοθρησκία (2:23) may also be connected contentwise, 2:23; Lohse, p. 184; Lähnemann, Kolosserbrief, p. 139.

[18]The negative connotation of ταπεινοφροσύνη is found only here and in 2:23 in the NT; Schweizer, p. 158.

[19]Jenni–Westermann, Handwörterbuch II:342.

[20]Cf. Percy, Probleme, p. 147ff.; Francis, "Humility," p. 114f.; see also § 12.

[21]E.g., in the Eleusian mysteries, Clem. Al., Protr. II, 21; Arnob., Adv. nat. 5, 26; Schweizer, "Christus," p. 310. On the gnostic meanings of humility, see § 12 above. There is little likelihood that humility here is connected with the humble minded (רוּחַ עָנִי = lit.: "poor in spirit") of Qumran (e.g., 1 QM 14.7), so N. Kehl, "Erniedrigung und Erhöhung in Qumran und Kolossä," ZKTh 91 (1969), pp. 364–394. The opponents were not an apocalyptically oriented Jewish group; § 12).

[22]On the teaching concerning the knowledge of deity via its pictures, see § 12 and cf. also Gos. Phil., NHC II/3; 67:10ff.; Iren., Adv. haer. II, 7, 4f.

[23]See § 12.

visions makes this comprehension quite feasible.[24] If we reconstruct
the heresy following the gnostic model (§ 12), we can also explain
the lack of concrete allusions to a mystery deity and its myth.

In his visionary journey through the elements of the world (spheres),
the myste of the Isis mysteries saw the upper and lower deities that
were subject to Isis, according to Apuleius (Metam. XI, 23). Perhaps
he also passed by her images and statues.[25] In the gnostic initiation,
which depicted the redemption from the material world,[26] the awakening from the spiritual sleep was connected with the revelation of
the light and with the unveiling of humanity's true situation under
the dominion of angels and demons, against whom the light is able
to protect (Ap. John, NHC II/1; 30:11–31:25).[27] The testing of the ascending soul by the great demon is also addressed in the Hermetic
tractate of Asclepius (NHC VI/8; 76:21–77:11 = Lat. Ascl. 28). Thereby
the opponents are not yet classified with regard to the history of religions, however; they are only classified with regard to the phenom-
enology of religion (§ 12). It is quite feasible that the author was able
to describe polemically the opponents' fear of and speculations about
angels, namely, as angel worship and the main object of their initiation, in order to abase them in their consciousness of superiority (2:16,
18, 23).

We do not consider the textual change to ἃ μὴ ἑόρακεν to be an acceptable alternative in the interpretation of this reference (C, Ψ, ℵ—
the second corrector, Byz., and a significant part of the Latin text tradition), nor the change to ἃ οὐκ . . . (F, G), namely, "taking a stand
on that which he did not see." In this case the opponents actually
would have seen nothing. But the author does not deny the opponents' visions,[28] he merely relativizes the quality of their content[29]
because they do not reveal the way to the true salvation (2:20).[30] As

[24]So e.g., Dibelius, "Isis Initiation," p. 88 (he rendered it roughly as follows: "who
enters (in the initiation) that which he saw." In Dibelius–Greeven the translation resembles ours.

[25]Dibelius, "Isis Initiation," pp. 80ff., 88; Pokorný, Epheserbrief, pp. 82–111.

[26]Cf. Pokorný, "Der soziale Hintergrund der Gnosis," in K.-W. Tröger, Gnosis und
Neues Testament, Berlin, 1973, pp. 77–87, esp. 84ff.

[27]G. MacRae, "Sleep and Awakening in Gnostic Texts," in U. Bianchi, ed., Le origini
dello Gnosticismo, Supplural Numen 12, Leiden, 1967, pp. 456–507, esp. 502f. The initiation may be restricted to the inner experiences and visions; W. Carr, "Two Notes
on Colossians," JTS 24 (1973), pp. 492–500, esp. p. 496.

[28]Lohse, p. 175.

[29]See esp. Haupt; Lohse; cf. Blass–Debrunner–Funk, § 154.

[30]The conjecture of J. B. Lightfoot is not convincing, according to which the text here
originally read αἰώρᾳ κενεμβατεύων = stepping into the empty space on the tight-
rope; so also Percy, Probleme, p. 172ff. Other conjectures also presuppose κενεμβατεύειν
(overview in Lohse, p. 175, note 4), e.g., ἀέρα κενεμβατεύων (= stumbling into the air),
so J. R. Harries, "St. Paul and Aristophanes," ET 34 (1922–23), pp. 151–156 and B. G.
Hall "The Second Chapter of Colossians," ET 35 (1923–24), p. 44, who collected pos-

soon as we admit that this may be a saying of the false teachers cited here, the need for conjectures disappears.[31]

The last part of the verse condemns the puffed up attitude and conceit of the opponents (cf. 2:16, 18a): They are conceited without reason (εἰκῇ); their behavior is indicative of their sensuous (σάρξ; →2:11, 13, 23) mind (νοῦς). In Gnosticism νοῦς was an important concept (e.g., Iren., *Adv. haer.* I, 1, 1); in Hermeticism it even was the divine, original principle (e.g., *Corp. Herm.* I, 6, 12) which leads the soul to understanding (X, 21). But here *nous* (mind, intellect) denotes precisely the fleshly, thisworldly entity. It may be a polemic against the role of *nous* in the heresy. In 2:23 ascetic wisdom is revealed similarly as an instrument of the flesh. More conspicuous here is the polemic point against the initiation of the opponents which might culminate in the contemplation of the heavenly deity (cf. the revelation of the deity in the form of light in Iren., *Adv. haer.* I, 29, 1; 30, 1; *Gos. Eg.*, NHC III/2; 40:15ff.; *Gos. Thom.* Log. 50, 61 et al.). Asceticism (humility) was to be preparatory for all of this, but here (and in 2:23) it is unveiled as something this-worldly.[32] Nearness to God is indeed not attained by the Christian's being liberated from relationships with other people (in the church), and especially not by relativizing the crucified and resurrected One as the head of the church. This is the theme of v. 19 in which the warning of this verse is substantiated. There the head is Jesus Christ[33] in his twofold authority as agent of creation and as head of the church (→1:18; →2:10; § 10 [c], cf. Eph. 1:22f.; on 2:18 see also after 2:19).

§14 *Excursus: Body of Christ (II)*

Christians recognize and confess Jesus Christ as their head and thus form the body which obeys the head. Since Christ is at the same time the agent of creation, we have to reckon with the conception of his twofold authority in Colossians: the objective authority over creation and the acknowledged authority over the church (1:18; 2:10). In Ephesians this conception is already developed (Eph. 1:22f.).

The picture of the church as the body of Christ was previously used by Paul (1 Cor. 6:15f.; 12:12–31; Rom. 12:4ff.). By means of it he established the unity of the church as local community, including all

---

sible parallels from Aristophanes for this, see also *Second Treatise of Seth*, NHC VII/2; 65:13.

[31]Lohse.

[32]Evans, "Mystics," p. 198f.

[33]Hence Gk. uses ἐξ οὗ (from whom), although κεφαλή (head) is feminine.

the diversity of the spiritual gifts (charisms), as well as its union with Christ (1 Cor. 6).[34]

The figure of society or the state as an organism was common in antiquity. We have become acquainted with it especially via the parable of Menenius Agrippa, which he supposedly told during the class uprisings in Rome (494 BCE; Liv. II, 32:8–12, cf. Plut., De Philopoem 8:3).[35] Colossians (1:24; 2:9b–10, 17, 19) and Ephesians (see § 11) are linked with the Pauline usage, but their understanding of the church as the body of Christ contrasts from that of the apostle in several typical points of issue.

(a) Whereas this figure is used as a comparison in Paul (1 Cor. 12:12; Rom. 12:4f.), it becomes an irreplaceable expression in Colossians and Ephesians. The comprehension of the cosmos as an organism, which we have already encountered in the hymn (§ 11), has contributed to this. If the false teachers were associated with Gnosticism, they thoroughly spiritualized this conception and transposed it to the spiritual world. Corpus Hermeticum XIII, 8, for instance, describes spiritual initiation as "alignment of the logos" and the gnostic god "Man" (anthrōpos) is frequently understood as the sum total of the world "above" (Hippol., Phil. V, 7:6).[36] If the church, according to the author's addition in 1:18a, is the body of Christ, the church is the organism in which—using a modern expression—the ultimate purpose of existence is focused. The church is not the body of Christ on account of its moral perfection, but because it is dependent upon Christ as its head. In distinction to every possible, spiritually mystical interpretation of being raised together with Christ (→1:12f.; § 13), it is here understood concretely as participation in the life of the church,[37] which means that it is also made concrete socially. This will be confirmed by the paraenesis (Part IV).

(b) In contrast to the main letters of Paul, Christ is here described explicitly as the head of the body. In terms of the history of religions, this motif has also been borrowed from the conception of the world as an organism, as found in the hymn of 1:15–20 (cf. e.g., Orph. Fragm. 168). This motif, too, may have played a part for the opponents,[38] but

---

[34]A. Wikenhauser, Die Kirche als der mystische Leib Christi nach dem Apostel Paulus, Münster, 1937, esp. p. 154ff., (he argues for the authenticity of Col., however); P. Bonnard, "L'église, corps de Christ," most recently in P. Bonnard, Anamnesis, Cahiers de la RThPH 3, Geneva, 1980, pp. 145–158.

[35]G. D. Kilpatrick, "A Parallel to the New Testament Use of σῶμα," JTS 13 (1962), p. 117.

[36]For further documentation see § 11; cf. Käsemann, Leib, pp. 65ff., 147ff., 157ff.; H. M. Schenke, Der Gott "Mensch" in der Gnosis, Berlin, 1962, p. 6ff.

[37]Merklein, "Theologie," p. 49ff.

[38]The heavenly head is mentioned explicitly e.g., in the Naassene sermon (Hippol., Phil. V, 8, 13) or in the Odes Sol. 17:14–16 which have a gnostic coloring, though not a gnostic imprint. The description of Jesus Christ as head in Ign., Trall. 11:2 may already

the only certainty is that the equation of Jesus Christ with the head underscores his central position.

(c) The image of the church as body in Paul refers primarily to life together within the Christian community and to its witness;[39] Colossians and Ephesians emphasize the worldwide unity of the church of Jesus Christ which joins all believers and those baptized into one body. The influence of the conception of the cosmic body is also discernible here, but the application is descriptive of the time in which Christians were already apart from Judaism and searched for their own identity as a social entity.[40]

(d) Finally, the motif of growth that is mentioned here as well contrasts the soma concept in Colossians and Ephesians against that of the Pauline homologoumena. This motif is likewise taken from the cosmological tradition and is applied to the church alone here.[41] The church grows by means of the love of Christ (Eph. 5:29)[42] and the charisms of the individual members (Eph. 4:16). Missions is the outward aspect of growth (Col. 1:6, 24ff.).[43] All of these motifs are also echoed here (Col. 2:19). This may be emphasized over against the opponents'[44] cosmic-metaphysical concept of salvation;[45] in any case, it relativizes the attempts to understand the theology of these two letters as the nullification of eschatology.[46] Although the futuristic eschatology is peripheral here, its function with reference to the believing community is expressed in terms of linking the Christian hope with faith, of dependence upon the cross and resurrection of Christ, of the paraenesis, and especially of linking it with the concrete social milieu of the church (cf. § 13). The growth motif guards the assurance of salvation against the danger of self-affirmation.

The argument against the Colossian philosophy, then, is cast in the form of a conflict regarding the interpretation of the notion of body–

---

be influenced by Eph. and Col.; on the issue as a whole, see Pokorný, *Epheserbrief*, pp. 33–69, esp. p. 67.

[39]The Pauline conception of the body of Christ is distinct from the cosmic conception especially when it is used in conjunction with Jesus as the Lord of the Supper: 1 Cor. 10:14–22, cf. Rom. 12:5; see H. Hegermann, "Zur Ableitung der Leib-Christi-Vorstellung," *ThLZ* 85 (1960), pp. 839–842.

[40]Mussner, *Christus*, p. 137ff.; Lohse, "Christusherrschaft," p. 215f.

[41]Gnilka, p. 152.

[42]Mussner, *Christus*, p. 142ff.

[43]Schweizer, p. 163; on the inward and outward dimension of growth, see Steinmetz, *Heils-Zuversicht*, p. 127f.

[44]The concept of growth is not characteristic for the spiritual and religious milieu of gnosticism, though it is found in *Corp. Herm.* I, 18, cf. IV, 11 and in part also in Ogd. Enn., NHC VI/6; 54:27.

[45]Merklein, "Theologie," p. 51, note 107: "As a historical organism the church has yet to become what it already is as an organism in Christ."

[46]So esp. Lindemann, *Aufhebung*, p. 239; Schenk, "Christus," pp. 147–151.

members (see § 11), which is also referenced in 1:15–20. The opponents spiritualized it while the author "socialized" it in dependence upon Paul, that is, he related it to the church and rendered it dependent upon Jesus Christ.[47]

19 Here the warning of 2:18 finds its substantiation. The opponents did not attain the divine head because Jesus Christ, as the head of the church, is the true head. However, this can be derived only from the context of 1:18, 24 and 3:15 (cf. also Eph. 4:1–16), since the concept of body per se can be understood similarly to that in 2:17. Yet we know that in the entire Pauline realm the concept of body often referred to the church and in particular we know that in Colossians growth describes the mission. (→1:6).[48] Hence the expression is congruent with 1:18a (incl. appositional genitive "of the church"). The emphasis on the joints and ligaments may indicate a polemic against the annulment of relationships and the elimination of the senses that were necessary in order to attain salvation in Gnosticism[49] (cf. *Corp. Herm.* XIII, 3[50]). The union with the immaterial light also occurs as the venue to overcome the pressure of the heavenly powers (Acts Andr. B, 6). In our context the joints and ligaments (originally also part of the cosmological conception, e.g., Philo, *Quis Her.* 246, δεσμός) depict the communication within the church through the word, the sacraments, and brotherly love (3:12–15). The opponents are "puffed up without reason" because they underestimate the church as the social structure of life in the faith. Phenomenologically their attitude was similar to that of those who were "strong" in Corinth who ate the food sacrificed to idols and thereby disrupted the unity of the Christian community. They too appealed to a higher knowledge (1 Cor. 8:1–13, esp. vv. 1 and 11, cf. 1 Cor. 4:6; 5:2).[51] The emphasis upon the new life in the framework of a special group which sociologically may lead to their isolation,[52] expresses primarily the social dimension of personal faith here.[53]

20–23 The following three verses form a minor subunit[54] in which the author outlines the consequences from the first, negative part of his argument. As far as content is concerned, the appeals and warnings are similar to those of Col. 2:6, 8, except that in place of the ref-

---

[47]Cf. S. Hansen, *The Unity of the Church in the New Testament*, Acta Sem. neotest. Ups. 14, Uppsala, 1946, p. 109ff.; Schweizer, "Kirche," p. 298ff.; Weiss, "Motive," p. 322f.
[48]Cf. also § 9 (c), note 83 on 1:15–20, and esp. →2:17.
[49]See also Pokorný, *Epheserbrief*, p. 57.
[50]Cf. Gnilka, p. 69.
[51]Lohse, p. 178.
[52]Meeks, "Body," p. 213.
[53]Pokorný, *Epheserbrief*, pp. 127f., 130ff.
[54]Regarding its structure, see Zeilinger, *Erstgeborene*, p. 59ff.; Gnilka, p. 55 — he anticipates the beginning of a new pericope here.

erence to faith's establishment (2:7), he argues on the premise of the first part of the Easter message, namely, the death of Christ (2:20). Dying (2:12 speaks of being buried) with Christ makes possible the liberation from the external demands — an echo of the argumentation in Gal. 2:19–3:5, cf. Rom. 6:2–7; 7:4–6. It does indeed mean that the one baptized is part of the new age in which the powers of this world no longer have any power.[55] For Paul it meant liberation from the demands of the Mosaic law, here from the external demands of the false teachers. The common denominator is that in both cases there was a dependence upon the intermediate beings; the law was proclaimed by angels (Gal. 3:19; cf. Acts 7:53), while the regulations of the false teachers (δόγμα, δογματίζειν[56]) are dependent upon the superhuman powers (→2:14f.). The two intermediaries are described as "elements" (στοιχεῖα, Gal. 4:3–5:9; Col. 2:8, 20). The theological accomplishment of the author of Colossians is to be sought in the analogous function of these diverse phenomena.[57]

If the message of the resurrection has been accepted, the gospel already begins with "dying with Christ" in baptism and in the exercise of faith. The death of Christ, the effect of which is being actualized in baptism, has led to the disarming of the superhuman powers (2:14f.; § 10). It has been shown that they are not able to gain entry into the presence of God, nor are they able to obstruct it. Hope, the object of which is already laid up in heaven (→1:5), makes a new life in this world possible; in spite of all the external influences, it is not determined by the latter but by faith (1:4). Every indirect summons not to live in the world has to be understood in this manner. Likewise the Gospel of John, with its conspicuous separation from the world, emphasizes that Christians are in the world, though not "of" the world. The latter is separated from the eschatological fulfillment by the boundary of temptations and of death. Here the eschatological proviso is expressed in terms of eschatology rather than of paraenesis.

21 The prohibitions are linked with the prohibition series of 2:16.[58] At least the second prohibition refers to food ("do not taste"). The remaining two are almost indistinguishable. The verb ἅπτεσθαι, which we translate "touch," is used to denote sexual relations in 1 Cor. 7:1. On account of 2:22 this can hardly be in mind here.[59] Rather, it re-

---

[55]The Pauline forensic notion that the death of the accused signals the cessation of the criminal procedure (Rom. 7:1) is secondary in comparison with this fundamental experience.

[56]Literally "to allow the imposition of regulations upon one," Gnilka, p. 157; "to acknowledge the obligating power of the δόγματα," Lohse, p. 180.

[57]Schweizer, "Elemente," p. 162f.

[58]Zeilinger, *Erstgeborene,* p. 60.

[59]See Schweizer; Martin.

fers to certain taboo requirements. Things which were taboo were associated with a particular ontological realm, regardless of whether it had positive or negative indicators, and contact with things taboo might have ominous consequences for the individual.[60] This is a history-of-religions phenomenon, and Christian faith effects the prerequisites for overcoming it. Only God, the Father of our Lord, is holy; everything else is his creation (1:16), hence it cannot be untouchable. In the OT only the sinner convicted by God can be declared untouchable (e.g., Is. 52:11, cited in 2 Cor. 6:17).[61] The desacralization of nature was one of the prerequisites of its scholarly investigation of much later times.[62] Although the observance of food regulations was not characteristic of the Gnostics with whom the opponents were associated (§ 12), in our opinion[63] it is compatible with their teaching. The Gnostic is able to see images of the divine—which for the Gnostic are untouchable—in a number of things (§ 12). In view of 2:23, according to which severity to the body (asceticism) is part of the program of the opponents, the ascetic concern could have been more important than the taboo character of things forbidden. Yet all of this does not need to be more than an emphatic expression[64] for the food regulations[65] addressed in 2:16.

22 This verse favors an interpretation such as this. That with which the demands are concerned is of no enduring value; it is merely food[66] intended for consumption. This is akin to the sarcastic and radical saying of Jesus in Mark 7:19, par., according to which foods cannot defile anyone, because they do not reach the heart. They only enter the stomach and then go to waste. Already in the pre–Markan tradition it was added that Jesus declared all foods pure thereby (Mark 7:19b, cf. 1 Cor. 10:30). A parallel to the traditions about the disputes between Jesus and the Pharisees can also be found in Col. 2:22b: In Mark 7:7, par., with the aid of the quotation from Is. 29:13 (LXX), the scribal interpretation of the Bible is rated as "human precepts and doctrines,"[67] and in Mark 7:9, par., it is described as a tradition in

---

[60]Behind this was the idea that the human world has its boundaries and overstepping them is hubris which the gods punish; Nilsson, *Geschichte* I, p. 374f.

[61]On the Jewish taboo requirements, see Letter of Aristeas 142 (cf. Ernst; Billerbeck III, 629).

[62]H. G. Fritzsche, *Lehrbuch der Dogmatik*, Pt. 1, Berlin, 1982², p. 320f.

[63]This would favor the argumentation of E. Schweizer who identifies the opponents with the Pythagoreans (see note 29 on 2:6–15 above), who adhered to food regulations. Yet there were also other Christian groups with an ascetic tendency: H. D. Betz, *Plutarch's Theological Writings and Early Christian Literature*, Studia ad Corpus Hellenisticum Novi Testamenti 3, Leiden, 1975, p. 307f.

[64]Cf. Bujard, *Untersuchungen*, p. 184.

[65]On ἅπτεσθαι in connection with food, see e.g., Xenoph., *Cyr.* I, 3, 5.

[66]Schweizer.

[67]τῶν ἀνθρώπων means "human" here; it does not refer to specific teachers.

conflict with the commandment of God, reminiscent of Col. 2:8. Thus the regulations[68] of the opponents are compromised. The use of OT quotations in the Christian tradition became common (e.g., Rom. 12:16–20),[69] similar to the minimizing of external regulations as human commands (Tit. 1:14). The affinity with Mark 7:19 indicates, however, that the author was also familiar with part of the Synoptic tradition.

23 Verse 23 adduces the final, summarizing (slightly demagogical) polemic against the Colossian philosophy, again in the form of an antithesis (as in 2:20, 22)[70] whose wording is not altogether clear and whose interpretation is rather difficult.[71] Again, this is probably the result of using some concepts from the opponents' teaching that were no longer understood by the later church. This may have led to text corruptions,[72] some which may be reflected in the extant MSS.

"These" (ἅτινα refers to the human precepts and doctrines, 2:22b),[73] not to the forbidden things, since v. 22a is merely an incidental remark. The actual syntactical crux is found in the conclusion of the verse, which sounds like an unnatural addition. According to some interpreters the latter refers to the beginning of the verse: "These have indeed an appearance . . . but they are of no value."[74] It is difficult to link the phrase οὐκ ἐν τιμῇ τινι (without honor, without value) with what follows, however. It lacks an adversative conjunction. Either the indulgence of the flesh has to be construed positively, or πρός (here translated "in") has to be taken to mean "against,"[75] for which there is little evidence in such contexts.[76] It is hardly convincing to understand the indulgence of the flesh positively,[77] since "flesh" (σάρξ) otherwise has negative connotations in Colossians (2:11, 13, 18).[78] Difficulties of this kind are avoided with the hypothesis that 2:22b–23a ("according to . . . severity to the body") is a parenthe-

---

[68]Grammatically 2:22b could also be linked with δογματίζεσθε in 2:20.

[69]Further references in Schrage, *Einzelgebote*, p. 233.

[70]Zeilinger, *Erstgeborene*, p. 127f., notes a further antithesis in 2:22b–23a: human precepts/appearance of wisdom. However, v. 23 is a unit grammatically as well as in the argumentation.

[71]According to Conzelmann it is impossible to translate.

[72]Cf. Haupt, p. 118.

[73]Haupt, Dibelius–Greeven; Bo Reicke, "Zum sprachlichen Verständnis von Kol. 2:23," *Stud. Theol. Scand.* 6 (1952), pp. 39–53; TOB. Both translations allow for both possibilities.

[74]Houlden, TOB, Schweizer.

[75]Lightfoot, v. Soden, RSV, NEB, GNB, TOB (alternate possibility), Moule, Caird, Martin.

[76]A summary of the evidence is found in Lightfoot.

[77]So must church fathers, e.g., Chrysostom, cf. B. Haussler, "Zur Satzkonstruktion und Aussage in Kol. 2:23," in *Wort Gottes in der Zeit*, FS K. H. Schelkle, Düsseldorf, 1973, pp. 143–148.

[78]This is also true of "satisfaction" (πλησμονή), cf. e.g., Hab. 2:16 (LXX).

sis,[79] but in this case the interruption would be too lengthy.[80] Other translations separate the two parts of 2:23b and link the conclusion with the first part: "These are here [ἅτινά ἐστιν] . . . [for] the indulgence of the flesh."[81] In this case the remainder of the verse is an insertion: ". . . though they have an appearance of wisdom . . . and severity to the body without any honor. . . ." For Paul the body is honorable (1 Cor. 12:23f., cf. 6:13). Thus the opponents' asceticism is criticized as a disregard for the body.[82] Our translation is also predicated upon this interpretation of the text.[83] Hence the verse says something like this: The precepts and doctrines of the opponents indeed have the appearance of wisdom because they look like additional worship, humility, and reckless asceticism, but in reality their purpose is physical satisfaction. Some of the conceptions and phrases which have been mentioned previously are reiterated here in conjunction with the polemic against the opponents.[84]

That which has the appearance[85] of wisdom does not refer to the individual precepts and doctrines which are the grammatical referent, but to the philosophy as a whole (→2:8),[86] which the author combats. Wisdom may be its self-designation or the name of a divine figure (§ 12). The reader knows from 2:3 already that this refers to an apparent wisdom only, because there it reads that the hidden treasures of wisdom and of knowledge are found in Jesus Christ.

The "rigor of devotion" (ἐθελοθρησκία) is probably a new linguistic formulation on the part of the author[87] and can also denote a self-made cult or despotism.[88] In this case one would have to consider

---

[79]Dibelius–Greeven. The flow which is interrupted by the parenthesis, would then be as follows: " . . . referring to things which all perish as they are used . . . but they are of no value in checking the indulgence of the flesh." On its critique, see Lohse, p. 183.

[80]For this reason some interpreters take 2:23b to be an augment (Abbott, Beare, Lohse, Gnilka et al.). But this again does not avoid the problems mentioned above. According to Ernst, the words about the value in 2:23b are part of the parenthesis.

[81]Reicke (see note 73 above); Blass–Debrunner–Funk, § 353, 2b.

[82]In this view, the absence of the second adversative conjunction (δὲ) in the final clause is not awkward. Its ommission is unusual in any case, but it is not impossible grammatically: Blass–Debrunner–Funk, § 477, 2c.

[83]For the grammatical substantiation, see B. Hollenbach, "Col. 2:23: Which Things lead to the Fulfillment of the Flesh," NTS 25 (1978–79), pp. 254–261, as well as in Alford or Peake. Haupt is in close proximity to this interpretation. The rest of the translations of this kind differ in the understanding of the phrase "of no value." Reicke (see note 73 above) takes τιμή to mean regard for the weaker brother in the Christian community (Rom. 12:10); for Lohse (p. 183f.) τιμή may denote the deification in the initiation of the false teachers; cf. Reitzenstein, Mystery Religions, pp. 320–322, appealing to Apul., Metam. XI, 22 (dignatio, dignatus); on the whole, see H. Hübner, EWNT III:856–860.

[84]Bujard, Untersuchungen, p. 99.

[85]On λόγος as rumor, see e.g., John 21:23.

[86]Bornkamm, "Heresy," p. 126ff.

[87]Blass–Debrunner–Funk, § 118, 2.

[88]Cf. ἐθελοδιδάσκαλος in Shep. Herm., Sim. 9, 22, 2.

this a polemical inversion of the opponents' term.[89] But since all the other terms mentioned in parallel (wisdom, self-abasement, severity to the body) are not negative per se, the reference is more likely to an additional act of devotion in the sense of a voluntary cult,[90] which is obviously identical to "delight in" or (RSV) "insistence on" (θέλων, 2:18) the worship of angels (θρησκεία τ. α., 2:18; § 12).[91] Hence the author qualified the self-imposed strictness of devotion of the false teachers as angel worship.[92] In contrast to the official religion of the Greek polis, to the Roman cult of the emperor, or to the cult of the Manes (gods of the dead), to which everyone adhered from birth, the "strictness of devotion" might describe the cult of the mystery deities, that is, the deities whose worship was a matter of personal choice and which were proclaimed by peripatetic prophets. However, the choice of deity here is described as an illusion — almost in the sense of Feuerbach's criticism of religion, which emerged from the need for self-gratification. In reality it is only the will (θέλημα of God (→1:9; 4:12) which affords entry to the way to life.

Asceticism (cf. 2:18), which is part of the cult of the opponents, is mentioned twice, for "severity to the body" is obviously the same thing.[93] Probably the phrase "of no value" refers to the severity in terms of reckless severity which diminishes the body's value as God's creation (see 1 Tim. 4:3). In fact, all of this serves "fleshly," sinful human existence;[94] it is the opposite of putting off the body of flesh (2:11), of the "old nature" (3:9). It is self-praise and has for its purpose the devaluation of noninitiate brothers and sisters, which is typical of the "sensuous mind" (2:18). The measuring stick of true and false selfdiscipline is whether it builds up or weakens the body of Christ, whether it receives with thanksgiving the grace which is offered or seeks its own praise. "Putting on the new nature" (3:10) is life in the fellowship of the church as body of Christ(→3:16f.).[95]

The critique of the overly pious group thus flows organically into the paraenesis which moulds the life of the community in concrete gratitude and common joy.

[89]According to Lohmeyer, the false teachers called it ἀγγελοθρησκία; cf. Lohse; Bornkamm, "Heresy," p. 134.

[90]Alford, Gnilka; cf. ἐθελοδουλεία (voluntary submission) in Plato, Sympos. 184C. We cannot discount a faint echo of a double entendre, however.

[91]See note 17 above.

[92]Schweizer, p. 159.

[93]p[46] and B do not have the conjunction "and"; they take the statement concerning the severity to be in apposition.

[94]Cf. προνοία τῆς σαρκός ("mindset of the flesh"), Rom. 13:14.

[95]It cannot be demonstrated that τιμή was linked polemically (ironically) with honoring the mystagogue and the gratification (satiety — πλησμονή) with pleroma (1:9, 19; 2:9), as a concept of the opponents' teaching; cf. Bornkamm, "Heresy," p. 133f.; Dibelius–Greeven; Gnilka, p. 161f.

Part Four: Paraenesis for the New Life (Exhortatio), 3:1–4:6

Two points of view overlap within the structure of the paraenetic portion: the rhetorical, in which the exhortation comes at the end of a speech, and the one regarding content, in which the appeals are the result of the argument; consequently the entire paraenesis is part of the major complex of considerations, itself pastoral in perspective, regarding the significance of the baptismal event (2:6–3:17; cf. Table 3). The gospel that the author endeavors to interpret (§ 13) through his argument (2:12f.) links the polemical and paraenetic parts; thus the segment of 2:20–23 serves as a transition. Both indicative and imperatival statements are derived from the concepts of dying with and being raised with Christ. In 3:9ff. the image of death and new life is replaced by the semantically isotopic metaphor of putting off and putting on (the old and new man). In all of this the Christian is to keep his or her focus upon the "firstborn from the dead" (1:18b), who is at the same time the agent of creation (1:15). The paraenesis, which picks up traditional material even in 2:5–17, concludes with the concrete instructions of the household code (3:18–4:1). The concluding summons (4:2–6) functions as a transition from the corpus of the letter to the personal notes and greetings.

1. Consequences of the gospel for the New Life, 3:1–17

(1) If then you have been raised with Christ, seek the things that are above, where Christ is, seated at the right hand of God. (2) Set your minds on things that are above, not on things that are on earth. (3) For you have died, and your life is hid with Christ in God. (4) When Christ who is our life appears, then you also will appear with him in glory.

(5) Put to death therefore what is earthly in you: fornication, impurity, passion, evil desire, and covetousness, which is idolatry. (6) On account of these the wrath of God is coming. (7) In these you once walked, when you lived in them. (8) But now put them all away: anger, wrath, malice, slander, and foul talk from your mouth. (9) Do not lie to one another, seeing that you have put off the old nature with its practices (10) and have put on the new nature, which is being renewed in knowledge after the image of its creator. (11) Here there cannot be Greek and Jew, circumcised and uncircumcised, barbarian, Scythian, slave, free man, but Christ is all, and in all.

(12) Put on then, as God's chosen ones, holy and beloved, compassion, kindness, lowliness, meekness, and patience, (13) forbearing one another and, if one has a complaint against another, forgiving each other; as the Lord has forgiven you, so you also must forgive. (14) And above all these put on love, which binds everything together in perfect harmony. (15) And let the peace of Christ rule in your hearts, to which indeed you were called in the one body. And be thankful. (16) Let the word of Christ dwell in you richly, teach and admonish one another in all wisdom, and sing psalms and hymns and spiritual songs with thankfulness in your hearts to God. (17) And whatever you do, in word or deed, do everything in the name of the Lord Jesus, giving thanks to God the Father through him.

The first three paragraphs begin with allusions to the argument of 2:12f. (Table 3). The entire pericope has one common concern: Because ultimate reality is linked with Jesus Christ (→2:17) and because the body of Christ is the church by virtue of its dependence upon him, there can be no way to God other than life joined with the church. To be with Christ has a social dimension.[1] The Lordship of Christ, which the powers exploited by sin (§ 10) do not have in perspective, is recognized by the Christian community (→1:13).[2] The paraenesis, therefore, is not moralizing at all; instead, it is a vehicle for the proclamation of the rule of Christ and almost borders on exorcism (3:5f., cf. Eph. 4:27; 6:11ff.). The summons is anchored in the proclamation of the gospel;[3] in 3:1–4 it comments on expressions of faith that perhaps belonged to the basic content of the catechism even then (resurrection of Jesus Christ, his exaltation to the right hand of God, the new life of the believers, their hope and the final revelation of the glory of God, 1 Tim. 4:1f.).[4] "As therefore you received Christ Jesus the Lord, so live in him" (→2:6).

The paraenesis accords surprisingly little attention to the actual situation of the letter. The polemic against the false teachers is present only in the constant references back to the argument and in the en-

---

[1]This is also the understanding of Eph. where this part is addressed in 4:1–5:20.
[2]Schweizer, "Mystik," p. 197ff.; idem, "Gottesgerechtigkeit," p. 474f.
[3]Wengst, "Versöhnung," p. 24.
[4]Wengst, Formeln, p. 126ff.

deavor to order the shared life. The author continues a paraenetic tradition originating in the common needs of broad circles in early Christendom.[5] At this point we see the second theological parameter in connection with the situation of the recipients. They are incorporated into the body of the church as a whole in which they no longer occupy center stage with their problems and temptations. This corresponds with the first parameter which we indicated in § 13, namely, that humanity's self-effort, including superpiety, is worthless; hope is bound up with Christ.[6] Only within these parameters can the gospel be adapted to the human potentialities of understanding.[7]

1 "Then" (οὖν) grammatically connects the paraenesis with the preceding pivotal pericope (Table 3). In terms of content the link is provided by the resumption of the second part of the argument of 2:12b (§ 13). The appropriation of salvation in baptism is emphasized in such a way that earthly death and the perfection of salvation to come are thus relativized. Hope is already prepared in heaven (→1:5); the goal is "above" (ἄνω; 3:1, 2); in comparison with Rom. 6, the notion of "not yet," relative to the eschatological future, recedes. It is not eliminated altogether, however. Life "with Christ" will be revealed only at the parousia (3:4; § 13). The writer obviously assumes that the full revelation will not come until after the recipients' death. In comparison with the soteriologically decisive death of Jesus, the death of the individual recedes into the background; theologically, it is not even mentioned. For Paul, who really reckoned with death as the "last enemy," the eschatological proviso was meant to guard against self-righteousness. In Colossians this function is carried out by linking salvation with Jesus Christ and by the developed paraenesis. The more radically the completion of salvation is emphasized, the more detailed the exhortation has to be (§ 13).[8]

"Seek" and "set your mind" (v. 2) are verbs expressing the attitude of life (Matt. 6:33, cf. Phil. 2:2 et al.). Similar to heaven, "above" is a metaphor for that which is transcendent and in the Bible is used concretely for God and his immediate presence. In Paul we encounter it in Phil. 3:20. Accordingly the exalted Jesus Christ sits at the right hand as Messiah, as articulated in Ps. 110:1 (LXX 111:1).[9] Early Christology associated this conception with statements concerning the exaltation of the crucified Jesus, and it was quickly disseminated (Mark

---

[5]M. Dibelius, *From Tradition to Gospel*, ET by John Steely, Philadelphia, 1965, p. 238ff.

[6]Grässer, "Kolosser 3," p. 137.

[7]Cf. ibid., p. 151.

[8]Cf. Kippenberg, "Vergleich," pp. 763–767; Lindemann, p. 54.

[9]This is one of the few allusions to the OT, in the form of a midrash or pesher on this reference in the Psalms; beyond this it was secured by the Christian tradition.

12:35–37, par.; 14:62, par.; Rom. 8:34; Eph. 1:20).[10] The right hand side of the ruler was the place of honor for those who were to carry out his will (1 Kings 2:19, cf. Zech. 3:1). Here the picture emphasizes the subordination of the superhuman powers to the power of the resurrected Christ (→2:15, 19).

2 To "set one's mind on things that are above" is tantamount to seeking the things "which are above" (v. 1a, cf. 1:5). "Above," in contrast to "on earth," does not merely denote spirituality here, but especially the fellowship with the exalted Jesus Christ (Phil. 3:19f.) who will be coming from heaven (cf. Mark 14:62, par.). "On earth" means everything that hinders fellowship with Jesus Christ, including the pious practices and, paradoxically, also the opponents' asceticism (→2:23) — an argument which has its parallel in Phil. 3:17–21.

3 Now the discussion returns to the first part of the argument, except that the terminology used here is that of dying, rather than that of being buried (2:12a) and of being dead (2:13a). The purpose of the expression is the same, however: By faith (cf. 2:12) the conquest of the boundary of death is anticipated in baptism, and human hope's dependence upon God's love and forgiveness (3:12f.), as revealed in Jesus Christ, is acknowledged and proclaimed. The sinful disposition of life, characterized in →3:5, 8, falls to the wrath of God (3:6). There is hope for humankind in the midst of this life only because Christ has opened up a new perspective. Just as this hope is laid up in heaven and is not yet revealed and made complete (→1:5), so the new life thus far is also contained only in the resurrection of Christ that is witnessed and proclaimed. In the framework of the letter the eschatological proviso is expressed most clearly at this juncture (cf. § 13).[11]

§15 Excursus: Ethical Consequences of the Argument

The life of Christians is described in terms analogous to Jesus' destiny: buried with and raised with. This is also reflected in the paraenesis.[12] In Col. 3:3, however, the analogy is suspended by the remarks about the eschatological proviso. This is demonstrated not only in that salvation is contingent upon Jesus Christ, but also in that the new life has the shape of fellowship with Jesus Christ (→2:19; 3:4, 15, cf. Gal. 2:20; Phil. 1:21ff.; Ign., Eph. 3:2). It is only Jesus Christ, therefore, that the Christian can confess to be raised from the dead, which means

---

[10]See W. Thüsing, Erhöhungsvorstellung und Parusieerwartung in der ältesten nachösterlichen Christologie, SBS 42, Stuttgart, 1970, p. 46ff.

[11]Bruce, "St. Paul," p. 272; Weiss, "Motive," p. 320; differently Schenk, "Christus," p. 150.

[12]Emphasized by Schenk, "Christus," p. 152.

among other things that, as the resurrected One, he is fully identical with the crucified Jesus of Nazareth. The other people are being transformed by the offer of fellowship with Jesus Christ. Paul says in 1 Cor. 3:13–15 that Jesus Christ is the foundation of the new life, and everything that is not in accord with this foundation falls to the fire of judgment. For the believer whose being is bound to Christ, the judgment of God no longer means condemnation, neither is it excluded (2 Cor. 5:10, cf. 4:4f.; →1:10). It is some sort of refining and enablement for the fellowship of the new life. We read of these daring ideas in Paul only peripherally, and the author of Colossians has not adopted them directly. Indirectly, however, they assist us in grasping the dialectic of the proclamation of salvation and of the appeals in Colossians. The believer cannot be robbed of his or her salvation, of this the believer can already be assured; but this new life is still covered up with many sins which cannot endure the judgment of God. The believer may "put them to death" and may know that the effort for personal renewal has meaning.[13] The more emphatic the completion of salvation becomes, the more the paraenesis expands (§ 13; →3:1).[14]

4 The sentence regarding the hiddenness of the new life in v. 3 indicates that the author conceives of two phases in the revelation in Jesus Christ: The revelation in the Easter event, which reaches people through the apostolic proclamation (1:26), and the revelation of the heavenly glory (1:11, 27), which is to come in the end. The first revelation signifies the real change in humankind's situation (cf. § 10). The other revelation, mentioned in this verse as the final epiphany, is to be a solemn unveiling of the condition revealed in faith. In both instances the verb φανεροῦν is used, which we translated as "made manifest" in 1:26, and here as "appear." Essentially the concept of a dual or "split" eschatology is characteristic for the entire New Testament. It reflects the fact that the revelation of God (coming of the Messiah) in Jesus Christ transpired in the framework of this age; it was not connected with a cosmic revolution, as it was anticipated in apocalypticism.[15] For Colossians, however, the description of the parousia as epiphany is typical (otherwise only in 1 John 2:28; 1 Pet. 5:4).[16] The first revelation means that the believers (the "saints," the church) receive the mystery of the gospel, while the second one means that, together with Jesus Christ, they will be presented to the rest of

---

[13]Käsemann, "Baptismal Liturgy," p. 162f.; cf. L. Nieder, *Die Motive der religiös-sittlichen Paränese in den paulinischen Gemeindebriefen*, Münchener Th. St. I/42, Munich, 1956, p. 35ff.

[14]See also note 8 above. Regarding the issue of the temporal test of faith, see Schweizer, "Gottesgerechtigkeit," esp. p. 475f.

[15]This dimension of Pauline eschatology has been expressed aptly by J. B. Souček, *Teologie apoštola Pavla*, Prague, 1982², p. 66ff., cf. note 37 on 1:3–8.

[16]Grässer, "Kolosser 3," p. 146.

creation in the glory of God. The author is likely thinking of the end-time carrying away (Gk. ἀπαργησόμεθα) as in 1 Thess. 4:17, which at the same time is to signify the subjection and "taming" of the powers begun with the resurrection of Jesus (→2:15; § 10). How he conceptualized it, cannot be said.[17] The concept favors an apocalyptic context (2 Bar. 39:7), but it may refer to an external influence; besides, it is not crucial in the framework of the soteriology of Colossians. The only thing which characterizes the new life is fellowship with Jesus Christ (§ 15). Christ is contemplated both here and in the hymn of 1:15–20, the form of which the author of Colossians corrected (§ 9 [c]).

Instead of "your life," some manuscripts have "our life" (B, Byz. MSS, sy, sa, et al.). Since this differs from the second person plural in the context (3:3), and since it is theologically more precise (the recipients are taken up into the perspective of the common Christian hope), the first person plural is often considered to be the more likely original reading.[18] However, the theological precision may also be a secondary feature, and since "your" has better attestation, we have retained it.[19] Hence the author describes the Christian hope from the recipients' perspective.

3:5–11 The second paragraph focuses upon the negative consequences of the argument. At the same time, the paraenesis per se begins at this point. Dying with Christ is to lead to "putting to death what is earthly." In practical terms this means overcoming the vices that are listed in two sequences of five elements each in 3:5 and 8f. "Putting to death" those vices is identical to "putting off the body of flesh" (2:11).

§16 Excursus: Lists of Virtues and Vices[20]

Similar to the lists of virtues (→3:12; Gal. 5:22f.; 2 Cor. 6:6; 12:20f.; Phil. 4:8; Eph. 4:2f., 32; 5:9; 1 Tim. 4:12; 6:11; 2 Tim. 2:22; 3:10; 1 Pet. 3:8; 2 Pet. 1:5–7), the catalogs of vices (→3:5; Gal. 5:19–21; 1 Cor. 5:10f.; 6:9f.; 2 Cor. 12:20f.; Rom. 1:29-31; Eph. 4:31; 5:3–5; 1 Tim. 1:9f.; 2 Tim. 3:2–5; Tit. 3:3; 1 Pet. 2:1; 4:3, 15, cf. Mark 7:21f., par.; Rev. 21:8; 22:15) are likewise influenced by the ethical traditions of the world around them.[21] This applies especially to the tradition of Stoic teaching in which virtues and vices were listed and sometimes also placed in juxtaposition (Diog. Laert. VII, 110–114; Plut., *Stoic. Rep.* 15, 1041A).

[17]Cf. Gnilka, p. 176.
[18]E.g., RSV, Lohmeyer, Peake, Houlden, Ernst, Schweizer, Gnilka.
[19]E.g., Dibelius–Greeven, Jer., TOB, Metzger.
[20]Additional sources and documentation in Wibbing, *Tugend- und Lasterkataloge*, pp. xff., 14ff., and Schweizer, "Gottesgerechtigkeit."
[21]Emphasized by B. S. Easton, "New Testament Ethical Lists," *JBL* 51 (1932), pp. 1–12.

Similar lists are also found in the Wisdom of Solomon (virtues: Wisd. 8:7; vices: 14:25); some Jewish writings are influenced by the schema of the two ways,[22] which had its origin in the fables of Heracles (Xenoph., Mem. II, 1) and which influenced the ethical traditions of Judaism and early Christianity in many places (e.g., Did. 1:1ff.). In TBenj. 6f. virtues and vices are viewed as works of the good or evil superhuman powers which seek to dominate humans. The catalogs of virtues and vices are even more clearly related to the relative anthropological and ethical dualism[23] in the rules of the Qumran sect (1 QS 4.2–12).[24] The ethical acts of a person demonstrate that he or she is elect and will endure the eschatological judgment of God (1 QS 4.18–26).[25] In distinction to the mainstream of the biblical witness in which the will of God is recognized in concrete historical events, the catalogs of virtues and vices are a relatively new vehicle of paraenesis[26] that need to be addressed theologically.

In contrast to the central role of ethics in hellenistic philosophy, in the NT ethics is part of the consequences of the fundamental disposition determined by God. In the logia source (Q) the demands were framed by a human apocalyptic orientation and motivated by the perspective of the kingdom of God. The NT lists of virtues and vices (esp. Gal. 5:21; 1 Cor. 6:9; Eph. 5:5) are in similar fashion linked with the eschatological hope.[27] The eschatological orientation of the lists in Colossians is indicated in 3:4, 6 and in 3:13 is interpreted as dependence upon the grace of God. Their concrete shape is the possibility of being united with the risen Lord. The virtues and vices are no longer conceived of as two possible venues; Jesus Christ, to whom the Christian belongs (→3:10), is the only perspective of creation (1:15, 20) to which he is also proclaimed (1:23b). By faith (1:23a) everyone is able to live in Christ's sphere of power (cf. 3:1, 11). This alone and no forced decision is the motive for the endeavor of a new life.

As far as the content of the lists is concerned, we note that:

(a) The lists are linked to the non-Christian ethical traditions (as already indicated).

(b) They are usually modified for use in the Christian context. Instead of virtues of rationality (moderation) and of love of friends, agape, which reflects the love of God, is emphasized.[28]

---

[22]Cf. Seeberg, Katechismus, p. 35ff.; Vögtle, Lasterkataloge, p. 113f.

[23]Wibbing, Tugend- und Lasterkataloge, p. 61ff.

[24]For this reason the Qumran parallel remains "in the general frame of late Jewish paraenetic content," Braun, p. 233.

[25]Wibbing, Tugend- und Lasterkataloge, p. 71ff.

[26]This is a secondary literary genre: Wibbing, Tugend- und Lasterkataloge, p. 24ff.

[27]K. Romaniuk, "Motywacja soteriologiczna w parenezie nowotestamentalnej," Roczniki theologiczno-kanoniczne 15 (1968), pp. 61–76, esp. p. 70.

[28]Cf. Vögtle, Lasterkataloge, p. 165ff.

(c) The lists were not formulated as rigidly as certain portions of the early Christian confessional and didactic tradition, so that, on the whole, it is more appropriate to speak of only one form of tradition (that is of a literary subtype) and of a number of frequently occurring terms. Among the vices, those surfacing often are sexual immorality (πορνεία) and idolatry (εἰδωλολατρία, unknown in the pagan vice catalogs); and among the virtues, they include faith (πίστις), patience/endurance (μακροθυμία) and love (ἀγάπη), which is considered to be a fundamental virtue (3:14) precisely because it reflects God's love for humankind (3:12f.).[29] Since patience/endurance is premised upon hope, there is a certain analogy here to the triad faith–love–hope (→1:4–5a). Differing catalogs are used in Colossians and Ephesians (4:2f.; 5:9; vices: 4:31; 5:3–5), two of which (Col. 3:5 and Eph. 5:3–5) agree in three of the elements (fornication, impurity, covetousness as idolatry; cf. 1 Thess. 4:3–6; 1 Cor. 5:9–11, cf. Rom. 1:29–31).[30]

(d) The changes in the NT catalogs over against the non-Christian models denote an approximation to Jewish thought (idolatry as a principal vice, which has its equivalent in covetousness (→3:5); humility as virtue →3:12);[31] the most conspicuous agreements are to be found between the catalogs of Colossians and the rules of the Qumran sect. On the whole the paraenesis in Colossians (list of virtues and vices, as well as household code; § 17) is particularly similar to the external shape of the paraenetic wisdom tradition of hellenistic Judaism (esp. Pseudo-Phocylides).

(e) The combination of the catalogs with the household codes, which structure the life of the particular group within the framework of society (which was not the case, e.g., in Qumran), is descriptive of those groups exposing themselves to society at least to the extent that they are able to communicate with it on the basis of some common norms and practices. If this is not to lead to the elimination of the group's identity, its fundamental concern has to be formulated clearly as the framework of its conduct. The paraenesis in Colossians is also theologically based and is raised to the level of thankfulness (3:15; 4:2, cf. 2:6f.).

(f) The reason for the potential communication with the ethics of the world around them is the key position of Jesus Christ as the agent of creation and redeemer (1:15–20). That which remains the destiny of the created order in spite of sin is discovered in faith. Turning to Christ is simultaneously the individual's finding of him- or herself.

---

[29]See note 28 above and Wibbing, Tugend- und Lasterkataloge, pp. 87f., 99f. On the combinations of virtues and vices in the lists, see Vögtle, Lasterkataloge, pp. 13–17.
[30]Schweizer, "Gottesgerechtigkeit," p. 462.
[31]Schrage, Einzelgebote, pp. 187–210.

Sin does not mean ignorance of what is good, but especially denotes the inability to fulfill the latter (cf. Rom. 1:18ff.; 2:17ff.).[32]

5 The listing of the vices has its most obvious parallel in Gal. 5:19f. (except for Eph. 5:3–5); in its form, it has similarities with Rom. 13:12b.[33] "The members" (RSV: "in you") are not the subject of the sentence but the object,[34] because the notion of head-members (in the sense of Col. 2:18f.; Eph. 4:15f.) does not occur in the immediate context.[35] In the background is the somewhat modified conception that members serve either that which is good or fornication (Rom. 6:13; 7:23). Here the members are to be exchanged altogether (3:12), signifying the new purpose of life with its expressions. Putting to death the sinful members can be a conception compatible with the claims of the heresy of 2:20–23[36] and is in tension with the statement in 3:3 of having died. What follows, however, indicates that the reference is not to an ascetic attempt to spiritualize life, but to its socialization within the framework of the church as the body of Christ.[37] The argument that the later Manichaean conception of the five spiritual members[38] is presupposed here is merely speculation. More likely at issue here is the understanding that the redeemed belong to the realm of the heavenly hope (1:5; § 13) and the idea of the "cutting off" of their sinful members (which are "earthly"). It might be one of the conceptions associated with the opponents, who understood it in terms of the gnostic interpretation of the Attis myth in the Naassene sermon (Hippol., *Phil.* V, 7, 15). There the cutting up of Attis denotes his liberation from bondage to this world.[39] In this case the reinterpretation of the conception of overcoming the "earthly" members would consist, outside of the christological framework (2:12f.), of actualizing the new life within the framework of the church. Everything, therefore, that deifies the earthly, sinful life is a vice. It is not cosmic humanity which is discussed here but, similar to Philo, actual humanity. Nevertheless they are categorically regarded as members of the church; their life is not evaluated on the basis of their effort,

[32]G. Bornkamm, "Glaube und Vernunft bei Paulus," most recently in idem, *Studien zu Antike und Urchristentum*, pp. 119–137.

[33]Cf. Sanders, "Dependence," p. 42f.

[34]In the opinion of Ch. Masson.

[35]The addition of "your" in A, D and other MSS confirms that "the members" were viewed as object.

[36]So C. F. D. Moule in *RevExp* 70 (1973), pp. 481–493, cited in Schweizer, "Forschung," p. 180.

[37]Schweizer, "Gottesgerechtigkeit," p. 475f.

[38]Cf. Dibelius–Greeven, p. 41; R. Reitzenstein, *Das iranische Erlösungsmysterium*, Bonn, 1921, p. 160f., esp. p. 161, note 2. Concerning the five spiritual members, see *Acts Thom.* 27.

[39]E. Schweizer has pointed out the five vices and five virtues mentioned in Philo and in a similar context (the spiritual ascent): *Ebr.*, p. 21f.

but on the basis of their willingness to live in togetherness in the church.

Fornication (πορνεία) designates prostitution[40] or incest (Lev. 18:6–23, cf. 1 Cor. 5:1ff.); since OT times it also was a term used for idolatry (e.g., Jer. 3:2, 9; Ezek. 23:8, זְנוּת; cf. Rev. 9:21). Paul sees in it an expression of the superhuman power threatening the church (1 Cor. 5:11–13). Eros is characterized in the same way both in Pseudo-Phocylides 194[41] and in Qumran (1 QS 4.10; CD 2.16 et al.). Jewish tradition links fornication with covetousness (TJud. 18:2–6[42]).

Likewise impurity (ἀκαθαρσία) often occurs in connection with idolatry (Gal. 5:19–21; 2 Cor. 12:21f.). This concerns cultic impurity (Lev. 11–15), impurity before God, which Jesus perceived to be inward and which he rendered independent of external conditions (contact with an impure object; Mark 7:1–23, par.). This is also reflected in Col. 2:16. Hence the reference is not to external cultic impurity; instead it is obviously referring to sexual deviations or promiscuity. According to Rom. 1:24f., such impurity is an affront to the creator.

In contrast to Stoicism, passion (πάθος), in Paul, again denotes erotic passion (1 Thess. 4:5; Rom. 1:26f., cf. PsPhocyl. 194).

Desire (ἐπιθυμία, here "evil desire"; cf. malice in 3:8) in the Jewish tradition (esp. Ex. 20:13, intensified in Matt. 5:28) is that yearning which God prohibits[43] (in the lists of vices also in Tit. 3:3; 1 Pet. 4:3; in Tit. 2:12 equivalent to godlessness). The removal of evil desire is also mentioned as an accompanying phenomenon of the new life in Gal. 5:16. Evil desire is explicitly a sexual desire in the Synoptic tradition (Matt. 5:28) and in Paul (Rom. 1:24f.)[44] The reason for the list's focus on sexual vices is not prudishness, but the realization that the husband-wife relationship is first and foremost the most profound human interrelationship in which faith has to be proved.[45]

Covetousness (the only vice carrying the definite article) is at once characterized as idolatry, as transgression of the first commandment (cf. Pol. Phil. 11:2; avaritia = idolatria), hence it is the main vice (cf.

---

[40]B. Malina, "Does Porneia mean Fornication?" NovT 14 (1972), pp. 10–14.

[41]Immediately following (p. 195ff.), however, love in marriage is highly esteemed.

[42]On this issue, see E. Reinmuth, "Geist und Gesetz. Studien zu Voraussetzungen und Inhalt der paulinischen Paränese," Diss. Halle 1981, according to the review in ThLZ 107 (1982), p. 633f.

[43]See also H. Hübner, EWNT II:65–71, esp. p. 69.

[44]On sexual perversion as the conduct which is not able to endure God's judgment, see e.g., 1 Thess. 4:3–6; 1 Cor. 5:10f.; 6:9; Rom. 1:18–32.

[45]On the ethics referring to this in the time of Jesus, see Vögtle, Lasterkataloge, p. 22f. Not all of the affections are rejected here (as among the Stoics), only the sinful affections are, idem, p. 211. On the liberal morals of the sexual life in the early imperial era, see Artemidorus, Onirocriticon I, 78–80.

Prov. 15:16f.), as Jesus also emphasized it in his warnings against mammon (Matt. 6:24, par., cf. Mark 10:17–31, par.). Similar to the sexual vices, covetousness[46] is likewise part of elementary human relationships and for this reason is particularly dangerous for life in unity in the church.

6 The negative side of the eschatological perspective is emphasized here for the first time. The wrath of God is the judgment of God (Eph. 5:6, cf. 1 Thess. 1:10; Rom. 2:5; 3:5f.; Matt. 3:7; Zeph. 2:3, יהוה־אַף). The term itself shows that the judgment of God does not mean human judgment according to standards next to or outside of God's, but that God, in his love and "wrath" against sin, is the standard and the most profound law.

Most manuscripts (incl. א, A, C et al.) add the words "upon the sons of disobedience," a Semitic idiom for "the disobedient," to which the continuation of ἐν οἷς (among them) follows logically. But since this phrase occurs in the parallel of Eph. 5:6 and is not found in the oldest manuscripts (p[46], B, sa, et al.) of Col. 3:6, we have to assume that it is a later addition.[47]

7 ἐν οἷς can refer to the individual vices (cf. δἰ ἅ, 3:6) and thus translates "in such things"; in this case ἐν τούτοις in 3:7b (in our translation "in them") is a tautology, although it may also refer to the "members" (3:5). Since walking denotes life (lifestyle), this verse describes the recipients' pagan past (1:27; 2:13) as a consequence of the old age, which, since their baptism, no longer dominates them (2:12f.). For this reason they are able to resist its effect (3:8ff.).

8 In the structure of the letter, the sentence concerning putting away the vices (cf. Rom. 13:12–14) has its parallel in 2:20 (dying to) and 3:5 (put to death).[48] At this point the negative ramifications of the argument are developed: The vantage point which ("now") unfolds the resurrection of Christ to those baptized enables them to resist the evil expressions of the superhuman powers. Semantically "putting away the vices" is related to disarming the powers (2:15), and especially to putting off the body of flesh (2:11), and is theologically derived from them. The positive side of putting off is putting on in 3:10 and 12 (the picture of the garment).[49] In this sequence of the argu-

---

[46]Vögtle, *Lasterkataloge*, p. 25f.

[47]So most commentators; less clearly Metzger, cf. Bénoit, "Rapports," p. 16f.

[48]The cosmic background (Philo, Fug. 110) has practically no part to play here; against Schweizer who relativizes his own assumption in this regard ("Gottesgerechtigkeit," pp. 468, 472, 474).

[49]On the ethical background of the metaphor of putting off (cf. Philo, Somn. I, 225), see P. W. van der Horst, "Observations on a Pauline Expression," *NTS* 19 (1972–73), pp. 181–187; the most significant example: Pyrrho, the skeptic, happened to be attacked by a dog one day. When he was blamed for it, he answered "it is difficult to put off the man," Diog. Laert. IX, 66.

mentation, "them all," represents the vices that in 3:8b are depicted by means of a new, different list of vices (five vices again; a certain parallel is found in Eph. 4:31; cf. § 16), so that 3:5–8 constitutes a chiastically structured subsection.

In contrast to 3:6, anger (ὀργή) here points to a human emotion in which the individual is capable of doing that which is wrong before God (Jas. 1:19f.).[50] Wrath (θυμός, lit. fury) is a virtual synonym of anger (2 Cor. 12:20). Malice (κακία, cf. רָעָה in 1 QS 4.11) is a common descriptor of human misconduct (1 Cor. 5:8; Eph. 4:31f., cf. the "evil" desire in 3:5). Slander (βλασφημία) here denotes defamation, abuse (cf. Mark 7:22, par.), hence a sinful breakdown of human inter-relationships, similar to foul talk or abusive speech (αἰσχρολογία, only here in the NT). The meaning of "blasphemy" is also contained in the first term, however (cf. Matt. 5:21–26). "From your mouth," in proper Greek, should actually refer to "putting away,"[51] but here it refers to the final (two) elements of the list of vices.[52] The emphasis of "from your mouth" obviously is one of the author's notations in-dicating, similar to 2:22 (the reference to the human tradition), aware-ness of the tradition behind the Synoptic pericope concerning things pure and impure (Mark 7:1–23, par.). In the process of the church's separation from Judaism, the latter gained special significance for Christians and proved itself also in the polemic of Colossians.

9a is a summary of the preceding list of vices, as well as of the en-tire subsection of 3:5–8: Do not lie to one another! Lying is the result of separation from God which Jesus Christ has indeed overcome (1:21f.). It is the opposite of the proclamation of the gospel as the word of truth (→1:5f.) and in early Christian literature denotes wrongheaded action (Rev. 20:8; Gos. Thom. Log. 6). The new life is a social reality in the deepest sense of that term, and the Christian community is the realm in which there are (God-given) conditions for overcoming that alienation (see esp. 3:11, 13).

9b–10 The following subordinate clause (par.: Eph. 4:22–24; simi-lar combination of metaphors in Rom. 13:12–14) reiterates the image of putting off in 3:8 via the related metaphor of putting off the old and putting on the new nature.[53] All of these are allusions to baptism (Gal. 3:27; Rom. 13:12, 14 et al.). ἀπεκδυσάμενοι[54] and ἐνδυσάμενοι are not to be construed as indicative[55] but, in connection with the

---

[50]W. Pesch, EWNT II:1294–1297, esp. p. 1294.
[51]So understood by Oltramare, Meyer, Abbott, and others.
[52]So most interpreters.
[53]See note 49 above.
[54]Here with a different meaning from that in 2:15.
[55]So e.g., Meyer, Ewald, v. Soden, Masson, Houlden, Wilckens, GNB, Bratcher–Nida, Ernst, EÜ, Gnilka.

phrase "do not lie," imperatively.[56] This is supported not only by
the phrase "with its practices," but also by the parallel in Eph. 4:24.
The contingency of this process upon the history of Jesus (2:11ff.) and
the relationship of the new humanity to him are expressed here with
a reference to the image of God (cf. Gen. 1:27; →1:15).[57] The theme
of the first stanza of the hymn is taken up again thereby (see § 5 [b]).
In their new life Christians rediscover the intention that God had in
creation.[58] The newness of their life is the newness of the new creation (Gal. 6:15; 2 Cor. 5:17); the inner tension of this process is also
expressed grammatically. The new person, characterized by baptism,
is continually renewed in that he or she always recognizes, thanks to
a new perspective, what the will of God is (1:9f.; Rom. 12:2).[59] According to Gen. 3, eating from the tree of knowledge led to the loss
of the image of God; here knowledge is associated with the new person (cf. 2:2) because it is obedient knowledge. This is a play of se-
mantics that the author of Colossians formulated with the help of the
motif he adopted from Phil. 1:9. He wanted to reinterpret the concept
of knowledge, which possibly played an important part for the opponents (→2:3; § 12).

11 "Here" (ὅπου) refers to the "new nature," not to the image of
God or to knowledge: The new person is a social entity (→3:9);[60] it
refers to the communion with Jesus Christ (→1:13) in which the contradictions of the old world are cancelled. The social dimension pro-
tects the cosmic view of redemption and new life from illusive
interpretation. The cancellation of the contradictions is a significant
theme in the Pauline baptismal paraenesis (Gal. 3:28; 1 Cor. 12:13).

The fundamental contradiction eliminated in the church is the
contradiction between the chosen nation (Israel) and the nations (cf.
Exod. 19:5). God alone is able to cancel it through his election (1:12f.),
which signifies the forgiveness of sins (1:14, 22) and is recognized by
faith. The Gentile world is described as "Greek"—a metonymy for
the entire culture, its value system, and its religious milieu. The mir-
acle of the new creation means that the people who were raised in
this environment have recognized their hope in the crucified and resurrected Jesus. In contrast to Gal. 3:28 the Greek is mentioned first

[56]So the Vulgate, Peake, Haupt, Dibelius–Greeven, Conzelmann, Schiwy, Lohse,
Schweizer and others.

[57]On the role of Jesus as the image of God in soteriology (cf. Rom. 8:29) and ethics,
see Lohse, "Imago" (Bibliography on 1:15–20); Jervell, *Imago*, pp. 232f., 239.

[58]R. Schnackenburg, "Der neue Mensch–Mitte christlichen Weltverständnisses. Kol.
3:9–11," most recently in *Aufsätze und Studien zum Neuen Testament*, pp. 130–148,
esp. p. 138ff. In distinction to Eph. and Col., the Pauline homologoumena refer only
to the old, not to the new man (Stegemann, "Alt und Neu," p. 520f.). Yet Paul speaks
of the figure of the new Adam which the believers bear: 1 Cor. 15:47–49.

[59]See esp. Lohse.

[60]Tannehill, "Dying," p. 24: "collective entity."

here; the distinction between Jew and non-Jew is expressed (perhaps on account of the circumcision rite of the opponents; →2:11; § 12) in terms of a contrast between circumcision and uncircumcision,[61] and the distinction between male and female (probably on account of the tension regarding 3:18; § 17) is not expressed.[62] The next couple of terms is not an antithesis but an escalation: barbarian-Scythian. Both are non-Jews, but from the Greek perspective the barbarians were in juxtaposition to the Greeks. The Scythians were held to be the wildest barbarians (e.g., 2 Macc. 4:47).[63] The final antithesis stated is that of slave-free, which is also cancelled in Christ (yet cf. 3:22ff. and § 17).

That Christ is "all and in all" does not point to a pantheistic dissolution in the shape of the Risen One; instead, similar to 1 Cor. 6:15, the reference is to the immediate communion with Jesus Christ and to the direct exercise of his rule (→1:13, cf. 1 Cor. 15:18).[64] He remains the head of the body of the church and as such he does not intend to dissolve the body. If the statement concerning equality in Christ in Gal. 3:28 was part of the theological argument (probatio), it is part of the paraenesis here. In both instances it has ecclesiological significance and indirect missionary implications.

12 The final one of the paragraphs (3:12–15) unfolding the argument concretely, begins here (see Table 3). In contrast to 3:5–11, the focus here is by means of a list of virtues, once again on the positive implications of the argument. It begins with the metaphor of putting on, which was already used in 3:10 and which prepared for the transition.

The recipients are addressed as the chosen ones, saints and beloved – all attributes expressing the dignity of the believers. According to 1:26 the saints are the recipients of the mysteries of God, and by their Christian existence they demonstrate the importance of the gospel. "Beloved" (cf. e.g., 1 Thess. 1:4) is an attribute reminiscent of baptism (→1:12). In the faith, the beloved are sons and daughters of God, just as Jesus himself. That which they are to "put on" is the opposite of what they "put off": Lying to one another has its counterpart in heartfelt compassion and in the remaining four virtues (which equals five again) listed here. Heartfelt compassion as a hu-

---

[61]Cf. Gal. 6:15: The new creation obliterates the distinction between circumcision and uncircumcision.

[62]This may be the result of the heretics' conception of the male–female character of the supreme deity; see Plato, Sympos. 189Cff.; Gos. Thom. Log. 22; Gos. Phil., NHC II/3; 69:24–70:4; Hippol., Phil. V, 14, 2; VIII, 9, 2, et al. On the issue, see W. A. Meeks, "The Image of the Androgyne: Some Uses of a Symbol in Earliest Christianity," History of Religion 13 (1974), pp. 165–208. In some MSS (e.g., D*, it) "neither male nor female" was imposed on the basis of Gal. 3:28.

[63]For an example of the intensification of barbarian–Scythian, see Ascl., NHC VI/8; 71:5.; Bengel: "Scythae . . . barbaris barbariores."

[64]Cf. Schnackenburg, "Der neue Mensch" (see note 58 above), p. 141.

man virtue (σπλάγχνα οἰκτιρμοῦ, cf. εὔσπλαγχνοι in Eph. 4:32) clearly has social implications (cf. Phil. 2:1); as a reflection of the mercy of God (Rom. 12:1, in terms of content similarly in Eph. 4:32–5:1; 1 Pet. 2:9), it belongs to the common life in the church.[65] Kindness (χρηστότης, cf. Eph. 4:32) is "the great experience that God's love which is revealed in Christ and shed abroad in the hearts of His people by the Spirit . . . works itself out in them . . . towards their neighbours."[66] It also occurs in the list of virtues in Gal. 5:22 and in 2 Cor. 6:6 (with reference to God, see e.g., Rom. 11:22; Tit. 3:4). Humility (ταπεινοφροσύνε, cf. Eph. 4:2) is also among the virtues that are particularly important in the mutual relationships within the church (Phil. 2:3). Heroism and surpassing others were the educational ideal in the Greek schools (Hom. II. VI, 208 = 11, 784). Humility has a positive meaning in the list of virtues, though different from that of the opponents where it denotes fasting or self-abasement before the heavenly powers (→2:18, 23; § 12). πραύτης (meekness) is closely associated with humility (so also in Eph. 4:2 and Gal. 5:23). Patience (μακροθυμία, forbearance) occurs frequently in lists of virtues (Eph. 4:2; 2 Cor. 6:6; 1 Thess. 5:14; 2 Tim. 3:10) and thus is part of typical Christian virtue (→1:11), the outworking of which is described in the following verse.

13 The Christian community lives by reflecting in its life the gospel which it proclaims. The gospel is formulated in 3:13b: The Lord has forgiven you (cf. 1:3–5). This is again directly reminiscent of the argument (2:12f., see esp. χαρίζεσθαι in 2:13 and 3:13). That it is Jesus Christ who forgives and not God is unusual. As the Lord[67] whom God resurrected and exalted, he represents God himself to the believers.[68] The consequence of this, on the one hand, is thankfulness (εὐχαριστία) to God (1:3; § 13) and, on the other hand, forgiveness of others. In the Synoptic tradition the parable of the unforgiving servant in Matt. 18:21–35 addresses this state of affairs. The principle of analogy plays a significant part in the ethics of Colossians.[69] There are several examples in the Pauline letters of situations in which the forbearance of another (1 Cor. 11, cf. Rom. 15) or the actual forgiveness (2 Cor. 2:7; Philem.) were the only real solutions. Forgiveness does not mean indifference in regard to evil. It is a constructive act which love is able to elicit (cf. Luke 7:47) and thus is able to separate the neighbor from

---

[65]We are not told here that this *communio sanctorum* also includes the angels (→1:12), as Lohmeyer (p. 145) suggests; 3:16 militates against it.

[66]K. Weiss, TDNT IX:483–492, on p. 491.

[67]In Paul the title Lord is used mostly in the paraenesis; Neugebauer, *In Christus,* p. 147ff. In terms of textual criticism, κύριος (p⁴⁶, A, B, D*) is the original reading; the other readings can be explained by the influence of Eph. 4:32; Metzger.

[68]Cf. Mark 2:1–12. Here the exalted Lord is in mind; Lohmeyer, p. 147; Schweizer.

[69]Wengst, "Versöhnung," p. 24ff.; Schenk, "Christus," p. 151f.

that which is evil.[70] In our context this verse is the way of overcoming the lie (→3:9); the author had in mind the seduction on the part of the false teachers (2:8).

14 Grammatically this verse is still dependent upon the appeal to put on the virtues (3:12). Love (ἀγάπη; →1:4; →2:2) is the fundamental virtue (Eph. 4:16; 1 Thess. 5:8; 1 Cor. 13; Rom. 13:8, 10)[71] reflecting God's love for humanity (→2:13; 3:12).

It "binds everything together in perfect harmony." The meaning of this phrase cannot be established unequivocally. It is not impossible that it develops the image of putting on. In this case the bond would be the belt which holds together the individual virtues like pieces of clothing.[72] Since Eph. 4:3 (1 Cor. 16:14) also discusses this bond apart from this metaphorical context and in the framework of the intra-church relationships, it likely also denotes in this instance the perfection of the virtues within the common life of the church (cf. →2:19).

Every kind of means of binding, from handcuffs to the metaphorical bonds among the members of the family, has been designated as σύνδεσμως (bond).[73] Here it also refers to the metaphorical bond which makes one whole entity[74] out of many members (i.e., people within the church).[75] Hence this is a genitive of purpose.[76] The binding with love leads to perfect harmony. As early as in 1:28 the "mature person" was the goal of the Christian proclamation. Mature is the one who is able to endure God's judgment (→1:28). And to love means to desire this maturity for other people (cf. Luke 6:27–36, par.). This type of conduct is more demanding inwardly than rigorous legal piety. It requires continual growth in the knowledge of the beneficent will of God (→1:9f.). In an empirical community such maturity is not there as a matter of course. The genitive "of perfection," therefore, also carries ultimate connotations.[77] Thus perfection (maturity) is (a) the eschatological (though here more "spatially" eschatological) goal of growth, similar to the idea in Eph. 4:13. It is also analogous to the comprehension of love as eschatological reality in 1 Cor. 13:8–13. Perfection is not moral infallibility but connotes reaching the goal and (b) the integrity of love which responds to God's love in such a man-

---

[70]The reference is to a more active understanding of virtue than in the five virtues mentioned by Epictetus, *Diss.* 2, 22, 36.

[71]Severian of Gabala (Staab, *Pauluskommentare*, p. 328). On the unity and diversity of the Pauline virtues, see Vögtle, *Lasterkataloge*, p. 158ff., 165; Schrage, *Ethics*, p. 249f.

[72]Ewald, v. Soden.

[73]Documentation in G. Fitzer, *TDNT* VII:856–859.

[74]E.g., in the *Corp. Herm.* I, 18 it also refers to the bond which holds together the universe in its male and female dimension.

[75]Haupt, Conzelmann.

[76]Blass–Debrunner–Funk, § 166, 1. Hence this is neither an objective genitive (one cannot bind perfection) nor a subjective genitive.

[77]Lohse, Martin.

ner that it views all relationships in its light (2 Cor. 5:14f., cf. Eph. 5:25–30).[78] An analogy to this is found in the Sermon on the Mount (Matt. 5:43–48, esp. v. 48) which deals with the love of one's enemies, whereas especially the love for fellow Christians is in mind here. This is not meant to limit it, but rather to make it concrete in the relationships among the various house churches of the recipients.

15 This verse is related to the tradition of the apostolic salutation (→1:2) occurring at the beginning and end of the epistles (e.g., 1 Thess. 5:23). Its affinity here is with the concluding benediction. The word of thankfulness, reiterated once more in 3:17, likewise picks up the theme of the first part of the letter (1:3ff.; Table 3). For this reason some scholars are of the opinion that the following household code was added later (§ 3 [c]). But since the author of Colossians may have been the first one to use the household code (§ 17), it makes sense that he attached this new element, together with the personal greetings, at the end of the epistle.

Peace is to decide, rule (βραβεύω; cf. →2:18) in the hearts (→2:2. cf. 3:16) of the recipients. If love is the cardinal virtue, peace is the condition of the eschatological goal (→1:2; →1:20) and encompasses human interrelationships, as well as the relationships between God and humankind ("his body"–see § 14 and cf. Eph. 2:14f.). The summons to thankfulness is in keeping with the word regarding love in 3:14. If mutual love represents one side of the response to God's love, thankfulness represents the other side, the disposition by which the love of God is perceived. At the same time 3:15b connects with the introductory prayer of thanksgiving (cf. also →3:17), similar to the connection between the salutation of peace at the beginning of this verse and 1:2, as well as 1:20.

16 3:16–17 seems to be an addendum which concludes with another call to thankfulness. But it is more likely a literary link, formulated like a supplement, which introduces the household code (cf. e.g., 3:17 with 3:23).

The "word of Christ"[79] is identical to the word (4:3) and to the "word of God" (→1:25; see 1 Thess. 1:8). According to 1:25–27 the presence of Christ in the Christian community ("Christ in you") is part of the word of God and leads to an ever new unfolding of the word of God. The author has taken the metaphor of dwelling from the hymn (§ 9 [d]; →1:19) and applies it to the Christian community.[80]

---

[78]An echo of the Heb. stem שׁלם is also involved here; cf. Wisd. Sol. 6:15.

[79]A genitive of content; Souček, Houlden, Schweizer.

[80]ἐν ὑμῖν refers to the community ("among you"; so Meyer, Abbott, Dibelius–Greeven, Gnilka); the reference is to the church as the body of Christ (→1:27). For Peake, Haupt, et al. it refers to the individuals ("in / everyone of / you"), analogous to "in your hearts."

In Christ dwells the fulness of God, while the word of Christ dwells
in the community; in other words, in the community one is able to
meet God, and the word of God is able to and meant to dwell in the
community "richly" (πλουσίως), that is, adequately for salvation (cf.
1 Tim. 6:17; Tit. 3:6).[81]

Among other things, the word of Christ is at work in the community by means of mutual instruction and admonition (→1:28; Rom.
15:14). The admonition was probably connected with the instruction
as a warning against possible misconceptions; it had the approxi-
mate function of correction (1 Thess. 5:12, 14; 1 Cor. 4:14, cf. Col. 1:28).
The phrase "in all wisdom" (on wisdom →1:18; 2:3) refers to the
phrase "teach and admonish one another" (so also in 1:28), not to
"dwell in you" (roughly analogous to 1:9).

The translators are not unanimous in their understanding of the rest
of 3:16. Some associate the psalms etc. with what follows, namely,
singing.[82] They find it difficult to conceive of exhortation through
hymns, though psalms and hymns are mentioned side by side in 1 Cor.
14:26. There are substantial reasons favoring the combination of teaching and admonition with the psalms etc.[83] In the parallel of Eph. 5:19
we read that the recipients are to speak with one another in psalms,
hymns, and spiritual songs. Moreover "singing with thankfulness"
is to be understood as fulfillment of "be(come) thankful" (3:15b),[84]
characterizing the entire Christian disposition of life (cf. 1:12ff.). In
this case the teaching is the teaching of the grace of God, and one
of the hymns to be sung as an expression of thankfulness is Col.
1:15-20 (cf. § 9 [d]). The gospel and admonition are closely related
in the Christian instruction and tradition;[85] the imperative is derived
from the good news with its corresponding teaching.

The psalms, hymns, and spiritual songs, whose respective parameters were already Calvin's concern,[86] are virtual synonyms here (§ 9 [d]).
The psalms are in line with the tradition of the OT and Jewish psalmody,
but they are new formulations of Christian texts, as in 1 Cor. 14:26.
In view of the description of the Christian worship in 1 Cor. 14:26-31,
it cannot be ruled out altogether that the "spiritual (→1:8; § 12) songs"

[81]On the emphasis of the fullness in terms of the sufficiency of the gospel, see 1:27;
→2:2.

[82]Roughly: "sing psalms . . . to God;" Dibelius–Greeven, RSV, NEB, Lohse, Schweizer.
Others take it as a second expression of the word of Christ, namely: "Let the word
of Christ dwell in you . . . , teaching . . . and singing psalms . . . "; Ewald, Alford,
Jer., Houlden, Schiwy, TOB.

[83]So Lightfoot, Meyer, Abbott, v. Soden, Peake, Scott, Lohmeyer, Souček, Masson,
Conzelmann, Ernst, Gnilka, et al.

[84]In conjunction with singing one might more likely expect an accusative: "Sing
psalms . . . ;" see Peake, et al.

[85]So correctly in Schrage, Einzelgebote, p. 131ff.

[86]See the materials in Lohse.

denote glossolalia,[87] which would be directed into the proper channels by means of the reference to instruction and grace. But this is
merely a supposition. If one sings to (for) God[88] (1:12), it is likely
something other than intellectual instruction, but has to do with singing "from the heart" (→2:2), hence with instruction and admonition
through common participation in worship. Peace in the heart is peace
experienced corporately in the framework of the church (3:15).[89]

17 In conclusion, thankfulness is described once more as the fundamental disposition of the Christian life (cf. →1:3). A similar char-
acterization of the Christian life as life to the glory of God can be found
as early as 1 Cor. 10:31. The phrase "in the name of the Lord" is to
be understood as the orientation of all of life in which one is exposed
to the spiritual authority of the exalted Lord. Humanity is placed into
the Lord's sphere through baptism "in the name"[90] of the Lord Jesus
Christ (1 Cor. 6:11). By means of mutual admonitions (3:16) Christians
guard against forsaking that sphere (cf. 1 Thess. 5:11). Thanksgiving
to God the Father frames the corpus of the letter (cf. 1:3).[91]

2. Household Code, 3:18–4:1

(18) Wives, be subject to your husbands, as is fitting in the Lord.
(19) Husbands, love your wives, and do not be harsh with them. (20) Children, obey your parents in everything, for this pleases the Lord. (21) Fathers, do not provoke your children, lest they become discouraged. (22)
Slaves, obey in everything those who are your earthly masters, not with
eyeservice, as men-pleasers, but in singleness of heart, fearing the Lord.
(23) Whatever your task, work heartily, as serving the Lord and not men,
(24) knowing that from the Lord you will receive the inheritance as your
reward; you are serving the Lord Christ. (25) For the wrongdoer will be
paid back for the wrong he has done, and there is no partiality.

(4:1) Masters, treat your slaves justly and fairly, knowing that you also have
a Master in heaven.

Bibliography: See especially the relevant excurses in the commentaries, esp.
in Dibelius—Greeven, Lohmeyer, Lohse, Ernst, Schweizer and Gnilka. Other

[87]In the *Gospel of the Egyptians* from Nag Hammadi (III/2; IV/2), whose author
probably was already acquainted with Col. (see →1:14), the hidden mystery is expressed,
among other things, through inarticulate sounds, pointing to the inexpressible (NHC
III/2; 44:2ff.). According to K. Gábriš who analyzed similar phenomena in the liturgy
of Mythra, this may be an attempt to put glossolalia into writing; "Charismatische
Erscheinungen bei der Erbauung der Gemeinde," *CV* 16 (1973), pp. 147–162.

[88]So the earliest MSS. The reading of "to the Lord" is influenced by the parallel
in Eph. 5:19.

[89]On the didactic and pastoral function of thanksgiving, see O'Brien, *Thanksgivings*, p. 101.

[90]The name represents its bearer and brings to mind his authority; summarization
in H. Bietenhard, *TDNT* V:242–283, on p. 242f.

[91]Cf. Schubert, *Thanksgivings*, p. 134.

sources: Crouch, J. E. *The Origin and Intention of the Colossian Haustafel*, FRLANT 109, Göttingen, 1972; Lührmann, D. "Woman nicht mehr Sklave oder Freier ist," in *Wort und Dienst* NF 13 (1975), pp. 53–83; Schrage, W. "Zur Ethik der neutestamentlichen Haustafeln," NTS 21 (1975–76), pp. 1–22; Weidinger, K. *Die Haustafeln. Ein Stück urchristlicher Paränese*, UNT 14, Leipzig, 1928. See also the sources in the notes to § 17.

§17 *Excursus: Household Codes*

Colossians 3:18–4:1 constitutes the so-called household code (*Haustafel*) which has its parallel in Eph. 5:22–6:9. The household code is also found in 1 Tim. 2:8–3:13; 6:1f.; Tit. 2:1–10; 1 Pet. 2:13–3:7; *Did.* 4:9–11; *Barn.* 19:5–7; 1 Clem. 21:6–9; Ign., *Pol.* 5:1; Pol., *Phil.* 4:2–6:3, similar to e.g., Philo, *Decal.* 165–167, or PsPhocyl., 175–227.[1] It was the environment of hellenistic Judaism, then, in which Christians encountered similar traditions.[2] The particular material in the texts mentioned indicates that they are diverse in form and that it is possible only with reservations to speak of a literary genre or subgenre. Even the term household code, which we retain as traditional designation, is misleading. The admonitions shape the common life of the Christian (or Jewish) family only indirectly; no concrete demands are made, as in Philemon, for instance, nor is there general (common, cf. § 16) advice given about developing the life of the Christian family;[3] instead, Christians are given patterns of behavior as members of their respective class. In the Pastoral Letters, for instance, the classes within the Christian community are considered as well.

The model of the household codes has been sought in the Stoic lists of obligations (e.g., Epict., *Diss.* II, 10, 1ff.; 14:8; Diog. Laert. VII, 108), in which the obligations of a cosmopolitan individual to other people or institutions are enumerated. By fulfilling them the Stoic attains inward perfection and enjoys contentment. Later attention was called to the tradition of domestic advice, to the oikonomia, in which the roles of the respective classes (father, mother, child, slave) are described (Sen., *Ep.* 94:1; Arist., *Pol.* I [3–7] 1253B–1255B).[4] Nevertheless this also remains a merely indirect parallel to the NT household codes, since the advice has an overwhelmingly economic motivation and its literary frame is much broader in the former. By contrast, in Colossians the church is the decisive social entity in the concrete

---

[1] Additional documentation in Weidinger, *Haustafeln*, p. 14ff.; Dibelius–Greeven, p. 48f.; Lohse, p. 221ff.; Crouch, *Haustafel*, p. 74ff., cf. Lührmann, "Sklave," p. 71ff.; Gnilka, p. 207ff.

[2] Schrage, "Haustafeln," p. 7.

[3] According to Aristotle, the "house" consists of those who spend the day together, *Pol.* 1252b.

[4] Lührmann, "Sklave," p. 75ff.

shape of the Christian community (3:15). The house is not always identical to the house church. The master of the house may also be a pagan (cf. 1 Tim. 6:2 with Col. 3:22ff., see also Rom. 16:10, 11).

Early Christian household codes, then, followed a certain model in literature and obviously also in the forms of the oral tradition of the hellenistic and Jewish surroundings. But even the differences in form which we have observed in the possible non-Christian models indicate that they contain new important elements that are—at least indirectly—linked with the gospel.[5]

Since the household code of Colossians is the earliest Christian evidence of this subgenre, we may learn something from this example about the motives that led to the incorporation of the household code in Christian paraenesis and that may have influenced their function in that new correlation.

(a) All household codes are intended for daily life. As a subgenre they are part of that milieu in which one reckons with a perspective that focuses upon years, if not generations.[6] The adoption of the household codes could not yet have taken place in the era of the apocalyptic expectation of an imminent return during which the main letters of Paul were written. Paul himself, however, already developed conditions to overcome the expectation of an imminent return by showing that an anticipation like this is not part of the essence of the gospel (1 Thess. 4:13–18). In the proximity of his explanations we also find the nucleus of a household code, namely, the appeal to an industrious and orderly life (4:11).

(b) In 1 Thess. 4 we also find one of the significant motifs for the later introduction of the full-fledged household code: The Christians' orderly life is the best apologetic in a non-Christian environment (→4:5f.). The reference to the conduct before "all people," in Phil. 4:5, introduces the appeal to do what is also deemed honorable and virtuous (cf. § 16 [f]). The same motif is formulated in conjunction with the household codes in Col. 4:5; 1 Tim. 6:1; Tit. 2:5 and 1 Pet. 2:12, 15; 3:1.

(c) Without commonalities in the model of social behavior there is no communication with the world around (see § 16 [e]). The Christian attitude is indicated most conspicuously with the phrase "in the Lord" (3:18, 20, 23, 24; 4:1). In the Pauline realm this often signals that being in Christ (→1:28) has its ramifications for conduct.[7] Thus

---

[5]Cf. K. Romanius, "Les motifs parénétiques dans les écrits pauliniens," *NovT* 10 (1968), pp. 191–207.

[6]Weidinger, *Haustafeln*, p. 6.

[7]L. Goppelt, "Die Herrschaft Christi und die Welt," in idem, *Christologie und Ethik*, Göttingen, 1968, pp. 147–164; Neugebauer, *In Christus*, p. 147ff., cf. →2:6).

it is not insight into the rationality of the world order[8] but the confession of Jesus Christ as Lord that makes possible the coexistence with the world around. "In him all things were created" (1:16), and the practice motivated by the recognition of Jesus Christ as Lord, affirms the eschatological peace restored by Jesus Christ (1:20). This results in the emphasis of love, service, and obedience—social (though not exclusively Christian) virtues.

(d) The accommodation to the environment,[9] which several exegetes judged negatively, is more conspicuous than the Christian foundation. In our context it is primarily the affirmation of slavery which contrasts with the explanation of Col. 3:11 (cf. Gal. 3:28) in principle.[10] Here the accommodation to the environment goes too far, to the very boundary of what may still be considered Christian. Yet, in my opinion, that boundary has not been overstepped. The life of Christians takes place prior to the unveiling of the true life with Christ in God (3:3). The Christian lives his or her new life in the old world. The believer's missions-oriented, apologetic accommodation to the world around (item [b] above) is not maintained with the intention of immortalizing the existing societal order. It is to demonstrate that in their otherness Christians do not threaten their fellow citizens (cf. the "odium generis humani" argument of later Roman antichristian propaganda). It is not merely an apologetic motif. This kind of communication with the world around is essentially part of the gospel.[11] On the one hand, the gospel leads to the believers' separation from the "world"; on the other hand, the tendency is inherent in the gospel to influence all of life, including the weekday, which in that society was not possible except by subjection and industriousness. In contrast to the mystery religions and other groups which were not identified either with the "house" or with the polis, in the Christian community the whole world comes into purview.[12] By their confession, by their new foundation of morals ("in the Lord"), by their new personal relationships (Philem. 16: master and slave as brothers), and by forming a new social realm in the Christian community, Christians relativized the respective orders of the world. In Rom. 16:21–23, for instance, men bearing the names of slaves, such as Tertius and Quar-

[8]Schweizer, p. 218f.

[9]Crouch, Haustafel, p. 122ff.

[10]On the situation of slaves in antiquity and on their role in the church, see Gnilka, Philemonbrief, pp. 54–81.

[11]With regard to human interrelationships, this is also the concern of the words of Jesus in Matt. 5:38–42, par., in our context esp. 5:41; on this issue see also U. Duchrow, Christenheit und Weltverantwortung, Forschungen und Berichte der evangelischen Studiengemeinschaft 25, Stuttgart, 1970, pp. 170–180.

[12]Cf. E. Käsemann, "Principles of the Interpretation of Romans 13," most recently in idem, New Testament Questions of Today, pp. 196–216, esp. pp. 205f., 211f.

tus, and higher officials are on the same level. This contributed only in an indirect manner to the dissolution of the order of slave maintenance, but since the church is a social entity at the same time, it was nevertheless more than a merely theoretical equality of all people, as proclaimed by the Stoic philosophy and as present among Christians as well (→3:11). This is already a secondary reflection which views the household codes in a broader historical and theological context. During the time when the Pauline corpus came into existence, there was no real societal alternative to slavery, and the main reason for introducing the household codes was to give an authentic witness to the gospel, to live life before God in the existing form, and to humanize it by reflecting the love of God.[13]

(e) I do not wish to deny thereby the dangerous tendencies of the NT household codes. 1 Tim. 6:2, for instance, limits the brotherhood between the Christian master and the Christian slave proclaimed in Philem. 16, though it does not eliminate it altogether. The slaves are not to obey their Christian masters any less because they are their brothers in Christ. The reason for this exhortation, however, is to avoid compromising the name of the Lord in the eyes of outsiders (6:1). But indirectly this is indeed a testimony of the real change in the master-slave relationship in the Christian households (see also →3:25). According to *Did.* 4:11 and *Barn.* 19:7, all masters are declared to be the image of God again, but conversely the brotherhood of Christians is already made concrete in *Barn.* 19:8f.: They are a community which also inculcates temporal possessions (cf. *Did.* 4:7). In the community codes the paraenesis of masters and slaves recedes while the hierarchical superordination of the bishops takes on prominence (Ign., *Pol.* 6:1). E. Schweizer stated that christianization and paganization[14] go hand in hand here.[15] These dangers, too, belong to the intrahistorical effect of the gospel and indirectly divulge something of the concern that motivated the author of Colossians to introduce the household code. The false teachers led to asceticism (→2:18, 21), escape from the world, and superiority (2:18; § 12). The household code is to shield the gospel from a spiritualistic misinterpretation like this.[16] The sacrifice of Christ which brings about peace (→1:20;

[13]Wengst, "Versöhnung," p. 25f.; Schrage, *Ethics*, p. 255f.

[14]In 1 Clem. 20:1ff. the household code, with its emphasis on humility, is predicated upon the creation order. On the ethos of analogy in Col., see Schenk, "Christus," p. 152f.

[15]Schweizer, p. 220.

[16]Crouch, *Haustafel*, p. 145f. Considering what we have said in § 3 and 4, the addition of the household code can hardly be explained as a later decision, after the "Onesimus case" (4:9, cf. Philem.; so several English commentaries). However, the similarities in the final salutations in Philem. and Col. (→4:10ff.; § 3) lead to the conclusion that the household code of Col., in its second part, presupposes Philem. and intends to comment upon it.

→3:15) also has revealed the true order of creation which is able to motivate the Christians' witness in society.[17]

(f) The fact that the household code of Colossians is the very first one we encounter in Christian literature explains in part its position in the framework of this letter, after the formal conclusion of the major themes (Table 3; →3:15). It cannot be demonstrated that it represents a later addition dependent upon the household code of Ephesians.[18] The household code of Ephesians (5:21–6:9) is more clearly Pauline,[19] but this can be explained as a deeper reinterpretation of the adopted elements in the framework of the Pauline school. In particular, the reinterpretation has its correspondence in Ephesians in the more consistent correlation of the household code with the theological context and with the literary structure of the letter.

18 ὑποτάσσεσθαι (subordinate) is also used in terms of (often emphatically voluntary, 1 Cor. 16:16)[20] fitting into a structure (e.g., 1 Cor. 14:32). In the Greek world the subordination of women (cf. Eph. 5:21–24) was considered a natural order (Soph., *Aias* 293: Keeping silent becomes the woman's adornment, cf. 1 Cor. 14:34).[21] In Judaism the status of women was no higher, despite the words of highest praise for the "industrious woman" as housewife in the proverbial literature (Prov. 31:10–31). Her subordinate position in 1 Tim. 2:11–14 is derived from the history of creation and the Fall (Gen. 2:22; 3:13), while in 1 Pet. 3:5f. it is predicated upon the Abraham-Sarah relationship; nevertheless, salvation is explicitly promised to them (1 Tim. 2:15; 1 Pet. 3:7). Otherwise their subordination was based on missionary (1 Pet. 3:1) and apologetic (Tit. 2:5) arguments. The phrase ὡς ἀνῆκεν (as is fitting)[22] in Col. 3:18 shows the influence of Stoic motivation of duty in keeping with the world order (τὸ καθῆκον), but at the same time the premise of this duty, namely, "in the Lord" (see § 17 [c] above), indicates that it also represents a token of humility and sociability as Christian virtue (cf. 3:12f.). In contrast to Gal. 3:28, Col. 3:11 does not say that the distinction between man and woman is eliminated in Christ. In Eph. 5:23f. the submission of women has its basis in the salvific order.

19 The exhortation to the husbands is the counterpart of the paraenesis concerning the women. Marital love was not emphasized in

---

[17]The reason for accomodation among the Jews was the Noahic law with which non-Jews must have been familiar as well, Crouch, *Haustafel*, p. 109f.

[18]So Munro, "Evidence," p. 437.

[19]See ibid., p. 434ff.

[20]G. Delling, *TDNT*, VIII:27–48; R. Schnackenburg, "Die Ehe nach dem Neuen Testament," most recently in *Aufsätze und Studien zum Neuen Testament*, pp. 149–169, esp. p. 161.

[21]Further material in Crouch, *Haustafel*, p. 109f.

[22]On the impersonal meaning of ἀνήκω, see e.g., Eph. 5:4; Philem. 8. The imperfect here carries no special significance, see Gnilka, p. 217, note 57.

antiquity,[23] regardless of the OT testimonials of spontaneous love in marriage (Gen. 24:67; 29:18 et al.). In this context the author views love, which is also described as the bond of marriage, e.g., in PsPhocyl., 196f., in conjunction with 3:14 (on love, →1:14; →2:2). This is the precondition for the more profound understanding of marriage in Eph. 5:22–33. There the husband's love of his wife is motivated directly by Christ's love (Eph. 5:25). The opposite of love here is bitterness (πικραίνειν), that is, lack of consideration, anger, and irritability;[24] it denotes the rejection of the other, the disruption of communication with others and with God (cf. the correlation of bitterness with the curse in Rom. 3:14). Bitterness is cited first in the list of vices in Eph. 4:31. Love is made concrete here by way of the negation of this kind of negative behavior. The husband is addressed as the one responsible for the shaping of marriage. And love is the means by which all orders of this world can serve the new life.[25]

20 Children-fathers (parents) is another pair of functions belonging together. Children are called upon to be obedient (ὑπακούειν)[26] "in everything" (cf. 3:23a), which is more than the subordination of the wives (3:18). The obedience of children is already anchored in the decalogue (Exod. 20:12, cited in Eph. 6:2); together with the emphasis of the individual's sinfulness "from youth" (Gen. 8:21), this has led to more directive and sometimes even brutal rearing (e.g., Sir. 30:1–13; Philo, Spec. Leg., II, 232ff.). The Stoics, too, raised children to absolute obedience (Epict., Ench. 30). What is novel in this instance is that children are addressed at all and thus are regarded as human subjects.[27] Their obedience is given positive valuation, it "pleases the Lord." "Pleasing" (εὐάρεστον) is a major term in the language of paraenesis.[28] According to Rom. 12:1, the Christians' whole life is to be lived as a living sacrifice, pleasing to God.[29] That which is pleasing is formulated more restrictively here; it is equivalent to "in the Lord" (§ 17 [c]), which has a function similar to the eschatological promise in 3:24, 25b and to the admonition in 4:1b.

---

[23]For a summarizing essay on this topic, see W. Grundmann, "Das palästinische Judentum," in J. Leipoldt and W. Grundmann, Umwelt des Urchristentums, Berlin, 1965, pp. 143–291, on p. 175ff.; H. Cancik-Lindemaier, "Gesellschaftliche Bedingungen der römischen Erotik," in L. Hieber and R. W. Müller, eds., Gegenwart der Antike, Frankfurt/New York, 1982, pp. 29–54.

[24]The original meaning of πικρός is "pointed," "sharp," here used figuratively.

[25]Cf. Schrage, Einzelgebote, p. 259f.

[26]In the Pauline homologoumena it is used exclusively of obedience to Jesus Christ and to the gospel. Its use here in conjunction with the orders of creation is a sign of the relatively later phase of Christian thought, cf. W. Schenk, "Die Gerechtigkeit Gottes und der Glaube Christi," ThLZ 97 (1972), pp. 161–174, esp. 165.

[27]Schweizer.

[28]EWNT II:186f.

[29]Gnilka, p. 220.

21 In contrast to Sir. 30 or to Philo, the exhortation to the fathers is addressed against the use of their authority (*patria potestas*). Of course the argument is not that the fathers are to relinquish it altogether; as v. 20 indicates, it (the authority) is assumed but not stressed.[30] In the forefront is the fear that the children might be "provoked,"[31] broken inwardly. "To lose heart" (become discouraged, RSV; ἀθυμεῖν) here may be the opposite of εὐθυμεῖν (to take heart), which is a promise of the undergirding presence of God, e.g., in Acts 27:22, 25, 36, similar to θάρσειν. Hence the author feared that inconsiderate treatment of the children might dissuade them from the faith. Could it be that the tradition of Jesus as the "friend of the children" (Mark 10:13–16, par.) played a part here?

22 Slaves[32] and their masters comprise the third complementary pair of concepts. The admonition to the slaves is more sweeping than the one to their masters, probably because there were more slaves than masters in the church. In any case, this exhortation is not intended to substantiate the subordinate status of the slaves.[33] It is significant that the slaves are addressed at all.[34] As in the case of both preceding pairs of concepts, the admonition also commences here with those who are "weaker." To begin with, this admonition parallels the exhortation to the children almost verbatim: The slaves, too, are to obey "in everything" (→3:20). Instead of the parents, the masters are here the superordinate authority (the slave owners) who, in contrast to Jesus Christ, are described as earthly (κατὰ σάρκα)[35] masters. This already relativizes their status. While the subordination of the slaves is internalized, the will of the earthly masters is no longer the supreme norm. At issue here is a conscious subordination and service from the heart (on heart, see →2:2; 3:16). This is the opposite of service "to attract attention" (ὀφθαλμοδουλία = "eyeservice," used only here and in the parallel of Eph. 6:6) and of service "to please men" (ἀνθρωπάρεσκος, also used only here and in Eph. 6:6). That slaves are to please their true Lord is reiterated in v. 23.

23 The phrase "whatever your task" here refers to the service of slaves, yet it represents an application of the general rule of the Christian life (→3:17). In this instance, "heartily" stands for the literal "from the soul" which also occurs in the twofold love commandment, for instance (Mark 12:30, par.; Deut. 6:5, LXX).

---

[30]Schrage, "Haustafeln," p. 15.
[31]In contrast to 2 Cor. 9:2, ἐρεθίζειν is used negatively here.
[32]See note 10 above.
[33]On this issue, see also § 17 (e).
[34]Schweizer.
[35]In 2:11, 13, 18, 23, σάρξ is used negatively. Here it has more the connotation of differentiation from the "heavenly" Lord; Gnilka.

24 The slaves' obedience, therefore, is intended primarily for Jesus Christ as the heavenly Lord. Their relationship to the earthly masters is freed from fear thereby. The admonition in 1 Pet. 2:18ff. indicates the strength the slaves drew from this, especially in the case of bad service.[36] Their service has taken on a new function, namely, through all of their conduct to point to their true Lord, from whom they also receive their true reward. It is their share in the new life which has been prepared "in the light" (→1:12, cf. 1:5), in the inheritance and the lot (κλῆρος, cf. Eph. 1:14, 18; 5:5, κληρονομία),[37] whose appropriation is already present in baptism (→1:12). The ending of 3:24 is reminiscent of Rom. 12:11, where appeals like these are addressed to all Christians, similar to Col. 3:17.[38]

25 The entire verse constitutes a "pronouncement of holy law," that is an assessment of humanity's current conduct in the light of the last judgment, usually following the principle that the eschatological punishment is commensurate with the type of sin ("lex talionis formula" e.g., in 1 Cor. 3:17).[39] This pronouncement constitutes an antithesis to the promise of eternal life in 3:24 and points out the possibility of damnation (cf. 3:6). This sentence, in conjunction with the preceding verse, has connotations similar to Rom. 12:19: "Beloved, never avenge yourselves . . . 'I will repay,' says the Lord" (Deut. 32:35). In the foreground is the reference to the higher norm which leads to the sublimation of aggression on the part of the oppressed. Indirectly the conclusion of this verse indicates that the earthly relationships are marked by sin: With God there is no partiality (προσωπολημψία — patronization; Rom. 2:11; Eph. 6:9, cf. e.g., Deut. 10:17). While the righteousness of God does not lead directly to the removal of unrighteousness in this world, the latter is placed under the judgment of God and unveiled as unjust. Partiality here does not refer only to the poor relationship between master and slave, but to the distinction between masters and slaves in general (3:11). In Ephesians the expression of no partiality is used in the admonition to the masters,[40] whereas here it only prepares for the admonition to the masters.

---

[36]Cf. K. Romaniuk, *Il Timore di Dio nella teologia di San Paolo*, Supplural Rev.Bibl. 2, Brescia, 1968, p. 82ff.

[37]Lindemann, *Aufhebung*, p. 199f.

[38]Schweizer.

[39]E. Käsemann, "Sentences of Holy Law in the New Testament," most recently in *New Testament Questions of Today*, pp. 66–81. K. Berger, "Zu den sog. Sätzen Heiligen Rechtes," NTS 17 (1970–71), pp. 10–40, contests that these sentences are part of the prophetic speech and construes them to be expressions of the wisdom tradition. This is not altogether convincing, since these pronouncements are distinct from the wisdom sayings by their specific form and by their function. They do not express wisdom regarding daily living, rather they confront the hearer with the question of life and death.

[40]In Eph. the entire admonition shifts even more in favor of the slaves; cf. Lindemann, "Bemerkungen," p. 243f.

The idea of judgment according to works (cf. 1:10) that echoes in the background is no antithesis of the argument that focuses upon the assurance of salvation (2:12f.) and that presupposes redemption by the grace of God (1:11–14, 21f.). The judgment of the baptized is part of their metamorphosis for the new life. The judgment consists of God "honoring" some of the works or attitudes of some while rejecting others,[41] so that one might be transformed when entering into the new life (see § 15). While it does not have to be construed like this here, the tradition of the Pauline exhortation emerged from this theological context in any case.

The social effect of Christianity within the early imperial era is an issue under dispute. On the one hand, the theological premise of the obedience of slaves has led to the internalization of their subordination and thus functioned as a release valve for possible revolutionary moods. On the other hand, the conditions for a fundamental change in the social order were not present at that time,[42] and by desacralizing them[43] via confrontation with the orders which apply "in Christ," their change was at least indirectly prepared. At the same time Colossians is a witness to the real change in the structure of society that the formation of the Christian community brings about. Within these, Christians spent considerable segments of their life, and in them their faith became a tangible social entity, in spite of inconsistencies and controversies (to which Col. also attests; see § 18, [d, e]).

4:1 The exhortation to the masters is relatively brief; it bears the imprint of 3:25. In Ephesians the admonition to the masters is expanded and made concrete. That which is just (τὸ δίκαιον)[44] and fairness (ἰσότης, equality) were the norms of the Platonic Stoic morals of popular philosophy. For the latter, equality was the mother of righteousness (cf. 2 Cor. 8:13f.), the principle of every commandment (Philo, Spec. Leg. IV, 231f.). Consequently the masters share in the responsibility for the life of the slaves. That which is just is everything necessary to sustain life (Matt. 20:4; explicitly on the living conditions of slaves, see PsPhocyl. 224–226).[45]

---

[41]Mattern, Verständnis (see note 15 on 1:9–11), pp. 151–215.

[42]On this issue, see Scott Bartchy, ΜΑΛΛΟΝ ΧΡΗΣΑΙ: First-Century Slavery and 1 Corinthians 7:21, SBLDS 11, Missoula, 1973, pp. 72–82. Also note the survey of sources there.

[43]Schrage, "Haustafeln," p. 22.

[44]Righteousness appears here as an ethical term only; Schrage, Ethics, p. 245.

[45]It is unlikely that an allusion to the regulations concerning slaves in Lev. 25:43, 53 is also in mind here.

3. Final Exhortations, 4:2–6

(2) Continue steadfastly in prayer, being watchful in it with thanksgiving; (3) and pray for us also, that God may open to us a door for the word, to declare the mystery of Christ, on account of which I am in prison, (4) that I may make it clear, as I ought to speak.

(5) Conduct yourselves wisely toward outsiders, making the most of the time. (6) Let your speech always be gracious, seasoned with salt, so that you may know how you ought to answer every one.

The first part of the paraenesis (3:1–17) focused especially on the life of the Christian community; the household code formed a certain transition (§ 18). The pericope before us concludes the paraenetic section and addresses the effect on the outside. There are two parallel subsections (4:2–4 and 4:5–6), each opening with an imperative, each addressing the word of proclamation, and each concluding with an "ought" statement.[1] The first subsection is concerned with the indirect support of the missionary proclamation through prayer, while the second is concerned with the direct support of their home front by the believers' lifestyle and conduct towards outsiders (on the more specific structure, see →4:5).

As a whole, this pericope connects with the conclusion of the first segment of Part IV (3:16f.). Themes in common are "the word," "thanksgiving," and the significance of the Christian lifestyle.

2 Calls to steadfast prayer were motivated by the imminent parousia; it was the pious form of vigilance (1 Thess. 5:6, 17; Luke 21:36). They occur frequently in the NT (Eph. 6:18; 1 Thess. 5:17; Rom. 12:12; Luke 21:36, cf. 1 Tim. 5:5 et al.) and are correlated with the idea of the sanctification of the life of faith in its entirety (1 Thess. 5:15ff.; Rom. 12:1ff.). Steadfastness and watchfulness in prayer in Colossians are probably emphasized due to the influence of an adopted tradition[2] with hardly more than an indirect reflection of apocalyptic expectation. The admonition to make most of the time in 4:5 indicates, however, that the new theological accents (2:12f.; § 13) have not completely shrouded the awareness of the eschatological vanishing point. It cannot be discerned from the formulation of this verse and its context (v. 3) that the steadfast prayer here might already have the form of a prayer vigil (vigilantia, earliest evidence in Ep. Apost. 15[3]), as it appears in Eph. 6:18. On the positive side it may be argued that, as with the frequent appeals of this kind, the reference is to prayer to accompany all activity, to prayer at every opportunity, to the urgency of prayer (1 Thess. 1:2; Phil. 1:3f.; Rom. 1:9; 12:12; Philem. 4;

[1]Details in Gnilka, p. 227f.
[2]Cf. O'Brien, Thanksgivings, p. 65.
[3]Cf. Schnackenburg, Epheserbrief, p. 289, note 743.

on the urgency cf. Luke 18:1–8), and to the whole disposition of life
to be defined as thankfulness. The theme of thanksgiving encompasses
the entire letter (→1:3, 12; 2:7; →3:17; Table 3).

3–4 A further key term of the letter recurs once more, namely, the
mystery (see Table 3) which denotes the gospel as the center of the
inclusive intention of God with his creation (→1:26f.; 2:2). The knowledge of this mystery is practically identical with faith (→1:23). The
Word, that is the Word of God, is another term for the gospel (→1:5).
Thus the recipients participate in the apostolic commission by sup-
porting it in their prayers. In this manner the work of the imprisoned
and absent apostle continues (2:1–5; 4:18, cf. § 3 [b, d] and § 4 [a]).
Fundamentally this is God's work. He "opens the door," he effects
the possibility of spreading the gospel. Door as a metaphor plays a
significant part in NT soteriology. It depicts (a) a narrow passage, the
present "strangeness" of salvation which is not yet unveiled (3:4, cf.
John 10:1, 2, 7), the mystery which must be proclaimed; (b) the possibility of shutting, the judgment and limitations on time; and (c) primarily the entrance into a new room, realm, or a new kingdom (Mark
13:29; 1 Cor. 16:9; 2 Cor. 2:12; Acts 14:27; Rev. 3:8). There may also
be an allusion here to the expectation that the Pauline gospel does
not remain in prison because the task of proclamation is subject to
the divine necessity (δεῖ, 4:4, cf. 1:23).[4] Hence the prayer influences
the *howness*, rather than the *thatness* of the fulfillment.[5] The mystery of God is to be made known to all nations (1:27).[6] The verb
φανεροῦν (become visible, reveal, make known) is significant for the
soteriology of Colossians and is used to express three dimensions of
the gospel: It describes the revelation of God in Jesus Christ (1:26),
the eschatological unveiling of the new life together with him (3:4),
and the proclamation of the gospel in between the two (4:4). In terms
of practicality, according to Col. 4, it appears that his fellow laborers
(1:7; 4:7ff.) assume the mission of the absent apostle (→2:1–5).

5–6 The final two verses of this pericope concern the home front
of apostolic proclamation. The term wisdom (σοφία) reflects only indirectly the theological meaning which it carries in →2:3. Here wisdom denotes the conduct commensurate with the knowledge of the
will of God (cf. 1:9; Eph. 5:15). The Christians' behavior is to support
the proclamation of the servants of the Word and indirectly to have
a missionary function. Centripetal mission such as this plays a significant role in the NT (e.g., Matt. 5:16; John 13:3). In the secularized

---

[4]Summary in W. Popkes, EWNT, I:668–671.
[5]Zeilinger, *Erstgeborene*, p. 112ff.
[6]The parallel of Eph. 6:20 emphasizes the free and open proclamation of the mystery of the gospel. Hence the recipients are to pray practically to this end that the Pauline heritage will not be suppressed in their environment.

world of today, when being Christian is no longer a matter of course, Christian conduct itself takes on a missionary function again. In NT times the missionary effect was an important motif for the shape of ethics (here expressed with the verb περιπατεῖν). From the Jewish perspective, those who are "outsiders" (οἱ ἔξω) were Gentiles.[7] The NT describes all non-believers in this manner (1 Thess. 4:12; 1 Cor. 5:12f.). In the formation of the Christian life they have to be considered as potential recipients of the proclamation (Phil. 4:5; 1 Pet. 2:12; on the question of common norms, see § 16 [f], cf. § 17 [b]). In this instance, "conducting oneself wisely" is roughly identical with the roles of the individual ranks characterized in the household code (3:18–4:1).

"Making the most of the time" (Eph. 5:16), addressed in a participial construction typical for Colossians, is not apocalyptically motivated by an imminent return here.[8] Making the most of time was the rule of general philosophical truth (Sen., *Epist.* 1:1).[9] The motif of the imminent return (καιρός denotes point of time or occasion) may at best be alluded to indirectly (cf. 3:4).[10] In this case time is to be used concretely for the purpose of mission.[11]

If v. 5 was concerned with the missionary effectiveness of Christian conduct, v. 6 emphasizes the significance of "passive proclamation," consisting of the ability to answer persuasively the questions of outsiders. The reference is not to questions pertaining to an official hearing, as may be the case in 1 Pet. 3:15, but to those questions which one's neighbors ("every one") pose to the adherents of minorities, sometimes with aggressive intent. The ability to use such discussions for the purpose of true communication is one of the most effective tools for doing missions and is an indicator of the fact that the respective Christian community is indeed the church, that is to say, that the church's separation from the world does not lead to its isolation. The ability to communicate is expressed via a commonly known saying, according to which graciousness, that is the persuasive and attractive power of speech is attained through its "salt" (Plut., *Quaest. Conv.* 685A).[12] Salt was an indispensable means for the preparation of savory meals and for their preservation (Job 6:6).[13] In the context of missions the image of salt occurs in Matt. 5:13–16, par.[14]

[7] Billerbeck, III, 362.

[8] So Lohmeyer.

[9] Lohse, further documentation in Dibelius–Greeven.

[10] The attempt to exclude the future dimension of eschatology from Col. and Eph. cannot be carried out consistently, despite the justification for the concern as a whole; see J. Baumgarten, EWNT, II:517–579, esp. p. 574.

[11] For other interpretive options, see Martin (NCBC).

[12] Further documentation in Dibelius–Greeven; Lohse, p. 238, note 10.

[13] Source material from Judaism in Billerbeck, I, 235.

[14] On the theological context of this picture, see J. B. Souček, "Salz der Erde und Licht der Welt," TZ 19 (1963), pp. 169–171.

χάρις in this context denotes the graciousness which overcomes the world's suspicion and contrasts the pride of the false teachers (2:18). Nevertheless the primary meaning of χάρις, namely, grace and thankfulness, may also be echoed here[15] (cf. Acts 14:3; 20:32;[16] Col. 3:16: word of Christ . . . with thankfulness).

In summary, the structure of this pericope, which describes the missionary effectiveness of a Christian community in the absence of the apostle, may be delineated as follows:

4:2	Prayer as support	Ia
3f.	of the apostolic proclamation	b
5	The Christians' life as support	IIa
6	of their arguments in dialogue with the world around them	b

Conclusion of the Letter:
Personal Notes and Greetings, 4:7–18

(7) Tychicus will tell you all about my affairs; he is a beloved brother and faithful minister and fellow servant in the Lord. (8) I have sent him to you for this very purpose, that you may know how we are and that he may encourage your hearts, (9) and with him Onesimus, the faithful and beloved brother, who is one of yourselves. They will tell you of everything that has taken place here.

(10) Aristarchus my fellow prisoner greets you, and Mark the cousin of Barnabas (concerning whom you have received instructions—if he comes to you, receive him), (11) and Jesus who is called Justus. These are the only men of the circumcision among my fellow workers for the kingdom of God, and they have been a comfort to me. (12) Epaphras, who is one of yourselves, a servant of Christ Jesus, greets you, always remembering you earnestly in his prayers, that you may stand mature and fully assured in all the will of God. (13) For I bear him witness that he has worked hard for you and for those in Laodicea and in Hierapolis. (14) Luke the beloved physician and Demas greet you. (15) Give my greetings to the brethren at Laodicea, and to Nympha and the church in her house. (16) And when this letter has been read among you, have it read also in the church of the Laodiceans; and see that you read also the letter from Laodicea. (17) And say to Archippus, "See that you fulfil the ministry which you have received in the Lord."

(18) I, Paul, write this greeting with my own hand. Remember my fetters. Grace be with you.

---

[15]Schweizer, p. 234, note 8.

[16]χάρις may have the same meaning in Luke 4:22: Jesus omits the words concerning the judgment in Is. 61:1f. and proclaims the grace of God which also applies to the Gentiles.

This concluding segment does not tie into the discussion in the body of the letter until v. 12. The characteristics of the persons mentioned here indicate, however, that they shared, or at least represented, the heritage of the apostle Paul and indirectly supported the concern and apostolic authority of the letter.

At this point we need to reconsider the significance of the agreements in the list of greetings between Philemon and Colossians.[1] Since it is unlikely that the two letters originated in close temporal proximity (§ 3 [d]; § 4 [a]), the agreements in the list of greetings have to be explained as an attempt to anchor Colossians in the life of Paul. The author chose Colossae as destination because it was a city (already destroyed by earthquakes) situated in the region threatened by the heresy. Since this was also the region to which the letter to Philemon had been sent earlier, it could not be any other letter but Philemon whose list of greetings was to be used as a model here.

In Rom. 16, which contains a similarly extensive list of greetings, the apostle's salutation is placed at the beginning. Here the apostle's fellow workers are in the forefront.

The following individuals cited in Colossians are also listed in Philemon: Onesimus, Aristarchus, Mark, (Jesus),[2] Epaphras, Luke, Demas and Archippus. The scholars who defend the authenticity of Colossians point out the other names that are not mentioned in Philemon and that cannot be accounted for on the basis of the explanation given above: Tychicus (Jesus), Nympha(s).[3] If Colossians is considered to be deuteropauline, they have to be regarded as people that the author knew (apart from a few mentioned in Philem.) continued to perpetuate the apostolic heritage during his lifetime and in the respective region.[4] On the handwritten greeting, see § 4 (a) and →4:18.

This section divides into four components:

4:7–9 Concerning the carriers of the letter
4:10–14 Greetings of the apostolic coworkers[5]
4:15–17 Greetings and instructions of the author
4:18 Greeting to all the recipients, including benediction which demonstrates the letter's apostolic authenticity.

---

[1]On the topic as a whole, see Lohse, pp. 246–248, and also note the synopsis of the lists of greetings in Philem. and Col.

[2]Provided we read Ἰησοῦς in Philem. 23, instead of Ἰησοῦ: Lohse, pp. 242f., 246, 288, note 2 (the conjecture of Th. Zahn).

[3]So esp. Peake.

[4]On this issue, see Lähnemann, *Kolosserbrief,* p. 181ff.; Ernst, p. 243; Zeilinger, "Träger," p. 186f.; Gnilka, "Paulusbild," p. 183ff.

[5]Zeilinger, "Träger," p. 180, associates this component with 4:10f. and 4:12–14.

The structure of vv. 7–9 is chiastic:

4:7 will tell you all about us
    beloved — faithful
4:8 sent — you may know — encourage
4:9 faithful — beloved
    will tell you everything about us.[6]

What the three verbs express in 4:8 applies both to Tychicus and to Onesimus. As mediators between Paul and the recipients they seem to have played a special role.

7 Acts 20:4, 2 Tim. 4:12, and Tit. 3:12 refer to Tychicus as one of the companions of the apostle. Earlier in 1:7 Epaphras is described as a "beloved (→1:5) fellow servant" (cf. "servant of Christ" in 4:12). The prominence of the faithful fellow workers who carry on the gospel as disciples of Paul (1:5ff.; 4:3ff.) frames the entire letter (Table 3). Epaphras is depicted as the founder of the Christian communities among the recipients (1:5; 4:12f.), but he is not the only link between Paul and the recipients. His return, similar to that of the apostle, is no longer anticipated (cf. →2:1, 5). Tychicus and Onesimus (v. 9) have taken over the torch of the fellow servants in the Lord and have faithfully represented the apostle, as his colleagues (in office), among the recipients (on the designation of servant, see →1:7). The parallel in Eph. 6:21f. mentions only Tychicus.

8 Tychicus is sent to the recipients;[7] together with Onesimus he is to be the one delivering the letter.[8] If this is a deuteropauline writing (§ 6; →2:1–5), the true recipients are to receive this epistle as an apostolic exhortation, which reached them only after a delay, because the Colossian community collapsed after the earthquake (§ 4 [b]) and which addresses their actual problems with prophetic acumen. Tychicus is to inform the recipients concerning Paul and his coworkers: "that you may know how we are,"[9] cf. "Tychicus will tell you all about my affairs" (4:7) and "They will tell you of everything that has taken place here" (4:9). This probably refers to information relative to the apostle's position and importance. Tychicus could attest to what has been said in 1:24–2:5 (cf. γνωρίζειν in 1:27).[10] The reference to Tychicus in Eph. 6:21f. is to be explained similarly.[11] The hearts of

---

[6]Ibid., p. 178.

[7]ἔπεμψα—epistolary aorist, describing the action from the perspective of the recipients of the letter; cf. Philem. 12; Blass–Debrunner–Funk, § 334.

[8]This is also how the tradition understands it which is reflected in the concluding remark of many of the Byzantine MSS.

[9]The variant reading "that I may know concerning you" (p^{46}, C, and others) is to be explained as a misunderstanding of the copyists; Metzger.

[10]Gnilka; Lindemann, p. 72 considers Tychicus to be the possible author; against this, see →4:10.

[11]Cf. Gnilka, "Paulusbild," p. 180.

the recipients are to be encouraged thereby (παρακαλεῖν), similar to →2:2, where the Christians in Laodicea are also mentioned explicitly. The teaching of the apostle conveys, among other things, the "word of Christ," which affects the admonition and directs faith into the proper channels (3:16f.). Hence in the absence of the apostle, Tychicus and Onesimus represented the apostolic heritage in the Lycus Valley.[12] Among other things, Colossians is to legitimize[13] their subsequent activity.[14] By canonizing Colossians the church has acknowledged this apostolic concern.

9 Onesimus (a common name of slaves = "the useful one," cf. the pun in Philem. 11) is on the same level with Tychicus. The individual in mind here is the slave Onesimus known from the letter to Philemon. He is described as the "beloved brother" of the apostle, which says essentially the same as "minister and fellow servant in the Lord" (4:7).[15]

Some interpreters argue that the commonalities with Philemon are merely intended to stir up the impression of authenticity and that it is not certain whether the individuals mentioned here, except for Epaphras, have any relations with the recipients (§ 4 [b]).[16] Our observations on 4:7f., where Tychicus, who is not mentioned anywhere else in the NT, and Onesimus are authenticated as bearers of the apostolic tradition, support the conclusion that they were known to the recipients and that among them ("who is one of yourselves") they continued to cultivate the apostolic heritage as successors to Epaphras. This applies to the alleged time of writing (→2:1–5). At the time of the actual writing they were no longer active among the recipients. That the author underscores their task here is meant to emphasize their position as links in the chain of the apostolic tradition.

(4:10–14) The following four verses cite (see →4:11) names which are also found virtually only in Philem. As the founder of the communities among the recipients (1:7), Epaphras represents the first link of the apostolic chain in the Lycus Valley. The other fellow workers, likewise introduced with the phrase "greets you," constitute two further groups (4:10f. and 4:14).

10 Aristarchus is mentioned in Philem. 24, and in Acts 19:29 and 20:4 he is referred to as one of the companions of Paul. Here he is described as fellow prisoner of the apostle, which is ascribed to Epaphras in Philem. 23. This is an attribute of honor (cf. Rom. 16:7) and

---

[12]Lohse, p. 240; Zeilinger, "Träger," p. 178ff.; Merklein, "Theologie," p. 36.
[13]Cf. Gnilka, "Paulusbild," p. 183ff.
[14]After the apostle's death, cf. Schille, *Paulusbild*, p. 54f.
[15]According to Harrison, *Paulines*, p. 65ff., Onesimus was the author of Col.; on this see § 4 (a).
[16]So esp. Schenke–Fischer, *Einleitung*, I, 167f.

also indirectly underscores the apostle's authority (→1:24). Mentioned next is Mark who, in contrast to Philem. 24, is identified more specifically as the cousin of Barnabas. Hence this refers to John Mark, the companion of Paul, according to Acts (12:12, 25), who deserted him (13:13, cf. 15:37). Following Philem. 24, however, he rejoined him later, and his position in the church is confirmed via his mention in 2 Tim. 4:11 and 1 Pet. 5:13 (with Peter).[17] Like his cousin Barnabas (Acts 4:36), Mark was perhaps also a Jewish GraecoPalestinian with bilingual education (Greek-Aramaic) and having both a Hebrew and Greek name (Acts 15:39 and here only named Mark; Acts 13:5, 13 only named John).[18] The instructions (v. 10b) likely refer to his acceptance among the recipients by means of a letter of recommendation.[19] Then the author addresses them directly: "if he comes to you, receive him"! Should Colossians be deuteropauline and thus written later (§ 4[a]), this note was to strengthen the position of John Mark, who did not come until after Tychicus. Of all those sending greetings, he could have been the only one still in contact with the recipients at this letter's actual time of writing.

11 Jesus (Heb. *Jehoshu'ā*)[20]—Justus (the righteous one) also has a double name whose second part is intended for the hellenistic-Roman world.[21] In this paragraph this name is the only one which does not occur in Philemon, if one does not read ᾽Ιησοῦς instead of ᾽Ιησοῦ in Philem. 23,[22] which is not unlikely, considering the numerous variations in the Christian tradition of "Jesus Christ" in the NT.[23]

Aristarchus, John Mark and Jesus-Justus are said to be the only[24] Jews assisting Paul in his work for (Gk. εἰς) the kingdom of God (they are his fellow workers, συνεργοί, cf. Rom. 16:3, 9, 21; Phil. 2:25; 4:3; Philem. 24). They assist him in the proclamation of the word, the gospel.[25] The concept of the kingdom of God, which for Jesus and in

[17]According to Papias (Euseb., *Hist. eccl.* III, 39) and Irenaeus (*Adv. haer.* III, 1, 1), whose authority was a presbyter, this Mark also wrote the Gospel of Mark—an assertion to which the salutation of Mark in 1 Pet. 5:13 obviously contributed to begin with. It probably had its inception in the tendency to link the writings which prevailed as canonical with individuals associated with the apostolic circle.

[18]On the Graeco-Palestinians, see Hengel, *Judaism and Hellenism*, p. 104f.

[19]Cf. 1 Cor. 3:1 with this; Gnilka.

[20]See W. Foerster, *TDNT* III:284–293.

[21]In this case a second name which sounds similar was chosen.

[22]See note 2 above.

[23]In Col. see 1:2, 28; 3:17; 4:12.

[24]The insertion of οὗτοι μόνοι in this sentence seems somewhat forced. It means that there were also other Jewish-Christian disciples of Paul who were either already dead or whose opinion differed from that of the author; for this reason the recipients, endangered by the heresy, were not to draw their orientation from them.

[25]This has nothing to do with a synergism; Lohse, p. 242, note 9. A synergism may be found in 1 Cor. 3:9 at best ("God's fellow workers"), but even there it stresses the fellow workers' dependence upon Paul; Steinmetz, *Heils-Zuversicht*, p. 32.

the Synoptic tradition is the sum total of the promised salvation, recedes in the NT letters. It does not vanish altogether, however, and is reinterpreted occasionally (Rom. 14:17). As fundamental content of the proclamation, without interpretation and outside the traditional terminology, this concept appears only here in the letters of the NT. These three men comprise a group of Jewish-Christian disciples of Paul with whom the recipients were acquainted and for whom they represented the ecumenicity of the Pauline heritage. They became the apostle's consolation. παρηγορία denotes comfort in the profoundest sense of the term[26] and is also documented as expression of comfort in death.[27] This meaning may be echoed here, provided we consider Colossians to be deuteropauline: The recipients ought to know that working together with the apostle and carrying on his heritage is the best way to honor him (→2:5).

12 Epaphras[28] (cf. Philem. 23), placed in the center of this section, is characterized as the one who carries out the apostolic function, though he is not an apostle. He is described in 1:7 as fellow servant of the apostle (cf. Phil. 1:1), and he administers the apostolic task "in his stead." Thus as a disciple of Paul he was the missionary of the Lycus Valley. The phrases "of yourselves" here and "of the circumcision" in v. 11 are analogous in form in Greek. One may deduce from this that Epaphras was not a Jew, in contrast to those mentioned previously. Hence he belonged to the recipients and to Paul at the same time: He is a servant of Christ; he strives so that the recipients might be filled with the will (→1:9) of God, as Paul and Timothy also do (1:9). He strives (→1:29; 2:1) for the sake of their completion (πληροφορεῖν, cf. πληροφορία →2:2), as Paul himself also does (→1:28f.). To the Colossians, therefore, he is "their apostle."[29]

13 As such he also receives a virtually juridical verification[30] of this apostolic mission. He labors and suffers[31] for the recipients (ὑπὲρ ὑμῶν) as does the apostle (→1:24). For this reason he is able to represent him to them (ὑπερ ἡμῶν; →1:7). On the Laodiceans, see § 4 (b). Thus for the recipients the apostolic line moves from Epaphras, via Tychicus and Onesimus, to Mark.

14 Luke and Demas are said to be fellow workers of Paul in Philem. 24. They are also cited together in 2 Tim. 4:10f., though Demas is depicted there as the unreliable coworker. Since the second century

[26]Only the logos is able to bring this about, according to Philo, Somn. I, 112.
[27]G. Kaibel, ed., Epigrammata Graeca, Berlin, 1879, Nr. 204, 12; 504, 2, et al.
[28]On Epaphras, see § 4, 2; →1:7.
[29]Marxsen, Introduction, p. 178.
[30]On μαρτύρειν meaning "to bear someone witness," see Rom. 10:2; Gal. 4:15.
[31]Both are echoed in the Gk. term πόνος. Some MSS have sought to weaken this expression; see Nestle–Aland.

Luke[32] (Muratorian Canon, Iren., *Adv. haer.* III, 1, 1) has been held to be the author of the Gospel of Luke and of Acts. Here he is described as the beloved (→1:7; 4:7, 9) and identified more specifically as physician—obviously an indication of the fact that the author still knew him. Whether or not he assisted Paul as physician,[33] we do not know.

(4:15-17) Finally there are the direct greetings and instructions, all of which[34] are probably intended for the Christians in Laodicea and therefore affect the actual recipients most directly. Our considerations in § 4 (b) are indirectly supported thereby. Why should the apostle send greetings to Laodicea via Colossae if he sent a letter to Laodicea at the same time?

15-16 On Laodicea, see § 4 (b). As indicated in § 12, it is likely that the heresy had already gained a foothold among the recipients at the time of writing and that the house church[35] of Nympha was one of the few bases of the disciples of Paul in the region of the recipients. Paul's letter to the Laodiceans is unknown.[36]

It cannot be inferred from the summons to read the apostolic letters in their worship gatherings that the letters had a normative role to play already then.[37] The author endeavored to have the letter read to the whole community, so that the individuals and groups infested with the heresy (the other house churches) could also hear it.

Whether or not the head of the Pauline house mentioned here was a certain Nympha (N . . . αὐτῆς—B, syr[h], sa, et al.) or one called Nymphas (from Nymphodoros?; N . . . αὐτοῦ—D, et al.)[38] is difficult to determine linguistically. The change to the masculine understanding

---

[32]The name Luke is derived from the Lat. *Lucius* or *Lucanus*; Luke is not to be identified with Lucius in Rom. 16:21.

[33]So Lohmeyer.

[34]Cf. Lindemann, "Gemeinde," p. 124.

[35]Concerning the house churches, see Philem. passim; 1 Cor. 16:15; Gnilka, *Philemonbrief*, pp. 17-33; W. Vogler, "Die Bedeutung der urchristlichen Hausgemeinden für die Ausbreitung des Evangeliums," *ThLZ* 107 (1982), pp. 785-794; A. J. Malherbe, *Social Aspects of Early Christianity*, Philadelphia, 1983[2], p. 60ff.—and further source material there.

[36]The noncanonical letter to the Laodiceans, extant in Latin, is a later elaboration. Only some of its terminology is Pauline; Hennecke-Schneemelcher, *Apocrypha*, II:128-132. It is unlikely that the letter to the Laodiceans is identical to Eph., as Schlier, *Epheser*, p. 31f., assumes; on this see also E. Käsemann, "Das Interpretationsproblem des Epheserbriefes," most recently in idem, *Exegetische Versuche und Besinnungen* II, Göttingen, 1965[2], pp. 253-261, on p. 255. Houlden, and others, assume that it could have been Philem.

[37]A similar summons is found in the Syrian Apocalypse of Baruch (86, 1-3) which is not much more recent than Col. (A. F. J. Klijn, in Kümmel, *Jüdische Schriften* V, p. 114). There the summons expresses the claim to the dignity of a prophetic writing; cf. Berger, "Apostelbrief," p. 216.

[38]ℵ, A, C, and others have the reading: N . . . αὐτῶν, that is . . . in their house.

in the course of the text transmission is more likely.[39] Since Nympha is not mentioned in Philemon, she must have lived among the recipients at the time Colossians was written and was personally acquainted with the author.

17 According to Philem. 2, Archippus[40] was part of the "house" of Philemon, probably as a member of his family,[41] and obviously the only one of the three recipients of Philemon mentioned by name living among the recipients at the time Colossians was written. In Philem. 2 he is described as a fellow soldier[42] of Paul.[43] No details are given of his ministry among the recipients. It could hardly be the diaconate in the later technical sense of the term, though it is already an office, a ministry which is "received" (παραλαμβάνειν). The reference is to receiving it "in the Lord," which does not exclude the outward form of the reception via succession of the bearer.[44] According to Eph. 4:12 "the ministry" (διακονία) is the upbuilding of the church as the body of Christ. It encompasses both the proclamation and the administration and coordination of the charisms. It may also be a specific ministry, but the proximity of Archippus to Philemon, his attribute of being a fellow soldier, and his position among those greeted directly, support the notion that this refers to an important ministry, most likely even the leadership of the communities in Laodicea.

The summons for him to fulfill his ministry is to be conveyed to him by all of the recipients. Thus he is admonished in the name of the Pauline tradition of the former community in Colossae. He is to place himself in the ranks of the faithful and beloved witnesses (→4:13). In the reflection of this epistle he is to discover how far away he has moved from the Pauline witness when he treats the heresy too carelessly. The summons can be understood as a warning,[45] but it may also be a more positive reminder [46] (cf. βλέπειν with ἵνα in 1 Cor. 16:10). In this case the letter intends to win the leadership of the community for the concern of the faithful Pauline houses (cf. § 4 [b]; § 12).[47]

---

[39]Metzger. Nympha as a woman's name, on the other hand, was more common; Haupt, p. 174; Lightfoot, Moule, Caird.

[40]The Gk. meaning of this name is stable administrator.

[41]His son, according to the older exegesis, see Gnilka, *Philemonbrief*, p. 16, note 20.

[42]So also Epaphroditus in Phil. 2:25, for instance. For Lohmeyer, *Philemon*, p. 175, it was an atttribute of the leaders of the community; cf. Zeilinger, "Träger," p. 185.

[43]On the motif of striving, see →1:29; →2:1; 4:12.

[44]Zeilinger, "Träger," p. 187f.

[45]So Masson, Hugédé.

[46]Gnilka.

[47]Conversely, Ollrog, *Paulus*, p. 237, argues that it is not possible to interpret Col. from a concrete church situation under the assumption of a postpauline origin.

18 The handwritten greeting is to confirm the personal relationship of the writer to the recipients (§ 4 [a]). In its wording, this sentence resembles that of the handwritten greeting in 1 Cor. 16:21, where the signature, along with the confirmation of the personal relationship, also authenticates the malediction of the false Christians who do not love the Lord (Christ). Here the signature may also have a function of identification, as in 2 Thess. 3:17. Particularly from the theological perspective the letter is thus confirmed as the Pauline message (§ 4 [a]). At the same time the signature emphasizes the admonition to Archippus (§ 4 [a]). The note concerning the fetters is meant to intensify the importance of the apostolic word. The reader is able to visualize how the apostle signs the dictated letter with heavy hand, his left hand shackled by a chain. "Remember . . . " refers to all of the apostolic suffering which was also addressed in 1:24. "Remember me when this letter is read, just as I also think of you always" is also written at the conclusion of the Syrian Apocalypse of Baruch (86:3).[48] Thus the apostolic message may and should constantly accompany the readers. This, too, points to the apostolic witness of a Paul who is absent "in body" (2:5).

The apostolic greeting which opens the letter (→1:2) also concludes it (in its shortest form).

[48]Translated by A. F. J. Klijn.

Concluding Observations

§18 History of Interpretation and Meaning of Colossians

The concluding observation is not intended to be a summary, nor is it to replace the delineation of the impact of Col. which Eduard Schweizer has presented in exemplary fashion.[1] It merely intends to reflect upon some of the primary trajectories of the theology of Col. in the broader historical and theological framework. Only in this context we shall refer to or augment the history of impact.

(a) Canonization and the polemic against heresy

Its canonization is the most significant historical success of Colossians. Indirectly it is already attested in Irenaeus, who appeals to Col. 4:14, for instance,[2] when he wants to prove that Luke (the author of the Gospel) was closely associated with Paul (*Adv. haer.* III, 14, 1). Irenaeus includes Colossians among the letters of Paul which he considers to be authoritative in the church (e.g., I, 27, 2). In *Adv. haer.* V, 14, 2, and frequently elsewhere the term οἰκονομία (office, plan of salvation; →1:25) occurs, which is influenced by Eph. and Col.; there Irenaeus argues against gnostic Docetism by using Col. 1:22f. (cf. also V, 14, 4, et al.).[3] Allusions to Col. are likely to be found as early as in the apostolic fathers,[4] though they refer to individual expressions only, mostly from the hymn (Ign., *Trall.* 5:2; Ign., *Rom.* 5:3; Ign., *Smyrn.* 6:1; *Barn.* 12:7; see also Just., *Dial.* 84:2 and others). They can only point to the fact that the hymn was known and the remaining two allusions to stability in the faith (Ign., *Eph.* 10:2; *Pol.* 10:1) may be a more general Christian expression. The influence of the con-

---

[1]Schweizer, pp. 345–289.
[2]See also Lohse, p. 257, note 3; Gnilka, p. 23, note 21.
[3]Schweizer, p. 262.
[4]See also Lohse, p. 257; Gnilka, p. 23.

cept of revelation of Col. (→1:27) is more clearly recognized in the
Epistle to Diognetus 8:9–11 (2nd cent.).[5]

The reason for its canonization was the Paulinism of Col. Its polemic against the heresy has indeed been considered relevant in the
arguments with the Christian gnosis; but Christian gnostics used Col.
earlier still: According to Irenaeus (*Adv. haer.* I, 4, 5) the Valentin-
ians quoted Col. 1:16; the *Epistle to Rheginos* (NHC I, 4; 45:25–28)
alludes to Eph. 2:5f. and Col. 2:12; the Sethians quoted Col. 1:20 and
perhaps Col. 2:14 in the *Gospel of the Egyptians* (NHC III, 2; 63:16;
64:4);[6] according to Hippol., *Phil.* VIII, 13, 1, the Arab Monoimos
quoted Col. 2:9, etc.[7] Clement of Alexandria clearly has Col. 2:8 in
mind when he asserts that the true Christian gnosis transcends Greek
philosophy (*Strom.* VI, 62, 1, 4). Thus it was not the basically anti-
gnostic polemic of Col. which led to its canonization. It is more correct to say that the Christian gnostics used this letter in their arguments
because, as a part of the Pauline corpus, it had gained authority in
the church. The words concerning the true mystery and its knowledge
were a welcome point of departure for them.

Hence it was the deliberate, proclaimed, and in part also accomplished Paulinism of Col. which brought about its canonization.[8]

(b) Pauline tradition

We have already observed (→1:7; →2:1–5; →4:7–18) that Col., in view
of the heresy being combatted, emphasizes the authority and the
"relatively representative" ministry (→1:24)[9] of the apostle Paul and
indirectly also develops a succession of authentic bearers of the Pauline teaching. In this regard Col. and Eph. move closer to the Pastorals, which explicitly speak of the authority of the Pauline heritage
in terms of "sound teaching" (ὑγιαινούσης διδασκάλους, 2 Tim. 4:3;
cf. παραθήκη, 1 Tim. 6:20) and of succession of "office" (1 Tim. 5:22;
1:6).[10] The difference is that in the Pastorals the principal emphasis
on the succession of office focuses attention upon the present office
bearers, while in Col. the emphasis on the actual disciples of Paul
and the reference to the apostolic foundation in Eph. 2:20 are only
accompanying phenomena of the bold attempt at reinterpreting the
Pauline witness (→2:12f.; § 13). On the one hand, the hope of the be-

---

[5]Lindemann, *Paulus*, p. 346.
[6]Cf. note 181 on 1:15–20, above.
[7]On this issue as a whole, see Lindemann, *Paulus*, p. 297ff.
[8]On Paul, see § 4 (a) and Lindemann, *Paulus*, pp. 401–403.
[9]Merklein, "Theologie," p. 32.
[10]On this see H. F. Weiss, " 'Frühkatholizismus' im Neuen Testament?" in J. Rogge
and G. Schille, eds., *Frühkatholizismus im ökumenischen Gespräch*, Berlin, 1983, pp.
9–26, esp. p. 16ff. Also consult the other contributions in this collection of essays which
summarize the discussion on "early catholicism."

lievers is being realized at the expense of the Pauline eschatological proviso; on the other hand, responses to the gospel are emphasized: faith (2:12), God's sympathy for the sinner (2:13f.),[11] and paraenesis (→3:1). In this regard the theology of Col. is Pauline.[12]

A comment on terminology may help here: The term "Pseudepigraphon," which contemporary scholarship uses to designate the deuteropauline epistles and other "canonical pseudepigrapha," can be misleading. Earlier only those writings which had never been acknowledged to be canonical were called pseudepigrapha, [13] while the canonical pseudepigrapha of the NT have stood the test as apostolic material because of their content or their actual impact upon the church.

On the issue of the church's accommodation in new historical settings and in the perspective of several generations, which links Col. with the Pastorals, see § 16 and esp. § 17 (cf. also →3:24f.).

(c) Cosmic dimension

We have already demonstrated that the key position of Christ in the cosmos, expressed in the hymn in 1:15–20, is applied by the author of Col. to the recipients' Christian community, hence ecclesiologically (see § 9 [c]; § 11 and § 14). When it is submitted to Christ as its head and carries the gospel, the church moves to the center of creation and history;[14] already in this aeon the community lives in fellowship with Christ, and through it the liberating power of Christ breaks into this world.[15] It was the concrete experience of baptism as incorporation into the body of Christ, including its social dimension, which inspired the author of Col. in the theological considerations mentioned above.

The cosmic dimension of salvation expressed by the hymn of 1:15–20 made it also possible for Christians of later centuries to resist feel-

[11]This, in a sense, contains a reference to the "heart of Scripture." On this issue, see J. Rohde, "Die Diskussion um den Frühkatholizismus im Neuen Testament, dargestellt am Beispiel des Amtes in den spätneutestamentlichen Schriften," in Frühkatholizismus (see note 10 above), pp. 27–51, esp. p. 29; A. Lindemann, Review of Kertelge, Paulus, in ThLZ 108 (1983), pp. 741–744.

[12]Indirectly the relationship with the Pauline homologoumena is also seen in the fact that the older Christian texts (esp. 1:15–20) are interpreted here via reference to the cross of Jesus (→1:20), similar to the way Rom. 3 and 5 interpret the formula of the son in Rom. 1:3f.; see also Lohse, pp. 254–257.

[13]On this issue, see A. M. Denis, Introduction aux Pseudépigraphes Grecs D'Ancien Testament, StVTPsepigr. 1, Leiden, 1970, p. XIff.

[14]Several interpreters also interpret the term "bodily" in Col. 2:9 with reference to the church; see →2:9, and on the history of interpretation, Schweizer, p. 274f.

[15]Indirectly associated with the emphasis on the role of the church, which is characteristic for Col., is the medieval substantiation of the practice of indulgencies on the basis of Col. 1:24, for instance; on this see Oltramare, p. 233; on the history of interpretation of Col. 1:24f., see Kremer, Leiden, I–VII.

ings of fatalism (Tat., *Orat.* 9),[16] which, in turn, led to the veneration of angels as mediators of salvation (Aug., *Conf.* X, 42).[17] On the
other hand, Col. 1:15f. made provisions for a positive conception of
the invisible powers, which could be considered proof of the power
of the creator who therefore cannot be a lesser demiurge (Iren., *Adv.*
haer. II, 30, 3f., 6, prefaces of the liturgy[18]). In the Cappadocian theology of reconciliation (Gregory of Nyssa and Gregory of Nazianzus)
it is rather Eph. which takes on prominence because it links reconciliation with the defeat of the devil. The Alexandrian Logos Christology, which likewise emphasizes the key position of Christ in the
cosmos, has sought its scriptural support especially in the Gospel of
John.[19]

Conversely the Arians used Col. 1:15 (→) as evidence for the relatively subordinate position of Christ, who for them was a superman
indeed, but nevertheless was part of the created order (Athan., *Contra*
Arian. I, 5, 35).[20] This is a secondary meaning, for the primary function of the hymn was to emphasize the dignity of Jesus. There the
"image" of God must be interpreted as invisible, pre-existent image
which stands in juxtaposition to the created order.[21] The position of
Jesus as agent of creation underscores the effectiveness of the reconciliation addressed in 1:20 (§ 9 [c]; § 12). Origen developed this motif
in his doctrine of the reconciliation of the universe (*Princip.* I, 6,
13).[22] The emphasis on the identity of the agent of creation and of
the redeemer (*Princip.* I Praef. 4) has exerted a positive influence upon
the history of dogma,[23] though Origen's speculation about the restoration of the cosmos (apokatastasis), which was influenced by Eph.
1:10, was not accepted.

[16]Orat. 5 and 16 indicate acquaintance with Col. and Eph., so that the argument of
Orat. 9, according to which Christians confess the Lord of the planets and thus are
above Heimarmene, is evidently also inspired by Col.

[17]Severian v. Gabala (Staab, *Pauluskommentare*, pp. 320f., 328), also conducts his
polemic against the veneration of angels explicitly on the premise of Col. 1:21f.; 2:3
and 3:5; further evidence is found in Schweizer, p. 280f.

[18]Following Kehl, "Erniedrigung," (see Biblio. on § 12 above), p. 391.

[19]On the logos doctrine, see Schweizer, p. 259f.

[20]Schweizer, p. 263ff., cf. Pokorný, *Gottessohn*, pp. 54–56. This conflict also influenced the translation of some of Origen's statements, e.g., *Princip.* I, Prefatio 4, where
Rufinus interprets Origen's reference to Col. 1:16 with an Arian slant.

[21]Chrysostom, MPG 62, 318; Oecumenius, according to Staab, *Pauluskommentare*,
p. 455; see Schweizer, p. 264; Gnilka, p. 80ff.

[22]Schweizer, p. 261f.

[23]It was not an obvious assertion. Even in modern times there are interpreters who
apply Col. 1:15–17 to the new creation; see Schweizer, pp. 266f., 290f. Marcion had
to eradicate the designation "the first-born of all creation;" v. Harnack, *Marcion*, p.
47f. For K. Barth, Col. 1:16 serves as evidence that Jesus Christ is the "first and eternal
word of God," *Church Dogmatics* IV/1, ET G. W. Bromiley et al., Edinburgh, 1955, p.
50; cf. W. Kreck, *Grundentscheidungen in Karl Barths Dogmatik*, Berlin, 1983, p. 242.

Later on Col. 1:15–20 and the Johannine Prologue provided the link for speculations about the fate of the pre-Christian generations; accordingly these may also be judged in the light of the grace of God.[24]

In modern thought[25] Col. has been a contributing factor in the inspiration of the theological, pedagogic work of Johannes Amos Comenius (1592–1670). In his late writing "Via lucis" which is preparatory to his incomplete main work (Consultatio catholica), he bases his thoughts on world mission (in the Reformation this was a largely neglected topic) on Col. 1:27–29 (Via Lucis IV, 13).[26] The same reference serves as the premise for his worldwide strategy of pedagogy which presupposes the proclamation of the gospel (idem., XVIII, 11).

The most elementary effect of Col., which is connected with its canonization, is its reading in public worship. According to the lections of the early church, Col. 2:9–15 (the segment with the argument of Col.) and 3:1–4[27] were to be read during the Easter liturgy, 3:12–17 (or to 21) on the fifth Sunday after Epiphany, and 1:9–14 was to be read[28] on the last Sunday of the church year.

(d) Interpretation of Colossians as an ecumenical issue

Colossians played a special part in the ecumenical discussion of the sixties. The essay of J. A. Sittler, "Called to Unity,"[29] which influenced the theological work of the third plenary session of the World Council of Churches in New Delhi, underscores the claim of the resurrected one upon the whole universe. Sittler has seen correctly that the most comprehensive scope of the Christian faith is sketched in Col. He correctly points out the heritage of the Eastern church which expresses in its theology and liturgy the neglected aspects of Eph. and Col. At the same time a similar concern motivated O. A. Dilschneider to write *Jesus Christus Pantokrator. Vom Kolosserbrief zur Ökumene* (1962). He begins with the interpretation of the superhuman "principalities and powers" in Col. and concludes with an analysis of the authentic "being in Christ."[30] He pleads for more adequate communication of the church with the world[31] which would correspond with the dependence upon Christ Cosmocrator. —This entire

---

[24]This question was also the concern e.g., of the interpretation of the Puritan P. Baynes, *A Commentary upon the First and Second Chapter of Saint Paul to the Colossians*, London 1635, reprint 1972, p. 118f.

[25]On the impact of Col. in the modern era, see Schweizer, p. 269f.

[26]*Via lucis* (1668), ed. by J. Kopecký et al., Prague, 1961.

[27]In the Common Prayer Book it is Col. 3:1–7.

[28]In the Common Prayer Book: Col. 1:3–12.

[29]*The Ecumenical Review* 14 (1961–62), pp. 177–187; cf. Gabathuler, *Jesus Christus*, p. 159ff. A summary presentation confronting the ecumenical discussion with the exegesis of Col. 1:15–20 is found in Ahrens, *Diskussion*, cf. Schweizer, p. 274ff.

[30]Dilschneider, *Pantokrator*, p. 191ff.

[31]Ibid., pp. 212ff., 216f.

cosmic Christology was (a) an intelligible result of ecumenizing theology and (b) a reaction to the encounter of Christian churches with non-Christian religions and with Marxist philosophy. This is correlated with the fact that cosmic Christology focused on the statements concerning Jesus Christ's agency in creation in Col. 1:15f.[32] The cosmic aspects of the Christology of Col. indeed express the preconditions and consequences of salvation; nevertheless, the beginning continues to be the concrete experience of baptism. The way to unity and reconciliation does not lead through the discovery of Christ's agency in creation, but through the commitment to the one who was crucified in this world, that is through "putting off" of sin—of all that separates people from God and from one another. It is also the way which leads through the concrete life in togetherness in the community that praises God and through the witness in the world, family and house.[33] Humanity is not permitted to limit the grace of God, of course, and humankind is also supposed to ponder its cosmic ramification. But if one were to obscure thereby that the cosmic Christ—the exalted one, the Lord—is to be declared clearly and unequivocally only through the witness of the concrete Christian community, or if the church were to attempt to take charge of redeeming the world by itself,[34] one would succumb to serving the superhuman powers and authorities, against which Colossians warns. This also means that the dignity and key position of the church in the cosmos consists precisely of its conscious and confessed dependence upon the crucified and resurrected Jesus Christ.

In spite of those possible misinterpretations, against which it is not adequately protected, the contribution of cosmic Christology remains undeniable. It has placed Western theology on notice that the goal of God's ways is not only the salvation of the individual. It is the new creation into which is to be received, out of this world, the community of men and women anchored in the grace of God. The church can be the nucleus of that community.[35] It can hardly be doubted that at least the judgment of human action and its consequences are part of the new creation, but this cannot be deduced from Colossians directly. In considerations such as this, the only point of departure is the investigation of the function of the principalities and powers which are at work supra-individually (§ 10) and with which humankind has

[32]Gabathuler, *Jesus Christus*, p. 163ff.

[33]One may object that "cosmic Christology" interprets particularly the older hymn which we reconstructed in § 10 (a). Yet we need to consider it inclusively, together with its function in the church, i.e. in practical terms: we have to read it in the canonical context of Col.; cf. Ahrens, *Diskussion*, pp. 95–98.

[34]Cf. the critical questions of ibid., pp. 27f.; 82f.; 85ff., et al.

[35]Schillebeeckx, *Christus*, p. 183f.

to deal, not only as individuals but especially as members of the Christian community (§ 14).[36] Further, a theology of nature as the creation of God can only be derived with reservations from Colossians. The statement about the agent of creation (1:15f.), in the context of the letter, emphasizes especially that the superhuman powers are not gods, but a creation of God. These powers cannot separate humankind from the creator and redeemer. The "reconciliation of all things" essentially is a metaphor expressing the new function of the superhuman powers in relation to humanity: For believers they lose their fate-like power (→1:20).

If we attempt now to trace, in summary, the boundaries between a legitimate and a false theological application of Colossians, we need to recall the two inseparably linked but distinct aspects of the theological task. In view of the intricate history of the impact of Colossians, this double "caveat" is particularly relevant.

(1) Theology is not meant to support faith via external evidence. Neither does Colossians have this intention, and in this sense it is also essentially Pauline.[37] The boundary of illegitimate appeal to this epistle is not overstepped where the process of thinking is encouraged or even exercised "boldly." But when speculation replaces faith, that is, when thinking is "Christianized," without proclaiming the crucified Messiah, without attending to the weak as well, without being concerned about everyday questions (cf. § 17), and without building upon the grace of God (Col. 1:6; 3:16 and εὐχαριστεῖν, cf. Table 3), the appeal to Colossians becomes illegitimate. Because Colossians wants to be Pauline in this regard, and because it is also essentially Pauline, we dare not, in its interpretation, forget Paul, the Reformation, and, in our opinion, also the positive heritage of dialectical theology.[38] Likewise, the individual is able to experience the

[36]Since the topic of the unity of the church is more prominent in Eph., we shall only discuss it in conjunction with that epistle.

[37]Lohse, p. 256f.

[38]In a certain sense, what K. Barth said about the twofold Lordship of Christ in the church and in the world is true of Jesus Christ as reconciler and agent of creation in Col. Those are not two independent kinds of rulership, rather they may be construed as two concentric circles. While the inner one is the church, the outer one is the world. Only through the church can the center, Jesus Christ, be witnessed to the world. In this manner the Lord and judge of the creation wants to work in the world now, K. Barth, *Christengemeinde und Bürgergemeinde*, ThSt (B) 20, Zürich, 1946. (On Col. 1 in the framework of this debate, see W. Schweitzer, *Die Herrschaft Christi und der Staat im Neuen Testament*, Zürich, 1948, ch. 4, 2; for a critique, see the review by H. Braun in *ThLZ* 78 (1953), p. 27f., cf. § 10 above.) Barth formulated this as some sort of a polemic against the Lutheran doctrine of two kingdoms. It does not affect Luther and his teaching per se, however, as much as it does its later formulations. On this issue, see U. Duchrow, *Christenheit und Weltverantwortung*, Forschung und Berichte der ev. Studiengemeinschaft 25, Stuttgart, 1970, pp. 461f., 575–588. In matters of "house discipline" Col., with its tension between Col. 3:11 and 3:22ff., conforms to the doctrine of two kingdoms, except that it delineates more clearly that God draws the authority of

encounter with the "cosmic" sphere of the Lordship of Christ (the conquest of fatefulness), expressed in the statements concerning the agent of creation and the reconciler of the world,[39] only by means of the witness of the community which confesses God and lauds his grace (e.g., 1:28). Hence the concrete expression of the Lordship of Christ over all things is the proclamation of the gospel,[40] which simultaneously causes a division that may even penetrate the human heart (3:5; 12). It is the tension between the grace of God and the alienation of humankind in sin (1:14, 21). In the light of the comprehensive concept of the gospel, this diastasis becomes even more distinct.

(2) Theology is to demonstrate the importance of the grace of God. Colossians accomplishes that by placing the Christian community's faith in the broadest framework of creation. Among other things, faith also grows by proving itself as the starting-point from which it is possible to interpret the broader contexts of life and the world (2:2f.). This tendency to reflect in terms of the broader contexts is inherent even in the most elementary testimonies of faith and cannot be imagined to be absent from the confession of faith. If faith does not dare to take this step to its own testing in the open field, it may be weakened unconsciously by an alien "beguiling speech" (2:4). We have already pointed out the dangers of the comprehensive reflection of faith (under [d] above).[41]

More distinctly than the ecumenical discussion of the sixties, it represents the thought of the scientist and priest Pierre Teilhard de Chardin (1881–1955),[42] which Karl Barth considered to be one of the greatest threats to theology.[43] This line of thought has at times been

---

the house into his service "through Christ" (see Duchrow's table on p. 573). Thomas Aquinas perceives the "dominationes, potestates et principes" objectively as intermediate authorities in the creation order (Summa theol. I, 18, 58); he does not address the issue of their alienation and of the defeat of their pressure in Jesus Christ; on this issue, see J. Smolik, "Die Mächte bei Thomas von Aquino," most recently in idem, Erbe im Heute, Berlin, 1982, pp. 79–82; Lindemann, pp. 81, 88f., compares the theology of Col. with proposition II of the Barmen Declaration of 1934 which emphasizes Jesus Christ as Lord and redeemer. In contrast to the German Christians, however, the Colossian opponents practiced more of an ascetic seclusion. Against this backdrop it is easier to grasp the differences in the theological argumentation. (I did not have occasion to read Lindemann's commentary until after the finalization of the manuscript of this interpretation.)

[39]Barth reflects profoundly on the manner of Jesus Christ's existence as ruler of all things: Dogmatics IV/3, ET G. W. Bromiley, Edinburgh, 1962, p. 752ff., cf. Gnilka, p. 86f.

[40]Cf. Gabathuler, Jesus Christus, p. 180; K. Barth, Dogmatics II/2, p. 104f. Based on Col. 1:15 he develops the concept of election and of God's benevolence to his creation which has its focus in Jesus Christ. Hence faith is the perception of God's predestination.

[41]It also applies to the "dynamic-historical" alternative of this trend, cf. Ahrens, Diskussion, p. 82.

[42]See also Schweizer, p. 273ff.; Gnilka, p. 85.

[43]K. Barth, Gesamtausgabe V. Briefe, Zürich, 1975, p. 172.

compared with the theology of Colossians.[44] Considering it on its own merits, Teilhard's vision of cosmic progress tends to deal with sin by interpreting it in the large framework of a positive perspective rather than through conversion.[45] But this is not the case in Colossians (1:14; 3:1ff.). Teilhard's thought can be received positively only on condition that the priority of grace and of faith is maintained.[46] As long as these are not severed, we are able to deem complementary the decision of faith, which the confession renders distinct from the environment, and the comprehensive theological reflection which discovers in Jesus Christ the perspective and ground of creation.[47]

(e) Contemporary significance of Colossians

Similar to that of most biblical books, the contemporary message of Colossians has to be rediscovered through interpretation; in so doing, the entire existence of the Christian community plays a part. The witness of Colossians is particularly effective in situations when a person feels threatened by fateful powers. In the global threat of nuclear weaponry such a feeling is understandable. Yet people are able to react against it by fleeing from the world, by resignation, or by aggression and hatred. With its witness Colossians seeks to liberate from the fascination with external ("cosmic") threats, to emphasize the finality of grace and to invite for concrete steps to be taken en route to reconciliation in everyday life[48] (the household code).[49] The picture of the church offered by Colossians is that of a community that is distinct from the environment by its relationship with Christ, and yet it does not exist in isolation because it is able, both through missions and its "active co-existence" in the "houses," to penetrate the world and to confess Jesus Christ as Lord in a concrete manner.[50]

---

[44]Daecke, *Teilhard*, p. 410ff.

[45]So e.g., "L'esprit nouveau," in *Oeuvres* V, Paris, 1959, pp. 107–126; on the incarnation of Christ permeating the universe, see esp. p. 123f.

[46]Teilhard de Chardin's understanding of the function of faith as assurance and acceptance of the grace of God was crystallized in his work "Le milieu divin," in *Oeuvres* IV, Paris, 1957, e.g., pp. 117ff., 155, where he interprets faith as a metamorphosis of man "in Christ." On the "primacy of faith" in Teilhard de Chardin, see Daecke, *Teilhard*, pp. 355ff.; 414ff.; W. Dantine, "Zur kosmischen Stellung des Menschen nach Teilhard de Chardin," *Acta Teilhardiana* 5 (1968), pp. 16–32, esp. p. 29ff. De Chardin's thought is assessed even more positively in S. Schneider, *Die "kosmische Grösse" Christi als Ermöglichung seiner universalen Heilswirksamkeit an Hand des kosmogenetischen Entwurfs Teilhards de Chardin und der Christologie des Nicolaus von Cues*, Bücherreihe der Cusanus-Gesellschaft 7, Munich, 1979, according to the review in *ThLZ* 106 (1981), pp. 517–520; cf. the legitimate objections by the reviewer, K. H. Kandler.

[47]Daecke, *Teilhard*, pp. 410–414, attempts to justify de Chardin's thought from the perspective of Col.

[48]On this see Schweizer, p. 282ff.; idem, "Christus," p. 312.

[49]Lohse, pp. 220–232; cf. § 17 and →3:25.

[50]Cf. Meeks, "Body," p. 213ff.; on the significance of ecclesiology in Col., see Francis, "Argument," p. 206f.

Index of Modern Authors

Index of Ancient Sources